INTERVENTIONS IN CONTEMPORARY THOUGHT

To my family,
as well as to all of my friends and mentors who have cultivated
practices of intervention

INTERVENTIONS IN CONTEMPORARY THOUGHT
History, Politics, Aesthetics

Gabriel Rockhill

EDINBURGH
University Press

Edinburgh University Press is one of the leading university presses in the UK. We publish academic books and journals in our selected subject areas across the humanities and social sciences, combining cutting-edge scholarship with high editorial and production values to produce academic works of lasting importance. For more information visit our website: www.edinburghuniversitypress.com

© Gabriel Rockhill, 2016, 2017

Edinburgh University Press Ltd
The Tun – Holyrood Road, 12(2f) Jackson's Entry, Edinburgh EH8 8PJ

First published in hardback by Edinburgh University Press 2016

Typeset in 11/13 Palatino Light by
Servis Filmsetting Ltd, Stockport, Cheshire

A CIP record for this book is available from the British Library

ISBN 978 1 4744 0535 5 (hardback)
ISBN 978 1 4744 2585 8 (paperback)
ISBN 978 1 4744 0537 9 (webready PDF)
ISBN 978 1 4744 0538 6 (epub)

The right of Gabriel Rockhill to be identified as the author of this work has been asserted in accordance with the Copyright, Designs and Patents Act 1988, and the Copyright and Related Rights Regulations 2003 (SI No. 2498).

CONTENTS

Acknowledgements   vii
Note on Sources   viii

Introduction: What Is an Intervention? Metaphilosophical Critique and the Reinvention of Contemporary Theory   1

I History

1 How Do We Think the Present? From Ontology of Contemporary Reality to Ontology without Being   37

2 The Right of Philosophy and the Facts of History: Foucault, Derrida, Descartes   55

3 Aesthetic Revolution and Modern Democracy: Rancière's Historiography   100

II Politics

4 Is Difference a Value in Itself? Critique of a Metaphilosophical Axiology   117

5 Castoriadis and the Tradition of Radical Critique   139

6 The Hatred of Rancière: Democracy in the History of Political Cultures   165

III Aesthetics

7 The Art of Talking Past One Another: The Badiou–Rancière Debate   193

| 8 | The Hermeneutics of Art and Political History in Rancière | 214 |
| 9 | The Forgotten Political Art Par Excellence? Architecture, Design and the Social Sculpting of the Body Politic | 243 |

Bibliography 262
Index 279

ACKNOWLEDGEMENTS

I would like to thank, first and foremost, Carol Macdonald. This book would not have been possible without her encouragement and insight. Special gratitude is also due to all of the friends and colleagues who took the time to read and comment on earlier versions of the texts printed below. Although an exhaustive list would be impossible, particularly because these were written over the span of nearly a decade, I am particularly indebted to Avram Alpert, Pierre-Antoine Chardel, Andrés Claro, Kevin Platt, Jean-Michel Rabaté, Julian Sempill, Ádám Takács, Annika Thiem and Yves Winter. I would also like to thank Axelle Karera and David Peña-Guzman for their comments on the introduction, as well as Steven Warren and the Department of Comparative Literature at SUNY Binghampton for their invitation to present the keynote address at their graduate student conference in 2014 (which was a unique occasion to present and receive feedback on a much earlier draft of the introduction). I am grateful, as well, to all of the other institutions and conference organisers who provided me with opportunities to publicly present various versions of these essays and receive critical feedback. Villanova University deserves particular mention in these acknowledgements, especially for the material support provided by the Office of Research and Sponsored Projects and the Board of Publications. I am grateful to the translators who took on the arduous task of rendering in English – for a native English speaker – texts that I had originally published in French: Sabine Aoun, Theodra Bane, Daniel Benson, Jared C. Bly, Sean Bray and Axelle Karera. Finally, I would like to express my sincere gratitude to Cathy Falconer for her unrivalled skills as a copy-editor.

Unless otherwise indicated, all translations are my own.

NOTE ON SOURCES

All of the texts printed below are circumstantial pieces anchored in specific moments and debates. I made an effort to keep modifications to a minimum in order to preserve the specificity of their conjunctural inscriptions. This is particularly important to emphasise in the case of chapters dealing with living philosophers (such as Badiou and Rancière). Updating these in order to integrate more recent publications would have required significant revisions, and the intellectual gain would have been minimal or none at all (particularly because their basic positions on the topics discussed have not changed). Moreover, it is true that I do not currently agree with all of the nuances of every individual position taken in the chapters below. However, attempted interventions always carry a certain risk with them, as well as their own specific historicity, and it is important for this project to accept both of these.

Earlier versions of these chapters have been printed in journals and books, and I would like to express my gratitude to all of the editors and publishing houses that have granted reproduction rights.

Chapter 1: 'Comment penser le temps présent? De l'ontologie de l'actualité à l'ontologie sans l'être', *Rue Descartes*, 75, 2012/13, pp. 114–26. All rights reserved. Republished by permission.

Chapter 2: 'Le Droit de la philosophie et les faits de l'histoire: Foucault, Derrida, Descartes', *Le Portique*, E-portique 5 – *Recherches*, December 2007. All rights reserved. Republished by permission. A slightly different version of this article appeared in Gabriel Rockhill, *Logique de l'histoire: Pour une analytique des pratiques philosophiques* (Paris: Éditions Hermann, 2010).

Chapter 3: 'Démocratie moderne et révolution esthétique: Quelques réflexions sur la causalité historique', in Laurence Cornu and Patrice

Vermeren (eds), *La Philosophie déplacée: Autour de Jacques Rancière* (Paris: Horlieu Éditions, 2006), pp. 335–49. The English translation by Sabine Aoun and Sean Bray was published as 'Modern Democracy and Aesthetic Revolution: Reflexions on Historical Causality', in Nadir Lahiji (ed.), *Architecture against the Post-Political* (New York: Routledge, 2014), pp. 31–40. All rights reserved. Republished by permission.

Chapter 4: 'La Différence est-elle une valeur en soi? Critique d'une axiologie métaphilosophique', *Symposium*, 17:1, Spring 2013, pp. 250–72. All rights reserved. Republished by permission.

Chapter 5: 'Eros of Inquiry – An Aperçu of Castoriadis' Life and Work', in *Postscript on Insignificance: Dialogues with Cornelius Castoriadis*, ed. Gabriel Rockhill, trans. John V. Garner and Gabriel Rockhill (London: Bloomsbury Continuum, an imprint of Bloomsbury Publishing Plc, 2011), pp. ix–xxxix. All rights reserved. Republished by permission.

Chapter 6: 'La Démocratie dans l'histoire des cultures politiques', in Jérôme Game and Aliocha Lasowski (eds), *Jacques Rancière ou la politique à l'œuvre* (Paris: Éditions Archives Contemporaines, Collection 'Centre d'Études Poétiques', 2009), pp. 55–71. All rights reserved. Republished by permission.

Chapter 7: 'Recent Developments in Aesthetics: Badiou, Rancière and their Interlocutors', in Alan Schrift (ed.), *The History of Continental Philosophy*, vol. 8: *Emerging Trends in Continental Philosophy*, ed. Todd May (Durham: Acumen Press, 2011), pp. 31–48. All rights reserved. Republished by permission.

Chapter 8: 'The Politics of Aesthetics: Political History and the Hermeneutics of Art', in Gabriel Rockhill and Philip Watts (eds), *Jacques Rancière: History, Politics, Aesthetics* (Durham, NC: Duke University Press, 2009), pp. 195–215. All rights reserved. Republished by permission.

Chapter 9: 'The Forgotten Political Art *par excellence*? Architecture, Design and the Social Sculpting of the Body Politic', in Nadir Lahiji (ed.), *The Missed Encounter of Radical Philosophy with Architecture* (London: Bloomsbury, 2014), pp. 19–33. All rights reserved. Republished by permission.

Introduction

WHAT IS AN INTERVENTION? METAPHILOSOPHICAL CRITIQUE AND THE REINVENTION OF CONTEMPORARY THEORY

INTERPRETATION AND INTERVENTION

This book is the result of a longstanding concern with the status and modalities of contemporary theoretical practice and, more specifically, the ways in which it engages with the intertwining themes of history, politics and aesthetics. Written over the course of nearly a decade, all of the chapters testify – to varying degrees and from diverse vantage points – to a profound and unresolved malaise with many of the established models of philosophical thinking. They each address particular issues and were written in specific contexts, as well as in two different languages and cultural milieus (francophone and anglophone). For this reason, they can very much be read autonomously. However, they all bear the marks of an ongoing preoccupation with the logic of practice of intellectual work, as well as with the possibility of radically reconfiguring it. In the pages that follow, I would like to tease out some of these deeper methodological concerns, as well as articulate the ways in which they contribute to a rethinking of the historical relationship between art and politics.

One of the central preoccupations of this book can best be described in terms of a heuristic distinction between two types of theoretical practice. An interpretation, first of all, abides by the rules of an established discourse. It works within the general normative, praxeological and epistemological framework of an institutionalised set of activities. An intervention, by contrast, seeks to contest these operative norms and guiding parameters in order to introduce alternative forms of intellectual practice. There are, of course, varying degrees of interpretation and intervention. The major difference between them remains, however, that an interpretation plays by the rules of a recognisable social ritual, whereas an intervention challenges them.

The activity that we might schematically refer to as normal theory strongly encourages the work of interpretation, and a weighty set of institutional mechanisms, social norms and professional pressures profoundly and often imperceptibly format intellectual work. These forces are anchored in a deep history that has normalised particular activities in which a set of self-evident givens has become sedimented. Interpretations, as innovative as they may be, nevertheless work within the implicit and unquestioned boundaries of a particular theoretical universe. Interventions, insofar as they seek to tap into a largely imperceptible scaffolding in order to reconfigure the very parameters of intellectual activity, are generally discouraged by the institutional apparatus. In fact, there are often powerful gatekeepers who maintain the sanctity of particular theoretical endeavours by refusing, dismissing or sidelining those who raise questions about the very nature of the social game that is being played. Interventions are therefore inherently dangerous, and even incendiary, not only because they call into question the rules of consecrated rites and customs (and those who benefit from them), but because they risk provoking the indiscriminate repression and suppression of those who undertake them.[1]

Since these are heuristic labels, it is important to insist on the fact that they have their source in a socially and historically specific theoretical proposition that is, itself, a form of intervention. These are not natural objects or transhistorical forms, but rather conceptual schematisations that, within the current conjuncture, hold the promise of gaining traction over the contemporary field of intellectual activity. In other words, they are specific tools for practical leverage rather than conceptual absolutes or rigid binary categories. In this regard, it is also essential to recognise that they are open to social negotiation, and that they are relational phenomena in the sense that their assessment depends on one's vantage point. There is no pure form of interpretation, nor is there something like a crystalline intervention. These pragmatic terms, as I propose to understand them, refer to an entire gamut of possibilities. Regarding interpretations, for instance, some are certainly more consensual than others, and there are often social values affiliated with those that appear more inventive within a certain spectrum. In theoretical circles, for example, new interpretations are often valorised as impressive forays into a particular game. However, these remain

Introduction

spectacular moves on a well-trodden playing field. Interventions, by contrast, seek to change the nature of the game by shifting the very terrain upon which one plays. This is not simply a matter of questioning presuppositions or thinking otherwise for what is ultimately at stake is changing the structural conditions of possibility of thinking and thereby altering the very activity of thought. In other words, interventions are never purely intellectual endeavours or thought experiments. They are practical incursions into the social rites and rituals of theoretical work.

Providing examples of interventions is a particularly delicate task because they are always forays into specific domains.[2] There is no such thing as an intervention in itself, which could be captured by an ideal exemplar, since any intervention is necessarily related to and intertwined with a given conjuncture. Its very comprehensibility requires, in fact, that it be socially legible (at least for some). It is, as the etymology of the term itself indicates – *intervenire* and not simply *venire* – a coming *between*, *in* or *among*. It needs to gain leverage *inter* a particular field of forces, to get a grip on them, to latch on. In challenging the rules of sanctified rites, an intervention thereby has to walk a fine line by putting forth alternative practices that 'come' from elsewhere and simultaneously attempting to gain traction over the situation into which it comes. It is in this sense that an intervention is never a purely speculative proposition, a leap of faith, or a philosophic programme invented from scratch. It is an anchored struggle to immanently reconfigure a socially and historically specific set of practices. Such reconfiguration is not, moreover, intermittent or ephemeral but requires a patient and resolute construction of alternative practices, communities and institutions.

In titling this book *Interventions in Contemporary Thought: History, Politics, Aesthetics*, it was not my intention to suggest that interpretation should be a thing of the past. This is an important practice for developing theoretical possibilities within particular parameters. However, there are socio-historical conjunctures that beckon for broader and riskier engagements that can potentially displace or even reconfigure the norms of intellectual practice. In the current case, there is no presumption to have invented something that is entirely new or to have magically reset the historical stage. The essays that follow have clear and identifiable limits, and they do not pretend to present a project that has sprung forth all at once, fully formed, from the mind of an isolated individual. Instead, they evince a trial and error method of struggle within and between particular intellectual communities, as well as a nomadic but resolute trajectory from the time of my doctoral studies and teaching in France to my present work in the American academy. Crossing and cutting across the roads of established social practice, they attest, above all, to an ongoing effort to chart out – in collaboration with a number of diverse theoretical projects, intellectual groups and alternative institutions – an orientation that parts ways with many of the extant models of intellectual life. It is in this sense that the title indexes the dual objectives that structure the book as a whole, even if certain aspects of these objectives still remain beyond the reach of the analyses that follow, like beacons on the horizon that beckon for future work. On the one hand, it aims at intervening methodologically in order to call into question a specific set of regularised activities and propose concrete alternatives, in part by drawing on important, but often less visible, counter-practices. On the other hand, it attempts to intervene thematically into a particular set of debates on history, politics and aesthetics. On both of these fronts, some of the essays are more interventionist than others. Indeed, in certain instances, it was necessary to articulate my claims in very close proximity to established hermeneutic strategies, and there is certainly still a place for this. Nevertheless, the overall thrust of the studies that follow is in the direction of a reconfiguration and reinvention of contemporary theoretical practice.

ARCHAEOLOGY OF THE DISCIPLINES AND THE CONSTITUTION OF CONTEMPORARY PHILOSOPHY

The disciplinary matrix, in our day and age, plays a crucial role in the formation and perpetuation of the institutionalised norms of intellectual life. Interesting interpretive work can be and is done within it, but the deep-seated conventions of the social rituals in place tend to function as structural givens. A given, it should be noted, is not the same thing as a presupposition. Whereas the latter refers to a theoretical assumption that could be made explicit, the former is a constitutive aspect of practice that is never questioned (or rather which cannot be questioned without seriously interrupting the practice itself, for it is akin to the act of pulling an intellectual emergency break). One of the significant limitations of much of the work that is referred to as interdisciplinary, multidisciplinary, transdisciplinary, cross-disciplinary or pluridisciplinary is

Introduction

that the givens of the disciplinary matrix largely remain intact. Certain presuppositions might be questioned or challenged, but the deep normative, praxeological and epistemological structures of disciplinary practice often remain the unquestioned playing field upon which these presuppositions are interrogated. As the terms themselves suggest, like many of the other neologisms that have been introduced, theoretical work is done between, across or within a plurality of disciplines, but the very categories of knowledge claims remain largely unaltered. There is a horizontal engagement in which one attempts to move between disciplines or even break down the walls that separate them. However, this type of lateral movement nonetheless tends to take them as given elements of the very practice of thinking.

Interventions, insofar as they affect the material practices of intellectual life, cannot avoid, at a certain level, incursions into the normalising procedures of disciplinary matrices (at least within our socio-historical conjuncture). Disciplines themselves have, of course, been forged over time and are largely bound up with the intricate history of the institutionalisation of knowledge. They have changed significantly over the years, and they are intertwined in important ways with a larger social, political, economic and cultural world. They are also deeply anchored within the institutional habitus of intellectuals. For all of these reasons, a vertical engagement is necessary that mines the disciplines in order to unearth both the deep history of their formation and their profound incorporation into the pre-theoretical dispositions of intellectual practitioners. Such a task aims at plumbing the depths by undertaking both an archaeology of the disciplines and an ethnology of ourselves, thereby introducing much-needed distance from present practices.[3] Rather than seeking a facile exit strategy, like many of the horizontal movements between or amidst disciplines, vertical engagements recognise that changing the disciplines is not like moving partitions or repainting walls, because the only real way out – which is a relative term – is actually down and through. Since disciplines are so profoundly anchored in the powerful institutional structures that sanction intellectual work and are intimately intertwined with the pre-theoretical inclinations shaping subjects, archaeological and ethnological work is necessary to reveal the historical contingency of these naturalised frameworks and bring to light the interstices in which one can gain leverage over them. This opens space, at least potentially, for architectonic displacement rather than sophisticated sidestepping.

Let us consider the case of contemporary philosophy, which in many ways is the result of a deep reconfiguration of the disciplines over the last two and a half centuries. The rising power and social prominence of modern natural science was one of the forces that significantly altered the field of philosophic inquiry. Whereas the practice of *philosophia* prior to the eighteenth century, and particularly the late eighteenth century, included what we would today qualify as scientific investigations into the natural world, philosophy today is no longer coextensive with what is now called science. To take but one noteworthy example, it is revealing that a seventeenth-century philosopher like Descartes wrote extensively on topics of natural science, and that these writings were considered a quintessential part of his *philosophia*. In our day and age, in spite of a renewed interest in cultivating a historical understanding of Descartes's scientific writings, it is still widely assumed that Descartes's philosophy was essentially expressed in so-called properly philosophic texts like the *Meditations* and the *Discourse on Method*. As I have argued in some detail in *Logique de l'histoire: Pour une analytique des pratiques philosophiques*, the very nature of philosophy as a theoretical practice has changed in the course of a few short centuries. It not only ceded the rigorous study of the 'natural world' to the so-called hard sciences, but it also gradually lost the stability of fixed reference points in the metaphysical realm (as well as in the socio-political world).[4] This is, of course, an extremely complex issue, and there was no overnight sea change, but we can say for the sake of argument that metaphysics became – at least within certain circles – an increasingly problematic field of inquiry. Moreover, the relative stability of the socio-political world and the naturalised structures of the *ancien régime* were called into question by modern social revolutions, as well as by significant changes ushered in by the so-called Industrial Revolution, the growth of modern capitalism, the expansion of colonisation, and so forth.[5]

It is within this context that institutions of higher learning began to take on their modern form and a new disciplinary matrix slowly emerged, in a complex force field of agencies that followed no simple pattern. The social sciences pushed through the widening crack between the natural sciences and the humanities, institutionally encroaching or building upon the territory occupied by philosophy. Indeed, as the Gulbenkian Commission has pointed out regarding the historical construction of the social sciences, 'it was primarily within the faculty of philosophy (and to a far lesser degree within the faculty

Introduction

of law) that the modern structures of knowledge were to be built'.[6] These new forms of analysis aimed at developing secular, systematic and empirically verifiable knowledge to account for the diverse features of a changing social world. The modern practice of history, for instance, parted ways with the tradition of chronicles – which focused on the works of supposed great men within a logic of repetitive exemplarity and circular temporality – by establishing largely linear accounts of an increasingly autonomous, denaturalised, archived, empirically verified and more 'egalitarian' past.[7] Economics, political science and sociology proposed novel tools of analysis that could help account for some of the transformations ushered in by industrial capitalism, modern nation-states and new social struggles. Although figures like Vico, Montesquieu, Rousseau and Wollstonecraft could surely be seen as forerunners, it was really through the course of the nineteenth century – especially the latter part – and primarily the early twentieth century that the social sciences consolidated their modern scientific form and were institutionalised.[8] It was also during this time that two other social sciences emerged in order to examine the supposedly undeveloped or underdeveloped regions of the world. Anthropology was formed, in part, in order to study groups perceived to be undeveloped, often lacking modern forms of technology and living in tribes. Since these peoples were frequently under real or virtual colonial rule, anthropology was seen as being able to provide 'information that could make the governors more cognizant of what they could and could not do (or should not do) in their administration'.[9] Orientalism developed as a discipline that focused on major civilisations outside the modern Western world – such as Persia, the Arabic-speaking world, China and India – that had purportedly arrived at a certain stage of development but never advanced to what is called modernity.[10] The new disciplinary framework, which of course included other fields as well, was enmeshed within the cultural structures of Euro-American colonialism, and it was generally assumed – explicitly or implicitly – that different disciplines were necessary to study the 'modern, developed world' than to analyse 'undeveloped' or 'underdeveloped' regions of the planet.[11] Moreover, as Immanuel Wallerstein has powerfully argued, the three social sciences forged for the analysis of contemporary life in the modern Euro-American world[12] – economics, political science, sociology – are founded on the presumption that one can meaningfully distinguish between three relatively autonomous spheres, which is one of the key tenets of liberalism: the market, government and civil society.[13] These can be studied, or so it is assumed, by privileging the present, whereas the past remains the special domain of historians. The modern disciplines are thus not only rooted in a very specific politico-cultural geography, but they are also bound up in important ways with a temporal distribution as well as a precise compartmentalisation of communal life. The world is at least implicitly aligned on a linear trajectory leading from the deep past still supposedly present elsewhere (anthropology and orientalism) to the authentic past qua past of the West (history), and finally to a largely dehistoricised present more or less frozen into three distinct spheres of social existence (economics, political science, sociology).[14] A rarely questioned meta-knowledge thereby undergirds the historical constitution of these fields of inquiry. This does not mean, of course, that all of the work in these areas can be reduced to the factors highlighted above. It is true, moreover, that many important changes have occurred since the mid-twentieth century, and numerous contemporary social scientists have sought to struggle against the inherited distribution of knowledge.[15] Nevertheless, for the continuation and intensification of this struggle, it is vital not to lose sight of the role that the larger politico-economic and cultural world played, and continues to play, in their development.[16]

It is within this changing social and institutional landscape that philosophy took on one of its modern forms in the Euro-American world. As a practice, it was increasingly embedded within institutions of learning, and the question of its shifting relationship to other institutionalised fields of inquiry – from the natural sciences and theology to the emerging historical social sciences (not to mention the traditional practical disciplines of law and medicine) – became crucial, as we will see.[17] Whereas many of the figures identified as major European philosophers in the seventeenth century exercised their professions outside of the academy, philosophers from the end of the eighteenth century increasingly worked as professors and teachers of philosophy.[18] This brought with it significant changes in the fields of inquiry as well as in the very activity of philosophical reflection. The structure and format of classes, the establishment of an institutionalised canon, the solidification of teachable narratives, the exigencies of the accreditation of thinking, the expansion of specialised publications, the formation of unique intellectual communities, the centralised and often circular audience of members of the academy, the branding of academic profiles

Introduction

and the political economy of ideas, the institutional competition with other disciplines – all of these factors and many more contributed in various ways to formatting extremely unique practices of philosophical reflection. These were intertwined, moreover, with a vast expansion of the archive. Through the increased availability and circulation of the written word, the development of modern libraries, the immense work of translators, the growth of the publication industry and other such phenomena, there was greater access to the texts of philosophic history.

It is within this force field, which is obviously much more complex than these few remarks might suggest, that the early forms of what is now called continental philosophy emerged. Although a lot more could be said about this, including the fact that there is not really a single practice of continental philosophy but rather a constellation of theoretical activities grouped under a problematic heading, I would like to simply highlight three features of the disciplinary configuration of these practices that will be important for what follows. To begin with, it is at this point in time that philosophy largely became a historical discipline in the sense that the very act of doing philosophy came to be increasingly identified with that of providing historical accounts of the work of past philosophers. In general, these narratives have been premised on forging a specifically Western tradition of philosophy, most often with an origin in ancient Greece, a characteristic modern turn around Descartes, and an end in the work of the philosophers recounting such stories. Secondly, philosophy gradually became a hermeneutic enterprise in which one of its primary tasks came to be that of interpreting the major texts of an established canon. Thirdly, the very practice of philosophy, at least in certain circles, morphed into an activity best described as exegetical thinking: philosophers think precisely by *thinking through* the canonised works of the past. These three changes have by no means followed the trajectory of a simple, linear development instigated by a sudden sea change. Moreover, there have been, and there continue to be, rival theoretical practices within the discipline of philosophy. Nevertheless, one of the major constellations of contemporary theoretical practice is indeed characterised by a historico-hermeneutic orientation in which philosophic thought in the present is intimately intertwined with reading and rereading the canonised texts of the past masters.

Although a number of problems plague this orientation, as we will see, it is important to recognise that this specific type of theoretical practice has particular advantages when it is well done. It can cultivate historical sensibilities, foster critical acumen in the meticulous analysis of texts in their original languages and promote intellectual practices that recognise the extent to which we are deeply enmeshed in the traditions informing our thought and practice. In relation to purely presentist philosophic practices, as well as those that ignore – often with an explicit but uncanny pretension to scientificity, as if excluding evidence was a sign of analytic rigour – the specificity of formulations and context in the name of abstract arguments, hermeneutic and historical approaches can provide extremely powerful tools for critically resituating ourselves, the work with which we engage, and philosophic claims in general.[19] Moreover, one of the major contributions of this philosophic modality is its critical dimension. It has refined various strategies for taking distance from established systems – not only systems of thought, but also political, economic, cultural and social structures – in order to critically interrogate their conditions of possibility, their presuppositions, their limitations, their exclusions. It is not the least surprising, in this regard, that one of the richest traditions of so-called continental philosophy has developed coextensively with various forms of critical theory, radical political economy, feminism, critical philosophy of race, decolonial thought, queer and trans theory, crip theory, animal studies, environmental philosophy, and so forth. This is probably one of the reasons that it has been institutionally marginalised, as Linda Martín Alcoff powerfully argued in her Presidential Address to the American Philosophical Association's Eastern Division Meeting in 2012.[20] Certain forms of what might more appropriately be called dialectical philosophy favour processes of investigation that remain open-ended, reflexive and potentially non-conclusive, and which are thereby capable of powerfully challenging any limits imposed on inquiry, including those of culturally specific notions of scientificity and their purported social and political neutrality.[21] The task of reinventing contemporary theory can – and I would argue *should* in the current conjuncture – draw on these resources in order to cultivate a deep critical sense of its colonisation by other forms of knowledge, as well as by social, political and economic forces.[22] Far from naively seeking to make it into the queen of the disciplines, such an endeavour aims at reinvigorating philosophic practice as not only the gadfly of disciplined thought but also the potential midwife for alternative theoretical practices.[23]

CRITIQUE OF EXEGETICAL REASON AND THE REINVENTION OF CONTEMPORARY THEORY

Since one of the important theoretical questions in the modern age has been that of the role of philosophy in a world characterised by the perceived successes of the so-called natural and social sciences, it is perhaps not surprising that philosophic practice in a certain tradition has increasingly come to orbit around historical and hermeneutic issues. In the new institutional setting, this appears to be one of the only domains in which philosophy can maintain its disciplinary legitimacy and hold out against the apparent power and social authority of the other disciplines, particularly in a world in which the metaphysical realm is arguably less secure than in other conjunctures. To a certain extent, this could be seen as philosophy having been driven into an institutional corner in which its only valid activity has become its own self-interpretation, that is, the endless exploration of the very textual tradition that it has constructed in order to historically legitimate itself.

This has brought with it a series of grave risks that are – or should be – cause for great concern.[24] To begin with, even though so-called continental philosophy is quintessentially historical, it tends to use impoverished models of historical analysis and explanation, which is at times directly linked to a haughty refusal to engage with the human and social sciences. We are often told that there is a sequence of – more or less disincarnated – ideas that are channelled from the ancient Greeks down to the present, and that we can have special access to this chain of extraordinary thoughts by studying a very small group of philosophic works written by the canonised 'great men' of the so-called Western tradition. This disembodied dialogue across the centuries – in which one often assumes that a fixed set of eternal big questions is debated – unfolds according to a central narrative that allows us to understand the totality of ideas from the Greeks to the present by using a single overarching framework. Perhaps the most widespread script is that there has been a shift from theocentric philosophy (beginning with Greek polytheism and continuing through the monotheistic traditions of the Middle Ages) to subject-centred philosophy (starting with Descartes and continuing through Kant, Hegel and phenomenology), eventually leading to a turn toward alterity and otherness – or, why not, a return of the subject or a turn toward objects – in contemporary thought. This schematisation knows a seemingly infinite number of variations, but the guiding principle remains the same: a single and often extraordinarily simple script permits us to understand all significant human thought in the West with a few very basic ideas.[25] It is true that in contemporary theory there is a widespread tendency to provide a two-dimensional account of history in which a dominant but incorrect way of thinking is either constantly challenged or ultimately overthrown by a superior mode of philosophising. This is the case, for instance, in the myriad histories in which the juggernaut of so-called Western metaphysics is curtailed or resisted by a repressed dimension of differential forces.[26] However, regardless of how these two dimensions are defined, this approach by no means significantly alters the core idea that the entire history of philosophy can be summed up in terms of a simple paradigm (which strikingly resembles fairytales of the perennial battle between the forces of good and evil). This leads to what I propose to call the contradiction of continental philosophy: a purportedly historical intellectual activity regularly relies on some of the most philosophically impoverished models of historiography, often without questioning them in the least (because they tend to operate as givens). The same is true, moreover, of the geographical models used for thinking the history of thought. It is generally assumed that philosophy is quintessentially a European phenomenon and that the history of properly philosophical thinking goes hand in hand with a history of Europe that stretches from the ancient Greeks to the present.[27] The rest of the world is implicitly or explicitly plunged into the abyss of non-thought, or at least non-philosophy.[28] Finally, the social models for structuring the supposed Western tradition of philosophy are embedded in a highly problematic hierarchical distinction between what Hegel called the 'heroes of thinking, of pure thinking' – that is, the great individuals who really philosophise, and who are most often white bourgeois western European males – and the unthinking or unphilosophical masses.[29]

In the face of these problems, and in a historical conjuncture where doing a certain type of philosophy still amounts primarily to examining the textual history of a particular philosophic tradition, the question of historical methodology should be at the forefront of theoretical debates. Indeed, the reinvention of contemporary theory – at least of this genre – requires a deep and expansive interrogation into its own historical methods (as well as their historical constitution).[30] It also necessitates a critical re-evaluation of its highly questionable cultural geography and operative social hierarchies. This work cannot simply be done within the historically constituted discipline of philosophy. It entails breaking with some of the unquestioned givens of disciplined thought and engaging extensively and profoundly with other modes of inquiry. This can not only enrich and transform philosophical inquiry, but it can also help reconfigure some of the givens of these other domains of investigation. Ultimately, this requires deep social and institutional reconfigurations that radically overhaul the contemporary knowledge economy.[31]

A second major risk has to do with the hermeneutics of isolated, disembodied and canonised texts, and a third with the perpetuation of exegetical thinking. The theoretical assumption that reflection is quintessentially a heroic endeavour in which a few privileged individuals chart the historical course of human thought is inherently problematic, and it ignores the deeply social and collective aspects of thought processes as well as the material formation of archives and individual bodies of work (which ultimately demonstrate that the very distinction between text and context is untenable).[32] It also creates a deep and almost insurmountable divide between the gods of thought, on the one hand, and philosophical acolytes on the other. Professional education in philosophy is almost exclusively oriented toward the latter, meaning that one is typically trained to be an interpreter, not a philosopher. In fact, attempting to cultivate the intellectual practice of a thinker, as opposed to a potential instructor of philosophy, is often perceived as deviant and presumptuous. Such acts are duly subdued or sidelined by an expansive system of naturalised institutional sanctions that serve to protect and preserve the intellectual division of labour.

The centre of gravity of so-called continental philosophy is exegetical thinking. The very practice of philosophising takes place within a framework of textolatry – to appropriate Vilém Flusser's felicitous neologistic reworking of idolatry – in which one reflects through the canonised words of the beatified saints.[33] Doing philosophy, in this regard, amounts to producing professional secondary, or even tertiary, literature aimed at providing an internal analysis of an elite pantheon of texts. There is, of course, a broad spectrum of possibility, including fidelity to original Ur-texts à la Pierre Menard, as well as readings that seek to undermine interpretive consensus and thereby transform commentary into original philosophy. In most cases, the *summum bonum* of such a practice is respectful originality: the interpreter introduces her or his own thought through a close reading of one of the crowned princes of philosophy.[34] Indeed, the professionalisation of philosophic discourse makes it resemble crackerjack forms of ventriloquism, in which the speaker's dummy – which needs to appear to speak for itself – is in fact a mummy produced out of the preserved paper shreds of the past.[35]

This can, in particular cases, perpetuate a specific form of intellectual imperialism insofar as it is almost exclusively the continental Europeans – and especially western Europeans – who are today recognised as the true originators of philosophic thought.[36] In fact, many forms of anglophone continental philosophy remain haunted by just such modes of Eurocentric theoretical colonisation, which is also intimately bound up with the perpetuation of class-based, racialised, patriarchal, ableist, urbanist and other hierarchies. For the masters of thought are, or at least appear to be – with a few important exceptions – white, bourgeois males from Europe.[37] There is thus a very specific intellectual and libidinal economy that is often at work in certain philosophic circles organised around European father figures.[38] According to a rarely questioned practical phallogocentrism and international division of labour, a handful of 'great men' from Europe are recognised as the only ones who can truly think, and they come to function – in certain communities – as the bearers of unquestionable philosophic realities.[39] This fosters, moreover, a unique form of authority epistemology, according to which a proposition is valid simply because a recognised authority stated it.[40] Argumentation, demonstration and the rigorous analysis of concrete particulars become secondary to faith in the father. The contemporary version of the scholastic expression *autos epha* – 'he said' meaning Aristotle, *the* philosopher, claimed it, therefore it is true – is 'my father figure said' or, more colloquially, 'my guy said'.[41] This type of philosophy as hero worship, or continental scholasticism, places thought at the feet of supposed philosopher kings, thereby imposing infantilisation as the consensual order orchestrating the thought and work of the droves of interpreters.[42] This theoretical *ancien régime* is often severely perpetuated, moreover, by the economy of the theory industry and the star system in their unrelenting search for a celebrity pool of bankable icons.

There are, of course, excellent examples that break with the colonisation of thought and the libidinal economy of authority epistemology.[43] Moreover, we should not unduly simplify the situation or essentialise thinkers based on what are sometimes superficial sociological classifications,⁴⁴ nor should we slip into a simplistic cultural geography according to which one inverts these categories by making Europe anathema and only recognising as valid those thinkers who are from a supposed outside.⁴⁵ The simple fact of writing on specific figures from a particular tradition does not, in itself, invalidate one's claims, just as the replacement of these thinkers by others – father figures by mother figures, for instance, or 'major' intellectuals by 'minor' ones, European theorists by non-European thinkers – does not necessarily alter the logic of practice at work.⁴⁶ Differences in form, when they are not combined with transformations in content and method, can produce false appearances of change according to the stereotyping logic of certain forms of identity politics, which concentrate more on an author's sociological categorisation than on what they actually say or how they say it. Moreover, it is not only that ideas cannot be invalidated due to their geographical provenance, but it is also important to recognise that references to intellectual work in continental Europe can actually function, in certain discourses and at particular times, as an appeal to a minority discourse resisting a mainstream consensus (as has certainly been the case in the relationship between much of 'continental' thought and the dominant institutions of Anglo-American philosophy during and after the Cold War).⁴⁷ In this book, it is true that the primary reference points remain some of the emerging or established philosophers of a particular tradition, and its author is fully cognisant of both the enormous critical power of this heritage and the persistent problems plaguing its historical constitution. As a series of interventions into an existing discursive field, what matters most for these writings is in many ways what is done with these figures. Far from blind embrace or dismissive rejection, far from hagiography or parricide (the inverted form of hagiography, in which the ideal saint of thought is the dead, eternalised saint), this book proposes a critique of exegetical reason by rigorously engaging with prominent philosophic positions precisely in order to develop a deep methodological intervention into contemporary theoretical practice, as well as propose an expansive and potentially innovative thematic analysis.⁴⁸ The metaphilosophical critique of continental scholasticism needs to mine this tradition and cull from it its major strengths, one of which is historico-hermeneutic rigour and precision. We need to move, however, from imprisonment to empowerment, from incarceration *within* the interstices of a socially constituted canon to an empowering historical elevation of thought that carefully works through – in order to think *with* and potentially beyond – some of the most prominent intellectual projects of a certain philosophic tradition.

With the aim of contributing, then, to the ambitious goal of reinventing contemporary theory, the chapters in this volume seek to propose alternative tools for thinking history, for engaging with the writings of the supposed masters, and, ultimately, for doing philosophic work. They develop a heterodox account of the history of contemporary thought, as well as an alternative rendering of the historical relations between art and politics. In general, the book proposes a form of radical historicism in which all of our most cherished values, concepts and practices are recognised as being historical through and through. This means that philosophy itself, rather than being an eternal form or even a unified enterprise in the history of the so-called Western world, is a socio-historical practice. In fact, one could even say that philosophy per se does not exist precisely because there are only various theoretical practices that are labelled – in different socio-historical conjunctures – as philosophical. It is therefore of the utmost importance to develop an understanding of history that permits us to map the chronological, geographic and socio-cultural dimensions of these practices. This allows us to break with the binary logic of epoch and event, or continuity and discontinuity, while elaborating an alternative account of historical change in terms of metastatic transformations that are unequally distributed across these three dimensions. Such a logic or order of history invites us to think in terms of overlapping constellations of theoretical practice within an expansive socio-cultural field. This book thereby proposes to radically part ways with many of the now-standard schematisations of the history of philosophy as well as of contemporary theory, which include both the movement model of philosophic sequences (in which, for instance, existentialism is followed by structuralism, which is in turn displaced by post-structuralism, and then why not by event philosophy or object-oriented ontology) and the individual paradigm that purports to simply rely on the supposed singularity of the work of each thinker.[49]

Hermeneutically, this project resists both the philosophical habitus that encourages us to identify the origin of thought with the mind of an individual philosopher – and to unduly rely on the constructed limits of his or her corpus as the limits of thought – and the reductive determinism that seeks to establish a single social determinant behind the work of a particular individual or group of thinkers. This has not only required an extensive engagement with other disciplines, but it has also necessitated working through the historical constitution of these fields in order to try and come to terms with some of their structural limitations. This has been important because in turning its back on authority epistemology, this book takes the writings of prominent philosophic figures as propositions within a vast cultural field that invite exploration rather than obsequious acquiescence. This means that philosophic hermeneutics is not simply a matter of participating in the institutionalised ritual of the internal analysis of canonised texts. Rather than taking philosophers at their word, this book invites us to diligently work through their writings by directly engaging with their objects of analysis in order to test claims, question deep-seated assumptions, advance counterpropositions, and elaborate alternative cartographies of the material in question. In the place of exegetical thinking, it advocates cultural theoretical engagements that call into question disciplined thought.

Although labels can often be problematic, this attempt to reinvent philosophic practice is not unrelated to what I have begun calling, through the insightful instigation of my friend and colleague Pierre-Antoine Chardel, *sociophilosophie*.[50] In addition to directly engaging with the analysis of socio-cultural phenomena *in concreto*, *sociophilosophie* attempts to rethink philosophy's relationship to the larger social, political, economic and cultural world. More specifically, one of the central methodological propositions of this book is that it is necessary to undertake a metaphilosophical critique aimed at reconfiguring the intellectual givens of theoretical practice. Rather than proposing another interpretation, in the sense of a move within a well-orchestrated game, it attempts to raise questions about the very nature of the game that is being played and its larger cultural and political relevance. This form of critique is by no means a purely intellectual endeavour that consists in proposing a philosophical analysis of philosophy, nor is it an attempt to unveil the theoretical presuppositions or individual leaps of faith operative in particular philosophies. It does not play the philosophic game against itself, so to speak, nor does it rely on the time-tested strategy of philosophic succession through the criticisms of the theoretical assumptions of one's predecessors. Instead, it seeks to change registers by scrutinising philosophy as a specific – and variable – type of intellectual social practice and examining the givens inherent within it. These elements, which go without saying for practising philosophers, are generally beyond the purview of philosophical analysis for one of two reasons: they either remain so implicit to the very act of philosophy that they are not recognisable as objects of inquiry, or they present themselves as so banally self-evident that they require no philosophical reflection or investigation. Unknown or too well known, the metaphilosophy of philosophic practice can hardly interest philosophers qua philosophers.[51] And this is with good reason: it can endanger faith in the philosophic game by raising troublesome questions regarding what it is that we do when we philosophise, and why, therefore, we do it.

RETHINKING THE HISTORICAL RELATION BETWEEN ART AND POLITICS

This is a collection of autonomous essays that does not claim to provide a historical survey of contemporary thought, nor does it purport to construct a single argument that develops sequentially through the course of the book. Each chapter is a specific intervention into a particular field, and some of the analyses are certainly more interventionist than others. The authors engaged with are not supposed to be representatives of particular schools of thought or movements. They have been chosen due to the major contributions that they have made to certain thematic debates, and in a number of cases they are thinkers with whom I had the opportunity to work directly (Derrida, Badiou, Rancière). Other philosophers could have taken their place or been added to the list, but circumstantial factors and structural coherence played an important role in circumscribing this project. This is in part because the analyses that follow are methodologically and thematically driven. They all seek to raise – from different vantage points – systemic questions regarding philosophical methodology and what it is that we do when we purport to engage in contemporary theory. These methodological preoccupations orbit, moreover, around three primary topics, which have been central to my research over the last fifteen or so years: history, politics and aesthetics. Although individual essays tend to focus on one of these issues, they all contribute in various ways to the overall project of developing alternative models for thinking the historical relationship between political forces and aesthetic practice. They are thereby preoccupied with one of the fundamental themes of critical theory in the broad sense of the term: what – if any – is the relationship between art and politics, and how can we make sense of their historical devel-

Introduction

opments? Rather than understanding these two spheres as separated by an insurmountable divide or linked by a privileged bridge, I argue that they are best understood as socially negotiated realms of practice that change radically over time, and whose various dimensions sometimes overlap, intertwine and even merge in specific socio-historical conjunctures.[52]

The opening chapter explores a philosophic question that reflexively sheds light on the orientation of the volume as a whole: how can we write the history of the present? Against the backdrop of the more specific concern with how to understand the present state of philosophy, it turns to the late work of Michel Foucault and his unique account of the ontology of contemporary reality (*l'ontologie de l'actualité*). It carefully reconstitutes his intriguing description of the event-like appearance of a new, modern attitude in the late work of Immanuel Kant. This attitude – which is more interrogative than declaratory – is precisely the same one that is at work in Foucault's own writings, for it consists in inquiring into the event-like status of contemporary reality by asking: what is the difference that characterises our present? In yet another act of performative repetition, Foucault thereby seeks to identify the event of event-based thinking, which he locates at the source of a historical trajectory leading to his own work. Although he obviously wants to part ways with periodic history insofar as it conceives of modernity as a time period rather than an attitude, this chapter raises a number of critical questions regarding the persistence of periodic history, the limitations of event-based thinking, the perpetuation of a Eurocentric cultural geography, and ultimately the very project of an ontology of contemporary reality. With brief forays into the work of figures such as Agamben and Kracauer (as well as Shakespeare, Vico, Montesquieu and Herder), it goes on to suggest that an alternative logic of history – founded on the three dimensions of time, space and social practice – would allow us to completely reformulate the way in which we approach the problem of the present. It suggests, in fact, that the present does not exist as a fixed and stable category, since it has no being per se. There are always multiple presents whose borders and definitions are negotiated in variable historical, geographic and social settings. The philosophic argument that is developed regarding the possibility of a historical ontology without being (*une ontologie sans l'être*) discreetly sets the theoretical stage for the rest of the chapters by suggesting that there is no single present of contemporary thought that could be grasped once and for all. Instead, there are various descriptive interventions that are more or less beholden to the metaphilosophical parameters of 'contemporary' theoretical practice.

The next chapter proposes a counter-history of what many take to be a seminal debate in the transition from structuralism to post-structuralism: the Foucault-Derrida controversy. It calls into question the widespread assumption that Derrida rejected Foucault's structuralist stranglehold by demonstrating that the meaning of a text always remains open. Through a meticulous examination of their respective historical models, methodological orientations and hermeneutic parameters, it argues that Derrida's critique of his former professor is, practically speaking, a call to return to order. His text performatively argues that the true task of philosophy is the endless internal analysis of the canonical texts of the Western tradition. In this way, it implicitly and explicitly criticises those trained philosophers like Foucault – and other so-called structuralists such as Lévi-Strauss and Bourdieu – who had been led astray from the philosophic fold by the social sciences. The ultimate conclusion is that the Foucault-Derrida debate has much less to do with Descartes's text per se (the proof thereof is that they both turn a blind eye to the patent fact that the mad speak, and in fact speak firmly and constantly [*constanter/constamment*], in the *Meditations*[53]) than with the relationship between the traditional tasks of institutionalised philosophy and the meta-theoretical reconfiguration of philosophic practice via the methods of the social sciences.

The final chapter of section I turns to the work of Jacques Rancière. He has, perhaps more than any other prominent living philosopher, extended the historical and historiographical work of Foucault by proposing an archaeology of aesthetics, with a particular concern for its relationship to politics. In doing so, however, he has avoided providing a genealogical account of the emergence of aesthetics, which appeared at more or less the same time as modern democracy. This chapter thereby sets as its task a critical reassessment of the genealogical limitations of Rancière's description of the historical relationship between art and politics. It is in this light that it advances an alternative account of historical causality by examining the variable conjuncture of determinants that contributed to the emergence of what Rancière calls the aesthetic regime of art. In order to do this, it implicitly calls into question Rancière's ultimate reliance on metaphilosophical parameters that keep him from seriously questioning a disciplinary matrix in which

Introduction

the purportedly anarchic power of philosophy is pitted against the supposedly reductive determinism of the social sciences.[54] In this regard, it functions as a transitional chapter that develops some of the historiographical, methodological and disciplinary arguments in the preceding chapters while simultaneously preparing for the next two sections on art and politics.

The opening chapter to section II returns to my interest in developing a counter-cartography of the present. It carefully outlines the implicit value system and binary normative logic – the valorisation of difference over and against identity – that has dominated what is called the philosophy of difference in France and played an important role in the politics of difference in the anglophone world and beyond. By detailing a series of surreptitious conceptual operations aimed, in part, at disguising the rigidity of this metaphilosophical axiology, it calls into question the sacralisation of difference, with special attention to its operative historiographical paradigms and its ultimate political consequences. It proposes, in this regard, a metaphilosophical critique of one of the deep-seated normative commitments that has dominated a significant portion of contemporary theoretical practice. This critical intervention thereby synthesises one of the central motifs of the book as a whole, which is to dismantle the metaphilosophical scaffolding of specific modalities of intellectual practice, and more specifically the more or less discreet attribution of value to difference in a seemingly endless number of domains.

The next chapter turns to the work of one of the major philosophic figures in francophone thought to have stalwartly resisted the theoretical constellation of the philosophy of difference: Cornelius Castoriadis. This is in part due to his identification with a tradition of radical critique that calls into question the standard academic role of philosophy and redefines it as the act of 'taking responsibility for the totality of the thinkable [*prise en charge de la totalité du pensable*]'.[55] Situating his work in relationship to Sartrean existentialism and the so-called structuralists or post-structuralists, whose publications have cast a long shadow over his own writings, it presents the fundamental stakes of a powerful but understudied intervention that sought to propose alternative theoretical practices (which largely cut across the grain of his socio-historical conjuncture). It thereby provides a succinct but comprehensive account of how his historical ontology and his defence of political autonomy form the backdrop for his writings on aesthetics, psychoanalysis and the philosophy of science. It also critically assesses the extent to which his departure from exegetical thinking did not lead to a broader critique of continental historiography and Eurocentrism, particularly in his account of the history of philosophy and politics.

The concluding chapter in this section examines Rancière's work on politics by calling into question his largely ahistorical formalisation, his strategy of hegemonic generalisation, his conceptual transcendentalism, his embrace of the value-concept of democracy, and his problematic positions on current events (which purport – in rather contradictory fashion – to distinguish between what is properly political and what is not). This critical reflection draws on a number of disciplines and weaves together both historical analysis and the study of the present in order to formulate an argument against the existence of politics proper. More specifically, it directly contests the thesis of works like *Hatred of Democracy* by sketching the broad outlines of an intransitive history of democracy in which there is no fixed, transhistorical object of analysis. It thereby seeks to open space for alternative histories of politics, which are not premised on identifying its true nature and then establishing binary scripts in which this nature is either preserved or debased.

Section III transitions from the question of politics to that of aesthetics by beginning with a chapter that explores what is arguably one of the most important contemporary debates between living French philosophers: the Badiou–Rancière controversy. This debate, which echoes in interesting ways the earlier exchange between Derrida and Foucault, is shown to have largely been an exchange in which they talk past one another (*un dialogue de sourds*). They each tend to criticise the other from a privileged citadel – politics for Badiou, aesthetics for Rancière – without responding to the criticisms of their opponent. Against this backdrop, the chapter seeks to provide a concise but comprehensive account of their respective positions on aesthetics and explain where their projects overlap as well as where they definitively part ways. In particular, it is concerned with distinguishing between two strategies for philosophically engaging with the arts: illustrative hermeneutics, which uses artwork as a representation of pre-existing philosophical concepts, and immanent cultural analysis that seeks to elucidate the specific aesthetic logic operative in concrete historical practices.

This investigation is followed by a chapter that outlines more broadly Rancière's major contribution to contemporary debates on art and poli-

Introduction

tics by situating it in relationship to the work of his predecessors, and more specifically the models of content-based commitment and formal commitment found respectively in Sartre and Barthes. It highlights the refreshing departure that he proposes from established paradigms for thinking art and politics. By unpacking his powerful thesis on their consubstantiality, it explores the idea that art can potentially configure and reconfigure the distribution of the sensible. At the same time, it underscores some of the limitations inherent in his resistance to fully historicising politics as well as in his tendency to succumb to what I call the ontological illusion and the social epoché.

The concluding chapter is organised around one of the major problems in contemporary theoretical debates – from Lukács and Adorno to Lyotard and Rancière – on art and politics. With a few rare but important exceptions, these discussions have favoured the visual arts and literature over and against architecture and urban design. However, as a few thinkers like Benjamin, Foucault and Lefebvre have suggested, if there is one art that appears to be prototypically political (in the sense that it is almost inevitably the site of collective decisions that directly shape the social body while simultaneously being subject to multifarious communal appropriations), it is probably architecture and public art. This paradox leads to a question of central importance, which guides the ensuing analysis: why have many of the foremost philosophic debates on the historical relation between art and politics sidelined what is perhaps – at least from a certain vantage point – the political art par excellence? By exploring the various facets of this question, this chapter proposes a critical re-examination of the metaphilosophical assumptions – including the hierarchical distinction between high art and low art, the intellectual and the material, and so forth – undergirding many of the standard historical narratives regarding the development of art and its relationship to politics.

Although they intervene in very specific debates and are anchored in a unique set of concerns, all of the chapters contribute – from various and motley perspectives – to a critical rethinking of the historical relationship between art and politics. This thematic dimension is, however, always combined with another, reflexive and performative aspect, which consists in critically interrogating the inner workings of philosophic practice and its deep-seated metaphilosophical framework. The central proposition is hence that it is not enough for us to revisit the question of history, politics and aesthetics with the same basic intellectual tools. It is necessary to intervene in such a way as to reconfigure the theoretical equipment and methods that we have at our disposal, for it is precisely the forging of new instruments, novel practices, different intellectual communities and ultimately alternative institutions that will allow us to reinvent contemporary theory.

NOTES

1. See Pierre Bourdieu's excellent essay on 'The Philosophical Institution', which concludes with the following lines: 'Thus, it is on condition that they take what is indeed the greatest possible risk, namely that of bringing into question and into danger the philosophical game itself, the game to which their own *existence* as philosophers, or their own participation in the game, is linked, that philosophers can assure for themselves the privilege that they almost always forget to claim, that is to say their freedom in relation to everything that authorises and justifies them in calling themselves and thinking of themselves as philosophers' (Montefiore (ed.), *Philosophy in France Today*, p. 7).
2. It would nonetheless be tempting to cite – as reference points for discussion rather than quintessential instances – Michel Foucault's account of the work of Marx and Freud as 'initiators of discursive practices [*fondateurs de discursivité*]' (Bouchard (ed.), *Language, Counter-Memory, Practice*, p. 131). They did not simply author works, according to Foucault, but they produced 'the possibility and the rules of formation of other texts' (p. 131). In the vocabulary used here, we might then say that they intervened in such a way as to create new spaces of practice, which gave birth to entire traditions. Foucault's own work – like the activities of the early Frankfurt School – could equally be seen as an intervention, though arguably of a different sort, that has contributed to the transformation of the very 'practice of thinking' via a 'de-disciplination' that has opened up new territories, methods and objects of analysis (see Ádám Takács's excellent analysis in 'Between Theory and History: On the Interdisciplinary Practice in Michel Foucault's Work'). We could add to the list of references for discussion the contributions made, in various ways, to the forging of new models of intellectual activity by figures such as Aimé Césaire, Frantz Fanon, Cornelius Castoriadis, Luce Irigaray, Samir Amin, Cornel West, Arundhati Roy, Anibal Quijano and Angela Davis.
3. Since traditional ethnology is often founded on an epistemological separation between the knower and the known, the subject of thinking and the object of action, this ethnology of ourselves might equally be described as a reverse ethnology, meaning an ethnology of the ethnographers.

4. On this point, see Gusdorf, *Introduction aux sciences humaines*, particularly pp. 346–7.
5. All of these changes were not unrelated to what we might call, in conceptual shorthand, a general temporalisation of the world. See Loren Eiseley's important work on this theme, including *Darwin's Century: Evolution and the Men Who Discovered It* and *The Firmament of Time*. Ernst Cassirer's *The Philosophy of the Enlightenment* is also a valuable source to consult.
6. Wallerstein et al., 'The Historical Construction of the Social Sciences', p. 7.
7. See Arendt, *Between Past and Future*, Hartog, *Régimes d'historicité*, Koselleck, *Futures Past*, Rancière, *Les Mots de l'histoire*, and Ziolkowski, *Clio the Romantic Muse*.
8. See Gusdorf, *Introduction aux sciences humaines*, Karsenti, *D'une philosophie à l'autre*, Manicas, *A History and Philosophy of the Social Sciences*, Wagner, *A History and Theory of the Social Sciences*, and Wallerstein et al., 'The Historical Construction of the Social Sciences', pp. 12–13.
9. Wallerstein, *World-Systems Analysis*, p. 8. Also see Asad, *Anthropology and the Colonial Encounter*, McGrane, *Beyond Anthropology*, and Wallerstein, *Unthinking Social Science*.
10. Although I am here drawing on Wallerstein's depiction of orientalism, Edward Said's magisterial work on the subject, *Orientalism*, which extends well beyond the discipline of orientalism, remains a crucial reference point.
11. There would, of course, be much more to say about other disciplines, such as geography and psychology, and all of these developments varied according to place and time. However, for the sake of concision, I have followed the general parameters put forth by the Gulbenkian Commission.
12. More specifically, these have as their common concern primarily five geographic regions, which correspond to the five colonial powers: France, Great Britain, the United States, and the territories that would later be called Germany and Italy.
13. See Wallerstein, *World-Systems Analysis*, p. 6: 'dominant liberal ideology of the nineteenth century insisted that *modernity* was defined by the differentiation of three social spheres: the market, the state, and the civil society. The three spheres operated, it was asserted, according to different logics, and it was good to keep them separated from each other – in social life and therefore in intellectual life.' See also 'The Present in the Light of the *Longue Durée*: Dialogue with Alfredo Gomez-Muller and Gabriel Rockhill', in Rockhill and Gomez-Muller (eds), *Politics of Culture and the Spirit of Critique*, pp. 98–112.
14. Despite painting in broad strokes at times and not developing a more radical politico-economic critique, Dipesh Chakrabarty's criticisms of 'historicism' and the deep-seated assumption that Europe is the sovereign

subject of all histories constitute an important contribution to the task of rethinking the disciplines: *Provincialising Europe: Postcolonial Thought and Historical Difference*.
15. The list of such endeavours would be too long to cite in full, but let us signal in passing the work of subaltern studies, postcolonial and decolonial theory, world-systems analysis and the 'ontological turn' in contemporary anthropology. In the last case, Eduardo Viveiros de Castro's forceful and innovative invitation to think anthropology as the 'permanent decolonisation of thought' is particularly noteworthy (*Cannibal Metaphysics*, p. 4).
16. Bruno Karsenti rightly emphasises the various ways in which the social sciences also empowered citizens with new tools of analysis, although this is arguably at the risk of significantly downplaying their negative effects. See *D'une philosophie à l'autre*, as well as the discussion of the book that took place on 11 July 2014 at the Critical Theory Workshop in Paris.
17. The precise topography of the institutional landscape, as well as the delimitation of the disciplines, depends on the specific socio-historical force field in question. Immanuel Kant's *Conflict of the Faculties*, for instance, provides revealing insight into the institutional struggles – between theology, law, medicine and philosophy – in the German-speaking world at the end of the eighteenth century. Theodore Ziolkowski has provided an enlightening institutional analysis of the same conjuncture in *German Romanticism and Its Institutions*.
18. See Levi, *Philosophy as Social Expression*, p. 166: 'From the birth of Francis Bacon in 1561 to the death of David Hume in 1776 – that is, for two hundred years – not one first-rate philosophic mind in Europe is permanently associated with a university.'
19. Kwame Nkrumah and Herbert Marcuse have both forcefully lambasted the conformism inherent in logicist and consensual practices of philosophy, which have not surprisingly been widely sanctioned and supported by mainstream institutions. They clearly have in mind some of the dominant forms of philosophy in the anglophone world. Nkrumah highlights, for his part, the social contention operative – explicitly or implicitly – in philosophy prior to the twentieth century and then writes: 'It is therefore not a little amazing that in the twentieth century, Western philosophers should largely disinherit themselves and affect an aristocratic professional unconcern over the social realities of the day' (*Consciencism*, p. 54). Marcuse fixes his sights on ordinary language philosophy and its extensions: 'Paying respect to the prevailing variety of meanings and usages, to the power and common sense of ordinary speech, while blocking (as extraneous material) analysis of what this speech says about the society that speaks it, linguistic philosophy suppresses once more what is continually suppressed in this universe of discourse and behaviour. The authority of philosophy gives its

Introduction

blessing to the forces which *make* this universe' (*One-Dimensional Man*, p. 175).
20. Alcoff, 'Philosophy's Civil Wars'.
21. There are some good arguments in favour of abandoning the expression 'continental philosophy', with all of its Eurocentric connotations (see, for instance, Maldonado-Torres, 'Post-Continental Philosophy'). It is nevertheless important to recognise that it operates as a social signifier within a larger force field, and that much of mainstream anglophone philosophy would welcome its disappearance or dissolution through internal critique, thereby allowing it to colonise the small remaining place that it precariously preserves within certain institutions. In this sense, thinkers like Amy Allen (in personal conversation) have made the equally significant argument that it can be necessary, in certain instances, to maintain the expression 'continental philosophy' as a – perhaps poorly named – place-holder for alternative spaces of thinking.
22. 'Today', as Alcoff poignantly asserted in 'Philosophy's Civil Wars', 'philosophy in the flesh has its back against the neo-liberal wall by those forces who want to know what value we add to higher education.'
23. These alternative practices need not necessarily be limited, of course, to ones inscribed within the historical and hermeneutic orientations of so-called continental philosophy.
24. The emergence of what is called analytic philosophy around the turn of the twentieth century surely cannot be separated from the ambition to modify the legitimate realm of philosophic activity, in part by at least partially calling into question this historical and hermeneutic orientation in the name of an examination of logically true statements in the present (which is largely modelled on certain scientific practices). This is not to suggest that we can thereby rely on a simplistic opposition between two different traditions (some philosophers trained in the 'analytic' tradition do the history of philosophy, and many of those trained in 'continental' philosophy engage with 'analytic' work), but rather that we need to be attentive to deep shifts in theoretical practice. It is also not to imply that the investment in identifying logically true statements in the present is purely laudable. The metaphilosophy of this practice is in dire need of a critical investigation that is as expansive and deep as it is structural and political. Although it is unfortunate that he does not seriously engage with the work of Frances Stonor Saunders and others on the minute details of the cultural Cold War, John McCumber has nevertheless made an important preliminary contribution to this project by foregrounding some of the links between the institutional domination of analytic philosophy, which began in the US in the early 1950s, and the post-war conservative hegemony summed up under the label 'McCarthyism'. 'The McCarthy

era', he writes, 'imposed an important restriction on just what kind of goal philosophers can pursue. It limited them to the pursuit of true sentences (or propositions, or statements)' (*Time in the Ditch*, p. xix). Moreover, he adds that 'there is also evidence suggesting that American philosophy largely remains, even today, what Joe McCarthy's academic henchmen would have wanted it to be' (p. xvii).

25. One of the significant pitfalls and limitations of certain forms of postcolonial and decolonial theory is precisely its tendency to maintain similar simplistic narratives regarding the history of 'the West'.

26. The very idea of Western metaphysics is perhaps the metaphysical notion par excellence since it is coterminous with the superstition that an eerie but omnipresent spectre is haunting the entire history of a particular 'culture'.

27. This tradition was invented in the late eighteenth and early nineteenth century, and was then projected back onto history as if it were a natural given, as I have argued in some detail in *Logique de l'histoire*. 'The great majority of early modern historians of philosophy', Peter K. J. Park adeptly writes, 'were in agreement that philosophy began in the Orient. It was in the late eighteenth century that historians of philosophy began to claim a Greek beginning for philosophy' (*Africa, Asia, and the History of Philosophy*, p. 2). Robert Bernasconi has powerfully and incisively made the same argument in a number of articles, and Park draws explicitly on his work (see, in particular, 'Philosophy's Paradoxical Parochialism: The Reinvention of Philosophy as Greek'). On the category of 'the West' and the construction of origin narratives in order to lay claim to certain civilisational commodities (democracy, philosophy, human rights, humanism, freedom, and so forth), see also David Graeber's essay 'There Never Was a West: or, Democracy Emerges from the Spaces in Between', in *Possibilities*.

28. Park cogently notes that 'the development of the modern discipline of philosophy and the exclusion of non-European philosophies from the history of philosophy are related phenomena' (*Africa, Asia, and the History of Philosophy*, p. 5).

29. Hegel, *Introduction to the Lectures on the History of Philosophy*, p. 62. The entire quotation reads as follows: 'The history of philosophy deals with Ideas in the form of *thinking*. It presents conscious thinking, puts before us the heroes of thinking, of pure thinking, for our consideration in their achievements. The achievement is the more excellent the less the particular character of its author has imposed its seal on it. It is in philosophy that the particular (i.e. the particular or private activity of the philosopher) disappears, and all that remains is the field of pure thought' (pp. 62–3). The suspicious and paradoxical nature of this type of attempt to disembody the

Introduction 29

history of philosophy, when the latter is in fact the history of very specific bodies thinking and bodies of thought, must not be lost on us.

30. 'For a philosopher', as Cornelius Castoriadis rightly pointed out, 'there *must* be a critical history of philosophy. If this history is not critical, he is not a philosopher; he is only a historian, an interpreter or a hermeneutician [...] Philosophy is a reflective activity that deploys itself at once freely and under the constraint of its own past. Philosophy is not cumulative – but it is profoundly historical' (*Philosophy, Politics, Autonomy*, pp. 17–18, translation slightly modified).
31. On this point, see Castoriadis, *Crossroads in the Labyrinth*, pp. 119–228.
32. In addition to *Logique de l'histoire*, where I make this argument in detail, see Nkrumah's trenchant criticisms of the museumification of canonical philosophic texts in the Western tradition, which is due to an 'academic treatment' that is 'the result of an attitude to philosophical systems as though there was nothing to them but statements standing in logical relation to one another' (*Consciencism*, p. 3).
33. See Flusser, *Towards a Philosophy of Photography*, p. 12.
34. Louis Pinto has provided insightful analyses of this and other related phenomena in *Les Philosophes entre le lycée et l'avant-garde* and *La Vocation et le métier de philosophe*.
35. Friedrich Nietzsche put his finger on a crucial aspect of this problem in his radical critique of professional philosophers' shortage of historical sense: 'You ask me about the idiosyncrasies of philosophers? ... There is their lack of historical sense [*ihr Mangel an historischem Sinn*], their hatred of even the idea of becoming, their Egyptianism. They think they are doing a thing *honour* when they dehistoricise it, *sub specie aeterni* – when they make a mummy of it. All that philosophers have handled for millennia has been conceptual mummies; nothing actual has escaped from their hands alive. They kill, they stuff, when they worship, these conceptual idolaters – they become a mortal danger to everything when they worship' (*Twilight of the Idols*, p. 35).
36. Gayatri Spivak poignantly and provocatively raised the crucial question of the relationship between Western intellectual production and Western economic interest in her canonical essay 'Can the Subaltern Speak?'.
37. This is surely one of the factors contributing to what Alcoff has aptly described as philosophy's demographic challenge: 'The world of philosophy today is, how shall I put it, "demographically challenged". In the United States, the discipline is less than 25% female (and women comprise less than 17% of full-time faculty, according to a recent study). African Americans, Asian Americans, Native Americans and US-born Latinos are rarities.' She attributes this to the West's 'universalist concepts': 'those who think themselves ahead of the historical curve have no need to worry

about the limitations of anything as quotidian as gender or ethnicity' ('Philosophy's Civil Wars'). Also see her essay 'A Call for Climate Change for Women in Philosophy'. See also Annika Thiem's extremely insightful call for institutional transformation in 'Queering Philosophy: How Can Queer Theory Inform and Transform the Practice of Philosophy?'.

38. This libidinal economy is the site of a form of cultural coloniality that perpetuates itself – as Aníbal Quijano has poignantly argued in a different context – through the seduction of Europeanisation rather than via repression. In his incisive essay 'Coloniality and Modernity/Rationality', he discusses the history of colonialism and underscores the moment when 'European culture was made seductive': 'beyond repression, the main instrument of all power is its seduction. Cultural Europeanisation was transformed into an aspiration [...] European culture became a universal cultural model' (Mignolo and Escobar (eds), *Globalisation and the Decolonial Option*, p. 23).

39. Parting ways with this institutionally inscribed cultural division of labour requires the cultivation of heterodox intellectual practices that cut across, and even leap beyond, the well-trodden paths within extant archives. Avram Alpert's important work is a case in point insofar as he seeks to redraw the established map of cultural and intellectual relations by providing prismatic readings of modern themes – such as the self in a global setting – that are refracted across modern European thought, American Transcendentalism, the black radical tradition and Zen Buddhism (see his dissertation 'Practices of the Global Self', part of which is currently being reworked into a book project entitled *Unbearable Identities: Essaying the Globe from Montaigne to Suzuki*).

40. This ideal-typical orientation knows a vast series of variations. For instance, Ian Hacking has identified a parallel but slightly different 'penfriend approach to the history of philosophy': 'A few heroes are singled out as pen-pals across the seas of time, whose words are to be read like the work of brilliant but underprivileged children in a refugee camp, deeply instructive but in need of firm correction' ('Five Parables', in Rorty, Schneewind and Skinner (eds), *Philosophy in History*, p. 103).

41. In relation to this highly problematic epistemology, it might be said that contemporary philosophy, in order to renew itself, needs to undertake an anti-scholastic revolution, parallel in certain ways to what took place in the seventeenth century in the writings of figures such as Sanches, Descartes and Hobbes. The last summed up one of the shared concerns of these and other authors at the time in the following terms: 'to forsake his own natural judgment and be guided by general sentences read in authors [...] is a sign of folly, and generally scorned by the name of pedantry' (*Leviathan*, p. 27).

Introduction

42. The battle of interpreters in many ways becomes a struggle over the relative status of the philosopher kings in which the elevation of one's *maestro* brings with it *osmosis legitimation*: the commentator, via mystical transfer, is ranked according to the ranking of masters.
43. Although I do not engage directly with their work in this book, the writings of the following figures all attest to a robust and diverse tradition of anglophone philosophy that works through but is by no means subservient to the 'recognised European masters': Seyla Benhabib, Wendy Brown, Judith Butler, Stanley Cavell, Dipesh Chakrabarty, Partha Chatterjee, Angela Davis, Nancy Fraser, Stuart Hall, Frederic Jameson, Richard Rorty, Edward Said, Gayatri Spivak, Charles Taylor, Cornel West.
44. Although he runs the risk of flattening the enormous discrepancies between different types of privilege, or even masking certain positions of privilege altogether, Gilles Deleuze nonetheless raises a very important point when he claims: 'The difference between minorities and majorities isn't their size. A minority may be bigger than a majority. What defines the majority is a model you have to conform to: the average European adult male city-dweller, for example … A minority, on the other hand, has no model, it's a becoming, a process. One might say the majority is nobody. Everybody's caught, one way or another, in a minority becoming that would lead them into unknown paths if they opted to follow it through' (*Negotiations*, p. 173).
45. The decolonisation of theoretical practice requires the development of a complex cultural topography based on a multidimensional conceptualisation of space. Rather than reducing the latter to a single, abstract background space or delimiting the world in terms of monolithic geographic blocs, the task of this radical geography is to denaturalise space and chart a multiplicity of different and overlapping spaces while being attentive to the stratifications and distributions operative within each of these heuristically delimited fields. This requires developing tools for a multivariate mapping that uses a multiplicity of factors to situate elements in spaces. Although this approach seeks to part ways with many of the now-standard but schematic geographic oppositions – the West and the rest, the North and the South, the core and the periphery, the First and the Third World, and so on – it should be emphasised that it does not in the least take the wind out of the sails of the critique of Eurocentrism. It simply identifies different levels of intervention by criticising what is heuristically labelled Eurocentrism while simultaneously recognising that Europe has no centre properly speaking, but is instead the site of striated, overlapping and contested spaces. The critique of Eurocentrism is thus recognised as a twin project to that of deconstructing the very idea that Europe has a centre. The latter does not exist *in itself* as a given reality but is rather a complex,

historically variable entity that forcefully persists *for itself* (or rather *for some*) and *for others*. The critique of Eurocentrism is thus simultaneously the critique of the centre of Europe, of centre-Europeanism. Finally, it is important to note that geographic synecdoche is an important rhetorical strategy in this dual endeavour, for it allows us to speak of certain entities – like Europe – while fully recognising that the part is being taken for the whole, that is, that this is a heuristic construction.

46. Nelson Maldonado-Torres has foregrounded this problem in the case of displacing the continent of reference from Europe to elsewhere: 'continentality may thus change its referent (Africa, America, Asia, Australia, or Latin America), but not necessarily its logic' ('Post-Continental Philosophy', p. 2).

47. Drawing on the important historical and political work of John McCumber, Maldonado-Torres has argued that continental philosophy in post-war America developed in part as a critical political and epistemological response to the conformism and consensualism of analytic philosophy, which was the preferred bedfellow of McCarthyism and conservative politics more generally (see 'Toward a Critique of Continental Reason', in Gordon and Gordon (eds), *Not Only the Master's Tools*, pp. 54–5).

48. This has nothing whatsoever to do with the theoretical bulimia that consists in ingesting work – often the latest trend of best-sellers – as quickly as possible in order to deliver it back to the public with the same rapidity in the form of an endless spate of theoretical purée.

49. The work of figures from an array of different fields has proven extremely helpful in parting ways with the standard philosophical schematisations of recent history. See, for instance, the writings of Anna Boschetti, Pierre Bourdieu, Michel Cressole, François Cusset, François Dosse, Jean-Louis Fabiani, Niilo Kauppi, Michèle Lamont, Albert William Levi, Pascal Ory, Louis Pinto and Jean-François Sirinelli.

50. See, for instance, his lecture at the École Normale Supérieure on 14 November 2013 entitled 'Socio-philosophie de la technique et de l'internet'. We are currently working on a book project together, tentatively entitled *Pour une sociophilosophie du monde actuel*.

51. Metaphilosophy is simultaneously among ($\mu\varepsilon\tau\acute{\alpha}$) and after or beyond ($\mu\varepsilon\tau\acute{\alpha}$) philosophy as such, for it is at once immanent to philosophic practice and generally beyond the scope of philosophers. This is not unrelated to what Pierre Bourdieu called 'philosophical doxa', which he defines as 'everything that goes without saying, and in particular the systems of classification determining what is judged interesting or uninteresting, the things that no one thinks worthy of being mentioned, because there is no *demand*' (*Sociology in Question*, p. 51). Also see the definition that he provides in *Pascalian Meditations*: 'a set of fundamental beliefs which

Introduction

does not even need to be asserted in the form of an explicit, self-conscious dogma' (p. 15). Although this is not the place to detail the differences between these two notions, let us signal one important discrepancy: where Bourdieu celebrates ordinary language philosophers as 'irreplaceable allies' in his sociological critique of philosophy (*Pascalian Meditations*, p. 31, translation slightly modified), I would argue that it is crucially important in our conjuncture to undertake a deep and expansive critique of the metaphilosophies operative in different philosophic practices. For that matter, we must equally bring critical attention to bear on phenomena such as metasociology and metahistory, even when we draw on and develop the work of researchers in these fields.

52. In this regard, the concerns of this book strongly resonate with the arguments I advanced in *Radical History and the Politics of Art*.
53. This argument is developed in the second section of *Logique de l'histoire*, which is the context in which this text takes on its full meaning, and in which it was originally published.
54. This is particularly apparent in the problematic position that he takes in 'Penser entre les disciplines: Une Esthétique de la connaissance'.
55. *The Castoriadis Reader*, p. 362 (translation slightly modified).

Section I: History

Chapter 1

HOW DO WE THINK THE PRESENT? FROM ONTOLOGY OF CONTEMPORARY REALITY TO ONTOLOGY WITHOUT BEING*[1]

EPOCHAL THOUGHT

From 'the postmodern era' to 'the post-industrial epoch' and 'the digital age', people have not ceased to offer labels for the present. To find *the* concept capable of defining the nature of it, and thus to speak truthfully regarding the characteristic feature of our age, is in effect one of the major theoretical concerns of numerous contemporary thinkers. But less attention is paid to the historical logic on which such a preoccupation depends. By historical order or logic, I mean the practical mode of intelligibility of history that provides us with temporal schemes, methodologies and patent positivities. In the case of the search for the concept most capable of grasping the core of our era, it goes without saying, for instance, that the present is a singular phenomenon, that it is identifiable and delimitable, that it warrants being interrogated in and for itself, that it has a proper nature, and that a single and unique concept would be capable of defining it. Such an investigation thus falls within a historical order dominated by what we can call epochal thought. This can be generally understood as the reduction of history to a periodical chronology, and more specifically as the attempt to grasp – perhaps even with a single epochal concept – the nature of an era, or of an important subset of it.

It can turn out that the investigation into the nature of the present proves itself to be more revealing of our historical conjuncture than the responses it provides. At least this is what Michel Foucault suggests in several texts written at the end of the 1970s and at the beginning of the 1980s. He initiates a reflection on what he proposes to call 'the

---

* This chapter was translated by Theodra Bane in close consultation with the author.

ontology of contemporary reality [*l'ontologie de l'actualité*]' by raising a fundamental question: where, historically speaking, does this interrogation into the very being of the present – so characteristic of our conjuncture – come from? In posing such a question, he attempts to historically resituate a certain form of historical questioning. In other words, he recognises that our relationship to the present, far from being invariable, is a thoroughly historical phenomenon. He thereby denaturalises our relation to contemporaneity along with our way of thinking of contemporary reality. In this way, he opens up the possibility of a historical critique of epochal thought.

His reflection on the ontology of contemporary reality revolves around Immanuel Kant, and notably around his essay 'Response to the Question: What is Enlightenment?' (1784).[2] He hopes to pinpoint in this text what is perhaps the first formulation of the question 'what is our contemporary reality?'.[3] Since the day Kant inquired into this question, philosophy has acquired, according to Foucault, a new dimension: 'it opened up a certain task that philosophy had ignored or that didn't previously exist for it, and which is to say who we are, to say what our present is, what that is, today.'[4] This task is simultaneously historical and anthropological because it is a matter of an ontology of contemporary reality that is at one and the same time an ontology of ourselves: 'I think that philosophical activity conceived of a new pole, and that this pole is characterised by the permanent and perpetually renewed question; "What are we today?"'[5] The philosopher from Königsberg had apparently responded to this central question in an almost entirely negative manner by defining the present 'as an *Ausgang*, an "exit", a "way out"': 'He is looking for a difference: What difference does today introduce with respect to yesterday?'[6] Thus it isn't at all surprising to see Foucault himself directly identify with this tradition of thought:

> Kant, Fichte, Hegel, Nietzsche, Max Weber, Husserl, Heidegger, the Frankfurt School have tried to answer this question. By inscribing myself in this tradition, what I am trying to do is thus to provide very partial and provisional answers to this question through the history of thought.[7]

It might seem that Foucault quite simply extends epochal thought to another level: rather than proposing a direct response to the question of the nature of the present, he suggests that it is precisely this question itself that constitutes the characteristic feature of our age. Indeed, he explains in a 1978 text that the historico-philosophic practice that he himself lays claim to:

> clearly finds itself in a privileged relationship to a certain period that can be empirically determined. Even if it is relatively and necessarily vague, this period is, of course, designated as a formative moment for modern humanity: *Aufklärung* in the broad sense of the term, to which Kant, Weber, etc. referred, a period without fixed dates, with multiple points of entry [...][8]

But in his 1984 article, whose title repeats verbatim that of Kant, he proposes to speak instead of an 'attitude of modernity'.[9] He even calls into question the identification between modernity and a period of history:

> Rather than wanting to distinguish the 'modern period' from 'pre' or 'postmodern' epochs, I think it would be better to try to find out how the attitude of modernity, ever since its formation, has found itself struggling with attitudes of 'counter-modernity'.[10]

For Foucault, an attitude is 'a mode of relating to contemporary reality [*l'actualité*]' that does not necessarily extend to the totality of an epoch.[11] On the contrary, it is the result of a 'voluntary choice made by certain people'.[12] Hence it appears that each historical period is potentially torn between several attitudes.

Foucault's reflection on the ontology of contemporary reality has the advantage of shedding light, up to a certain point, on the historicity of temporal experience and of its privileged categories. Instead of thinking of the present as an invariable formal category whose contents would change over the years, he actually inquires into the historical reconfiguration of the very category of the present. He thus invites us to reflect on the relationship between opposing historical attitudes rather than accept as such the presupposition according to which there could be a single and unique experience of contemporary reality. This being said, his discussion of the attitude of modernity remains somewhat ambivalent because he nonetheless wishes to locate it at the opening of a new epoch of thought, which is in fact the age of the advent of event-based thinking (*la pensée événementielle*).[13] He thereby traces a line of demarcation, in what appears to be an abstract temporality, between the age opened by the modern attitude and preceding epochs. He even says that the response to the Enlightenment question establishes a reciprocal, intertwining relationship between philosophy and its age:

> *Aufklärung* was made into the moment when philosophy found the possibility of establishing itself as the determining figure of an epoch, and when that epoch became the form of that philosophy's accomplishment. Philosophy could also be read as being nothing else than the composition of the particular traits of the period in which it appeared, it was that period's coherent figure, its systematisation, or its conceptualised form; but, from another standpoint, the epoch appeared as being nothing other than the emergence and manifestation, in its fundamental traits, of what philosophy was in its essence.[14]

We can therefore ask ourselves if Foucault went far enough in critically distancing himself from epochal thought, at least in his writings on the ontology of contemporary reality towards the end of his life.

The same is true of the brief reflection that Giorgio Agamben proposed on the contemporary, in which he relies in many respects on Foucault's analysis (with Heidegger and Nietzsche as subtexts). For it is equally a case of a courageous attitude – judged to be rare – with regard to the present: 'to be contemporary is, first and foremost, a question of courage'.[15] The contemporary is more precisely the one who dares to swim against the current of the times by having the courage to be untimely, occupying a position between the 'not yet' and the 'no more' (like fashion, according to Agamben).[16] He writes:

> Contemporariness is, then, a singular relationship with one's own time, which adheres to it and, at the same time, keeps a distance from it. More precisely, it is *that relationship with time that adheres to it through a disjunction and an anachronism.*[17]

And it is precisely such an untimely relation with the present that would allow contemporaries – according to the paradox extolled by Agamben – to grasp their moment better than anyone else:

Those who are truly contemporary, who truly belong to their time, are those who neither perfectly coincide with it nor adjust themselves to its demands. They are thus in this sense irrelevant [*inattuale*]. But precisely because of this condition, precisely through this disconnection and this anachronism, they are more capable than others of perceiving and grasping their own time.[18]

Yet such a paradox does not part ways in the least with periodic chronology. Quite the opposite: it presupposes it. For there is only a paradox provided that the present is thought in its epochality and the contemporary is defined as that which grasps the underlying nature of it precisely by moving away from it. Without the delimitation of the present – even if it be very general – and the relative coherence of epochs, anachronism would be incomprehensible. Moreover, the act of making distance from contemporary reality into the condition *sine qua non* of its conceptual seizure changes absolutely nothing with regard to the structuring of historical temporality. In the depths of this apparent questioning of chronology, we discover its endorsement. For the true paradox of this untimely anachronism, it might be said, is by no means situated at the level of a short circuit between proximity and distance with regard to the present. The true paradox is that the recognition of anachronism as such depends very precisely on well-structured time.

RETHINKING THE PRESENT

To rethink what is called 'the present', we must definitively part ways with epochal thought, that is the reduction of history to a periodic chronology and – more precisely – the effort to identify the underlying nature of each period, potentially resorting to a single and unique epochal concept. It is not enough to criticise this or that manifestation of it, or to slightly modify a few aspects. It is necessary to dismantle the historical order on which it depends. This entails, at the same time, the creation of an alternative logic of history that organises the problematic of the present entirely differently, and that abandons once and for all the chimerical quest for the epochal concept that is the most capable of grasping the distinctive feature of contemporary reality. This is because, to begin with, there is neither a nature of the present nor a conceptual essence of our moment. Nor are there merely two rival attitudes opposing one another since 1784.

For purely heuristic reasons, we should distinguish between three dimensions of history: the chronological dimension of temporality, the geographic dimension of space, and the social dimension of practices. As far as the first dimension is concerned, which often casts a shadow over the other two, it is important to recall that temporality is itself a historical element through and through.[19] Given that time, as we know it, is a human phenomenon, it varies in accordance with the three heuristic dimensions of history. There is thus no time in general, except through the projection from a specific structuring of temporality. What we can call *the perennial problem* consists precisely in thinking of the temporal from the atemporal, the historical against the background of the ahistorical. This is a quasi-permanent problem in the history of thought, which directly results from the supposed permanence of temporality, understood as the invariable formal structure framing the flow of time.

Moreover, in the abstract temporality of what is called the scientific age, there is no reason to expect that each period display an internal coherence. As Siegfried Kracauer has shown, there may be other forms of coherence that do not depend on chronological parameters at all. The existence of an abstract temporal framework based on modern forms of dating by no means implies a fundamental homology between all phenomena situated therein: simultaneity does not necessarily mean unification, cohesion or even coherence. Incidentally, it is not at all necessary that time – and, more precisely, the scientific chronology of the 'modern age' – be the most fundamental mode of historical organisation.

For all these reasons, Kracauer is absolutely right to proclaim 'the *Zeitgeist* is only a mirage'.[20] 'Cross-influences', he writes, 'are often counterbalanced by sundry inconsistencies.'[21] He thus calls into question the historical category of the epoch: 'the typical period is not so much a unified entity with a spirit of its own as a precarious conglomerate of tendencies, aspirations, and activities which more often than not manifest themselves independently from one another.'[22] And he is absolutely right to add: 'This is not to deny the existence, at any given moment, of certain widespread and even prevailing beliefs, goals, attitudes, etc.'[23] Yet, rather than completely abandon the category of the epoch, the author of *History: The Last Things Before the Last* affirms that we must defend two apparently contradictory and incompatible positions. On the one hand, he states that 'measurable time dissolves into thin air, superseded by the bundles of shaped times in which the manifold comprehensible series of events evolve'.[24] But he immediately adds: 'dating retains its significance inasmuch as these bundles tend to coalesce at certain moments which then are valid for all of them.'[25] Hence his critique of periodic history does not entirely break with periodic historical logic. Rather, he makes an effort to rethink the category of the epoch by abandoning the presupposition that assumes it would result from the homogeneous flow of time particular to abstract chronology. A period would thus presuppose neither a homogeneous temporality nor a unifying spirit. It would be, properly speaking, a spatio-temporal unity with its own rhythm:

> As a configuration of events which belong to series with different time schedules, the period does *not* arise from the homogeneous flow of time; rather, it sets a time of its own – which implies that the way it experiences temporality may not be identical with the experience of chronologically earlier or later periods.[26]

Time is only one dimension of history, and the latter is never reducible to its temporality alone. Otherwise it would remain imperceptible and intangible. If there were no agents, objects or elements situated in space, we would only be dealing with the elusive unfurling of an ephemeral phenomenon. Without space, history would quite simply not take place. The *nunc* is always a function of the *hic*, and vice versa. 'Chronology and geography', writes Giambattista Vico, 'are the two eyes of history.'[27] It is for this reason that it is absolutely necessary to provide an account of the horizontal dimension of history, that is to say the distribution of phenomena in space.[28] It is precisely by emphasising the spatial dimension that we can avoid the homogenisation of historical space particular to the purely chronological conception of history, which reduces it to the sole vertical dimension of time.

This is what Foucault has a tendency to do in his diverse writings on Kant and the *Aufklärung*, which grant a considerable privilege to historical discontinuity. For he suggests over and over again that the philosopher from Königsberg opened a new age, and more precisely that his essay on the Enlightenment was the advent of event-based thinking. He thus finds in Kant the starting point that was at the origin of his own project: the inquiry into the ontology of our contemporary reality. Such an interpretation inevitably presupposes a socio-historical compression (the *sine qua non* condition of epochal thinking). The variability and complexity of the social and historical world, as well as the effective circulation of Kant's article, are largely bracketed in the name of a vertical conception of history in which the latter comes to function more or less like a single thread susceptible to being severed at precise moments due to the simple existence of one written work.

This being said, there is at least one place where Foucault points out the geographic dimension of the history of the modern attitude regarding contemporary reality. Although he still keeps to the European tradition, he highlights, in an article on Georges Canguilhem, the differences between three cultural contexts:

> It would be necessary no doubt to try and determine why this question of *Aufklärung* has had, without ever disappearing, such a different destiny in the traditions of Germany, France, and the Anglo-Saxon countries; why has it taken hold here and there in so many and – according to the chronologies – such varied domains?[29]

He notably juxtaposes the 'historical and political reflexion on society' particular to the German tradition with the history of sciences in France.[30] But the same kind of questioning appears in different cultural conjunctures. Hence the Enlightenment question remains the unifying spirit of diverse orientations, that is to say the general theoretical framework whose contents vary according to context.

It is not sufficient to chart historical phenomena in the vertical dimension of chronology and the horizontal dimension of geography. It is equally necessary to account for the stratigraphic dimension of social practices. For each space-time is the site of diverse activities, and there can be absolutely divergent practices in the same chronotopic framework. It is thus just as important to think the sociality of history as to reflect on historical geography because geography always has a specific topography, composed of diverse strata of social practices. Victor Hugo provided an excellent illustration of this in the chapter of *Les Misérables* entitled 'The Year 1817', where he presents a long list of so many diverse details neglected by history:

> Such was the confused mass of the now-forgotten events that floated like flotsam on the surface of the year 1817. History ignores

almost all these minutiae: it cannot do otherwise; it is under the dominion of infinity. Nonetheless, these details, which are incorrectly termed little [...] are useful. It is the features of the years that make up the face of the century.[31]

Despite his critique of the blackmail of the Enlightenment, Foucault tends to think social space, in his reflection on the ontology of contemporary reality, in terms of an opposition between two attitudes: that of modernity and those of counter-modernity (the same applies *mutatis mutandis* to Agamben). Such a dichotomy reduces the complex topography of diverse social force fields to a binary logic opposing the Kantian tradition, with which Foucault identifies, to that of its rivals. A procedure of historical legitimation is operative here that is well attested in contemporary philosophy. History divides itself in two in accordance with an epistemological-normative division: the true thinkers of this or that purportedly crucial issue (contemporary reality, discontinuity, the contemporary, difference, alterity, incommensurability, indiscernibility, etc.) oppose all of those who are grappling with ideas judged to be dangerous, obsolete or inauthentic (counter-modernity, continuity, the non-contemporary, identity, and so on). Incidentally, it is assumed that the former are more sophisticated, profound or penetrating than the latter, even in cases where a certain idea of historical progress is called into question, while relying on a purely vertical history, structured by the more or less eternal repetition of a conceptual battle seemingly without end.

It is also notable that Foucault individualises the question of the modern attitude, edging even closer to a simplified form of historiography that is omnipresent in philosophy. It is not only that the history of the modern attitude is a heroic history (Hegel) or a monumental history (Nietzsche) of the great men of the European past, from Kant and Hegel to Weber, Nietzsche and the Frankfurt School. It is also that the anthropological question 'what are we today?' is largely thought of within the individual framework of the constitution of an autonomous subject.[32] Far from offering us a truly social anthropology, Foucault brings the question of *our* contemporary reality back to one of an individual decision within a binary social space: either we adopt the modern attitude in daring to ask ourselves about the difference of our historical moment like Kant, or else we display an anti-modern attitude by turning our backs on it.

As I have already had the opportunity to emphasise elsewhere, this individualisation of the question of the *Aufklärung* is particularly problematic in Kant's case. For, contrary to what Foucault would like us to believe in some of his writings, the philosopher from Königsberg insisted precisely on the properly social dimension of the Enlightenment. He writes:

> For any single individual to work himself out of the life under tutelage which has become almost his nature is very difficult [...] But that the public should enlighten itself is more possible; indeed, if only freedom is granted, enlightenment is almost sure to follow.[33]

Incidentally, it is the transformation of the community – if not of humanity as a whole – that is at the heart of the project of the *Aufklärung* according to Kant. Far from being a personal question or an individual affair of historical attitude, it is a reconfiguration of society due to the public use of reason. Given that such a transformation is necessarily a long-term task ('the public can only slowly attain enlightenment'), there cannot be an event-based discontinuity in the history of the Enlightenment according to Kant: 'Perhaps a fall of personal despotism or of avaricious or tyrannical oppression may be accomplished by revolution, but never a true reform in ways of thinking.'[34] It is probably for this reason that Foucault neglects the vitally important distinction that Kant proposes between the age of Enlightenment (*Aufklärung*) and the enlightened age (*aufgeklärte Zeitalter*).[35] To the question 'Do we now live in an *enlightened age*?', Kant responds, 'No, but we do live in an *age of enlightenment*.' And he immediately recalls the properly social dimension of the *Aufklärung*:

> As things now stand, much is lacking which prevents men from being, or easily becoming, capable of correctly using their own reason in religious matters with assurance and free from outside direction.[36]

Taking into account the social dimension of the Enlightenment, we must ask ourselves how many people were really interested in the *Aufklärung* debate. There were many who had not read Kant, Mendelssohn, Erhard and the other participants in the debate.[37] And as far as their readers are concerned, is it really legitimate to speak of a division between the attitudes of counter-modernity and an attitude – judged to be novel – of modernity? Let us briefly linger on the revealing case of J. G. Herder, who is not only situated in the same space-time as Kant, but was also described by the latter – despite his severe criticisms – as a thinker having had the courage to go beyond the superstitions of his profession. Herder called into question the ethnocentric idea of a linear and universal progress leading straight to European, that is to say 'enlightened', culture. Indeed, insisting on the diversity of cultural conjunctures, he lashed out directly at ethnocentrism and epochal thinking, and more generally at the historico-geographic abstraction on which they rely. 'No one in the world', he writes, 'feels the weakness of general characterisation more than I. One paints an entire people, age, part of the earth – whom has one painted?'[38] Emphasising the epistemological limits of finite beings, he fittingly highlights the gap between historical, geographic and social diversity on the one hand, and the generality of our categories of classification on the other:

> I know by the way, like you, that every general image, every general concept, is nothing but abstraction – the Creator alone is the one who conceives the full unity of any one and of all nations, in all their great diversity, without thereby losing sight of their unity.[39]

Epochal thinking presupposes an epistemological mastery of time, of space, and of social topography. This is exactly what Herder calls into question. In light of such a critique, situated precisely in the space-time of Kant, it behoves us to inquire into the Foucauldian thesis regarding the unprecedented nature of the latter's historical reflection. Was the author of 'What Is Enlightenment?' truly the first in the entire world to raise the question of contemporary reality in terms of event-based difference? Methodologically, we must first emphasise that it is impossible to know this with precision, since we quite simply do not have access to the thought of the totality of individuals at a given moment. And even the textual archives that we have at our disposal for this period are extremely vast, especially if we take into account publications in all of the languages of the world. Even if we restrict ourselves to the three linguistico-cultural spaces privileged by Foucault, numerous potential counter-examples come to mind. Due to lack of space, it is hardly possible to begin an exhaustive analysis here. We must then limit ourselves to indicating some cases that would merit closer examination, without pretending to have definitively proven, in the present framework, that these are pre-Kantian 'ontologies of contemporary reality'.

Let us begin with a position on the issue that was staked out well before Kant's. I have in mind the description of the theatre, and more precisely of theatrical performance, by Shakespeare in what is without a doubt his most well-known play. When addressing a troupe of actors, whom he defines in general as 'the abstracts and brief chronicles of the time', Hamlet advises them not to deviate from 'the purpose of playing':

> Whose end both at the first, and now, was and is, to hold as 'twere the mirror up to nature, to show virtue her own feature, scorn her own image, and the very age and body of the time his form and pressure.[40]

Claudius's nephew is not only providing a general description here. By making such a declaration while a brief play is being prepared to be performed before the new king (Claudius) and his wife (Hamlet's mother), he confesses his true intention: to conjure forth the hidden essence of contemporary reality, to lift the veil of history by showing the true nature of the present moment (which proves to be a disjointed time due to the fratricide committed by Claudius). Through a reversal so characteristic of Shakespeare's plays, it is the game of appearances that reveals the hidden depths of things: 'The play's the thing / Wherein I'll catch the conscience of the king.'[41] It is theatrical performance, Shakespeare seems to suggest in this spectacular *mise en abyme*, that is capable of unveiling the present reality that has been concealed by the false theatricality of life.

Since one might say that this is more a calling into question of the true nature of the present than an investigation centred on the question 'who are we today?', let us turn to the Enlightenment, where other examples come to mind. Although Giambattista Vico does not open an inquiry into contemporary reality as such in the *New Science* (1725 and 1744), he bases his entire project on the need, in his age, for a new science of human institutions. He thus takes on board the scientific method of Francis Bacon in order to establish a science of history and of society. Such a task uses a 'new critical art' that links philosophy to the historical analysis of the languages, customs and activities of diverse peoples ('philology' is the name he gives to such an analysis).[42] While it is true that Vico's project is not specifically centred on the study of contemporary reality, his new science clearly originates in his own present and advances a method for analysing history in its entirety, whether it be the past or the present. Evidence can be found for this, for example, in his references to the 'latest times of the civilised nations' and to 'the humanity of our day'.[43] This is more explicit in *On the Study Methods of Our Time* (1709), where he aims precisely at pinpointing the difference between his age and that of the ancients by comparing 'the advantages afforded by the study methods of the two epochs': 'My goal [...] is to indicate in what respect our study methods are superior to those of the Ancients; to discover in what they are inferior, and how we may remedy this inferiority.'[44]

We should also consider the role of contemporary reality in the work of Montesquieu, and notably in the *Persian Letters* (1721), where he describes the society of his time from diverse perspectives. In this regard, it is very revealing that he himself makes reference to contemporary reality (*l'actualité*) in 'Some Reflexions on the *Persian Letters*', which was added to the 1754 edition: 'novels of this type are usually successful because *one provides an account oneself of one's current situation* [*on rend compte soi-même de sa situation actuelle*], which means that emotions are conveyed more powerfully than any narrative accounts of them could do.'[45] As a final example, Jean-Jacques Rousseau seems to directly anticipate the conceptualisation of the present as a moment of outlet or exit (*Ausgang*), as well as the motto proposed by Kant for the *Aufklärung*, which in fact dates back to Horace: *aude sapere* (have the courage to know). In the preface to the *First Discourse* (1750), he writes:

> There will always be men destined to be subjugated by the opinions of their century, their Country, their Society: Some men today act the part of the Freethinker and the Philosopher who, for the same reason, would have been but fanatics at the time of the League. One ought not to write for such Readers when one wants to live beyond one's century.[46]

Moreover, like Herder after him, he proposes a critique of the idea of ethnocentric historical progress, which is so characteristic of his contemporary reality, and he summons us to shake off the yoke of historical myopia and of national prejudices: 'the whole earth is covered with Nations of which we know only the names, and yet we pretend to judge mankind!'[47]

TOWARDS A TOPOLOGICAL SEIZURE OF HISTORICAL PHASES

It is in obscuring the spatial and social variations of historical phenomena in the name of synthetic blocks and homogeneous units of practices that some people pretend to be able to establish sovereign concepts capable of grasping the totality, or the quasi-totality, of what takes place at a given moment. It is as if everything was miraculously linked – be it only within a specific region or for a particular tradition – by a sole and unique spirit of the times. Once we bring to light the geographic and social variability of practices, it must be recognised that there is no unifying spirit of the times, that there is no *Zeitgeist*. Time is, moreover, only one dimension of history, and there is no metaphysical force organising it into more or less homogeneous units. The consideration of the three dimensions of history therefore necessitates the abandonment of the traditional categories of epochs and events, as well as those of continuity and discontinuity. To be sure, it can sometimes be useful to make heuristic references to temporal phenomena of this kind without being obliged to reconstruct a more complex historical logic each time (evidence for this can be found in a few of the references in this chapter), but we must not forget the purely pragmatic status of these references. In general, then, we should think instead in terms of phases and metastatic transformations. A phase, contrary to a historical period, always distributes itself in a singular manner in the three dimensions of history. And a metastatic transformation, as opposed to an event, attests to a specific propagation at variable rhythms, spreading in social space-time through waves of progression or regression.

That is not at all to say that we are condemned to remain silent in the face of temporal complexity and spatial diversity. It is absolutely possible to rethink contemporary reality from the alternative logic of history outlined above. To this end, we must abandon epochal thinking in the name of a topological intervention that proposes, from a very precise point in space-time, a cartography of diverse constellations of practices. And just as a constellation is neither a raw positivity nor a pure invention, a topological seizure is neither purely objective nor absolutely subjective. It is the attempt on the part of a socio-historical agent to grasp the broad lines of a historical conjuncture by mapping, as far as possible, its phases and its metastases in the three dimensions of history. A conjuncture is not a homogeneous space-time or an epoch susceptible to being enclosed within a single container concept. It is a socio-historical field of forces. Such a seizure thus proposes a three-dimensional chart that functions as a modifiable navigational map orienting us in the conjuncture.

Ultimately, what is interesting about Foucault's thesis is not his claim to have grasped the nature of the modern attitude from its moment of initiation by the genuine thinker of the Enlightenment. What makes his position interesting is much rather that he proposes *nolens volens* a topological seizure of Kant's conjuncture, and more precisely of a very specific constellation of theoretical practices centred on the present. Like any constellation, it does not at all dominate the totality of the conjuncture, but it shares the historical sky with numerous other constellations (that do not necessarily organise themselves into a binary opposition). Foucault thus poses a question that is very much worth pursuing: was there, in a certain constellation of theoretical practices situated in the European culture of the end of the eighteenth century, a relatively singular interrogation into the specificity of the present?

By way of conclusion, let us return to the question pinpointed by Foucault in Kant in order to propose an entirely different solution. As we have seen, the author of *The Archaeology of Knowledge* sees in Kant an ontology of contemporary reality in the sense of a novel investigation into the very being of the present. It is certainly interesting that it is about an inquiry, but it is precisely this element that, through a conceptual reversal, comes to define the nature of the present. Moreover, this present strictly distinguishes itself from other 'presents' that preceded it. Foucault thus supplies us with a discontinuous history founded on a largely chronological conception of history, which generally eliminates the geographic and social dimensions. Once one accounts for these, it is necessary to recognise that we can only do an ontology of contemporary reality provided that we recognise that being is lacking: there is no 'present' in the singular, there is no single 'we'. This means that the ontology of contemporary reality must become, properly speaking, an ontology without being or an ontology without being an ontology (*une ontologie sans l'être*). Without unicity, 'our present' cannot be grasped by an epochal concept, or any other container concept claiming to lay hold of the essential core of a historical moment. Thus, instead of desperately searching for *the* concept of *our* era, we should develop – from specific anchoring points and relying on a completely different historical order – topological seizures of the phases and metastases of diverse constellations. Rather than rethinking the nature of the present by proposing the umpteenth epochal concept, what is at stake, more profoundly, is the task of rethinking the very way in which we think the present by recognising that there is no being at the heart of time.

NOTES

1. I would like to express my gratitude to Mogens Laerke and Diogo Sardinha for their comments and suggestions.
2. It is interesting to note that Foucault traces the critical attitude, defined as 'the art of voluntary inservitude', much further back than Kant in a text from 1978 entitled 'What Is Critique?' (in *The Politics of Truth*, pp. 41–81).
3. Foucault, 'What Our Present Is', in *The Politics of Truth*, p. 129 (translation slightly modified).
4. Ibid., pp. 129–30 (translation slightly modified).
5. Foucault, 'The Political Technology of Individuals', in *Power*, p. 403 (translation slightly modified).
6. Foucault, 'What Is Enlightenment?', in *The Foucault Reader*, p. 34. See also ibid., p. 38: 'It is in this reflexion on "today" as difference in history and as motive for a particular philosophical task that the novelty of this text appears to me to lie.'
7. 'The Political Technology of Individuals', p. 403 (translation slightly modified). See also Foucault, *The Government of Self and Others*, pp. 19–21, and 'What Our Present Is', p. 10.
8. 'What Is Critique?', p. 57 (translation slightly modified).
9. 'What Is Enlightenment?', p. 38.
10. Ibid., p. 39 (translation slightly modified).
11. Ibid., p. 39.
12. Ibid., p. 39.
13. I take the liberty of referring the reader to my own analysis of this problematic in 'Avènement de la pensée événementielle? *Aufklärung* entre Kant et Foucault', in *Logique de l'histoire*, pp. 363–84.
14. Foucault, 'Life: Experience and Science', in *Aesthetics, Method, and Epistemology*, p. 467 (translation slightly modified).
15. Agamben, 'What Is the Contemporary?', in *What Is an Apparatus?*, p. 46.
16. Ibid., p. 49.
17. Ibid., p. 41.

18. Ibid., p. 40.
19. See Elias, *Time: An Essay*.
20. Kracauer, *History: The Last Thing Before the Last*, p. 183.
21. Ibid., p. 183.
22. Ibid., p. 66.
23. Ibid., pp. 66–7.
24. Ibid., p. 154.
25. Ibid., p. 154.
26. Ibid., p. 155.
27. Vico, *The New Science of Giambattista Vico*, p. 11.
28. Space as we know it is, of course, a historical phenomenon like time, and it is therefore variable.
29. 'Life: Experience and Science', p. 468. See also 'What Is Critique?', pp. 50–5.
30. 'Life: Experience and Science', p. 468.
31. Hugo, *Les Misérables*, p. 118.
32. 'What Our Present Is', p. 137. It should be noted that Foucault insists more on the public dimension of the *Aufklärung* in *The Government of Self and Others*, pp. 7–12.
33. Kant, *On History*, p. 4.
34. Ibid., p. 4.
35. To my knowledge, there is a single place where Foucault edges closer to this distinction, without actually announcing it explicitly and entirely. He recalls in one of his courses at the Collège de France that 'the German text says very precisely: We are in the period, in the *Zeitalter*, in the age of *Aufklärung*', without however adding that it is not yet an 'enlightened age' (*The Government of Self and Others*, p. 37).
36. Kant, *On History*, pp. 8–9.
37. In 1800, Jean Paul estimated the German 'literary' public at 300,000 people, which constitutes an important change as compared to 1700, but still only amounts to 1.5% of the population. See Wittman, 'Was There a Reading Revolution at the End of the Eighteenth Century?'.
38. Herder, *Another Philosophy of History*, p. 23.
39. Ibid., p. 27.
40. Shakespeare, *Hamlet*, II, ii, 484–5; ibid., III, ii, 17–20.
41. Ibid., II, ii, 561–2.
42. Vico, *The New Science of Giambattista Vico*, pp. 5–6.
43. Ibid., pp. 111 and 16.
44. Vico, *On the Study Methods of Our Time*, p. 5; ibid., p. 6.
45. Montesquieu, *Persian Letters*, p. 258 (translation slightly modified and emphasis added). In the chapter entitled 'On the Right of Conquest' in *The Spirit of the Laws*, he declares without beating around the bush: 'Here

homage must be paid to our modern times, to contemporary reasoning, to the religion of the present day, to our philosophy, and to our mores' (*The Spirit of the Laws*, p. 139).
46. Rousseau, *The Discourses and Other Early Political Writings*, p. 4.
47. Ibid., p. 211.

Chapter 2

THE RIGHT OF PHILOSOPHY AND THE FACTS OF HISTORY: FOUCAULT, DERRIDA, DESCARTES*

THE MODESTY OF HISTORY

Michel Foucault's first book, *History of Madness* (1961), is slightly reminiscent of a short story by Jorge Luis Borges entitled 'The Modesty of History' (1952).[1] The narrator in this work inquires into the more or less discrete nature of 'historic days', that is, moments that disrupt the course of history by opening a new era. Casting doubt on the role of great events in the appearance of such days, he suggests that history is actually modest, only revealing itself in minute changes, which can be identified in particular in a few apparently insignificant words. Foucault seems to provide the perfect example of this 'modesty of history' in his work on madness when he analyses a few words by Descartes as the sign of an epochal change. He pinpoints, in a few phrases of the first *Meditation*, an index of the historical event situated at the opening of the classical age: the exclusion of madness and its reduction to silence.

Let me cite the key passage where Foucault discovers the 'advent of a *ratio*':[2]

> How could it be denied that these hands or this whole body are mine? Unless perhaps I were to liken myself to madmen, whose brains are so damaged by the persistent vapours of melancholia that they firmly maintain they are kings when they are paupers, or say they are dressed in purple when they are naked, or that their heads are made of earthenware or that they are pumpkins, or made of glass. But such people are insane, and I would be thought

* This chapter was translated by Daniel Benson in close consultation with the author.

equally mad [*extravagant*]³ if I took anything from them as a model for myself (AT, VII, 18–19/AT, IX, 14).⁴

Foucault's reading depends on establishing a dividing line between, on the one hand, the errors of the senses and the illusions of dreams, and, on the other, the perils of madness. The senses are only deceitful when they confront very distant and scarcely perceptible objects, while dreams create their illusions without producing the material reality that serves as their source. In both cases, doubt does not reach its extreme point, for the truth of simple and universal things is never called into question. The situation is entirely different with respect to madness. What is fundamentally at stake is not, however, the truth or falsity of an object. Rather, it is the very status of the thinking subject that is at issue. If madness is rejected as soon as it is invoked, this is because it is impossible that the thinking 'I' be mad:

> It is not the permanence of a truth that ensures that thought is not madness, in the way that it freed it from an error or a dream; it is an impossibility of being mad, which is inherent in the thinking subject rather than the object of thought.⁵

Such an exclusion of madness, immediately dismissed from the thinking subject, is the sign of an event-based displacement of madness 'outside the domain of belonging where the subject is in possession of its rights over truth'.⁶ Foucault does not delay in naming this domain that of reason itself. From this point on, madness and reason constitute two fundamentally distinct regions, with madness now banished from the sphere of reason: 'While *man* can still go mad, *thought*, as the sovereign exercise carried out by a subject who sets out to perceive the true, can not be devoid of reason. A dividing line is drawn that will soon render impossible the experience – so familiar to the Renaissance – of an unreasonable Reason, or reasonable Unreason.'⁷ A single sentence from Descartes's *Meditations* thus seems to be the – almost imperceptible – sign of a historic event. However, it should be remembered straightaway that it is only one sign among others, and that it does not single-handedly represent all aspects of the classical event. It is thus more accurate to speak of a structural synchrony between the exclusion of madness in Descartes and the 'great confinement' in the middle of the seventeenth century.⁸

If I have chosen to focus on only one historical sign and isolate it from the hundreds of pages that surround it, it is not an innocent gesture. For I am reproducing very precisely, in order to analyse it in turn, Jacques Derrida's strategy in his famous study of the few pages that Foucault devoted to Descartes. Let us recall the precise formulation of the economical principle of interpretation announced in this text:

> In alleging – correctly or incorrectly, as will be determined – that the sense of Foucault's entire project can be pinpointed in these few allusive and somewhat enigmatic pages, and that the reading of Descartes and the Cartesian cogito proposed to us engages in its problematic the totality of this *History of Madness* as both its intention and its feasibility [...].[9]

Whereas Foucault proposes to read a few paragraphs by Descartes as an indication of a historical decision, Derrida selects a few pages of a colossal work on the history of madness in the classical age, drawing conclusions from them regarding 'Foucault's entire project'.[10] It therefore seems legitimate, if not necessary, to reverse some of the questions Derrida addressed to Foucault regarding the exemplarity of his object of analysis, thereby addressing them to Derrida himself: 'what is the exemplarity of these pages by Foucault, while so many other pages of the same work dealt with the question of madness?'[11] 'Is this one example among other possible examples, or a "good example", an example that is privileged as revelatory?'[12] It is not certain that one will find a better response than the one proposed by Derrida to the questions he addressed to Foucault: 'Formidable and infinitely difficult problems that haunt Foucault's book [and Derrida's article].'[13]

Moreover, when it is a question of rereading Descartes 'over Foucault's shoulder' in order to come closer to the manifest meaning of the text that Foucault supposedly obscured, Derrida limits himself to the same few paragraphs of the *Meditations* that Foucault analysed.[14] And he finds in these words much more than the opening of a new era. He discovers, implicitly in the text, historicity itself, that is, 'the origin of history' and 'the condition of meaning and of language, the condition of the tradition of meaning, the condition of the work':

> The historicity proper to philosophy is located and constituted in the transition, the dialogue between hyperbole and the finite

> structure, between that which exceeds the totality and the closed totality, in the difference between history and historicity; that is, in the place where, or rather at the moment when, the cogito and all that it symbolises here (madness, derangement, hyperbole, etc.) pronounce and reassure themselves then to fall, necessarily forgetting themselves until their reactivation, their reawakening in another statement of the excess which also later will become another decline and another crisis.[15]

Despite the difference in scale, no doubt of significant importance, Derrida and Foucault are thus in agreement in using almost the same reading method, which consists in exchanging detail for totality by using a few pages, paragraphs or words for the entirety of a work, the sign of an epoch or the trace of the very origin of the history of philosophy. In both cases, they employ what can be called, for the sake of convenience, symptomatic readings. However, one should not be too hasty in linking such approaches to a preconceived framework in which a single law would determine the passage from the signifier to the signified or from the text to the concept.[16] Foucault and Derrida each have their own way of connecting their objects of analysis to a conceptual framework, and this would be deserving of a separate study.[17] Here it will suffice to say that the historical signs in Foucault are not simple epiphenomenal indications of more fundamental developments, nor are they historical causes setting in motion a whole series of changes. It appears, rather, that there is a relation of circular solidarity or structural synchrony between signs and history, between the words of Descartes and the classical age.[18] In the case of Derrida, he proceeds by a lengthy process of translation or transmutation that moves from textual traces to an entire theoretical architectonic that is supposed to be consubstantial with them. His first gesture consists in going back to what he calls the manifest meaning of the text and to the 'properly philosophical intention' that it contains.[19] Only after this 'rigorous and exhaustive internal analysis' of the text can one eventually broach the question of the 'latent historical meaning'.[20] Yet, if Derrida does indeed undertake to ascertain the manifest meaning of Descartes's text starting from the blank space that is found on page 45 of his article, no other blank space distinguishes the manifest meaning from his interpretation of it. Everything Derrida says thus seems to naturally follow from Descartes's writings, and there is no visible transition between the manifest meaning and the latent meaning of the text. Without saying more for the moment, let us simply note that the conceptual systematics that he finds in the author of the *Meditations* is supposed to be precisely situated at the level of the manifest meaning, and thus to be consubstantial with what Descartes says – and even with what he does not say, as we will see.[21]

CALL TO PHILOSOPHIC ORDER

Before advancing too far in my analysis, it is important to recall the circumstances of the debate between Foucault and Derrida. When the former published *History of Madness* in 1961, he proposed a thoroughly historical delimitation of his object of analysis. Madness was not understood as having a psychological, physiological or conceptual essence. It is first of all a type of relation between a human being, other human beings and the historical situation in which they find themselves. While at times Foucault seems to invoke madness as a general, or generalisable, phenomenon, he mobilises all of his talents as a historian in order to show that the experience of madness is always anchored in specific historical structures, such that, strictly speaking, there is only the experience of madness in the Renaissance, the experience of madness in the classical age, and so on.[22] If philosophy, or rather the philosophical object, plays a part in his study, it is not because he is interested in the philosophical concept of madness. On the contrary, philosophical documents are arranged among all of the other signs of history without being privileged in the least. With respect to Descartes, the supposed father of modern philosophy, his words are examined as historical indicators among others and, judging from the slim number of pages that he devoted to them, they are not the most important ones.[23] Foucault thereby deposes philosophical discourse from its exceptional vocation by neutralising it with the equalising discourse of the historian. He thus calls into question – at least implicitly – the capacity of philosophers to free themselves from the intellectual constraints of their time.[24] Philosophy's sacrosanct discourse is no longer separated from the unsophisticated chatter of the naive, nor from the mumbling of the mad, since the speech of savants is drawn from a discourse that is itself tightly regulated by historical formations. Such a desacralisation of philosophy did not have to wait long before receiving its rebuttal. But the form that this took was so singular that it remains partially obscured to this day. To borrow an image from Derrida: it was a Trojan horse, but a very original one.

On 4 March 1963, the young Jacques Derrida gave a talk at the Collège philosophique, which is not an incidental detail. Derrida's lecture, following Jean Wahl's proposition, was published in a journal that is also not without significance: the *Revue de métaphysique et de morale*.[25] The text was then incorporated into *Writing and Difference*, the first edition of which appeared in the collection *Tel Quel*. Derrida had been, as he himself recalled at the beginning of his lecture, Foucault's student. His critique of the latter's book is most often read as an act of calling into question his former master's structuralist method in the name of a deconstruction of the history of metaphysics that has the ambition of being 'neo' or 'post-structuralist'. According to this scenario, the debate is reduced to a generational conflict in which the philosophical youth looks to liberate itself from the straightjacket of structuralism imposed by those with intellectual power.[26] For Foucault apparently renewed, perhaps unwittingly, the Cartesian exclusion of madness by relying upon the totalising discourse of structuralism that systematically masked the hyperbolic moments of Descartes's text.[27] Derrida's strategy thus consisted in liberating such moments from the order imposed upon them by Foucault, creating a space for all that was repressed by his properly Cartesian reading, for all of the differences that had been pushed aside by his rigid, totalising structure. It is easy, in thus summarising the debate initiated by Derrida, to slip into caricature: in one camp is Foucault the naive Cartesian rationalist of the structuralist generation that purports to welcome the outside of thought – madness – by writing the history of its exclusion, without, however, accounting for the way in which history and language end up leading the outside of reason back into Reason's bosom. In the other is Derrida, the unruly student who refuses the master's voice within himself, the young rebel who knocks at the door of the philosophical citadel in order to surreptitiously bring in what Foucault and all the other secret defenders of metaphysics keep turning away, in spite of their claimed hospitality towards the outside of philosophical language: the extravagance of madness.

If there is a 'post-structuralism' in Derrida's text that is opposed to a bygone structuralism[28] – and this is surely the case up to a certain point – it cannot simply be reduced to this. For there is, perhaps above all, a philosophical call to order.[29] In the first place, Derrida reminds Foucault of the traditional delimitation of the philosophical object, since his commentary limits itself essentially to the few pages of Foucault's vast work dedicated to a renowned philosophical author.[30] Without explicitly stating so, Derrida brings the whole debate back to the traditional philosophical object, that is, to the canonical texts of philosophical masters.[31] And he seizes this object as closely as possible, not only by concentrating on a few paragraphs of the *Meditations*, but also by reminding Foucault of the need to return to the original Latin text. For if historians are allowed to read Descartes in the vernacular, true philosophers must read him in the classical language of erudition. Thus, instead of letting the reader follow the path traced by Foucault, which would consist in treating the words of the philosopher as historical signs among others, Derrida invites us to disassociate Descartes's text from the other historical documents brought together by Foucault, in order to reread it in a philosophical manner and bring out the 'properly philosophical intention' abusively distorted by the historian.[32] Once the philosophical text has been isolated, Derrida reminds Foucault – this is the second call to order – of the properly philosophical method: internal analysis. While historians quickly ascertain the manifest meaning of their documents so as to move on to the latent historical meaning, the task of philosophers is to linger patiently, and for a long time, over the manifest meaning of works without naively relying on external analysis:[33] 'I do not know to what extent Foucault would agree that the prerequisite for a response to such questions is first of all the internal and autonomous analysis of the philosophical content of philosophical discourse.'[34] We thereby arrive at the third call to order, which has the most far-reaching consequences: philosophical discourse eludes historians' discourse in fact and in principle.[35] I have already indicated the way in which Derrida's interpretation aims at extracting philosophical texts from the historical structure imposed by Foucault. But the liberation of the Cartesian text from the straightjacket of 'structuralist totalitarianism' is also something completely different: it marks the coronation of philosophical discourse as first discourse, and the condemnation of historical discourse as blindly metaphysical. For Derrida gives Foucault a very long lesson on the true relationship between philosophy and history over the course of which the former takes back all of its rights over the latter.[36] Let us attempt, then, to follow the broad lines of this lesson, identifying therein what seems justifiable in the rereading of Descartes proposed by Foucault's former student.

The principal thesis of Derrida's internal analysis seems to be the following: Descartes never excluded madness in the way Foucault describes. In the Cartesian text, according to Derrida, madness is only presented as a particular case of sensory error. It thus enters into consideration at the level of natural doubt, and in this way it is comparable to dreaming, although it is less radical than the latter because madness is less common and less universal.[37] In fact, Descartes at no point avoids the possibility of entirely erroneous sensory knowledge. If he seems to exclude the extravagance of madness, he immediately accepts it afterwards, in an even more profound form, as the possibility of dreaming. The exclusion of madness would thus only be a feigned exclusion leading to an increasingly hyperbolic epistemological extravagance. One of the key indications of this is found, for Derrida, in the first words of the paragraph on madness: *sed forte* (unless perhaps). This expression, to which Foucault apparently did not pay enough attention, announces Descartes's feigned objection in which the philosopher pretends to 'put to himself the astonished objection of an imaginary non-philosopher who is frightened by such audacity [the questioning of the sensory foundations of knowledge] and says: no, not all sensory knowledge, for then you would be mad'.[38] If Descartes acquiesces on this point, it is not in order to avoid putting into question knowledge arising from the senses. It is to propose to his fictive interlocutor a still more ruinous hypothesis for sensory knowledge, but one which his questioner cannot but accept because it appears so natural. For the existence of dreams is not only known, in principle, by everyone, it definitively undermines all of the sensory supports of knowledge. The dreamer, as Derrida says, is 'madder than the madman' or at least 'further from true perception than the madman': 'it is in the case of sleep, and not in that of insanity, that the *absolute totality* of ideas of sensory origin becomes suspect'.[39]

There is more: Descartes does not stop at the madness of the dreamer that ruins all sense-based knowledge. He then attacks the intellectual foundations of certainty with the hypothesis of the evil genius. It is only here, according to Derrida, that one encounters the possibility of a '*total madness*' that would be capable of destroying all forms of knowledge.[40] And, once again, this extravagance is not pushed aside from the philosophical path laid down by Descartes. On the contrary, the latter insists precisely on putting himself to the test of this madness that is much more profound than the madness of the dreamer and much more extravagant than the madness of the simple mad person. Foucault would thus have been wrong to privilege the reference to madness in the first phase of doubt, and before its ultimate instance. The true madness of Cartesian doubt would only come at this hyperbolic moment when all knowledge is ruined by the hypothesis of the evil genius: 'ideas of neither sensory nor intellectual origin will be sheltered from this new phase of doubt, and everything that was previously set aside under the name of extravagance is now welcomed into the most essential interiority of thought.'[41]

Descartes's entire philosophical approach would thus consist in putting himself to the test of a total madness beyond the limits of a mere factual madness, which would only call sensory knowledge into question (and only partially and contingently at that). In so doing, Descartes 'in principle refuses to let any determined knowledge escape from madness': 'at no point will knowledge alone be able to dominate madness, to master it, that is to say to objectify it'.[42] And if the act of the cogito eventually manages to escape madness, it does not establish a definitive exclusion of it. For the instant of the cogito (the expression is Derrida's) does not happen outside the grip of madness:

> The cogito escapes madness only because at its own moment, under its own authority, it is valid *even if I am mad, even if* my thoughts are completely mad. There is a value and a meaning of the cogito, as of existence, which escape the alternative of a determined madness and a determined reason.[43]

Total madness – exceeding or falling short of any determined madness – is thus not at all external to the cogito. It is, properly speaking, its *sine qua non* condition: 'The certainty thus attained need not be sheltered from an imprisoned madness, for it is attained and assured within madness itself.'[44] What Derrida calls the 'hyperbolic audacity' or the 'mad audacity' of the Cartesian cogito consists precisely in a return towards this 'original point which no longer belongs to either a *determined* reason or a *determined* unreason, no longer belongs to them as opposition or alternative'.[45] This point exceeds the totality of the thinkable and surpasses the entirety of factual history; it constitutes the point where the project 'of thinking this totality while escaping it' takes hold, qualified as mad by Derrida.[46] In short, the total madness of an originary point where reason and unreason are not at all determined as such persists at the very heart of the Cartesian cogito. In fact, this madness is the cogito in its inaugural moment:

> It is therefore a question of drawing back toward a point at which all *determined* contradictions, in the form of given, factual historical structures, can appear, and appear as relative to this zero point at which determined meaning and nonmeaning come together in their common origin [...], determined by Descartes as cogito.[47]

Instead of reading in the first *Meditation* the advent of a new epoch founded on the exclusion of madness by reason, Derrida affirms that the cogito – in its inaugural moment and even before it is said – is situated at the apogee of an absolute madness, outside of time and history, as the common origin and the origin by principle of all possible partitioning between reason and unreason, that is, of all factual partitioning. The Cartesian text thus would hardly be able to serve as a simple historical sign indicating the 'great confinement' of the classical age, for it carries within itself the trace of the originary point from which all possible historical delimitation between reason and madness proceeds.[48]

And yet, one might claim that Derrida refers explicitly to an exclusion of madness in Descartes's text. While this is true, it is necessary to specify straightaway that this exclusion is not related to an independent philosophical decision. It is a product of philosophical discourse as a whole:

> *In principle* nothing is opposed to the subversion named insanity [*extravagance*] in the first phase of doubt, although *in fact* and from a natural point of view, for Descartes, for his reader, and for us, no natural anxiety is possible regarding this de facto subversion. (Truthfully speaking, to go to the heart of the matter, one would have to confront directly, in and of itself, the question of what is *de facto* and what *de jure* in the relations of the cogito and madness.) Beneath this natural comfort, beneath this apparently prephilosophical confidence is hidden the recognition of an essential and principled truth: to wit, if philosophical discourse and communication (that is, language itself) are to have an intelligible meaning, that is to say, if they are to conform to their essence and vocation as discourse, they must simultaneously in fact and in principle escape

madness. They must carry normality within themselves. And this is not a specifically Cartesian weakness (although Descartes does not confront the question of his own language), is not a defect or mystification linked to a determined historical structure, but rather is an essential and universal necessity from which no discourse can escape, for it belongs to the meaning of meaning. It is an essential necessity from which no discourse can escape, even the discourse which denounces a mystification or an act of force.[49]

While Descartes himself does not exclude madness from methodological doubt, the language that he employs exiles unreason by an internal necessity. It is an implacable law of discourse: madness remains fundamentally heterogeneous to language. There is thus no reason for anxiety when confronting madness and questioning the basis of sensory and intelligible knowledge. Language itself provides the guarantee of meaning and, what is more, the moment of explicit exclusion is quick to follow (if it has not always already taken place). In Descartes's text, it happens at the enunciative moment of the cogito:

> I understand that within the movement which is called the *Cartesian cogito* this hyperbolic extremity is not the only element that should be, like all pure madness in general, silent. As soon as Descartes has reached this extremity, he seeks to reassure himself, to certify the cogito itself through God, to identify the act of the cogito with the act of a reasonable reason. And he does so as soon as he *proffers* and *reflects* the cogito. [...] For if the cogito is valid even for the most insane mad person, one must, in fact, not be mad if one is to reflect it and retain it, if one is to communicate it and its meaning.[50]

Derrida links this exclusion to the guarantee provided by God since only he allows me to leave the immediate experience of a mad and silent cogito, only he resituates me in time and 'insures my representations and my cognitive determinations, that is, my discourse against madness'.[51] It should be noted that God, according to Derrida, 'is the other name of the absolute of reason *itself*, of reason and meaning in general'.[52] If it is thus quite correct to say that Derrida also finds an act of exclusion of madness in Descartes, it must be pointed out that it is the absolute of discursive meaning that protects us against the extravagance of hyperbolic doubt more than Descartes himself by his philosophical verdict. As we have already seen, Descartes's thinking subject is committed to face the most complete madness, and it is his discourse that ultimately acts as a safeguard. More than a factual exclusion that would arise from an individual decision or a particular historical moment, it is here a question of a *de jure* exclusion: the act of writing a meditation in which one confronts madness leads to its exclusion, necessarily and by a principle of law.[53] Ultimately, one simply repeats the act of exclusion that characterises all philosophical discourse. Strictly speaking, such an exclusion – never entirely completed since the moment of excess continues to haunt all determined thought – can only appear in history because it is the product of the philosophical order, the order of law. In other words, if an exclusion of madness is found in Descartes's text, it only reproduces the same model of exclusion that dominates the entire history of Western philosophy, for it is an exclusion by principle.

Before studying more closely the relationship between history and historicity, let us pause to consider some of the methodological aspects of Derrida's reading, which, in his own words, is to be 'the most classical reading'.[54] The attention that the latter brings to the text's minutiae tends to conceal, at times, an entire series of operations that aim at reconstituting a conceptual foundation that supposedly falls directly within the scope of the text's manifest meaning. Despite the considerable number of pages that Derrida devotes to a few lines by Descartes, his subtle rewriting of the latter's argument does not entirely mask a conceptual translation that will need to be brought to light.[55] Let us begin with the hypothesis of the fictitious interlocutor. If more than one interpreter has found this hypothesis convincing, and if it does not seem to wrongly contort the meaning of the first *Meditation*, we should recall that Descartes never directly refers to it and, importantly, never speaks of the 'non-philosopher'. The 'novice in philosophy' is a pure invention of Derrida, and it serves several ends. Firstly, it situates Foucault's interpretation on the side of non-philosophy by making the historian into someone who confused the voice of the non-philosopher with that of the philosopher. This inability to distinguish between philosophy and non-philosophy in Descartes's text attests to the way in which Foucault, by employing the perspective of a historian, shut his eyes to the subtle framework of the properly philosophical object: only the non-philosopher is troubled by the extravagance of factual madness and calls for its exclusion, while the philosopher audaciously faces the most total madness. That the philosophical novice is the one who wants to exclude madness largely anticipates, moreover, Derrida's thesis: only philosophy confronts madness in its most absolute form. It leads factual madness, which troubles the non-philosopher, back to the principle madness that is its source. It is indeed very difficult not to read here an implicit reference to the relationship between the historical study proposed by Foucault and Derrida's properly philosophical analysis. This brings me to my third point: given that Foucault remains blind, according to Derrida, to the absolute madness at the extreme point of the cogito, he only manages to renew what Derrida qualifies as the Cartesian gesture. In fact, his entire project of a history of madness consists in recuperating the negativity of reason's outside by inscribing it in the language of history, and thus in the discourse of reason: 'I would be tempted to consider Foucault's book a powerful gesture of protection and confinement. A Cartesian gesture for the twentieth century. A recuperation of negativity.'[56] Foucault risks, more specifically, doing violence to Descartes's text by enclosing it within a determined historical structure that causes him to lose the 'meaning and the origin of meaning': 'It [every endeavour that attempts to reduce a project of undetermined excess] risks erasing the excess by which every philosophy (of meaning) is related, in some region of its discourse, to the bottomlessness of nonsense [*au sans-fond du non-sens*].'[57] To summarise: the historian, who is philosophically naive, confused the voice of the non-philosopher and that of the philosopher in such a way that he obscured the madness inherent in all philosophy, that is, the madness of a moment of excess prior to the determination of concepts, prior to every definite historical gesture. By reading Descartes from a historical point of view, Foucault thus excluded the trace of the origin of meaning and of history found within his text. He attempted to confine historicity itself within a history of meaning by excluding the extreme point of indetermination, the 'total madness' that only the philosopher can experience.

One might object that I have unfairly propped up, on a few precarious words, an entire argument concerning the relationship between philosophy and history. But these few words participate in a larger set of operations that I will reconstruct as I proceed in my analysis. As we will see, Derrida's interpretive strategy consists in undertaking a subtle and patient conceptual translation that eventually diverges considerably from Descartes's text, all the while claiming to be drawing closer to it.

Consider the example of the transition that leads, in the first *Meditation*, from the word *madness*, or more precisely 'the insane', to what Derrida calls 'total madness'. The latter term is obviously not Descartes's, and the first *Meditation* does not associate the evil genius or the cogito with some form of absolute madness.[58] All of this comes only from Derrida's reading and an epistemological definition of madness that allows him to move from the word *madness* to the general idea of calling into question sensory or intellectual knowledge, and then on to the point of the indetermination of concepts. The term *madness* – the same is true for the word *extravagance* – is thus charged with a fundamentally epistemological signification, which is quite far from the Cartesian definition of madness. Whereas Descartes very explicitly defines the latter term as a physical state (the brain clouded by the vapours of bile) that produces a discrepancy between words and reality, Derrida does away with this factual definition so as to rely on a definition of principle, which, in his view, comes closer to the proper meaning of Descartes's discourse: 'Descartes is concerned here not with determining the concept of madness but with utilising the popular notion of insanity [*extravagance*] for juridical and methodological ends, in order to ask questions of principle regarding only the *truth* of ideas.'[59] By recentring Descartes's remarks on definitions of principle, Derrida doubly distances himself from the 'manifest meaning' of the text: he finds madness where it is not mentioned, and he denies its presence where it actually is named in the text. Concerning the principal paragraph of the first *Meditation* in which Descartes explicitly mentions madness, Derrida affirms: 'what is significant is that Descartes, at bottom, never speaks of madness itself in this text. Madness is not his theme. He treats it as the index of a question of principle and of epistemological value.'[60] True madness, on the other hand, madness of principle, is located where madness is never mentioned. This is not only during the hypothesis of the evil genius, but even more so in the instant of the cogito, at this extreme point of hyperbolic excess that is the condition of possibility of all division between reason and unreason. Yet if the madness of the ultimate point of the cogito is never named in Descartes's text, if Derrida has no text to rely on, if he is obligated to refer to the intention of the philosopher (lacking written proof), this simple fact is conveniently explained away by a *de jure* principle: the most extreme madness is necessarily incompatible with language and must remain silent ('I am sure that within the movement which is called the *Cartesian cogito* this hyperbolical extremity is not the only element that should be, like all pure madness in general, silent').[61] It is ultimately a question of two operations that mutually reinforce one another. Where the words of the factual text contradict the principles of the *de jure* text, they must be excluded. Where the principles of the *de jure* text find no support in the *de facto* text, the unsaid must be explained by a necessity of principle, thereby changing a vice into a virtue. Obviously, nothing prevents occasional convergences between fact and principle, but in the case of madness in the first *Meditation*, it is clear just how much the lack of convergence in no way inhibits Derrida's 'internal analysis', which consists in reworking from top to bottom Descartes's 'text' in order to be able to speak of madness where Descartes does not offer the least word, and vice versa.[62] In the end, Derrida denies fact in the name of principle and affirms principle independently of fact, all the while claiming that fact and principle are inextricably linked in fact and in principle.

TWO MEANINGS OF CARTESIAN CLASSICISM

Let us return to the historical division proposed by Foucault and Derrida's critique of it. Given that the latter categorically refuses the idea of a rupture between reason and madness in the classical age, one might expect him to bring up historical examples that contradict Foucault's thesis. But there is essentially only one. And it is not, strictly speaking, a historical example. He takes one of Foucault's formulas ('the Greek Logos had no contrary') and compares it to the Socratic dialectic, affirming that there are only two possible alternatives:

> It must be *either* (a) that the Socratic moment and its entire posterity immediately partake in the Greek logos that has no contrary; and that consequently, the Socratic dialectic could not be reassuring [...]. *Or* (b) that the Socratic moment and the dialectical victory over the Caliclesian hybris already are the marks of a deportation and an exile of logos outside itself, and the wound left in it by a decision, by a difference; and then the structure of exclusion which Foucault wishes to describe in his book could not have been born with classical reason. It would have to have been consummated and reassured and ruminated for centuries in philosophy. It would be essential to the entirety of the history of philosophy and of reason.[63]

Three remarks are needed regarding this seemingly historical critique. First of all, the necessity that Derrida invokes is a necessity of principle – 'it must be *either* … *or* …' – and Derrida does not provide any specific textual or factual example in this passage.[64] Moreover, it is regrettable that, when speaking of Caliclesian *hybris*, he avoids discussing – to take but a few examples – *aphrosunē* (unreason, insanity, madness) in the *Meno* (88) and in the *Protagoras* (332e), as well as *mania* (madness, delirium, fervour) in the *Meno* (91c) and in the *Phaedrus* (245a, 256b, among others). Secondly, in both cases, the sole 'example' of the Socratic dialectic carries the totality of history or 'its entire posterity' along with it: 'It would be essential to the entirety of the history of philosophy and of reason.'[65] Thirdly, Derrida brings the two alternatives mentioned above back to their common root, which contradicts Foucault's entire historical thesis:

> Truthfully, for one or the other of these hypotheses to be true and for there to be a choice between them, it must be assumed *in general* that reason can have a contrary, that there can be an other of reason, that reason itself can construct or discover, and that the opposition of reason to its other is *symmetrical*. This is the heart of the matter.[66]

As was the case with madness in Descartes, Derrida relies on rules of principle without attempting to provide factual evidence, which allows him to challenge the historical delimitation proposed by Foucault without bringing up a single historical example.[67] Indeed, after briefly invoking the question of the translation of the term *hybris* in various Platonic dialogues, and without drawing any conclusions, Derrida is quick to affirm that:

> No matter what the relationship of the Greeks to *hybris*, and of Socrates to the original logos, it is in any event certain that classical reason, and medieval reason before it, bore a relation to Greek reason, and that it is within the milieu of this more or less immediately perceived heritage, which itself is more or less crossed with other traditional lines, that the adventure or misadventure of classical reason developed.[68]

This sentence perfectly encapsulates Derrida's approach: *whatever the historical and textual facts may be, it is in any case certain* that they are governed by *de jure* principles regarding the nature of reason.

Derrida thus replaces Foucault's event-based history with a history of recurrent structures that stem from an archi-originary conflict between reason and its outside.[69] He maintains that the crisis of reason and madness, whose trace is found in Descartes, has always existed: 'It suffices to say that, if it is classic, it is perhaps not so in the sense of the *classical age* but in the sense of eternal and essential classicism, albeit historical in an unusual sense.'[70] His historiographical debate with Foucault could thus be summarised as a debate over two different understandings of Descartes's 'classicism': either the term refers to a clearly demarcated era in which reason opposes itself to madness, or it makes reference to an immemorial era of thought in which reason and madness have always been engaged in an interminable struggle.[71] The question of language is particularly useful for illustrating the difference between Foucault's historical classicism and Derrida's philosophical classicism. The latter finds in Foucault's text the trace of the truth that he himself attempts to bring to light: 'But madness is what by essence cannot be said: it is the "absence of work [*œuvre*]", as Foucault profoundly says.'[72] Foucault's error would consist in interpreting this antagonism founded on principle in a narrow, overly historical manner. It is, moreover, interesting to note that Foucault, in both of his responses to Derrida in 1972, uses Descartes's own language, his lexical choices, as the sign of the advent of the classical age. In this regard, Foucault observes that the word *insanus* is used in order to emphasise the implausible imagination of the mad, whereas the words *demens* and *amens* are 'terms that are legal before being medical, and which designate a whole category of people who are incapable of certain religious, civil and legal acts'.[73] Thus it is not at all by chance that the word *demens* appears in the paragraph on madness in the *Meditations*, for 'the *dementes* were disqualified whenever it was a question of acting, going to court or speaking'; they 'do not have all their rights in matters of speaking, promising, committing themselves, signing, bringing legal actions, etc.'.[74] In addition, the term *demens* already indicates the profound discrepancy that Descartes establishes between madness and language, and more precisely the exclusion of the mad from the domain of discourse: in the classical age, the mad no longer have the right to truthful speech; they no longer have the right to speak and be taken seriously.

It is precisely this disparity between madness and discourse that Derrida emphasises in his critique of the Foucauldian project: how is one to write the history of madness, he asks, the history of what is fundamentally allergic to language, the history of what does not inscribe itself in written discourse? Foucault himself had underscored this difficulty, but Derrida insists, for his part, on distinguishing between the recognition of a problem and its solution: 'to state the difficulty of stating, is not yet to surmount it – quite the contrary.'[75] There are two possible conclusions: either maintain the silence proper to madness and abandon the project of writing its history, or else accept that the only language available is that of reason, and that all history is necessarily rational, whatever its proposed object of analysis.[76] This is a division of principle:

> By its essence, the sentence is normal. It carries normality in itself, that is, *sense* [*le sens*], in every sense of the word – Descartes's in particular. [...] And if madness in general, beyond any artificial and determined historical structure, is the absence of work [*œuvre*], then madness is indeed, by its essence and in general, silence, stifled speech, within a caesura and a wound that *open up* life as *historicity in general*. [...] Within the dimension of historicity in general, which is to be confused neither with an ahistorical eternity, nor with some empirically determined moment of the history of facts, silence plays the irreducible role of that which bears and haunts language, outside and *against* which alone language can emerge – 'against' here simultaneously designating the content from which form takes off by force, and the adversary against whom I assure and reassure myself by force.[77]

This situation perfectly summarises the fundamental aporia that haunts Descartes's text: while he does not exclude madness, since he integrates it into his most internal thought so as to attain the extreme point of the cogito, language itself necessarily excludes it, and this is the source of the 'natural comfort' and the 'apparently prephilosophical confidence' that we all have when reading the first *Meditation*.[78] Even if one faces the danger of madness and extravagance, one remains in the reassuring framework of language.[79] Unsurprisingly, the Foucauldian confrontation with madness is seen in the same way, with one difference. While he attempts to approach madness through a manifest sympathy for the outside of reason, he cannot prevent himself from repatriating it, from the first sentence of his history of madness, back into the world of reason. The only difference – and it is a major one, since in spanning Derrida's entire lecture it constitutes, one could say, the *différance* that determines all the differences and all the distinctions at work in his article – is the difference between the properly philosophical experience of madness and the historical exclusion of philosophical extravagance. Philosophy directly confronts the madness of exceeding totality while history circumscribes madness within determined configurations and confines the excess within totalitarian structures:

> To define philosophy as the intent-to-speak-hyperbole [*vouloir-dire-l'hyperbole*] is to confess – and philosophy is perhaps this gigantic confession – that by virtue of the historical enunciation through which philosophy tranquilises itself and excludes madness, philosophy also betrays itself (or betrays itself as thought), enters into a crisis and a forgetting of itself that are an essential and necessary period of its movement.[80]

Historical enunciation, we should understand, marks the forgetting of philosophy and its experience of madness; it is the – structuralist – confinement of its insane attempt to seize the totality of being while escaping it.

Here I would like to pause to consider literary language in Foucault's work. It is very odd that a thinker like Derrida – who reflected extensively on the relationships between philosophy and literature, and who himself employed a writing practice of a distinctly 'literary' orientation in order to deconstruct the traditional dichotomy between true discourse and fictive discourse – never inquires into Foucault's literary language or the role of literature in *History of Madness*.[81] It is all the more surprising when one considers that Derrida actually brought up the status of the historian's language, in a passing remark accusing Foucault of skirting the question himself:

> Hence, one can inquire – as Foucault does also, at moments other than those when he contrives to speak of silence (although in too lateral and implicit a fashion from my point of view) – about the source and the status of the language of this archaeology, of this language which is to be understood by a reason that is not classical reason.[82]

But Derrida already knows the response, and he is not interested in seeking out Foucault's proposed solution, whether successful or not (for that is not the question: it is a matter of distinguishing between fact and principle):

> Our *entire* European language, the language of everything that has participated, from near or far, in the adventure of Western reason – all this is the immense delegation of the project defined by Foucault under the rubric of the capture or objectification of madness.[83]

Against the backdrop of this absolute principle, Derrida brings Foucault's proposed archaeology of silence back to a single alternative: '*Either* be silent of a certain silence (a *certain* silence which, again, can be determined only within a *language* and an *order* that will preserve this silence from contamination by any given muteness), *or* follow the madperson down the road of his or her exile.'[84] This alternative, which obviously is not really one, leads straight to the major contradiction that undermines Foucault's whole project: he reduces madness to reason by writing its history. However, such a paradox – and this is the point I wanted to come to – can only subsist by systematically eliminating the question of literature, which obscures Foucault's entire effort to differentiate between the language of reason and literary language.[85] In the numerous instances where the author of *History of Madness* insists on distinguishing between two kinds of fundamentally distinct languages, Derrida abolishes in advance, by an essential principle, the difference that Foucault sought to marshal precisely in order to avoid producing a simple rational history of madness. This effort is twofold. Firstly, there are all of the passages on the writers and artists that confronted madness in one form or another. According to Foucault, in the modern age – to which Foucault still belongs – literature is very precisely a language written through a direct confrontation with madness and silence. It is clear that Foucault's own historical writing sought to reconnect, in a new manner, with this literary language, precisely in order to break with rational history.[86] Derrida seems to recognise this fact in one of the only passages where he approaches the question of literature, even though he appears to refer to it only in order to push it even further aside. When he considers the way in which Descartes could only invoke madness in the language of fiction, thus ensuring himself against factual madness, Derrida adds:

> But this is not a weakness or a search for security proper to a given historical language (for example, the search for 'certainty' in the Cartesian style), but is rather inherent in the essence and very project of all language in general; and even in the language of those who are apparently the maddest; and even and above all in the language of those who, by their praise of madness, by their complicity with it, measure their own strength against the greatest possible proximity to madness. Language being the break with madness, it adheres more thoroughly to its essence and vocation, makes a cleaner break with madness, if it pits itself against madness more freely and gets closer and closer to it: to the point of being separated from it only by the 'transparent sheet' of which Joyce speaks, that is, by itself – for this diaphaneity is nothing other than the language, meaning, possibility, and *elementary* discretion of a nothing that neutralises everything.[87]

Derrida rejects in a few sentences, in a few principles, all of Foucault's attempts at finding a language that would challenge the rational language of history.[88] One could say, if one wanted to take up the somewhat dull critique that Foucault himself marshals as much as Derrida, that this is a veritable exclusion of the voice of madness by the principles of reason.[89]

Once again, Derrida brings what is said in the text back to the unstated principles that govern it. Have I brought in enough examples in order to move from the level of facts to that of reasons, thereby drawing definitive conclusions regarding Derrida's entire project? The latter had already effectively demonstrated, in his analysis of historical exemplarity in Foucault, that there is never a sufficient number of facts allowing for a transition to the level of principle. These two domains are fundamentally distinct, since time immemorial. Strictly speaking, history only exists from the moment when the two are distinguished, and thus history itself has been trapped in a ruinous contradiction since its origin: while its existence depends on preserving the gap between principle and fact, its success – if not its simple realisation – depends on overcoming this gap and passing from the factual order to the rational order. Here one encounters the aporetic logic that Derrida will employ in numerous other cases: the condition of possibility of history (the division between principle and fact) coincides very precisely with its condition of impossibility. And this is quite natural because the domain of principle is the rightful domain of philosophy. Only the latter has the right to speak of principle. It is pertinent to recall in this regard the definition that Derrida gives to philosophy in his text on Descartes and Foucault: philosophy is the 'intent-to-speak-hyperbole', the intention to speak about that which surpasses the totality of facts, to 'think this totality while escaping it', 'to exceed the totality of the world, as the totality of what I can think in general'.[90] And – this is what must finally be clarified – this applies as much in the case of Descartes as it does in the case of Derrida himself: 'Even if I do not *in fact* grasp the totality, if I neither understand nor embrace it in fact, I still formulate the project of doing so, and this project is meaningful in such a way that it can be defined only in relation to a precomprehension of the infinite and undetermined totality.'[91] The excess of the philosophical project consists precisely in surpassing the world of facts towards a world of principle so as to seize the latter in its absolute totality instead of attempting to recompose it from the fragments of concrete phenomena (as the historian does, or rather as the historian attempts to do without success, since failure is inscribed in their very project as an essential necessity): 'This is why, by virtue of this margin of the possible, the principled, and the meaningful, which exceeds all that is real, factual, and existent, this project is mad, and acknowledges madness as its liberty and its very possibility.'[92] Derrida sees in the intentional meaning of Descartes's philosophical project the philosophical intent-to-say [*vouloir-dire*] par excellence, and this intent-to-say is at the origin of Derrida's own work. Like Descartes, he wants to approach this extreme point that exceeds the totality of facts; he wants to experience the madness that consists in exceeding the finite world towards the beyond.[93] I have already given numerous examples of this excess of principle over fact by following, to all appearances, the path of the naive historian. It would have sufficed, as a good philosopher, to enumerate the principles once and for all: 'that all history can only be, in the last analysis, the history of meaning, that is, of Reason *in general* [...]'; 'there is no Trojan horse over which Reason (in general) does not have the upper hand'; 'the concept of history has always been a rational one'; 'madness is what by essence cannot be said'; 'by its essence, the sentence is normal'; 'madness is indeed, by essence and in general, silence, stifled speech, within a caesura and a wound that *open up* life as *historicity in general'*; and so forth.[94] The difficulty with this list, and it is far from exhaustive, is that it contains principles of law brought back into the language of facts. None of them touch then upon the extreme point of the philosophical project, which necessarily must withdraw from the phenomenal world and forever remain silent (like the *a* in *différance*). Therein lies the contradiction of philosophy: one must continue to philosophise, to attempt to say what exceeds the totality of determined structures, in order to stretch towards the silent origin of all delimitation, the source of all history, the archi-origin of the world, despite the fact that the properly philosophical intention is required to translate itself into finite language, into determined utterances that inevitably part ways, according to an implacable law, with purely philosophical meaning. It is thereby necessary to incessantly deconstruct all determined statements so as to return to the philosophical intention that resides in them. But just as the philosopher alone seeks to speak the silent origin of the world in its absolute totality, only the philosopher can hear, within the murmurs of factual language, the originary meaning of a beyond. For the simple historian, the latter is necessarily concealed.

The following conclusion seems to impose itself: the true subject of Derrida's lecture is not the first *Meditation*. Descartes's text is only the finite occasion to debate something much more essential: the right of philosophy to speak the truth of history. And it is a right in the full sense of the word, a right that escapes all historical determination: 'I think, therefore, that (in Descartes) everything can be reduced to a determined historical totality except the hyperbolic project.'[95] If this project escapes in principle from the historian's analysis, it is precisely because the latter is not equipped with the necessary means to move from a factual statement to the intentional meaning that determines it. This is what is really at stake in Derrida's 'internal analysis': the reminder that the proper role of philosophy is to determine the conditions of possibility of history in its totality, while philosophy itself escapes history in fact and in principle.[96] The title of his lecture means exactly that: 'Cogito and the History of Madness' opposes the right of philosophy to the facts of history. Therein lies what one could call, playing on Derrida's words, his 'originary intention'.[97]

ANTINOMIC RESPONSES TO DERRIDA

Foucault would wait almost a decade before responding to Derrida. Let us briefly recall the circumstances. Mikitaka Nakano contacted Foucault in 1970 concerning a special issue of the Japanese journal *Paideia* on the relations between philosophy and literature in his work. Nakano planned to include Derrida's article 'Cogito and the History of Madness' as well as an article by J. Miyakawa on Derrida and Foucault. Miyakawa suggested that Foucault respond to Derrida's 1963–1964 critique. The first 'Reply to Derrida' thus appeared in 1972, before being reworked under the title 'My Body, This Paper, This Fire' and published in an appendix to the complete re-edition of *History of Madness* by Gallimard in 1972. There is, however, a remarkable difference between these two documents that I would like to take the time to consider here. In the first pages of the 'Reply to Derrida', one finds a long, dense socio-historical critique of the philosophical practice of which Derrida is identified as one of the most skilled practitioners. It should not be forgotten that between 1963 and the beginning of the 1970s, Derrida published *Writing and Difference* (1967), *Of Grammatology* (1967) and *Speech and Phenomena* (1967). Foucault, meanwhile, had published *The Birth of the Clinic* (1963), *Raymond Roussel* (1963), *The Order of Things* (1966) and *The Archaeology of Knowledge* (1969). These simple bibliographical indications suffice to show that many things had changed for both thinkers, and it seems legitimate to say that the goal for Foucault, in the first pages of his 'Reply to Derrida', was to resituate Derrida's interpretive practice within the strict limits of the 'framework of the teaching of philosophy in France', which he had never ceased to call into question in his own work: '*History of Madness* and the texts that have followed it are exterior to philosophy, as it is practised and taught in France.'[98] This 'framework of the teaching of philosophy' is formed, according to Foucault, by three postulates that Derrida upholds in his article 'Cogito and the History of Madness':

1. 'He [Derrida] supposes first of all that all knowledge, or in an even broader sense all rational discourse, entertains a fundamental relation with philosophy, and that it is in this relationship that this rationality or this knowledge have their foundation.'[99]
2. 'In relation to this philosophy, which eminently holds the "law" of all discourse, Derrida supposes that one commits "faults" of a

singular nature: not so much faults of logic or reasoning, which bring errors that might be isolated in a material fashion, but rather faults that are something like a blend of Christian sin and a Freudian slip.'[100]

3. 'Derrida's third postulate is that philosophy is on the far side and the near side of any event. Not only can nothing happen to it, but everything that can happen is already anticipated or enveloped by it. In itself, philosophy is only the repetition of an origin that is more than originary, and which infinitely exceeds, in its retreat, anything that it could say in any of its historical discourses.'[101]

At the core of this disciplinary battle, one finds two fundamentally different conceptions of knowledge: the conceptual order as a historical form that changes over time, and the conceptual order as a set of extra-temporal relations.

In the revision of his 'Reply to Derrida', Foucault removed the entire first part of his article. He simply added, after an asterisk and at the very end of his analysis, a few remarks concerning the 'historically well-determined little pedagogy' that appears in Derrida's article.[102] However scathing these remarks might be, they do not reach the depth of the opening pages of the first version of the text. For instead of a socio-historical argument carried over several pages, here there is merely a critical observation contained within three paragraphs. Moreover, the second version is largely dominated by a detailed confrontation between quotations from Derrida and citations from the first *Meditation*, a confrontation that very clearly distinguishes itself from the final paragraphs. Foucault makes no reference to other texts by these two authors, and he limits himself, even more than Derrida, to a comparison between two perfectly isolated texts. Outside of the above-mentioned comment regarding the Derridean method, there is absolutely no reflection on the historical context of the writings in question. The title ('My Body, This Paper, This Fire') and the structure of the article (the decision to begin each of the first five sections with a citation by Derrida, for example) perfectly summarise the reorientation: it is a matter of returning to the words of Descartes in the first *Meditation* and of scrupulously confronting them with the supposed internal analysis by Derrida.[103] In other words, Foucault proposes to directly contest the latter's reading by closing in on the facts of the text alone, in order to explain how the philosopher erred in his attempt to find the law of discourse beyond words. He thus brackets, as it were, historical contextualisation so as to better isolate the words of Descartes.

Foucault categorically rejects Derrida's idea according to which one should distinguish between the definitive thought of Descartes and the objection of the non-philosopher. Descartes supposedly invoked the latter in order to express the astonishment of the novice at the mad suggestion that doubt could reach such things as clearly and immediately perceptible as having a body, being next to a fire, holding a sheet of paper, and so forth. Breaking with Derrida's 'imaginary' hypothesis, Foucault proposes a 'double reading' of the *Meditations* by taking into consideration both the system of propositions that are found therein and the exercise of the thinking subject that passes through a series of modifications. While there are certain passages of the *Meditations* where one can simply follow the systematic sequence of propositions that succeed one another, there are others, according to Foucault, 'where the two forms of discourse intersect, and where the exercise modifying the subject orders the succession of propositions, or commands the junction of distinct demonstrative groups'.[104] The few lines on madness would figure among this latter group of passages insofar as they do not constitute a demonstrative progression of methodological doubt, but rather come within the exercise of the thinking subject. For when confronted with an obstacle to doubt – sensory objects as evident as 'my body, this paper, this fire' – Descartes returns to the condition of the meditating subject: would I still be reasonable if I doubted such things? Thus, we find ourselves here at the intersection of the two discursive forms, the system and the exercise, and it is the latter that governs the meditation that follows. For the doubting subject cannot reasonably call into question their most immediate contemporary reality without renouncing at once all the guarantees and safeguards of a reasonable meditation. In other words, if something resists the doubting of the subject's system of contemporary reality, it is less a series of demonstrable things than the exercise of meditation itself. It is obvious that a universally doubting thinker could easily question, as one more step in the demonstration, the certainty of the existence of the most evident, sensible things, but (this *but* marks the junction between system and exercise) such a move would compromise the ascetic framework of the *Meditations*. This is why it is necessary to exclude immediately and without delay this unreasonable extravagance that would risk carrying off with it all of the guarantees of the meditative exercise:

The Right of Philosophy and the Facts of History

> That madness be posited as disqualifying in any search for the truth, that it should not be 'reasonable' to call it to oneself to carry out the necessary doubting, that one cannot feign it even for an instant, and that the impossibility appears immediately in the very assignation of the term 'demens'; this is indeed the decisive point where Descartes departs from all those for whom madness may be in some way or other a bearer or a revealer of truth.[105]

Once madness is excluded as 'excessive and impossible', Descartes invokes the case of the dream that proves capable of casting doubt on the subject's system of contemporary reality, without, however, compromising the exercise of the *Meditations*.[106] For it is possible while dreaming, for instance, that one believes oneself to be sitting next to a fire even though one is really in bed. The experience of dreams does not threaten the very rationality of the meditative exercise itself:

> These two sides of the successful test (an uncertain stupor and a manifest vision) constitute very well the subject as *effectively doubting* his or her own contemporary reality, and as *validly continuing a meditation* that disregards all that which is not manifest truth.[107]

This forms the basis of the whole distinction between madness and dreams, according to Foucault: whereas madness is too powerful an ordeal for the contemporary reality of the subject, which must be excluded from the meditative exercise since it risks compromising it entirely, dreams are a measured experience that allows the subject to doubt its contemporary reality without endangering the reasonable nature of its philosophical undertaking.

Without denying the instructive aspects of such an interpretation, it is worth bringing up certain methodological questions concerning the double reading proposed by Foucault. First of all, it is debatable whether it is legitimate or fruitful to limit oneself to only a few paragraphs by Descartes in order to explain his combination or differentiation of reason and madness. Descartes speaks so little of madness in the first *Meditation* that it would seem advisable to study other passages where he mentions it. The theme of madness would obviously not be the only one that could benefit from the widening of such strict bibliographical limits. All the subjects discussed could, in principle, find clarification in other writings by Descartes. Take, for example, the way in which Foucault emphasises the importance of the title of the *Meditations*, which he sees as valorising the meditative exercise of the subject. It so happens, as one reads in a letter to Mersenne on 11 November 1640, that Descartes had entrusted the latter with fixing the definitive title of the book: 'I am finally sending you my work on metaphysics, which I have not yet put a title to, so that I can make you its godfather and leave the baptism to you' (AT, III, 238–9). One might respond that the nature of the text itself counts more than the title or the manner in which it was attributed (did not Descartes suggest the title *Meditationes de prima Philosophia* in the same letter?). But this brings me to my second question: instead of speaking of the philosophical meditation as a definitive and fixed form, would it not be better to examine the meditation as a thoroughly historical discursive form? The same is obviously true for all of the other objects of investigation. For what seems to be lacking in Foucault's discursive analysis, in the form it takes here, is precisely a historical investigation. Given that Foucault, for example, studied at length the relationship between the system and the exercise in Descartes, would it not be worthwhile to examine the role of these discursive forms in the seventeenth century? Is not the same true for the literary and philosophical genres of this period? Even the Latin terms that Foucault carefully distinguishes (notably *insanus/demens* and *amens*) are more or less presented in an ahistorical manner. Instead of questioning the history of Descartes's discursive practices, Foucault was content to accept, with a few exceptions, the rules of the game fixed by Derrida in his article from 1963: (1) the delimitation of the object of research: a few paragraphs by Descartes; (2) the use of the properly philosophical method: internal analysis; Foucault seems to have wanted to employ the latter in order to break with Derrida's third axiom: (3) the superiority of philosophical discourse, which is the only discourse that has the right to speak of right. The problem with such an approach is that, by confronting Derrida 'on his own terrain', Foucault ends up implicitly assenting to these three interpretive axioms. For his second reply to Derrida closely resembles the type of discourse that he himself called into question in his first reply: the pedagogical method of *explication de texte* that dominates academic philosophy in France. It is the response of the philosophical master who, in order to protect genuine gnosis, takes on the task of revealing the true meaning of the text to the student who lost their way.

CONCLUSION

The preceding analysis leads to the conclusion that the traditional historical patterns used to explain the transition from 'structuralism' to 'neo-' or 'post-structuralism' are incapable of explaining certain essential issues concerning the relationship between philosophy and the social sciences in the post-war period. The same applies to the sociological paradigm that opposes rebellious youth to the holders of power. Instead of reducing historical change to a linear succession of dominant theoretical movements, or restricting the intellectual field to a binary space opposing the *haves* to the *have-nots*, it is necessary to undertake a micro-analysis of debates in order to carefully detail each position and all of the strategies that are mobilised in them. Such a micro-analysis cannot, however, be disassociated from a socio-historical macro-analysis of the division of positions within the spheres of knowledge.[108] Such a method allows us to see the fundamental stakes of the debate between Derrida and Foucault. For it is less a question of a few words of Descartes than it is of the relationship between philosophy and the social sciences, that is, of the relation between two hermeneutic methods, two conceptions of history, two images of thought, two ways of conceiving the relation between principle and fact, and so forth. Such an approach has also allowed us to shed light on the normative, metaphilosophical logic that serves as the implicit arbiter in this debate. It is a logic that opposes the alterity of madness, imbued with an intrinsic value that is never explicitly stated or justified, to the debilitating sameness of reason. The principal strategy of each author consists in showing that his adversary is complicit with a rationality that is so diabolical that it convinces him that he can escape, however minimally, its conceptual straightjacket. Ultimately, it is a question of knowing who is capable of putting himself to the test of the outside of Western reason: the philosopher who bids farewell to a determined madness in order to approach the extreme point of the indetermination of concepts, 'before' all factual division between madness and reason, or the historian who takes leave of a historically constructed pedagogy in order to devote himself to a logically impossible task, which consists in writing the history of that which resists the language of reason. I hope the reader will excuse me for not definitively taking sides in this debate, for such an act would be equivalent to accepting its logic without questioning its source, its modes of functioning, its implicit values and its limits.

NOTES

1. Foucault, *History of Madness*, trans. Jonathan Murphy and Jean Khalfa (London and New York: Routledge, 2006 [1961]). The original 1961 French title was *Folie et déraison: Histoire de la folie à l'âge classique*. It was re-edited in 1972 by Gallimard under the title *Histoire de la folie à l'âge classique*. The short story by Borges was published in *Other Inquisitions, 1937–1952*, trans. Ruth L. C. Simms (Austin: University of Texas Press, 1964 [1952]), pp. 167–70.
2. Foucault, *History of Madness*, p. 47.
3. Translator's note: the French terms *extravagant* and *extravagance* are essential to Rockhill's argument that follows. As a general rule, I translate the terms into their homographic English equivalents 'extravagant' and 'extravagance' whenever they appear in the author's text. This conceptual rigour is necessary, particularly in the subsequent discussion of Derrida's article. Derrida uses *extravagance* to capture the hyperbolic, excessive quality of madness that escapes language and reason. Thus, the term has a conceptual importance that I have chosen to keep in English, at the expense of more colloquial renderings. However, in the English translations of Descartes, Foucault and Derrida, the words are sometimes translated as 'mad', 'eccentric', 'eccentricity' or 'insanity', among other terms. When these translations are cited (in actual practice, this only occurs in Descartes's text above and in citations of Derrida), I leave the words translated as such as long as they do not interfere with Rockhill's argument; otherwise I take the liberty to modify them or put the French word in brackets as I have done here with *extravagant*.
4. *The Philosophical Writings of Descartes*, vol. 2, p. 13.
5. Foucault, *History of Madness*, p. 45 (translation slightly modified).
6. Ibid., p. 46 (translation slightly modified).
7. Ibid., p. 47 (translation slightly modified).
8. As is well known, Foucault revisits the delimitation of the classical age in *The Archaeology of Knowledge*. He adds crucial precisions, notably on pages 176–7. It is interesting to note in this respect that Foucault had situated Pascal's (1623–62) stated position in his *Pensées* on the side of the pre-Cartesian division between the Renaissance and the classical age, even though the work was written at the end of his life and published after his death in 1670 (see Foucault, *History of Madness*, p. 35).
9. Derrida, 'Cogito and the History of Madness', in *Writing and Difference*, p. 32.
10. Foucault himself highlighted this dubious methodology in his 'Reply to Derrida', to which I will return later: 'I believe, however, that Derrida's analysis is inexact. In order to be able to show that these three pages of

my text would carry away with them the 650 other pages, in order to be able to criticise the totality of my book without saying a single word about its historical content, its methods, its concepts, its hypotheses (where there would undoubtedly be ample room for criticism), it seems to me that Derrida was led to falsify his own reading of Descartes, and also the reading that he made of my text' ('Reply to Derrida', *History of Madness*, Appendix III, p. 578, translation slightly modified).
11. Here is Derrida's original sentence, which I have paraphrased: 'What is the exemplarity of Descartes, while so many other philosophers of the same era were interested [...] in madness [...]?' (Derrida, 'Cogito and the History of Madness', p. 44).
12. Ibid., p. 42.
13. Ibid., p. 42.
14. Ibid., p. 45.
15. Ibid., p. 42; ibid., p. 60.
16. Foucault describes his study as an attempt to show that 'the systematicity which links together forms of discourse, concepts, institutions, and practices is not of the order of a forgotten radical thought that has been covered over and hidden from itself, nor is it a Freudian unconscious, but that knowledge has an unconscious that has its own specific forms and rules' (Foucault, 'Reply to Derrida', p. 578). With respect to Derridean deconstruction, Bernard Flynn correctly notes its debt to psychoanalysis (see 'Derrida and Foucault: Madness and Writing', p. 202; see also Derrida's clarifications in *Of Grammatology*, pp. 157–64). It seems, however, that symptomatology, here understood in all its generality, reaches back further than Freudian psychoanalysis, and is not unrelated to interpretive methods of the nineteenth century. On this point, I refer the reader to Jacques Rancière's insightful research, notably in *The Aesthetic Unconscious* and 'The Politics of Literature'.
17. Such a study should also take into account Heidegger's reading of the cogito (see in particular *Nietzsche Volume IV: Nihilism*, pp. 102–18.
18. Derrida is perfectly conscious of this: 'Without knowing, moreover, whether an event such as the creation of a house of internment is a sign among others, whether it is a fundamental symptom or a cause. This kind of question could appear exterior to a method that intends precisely to be structuralist, that is, a method for which everything within the structural totality is interdependent and circular in such a way that the classical problems of causality themselves would appear to stem from a misunderstanding. Perhaps. [...]' ('Cogito and the History of Madness', pp. 43–4, translation slightly modified). Let us recall, however, the 'manifest meaning' of Foucault's first sentence just after the pages that constitute Derrida's object of analysis: 'More than one sign gives it

[the classical event] away, and they don't all come from a philosophical experience nor from developments of knowledge. The one we would like to discuss belongs to a very broad cultural surface' (Foucault, *History of Madness*, p. 47, translation slightly modified). The creation of houses of internment would thus be precisely 'a sign among others', which is to be counted along with the historical sign that is Descartes's 'philosophical experience'. The sentence that I have just cited by Derrida is all the more curious since he affirms further on: 'Foucault leaves Descartes there, to go on to the historical (politico-social) structure of which the Cartesian act is only one sign among others. For "more than one sign", Foucault says, "betrays the classical event"' (Derrida, 'Cogito and the History of Madness', pp. 47–8, translation slightly modified).
19. Derrida, 'Cogito and the History of Madness', p. 45.
20. Ibid., pp. 44–5. It is however very significant that Derrida acknowledges, in an apparent act of intellectual modesty, that it is nonetheless impossible to make manifest in its meaning the totality of the content of philosophical discourse. This ultimately means that textual interpretation is without limit and that one never has the right to move on to the historical meaning. Thus there is never a legitimate way to reinsert philosophical discourse into history, that is, never a reinsertion which does not do violence to it. The entire reflection on the reinsertion (this is Derrida's word) of the content of the text into history obviously supposes that the text is already exterior to history, or autonomous in some way. Such a distinction is not merely illegitimate, but it depends itself on a very specific historical situation, as I have attempted to show in my study *Logique de l'histoire*.
21. I would like to highlight, anticipating the analyses to come, the subtle slippage identifiable in the sentences that introduce Derrida's internal analysis of Descartes, a slippage between the 'manifest meaning', which 'is not legible in the immediacy of a first encounter', and what he calls the 'properly philosophical intention' (Derrida, 'Cogito and the History of Madness', p. 45). To assure himself of the manifest meaning, Derrida already seems to anticipate the need to rely on the philosophical intention of the text in the places where the meaning is less evident. This impression is confirmed in the long note in the middle of page 58, where Derrida describes the 'intentional meaning' of the text as that which surpasses all finite totality and all factual determination, as that by which the philosophical project presents itself originally and independently of the finite world: 'One cannot allege that the philosophical project of the "infinitivist" rationalisms served as an instrument or as an alibi for a finite historico-politico-social violence (which is doubtless the case) without *first* having to acknowledge and respect the intentional meaning of this

project itself. Now, within its own intentional meaning, this project presents itself as the conceptualisation of the infinite, that is, of that which cannot be exhausted by any finite totality, by any function or by any instrumental, technical, or political determination' (ibid., p. 58).

22. On this point I refer the reader to Roger Chartier's excellent study entitled '"La chimère de l'origine": Foucault, les Lumières et la Révolution française': 'After him [Foucault], it became impossible to consider the objects of the historian as "natural objects" of history, as universal categories of which one need only track the historical variations – whether they go by the name of madness, medicine, the state, or sexuality' (*Au bord de la falaise*, p. 156). Alan Sheridan says as much about *History of Madness* ('Madness, Death, and the Birth of Reason', in *Michel Foucault: The Will to Truth*, pp. 11–45), as does Roland Barthes: 'He [Foucault] has not written the history of madness, as he says, *in a style of positivity*; from the start he has refused to consider madness as a nosographic reality which has always existed and to which the scientific approach has merely varied from century to century. In fact, Foucault never defines madness; madness is not the *object* of knowledge, whose history must be rediscovered. One might say instead that *madness is nothing but this knowledge itself*: madness is not a disease, it is a variable and perhaps heterogeneous *meaning*, according to the period' ('Taking Sides', in *Critical Essays*, p. 164, translation slightly modified).

23. That being said, Foucault admits in his 'Reply to Derrida' that placing his analysis of Descartes at the front of the chapter was not in accord with his general devalorisation of the philosophical object in *History of Madness*: 'But I had not yet managed to free myself sufficiently from the postulates of philosophical teaching, as I was unable to resist placing at the head of one chapter, and therefore in quite a privileged place, the analysis of a text by Descartes. This was no doubt the most expendable part of my book, and I willingly admit that I should have omitted it, had I been more consistent in my casual indifference towards philosophy' (Foucault, 'Reply to Derrida', p. 578).

24. Foucault writes in 1972: 'What I have tried to show (but it was probably not clear to my own eyes when I was writing the *History of Madness*) is that philosophy is neither historically nor logically a foundation of knowledge; but that there are conditions and rules for the formation of knowledge to which philosophical discourse is subject, in any given period, in the same manner as any other form of discourse with rational pretension' (ibid., pp. 577–8).

25. The introduction to the first issue is very telling regarding the orientation of the review. While philosophy is declared to be 'independent of science, of religion, and of common sense', the author maintains: 'It [philosophy]

is not entirely independent of history; but even here it remains separate from the history that considers ideas of thinkers as historical facts and is merely a question of erudition. Philosophy is only concerned with the history of systems or rather it connects itself to this history as being part of its idea' ('Introduction', *Revue de métaphysique et de morale*, 1, 1893, p. 3; my translation). It is Darlu, as François Azouvi notes, who wrote this unsigned 'introduction' (*Descartes et la France*, p. 341).

26. The usage of such an explicative framework encounters two immediate problems (in addition to those highlighted below): (1) Foucault had yet to enjoy the success of *The Order of Things* (1966); he was teaching at the University of Clermont-Ferrand and had just returned to France after five years abroad (1955–1960); and (2) the generational gap between Derrida and Foucault was only four years (1926/1930).
27. Recall Derrida's words: 'In this sense, I would be tempted to consider Foucault's book a powerful gesture of protection and internment. A Cartesian gesture for the twentieth century. A reappropriation of negativity' ('Cogito and the History of Madness', p. 55).
28. Derrida recalls in the first pages of 'Force and Signification' (an essay published in *Critique* in June–July 1963, before being collected in *Writing and Difference*) that structuralism, 'by virtue of its innermost intention, and like all questions about language', 'escapes the classical history of ideas' (*Writing and Difference*, p. 4). Indeed, the struggle between structure and force has an interminable quality: 'The structuralist stance, as well as our own attitudes assumed before or within language, are not only moments of history' (ibid., p. 10; see also ibid., pp. 28–9). And the development of 'this structuralist passion, which is simultaneously a frenzy of experimentation and a proliferation of schematisations', coincides with periods of 'historical *dislocation*', phrases that unmistakably refer to the events of the war and the immediate post-war period (ibid., p. 6).
29. In an article that carefully examines three ways of escaping university orthodoxy, Louis Pinto provides valuable insight into the socio-discursive insertion of Derrida and Foucault within the philosophical discipline ('Volontés de savoir: Bourdieu, Derrida, Foucault'). Nevertheless, it is unfortunate that the association of Foucault with philosophical discourse – which is justified to a certain degree – caused the author to lose sight of the call to order issued by Derrida.
30. Foucault perfectly described Derrida's strategy in the first pages of his 'Reply to Derrida': 'Derrida thinks that he can capture the meaning of my book or its "project" from the three pages, the only three pages that are given over to the analysis of a text that is recognised by the philosophical tradition' ('Reply to Derrida', p. 575).

31. Derrida had asked Foucault to attend his lecture at the Collège philosophique in these terms: 'I believe that I will basically try to show that your reading of Descartes is legitimate and illuminating at a profound historical and philosophical level that does not seem to me to be immediately indicated or signalled by the text that you use, and also, I don't believe that I will read it exactly as you do' (Letter of 3 February 1963, cited in the chronology prepared for Foucault's *Dits et écrits*, vol. 1: 1954–1969, p. 25; my translation).
32. Derrida, 'Cogito and the History of Madness', p. 45. Derrida again attacks Foucault's rejection of internal analysis in his article 'To Do Justice to Freud': 'he [Foucault] never, to my knowledge, cites or analyses any text by Freud, or by any other psychoanalyst, not even any contemporary French psychoanalysts' ('"To Do Justice to Freud": The History of Madness in the Age of Psychoanalysis', in *Resistances of Psychoanalysis*, p. 124, note 8, translation slightly modified). I will make a small correction here of a slight inadvertence on Derrida's part, without trying to oppose the general rule he establishes, by referring to the quotation from Freud on page 82 of the second edition of Foucault's *Mental Illness and Psychology* (1987 [1962]).
33. One easily recognises here the disembodied text so familiar to academic philosophy.
34. Derrida, 'Cogito and the History of Madness', p. 44. Among the questions brought up by Derrida, it is not surprising to find the following: 'Do philosophical notions have a privilege?' (ibid., p. 44), even though Foucault did not speak of philosophical notions in the passage cited by Derrida: 'To write the history of madness thus will mean the execution of a structural study of an historical ensemble – notions, institutions, juridical and police measures, scientific concepts – which holds captive a madness whose wild state can never in itself be restored' (ibid., p. 44). Note also the revealing persistence of the adjective 'philosophical' in the two paragraphs that introduce the internal analysis of the first *Meditation*, where Derrida uses it five times in five sentences (ibid., pp. 44–5).
35. Translator's note: the distinction that Rockhill makes here between fact and principle is essential to his argument throughout the text. However, there is a multitude of French terms that the author employs to make this distinction, each with nuances of meaning that are difficult to translate into English. There is a constellation of terms used to refer to the order of principle, notably *principe*, *principiel*, *de droit* or the Latin *de jure*. Because the terms have distinct though overlapping meanings, depending on the context, it is impossible to consistently translate each word with a single English equivalent: 'by principle', 'in principle', 'of law' and '*de jure*' are the most common terms that I use. Similarly, *de fait* is often used to signal

a shift to the order of facts, which I variably translate as 'factual', 'in fact' or, occasionally, *'de facto'*.

36. At some point, a study needs to be undertaken concerning the relationship between the simplistic historical schema of 'post-structuralist liberation' and the call to order announced by some of the young philosophers of Derrida's generation. For one must not forget that Lévi-Strauss, Foucault, Bourdieu and numerous other thinkers that were placed – voluntarily or otherwise – under the structuralist label threatened to dissolve the properly philosophical object and method into the social and human sciences, depriving the philosopher's discourse of its sovereign right to speak the truth of the other sciences. It no doubt appeared necessary to some of them to protect philosophy against the risk of becoming a historical object among others. On the particularly strained relationship between philosophy and the social sciences in the post-war period, see Fabiani, 'Sociologie et histoire des idées', Bourdieu and Passeron, 'Sociology and Philosophy in France since 1945', and Boschetti, *The Intellectual Enterprise*, pp. 59–87. Michèle Lamont is correct to see, in the criticisms put forth by Derrida against some of the established intellectuals of the 1950s and 1960s, a strategy of legitimation that consisted in opposing the structuralism of the past with a new philosophical approach (see 'How to Become a Dominant French Philosopher', pp. 599–600). For in attacking the leading thinkers of the moment, Derrida overtly positioned himself as the next candidate to succeed them. This opposition is blatantly clear in his article on Foucault, especially when Derrida makes reference to what he calls, openly playing with the political meaning of the term, 'structuralist totalitarianism' ('Cogito and the History of Madness', p. 57).
37. It is true that Foucault never provided, in my opinion, an exhaustive and convincing explanation of the following phrase, even in his two replies to Derrida: 'As if I were not a man who sleeps at night, and regularly has all the same experiences while asleep as madmen do when awake – indeed sometimes even more improbable ones' (*The Philosophical Writings of Descartes*, vol. 2, p. 13 (AT, VII, 19/AT, IX, 14)).
38. Derrida, 'Cogito and the History of Madness', p. 50.
39. Ibid., p. 51.
40. Ibid., p. 52.
41. Ibid., p. 53 (translation slightly modified).
42. Ibid., p. 55 (translation slightly modified).
43. Ibid., p. 55 (translation slightly modified).
44. Ibid., p. 55 (translation slightly modified).
45. Ibid., p. 56.
46. Ibid., p. 56 (translation slightly modified).

47. Ibid., p. 56.
48. See ibid., p. 57 (translation slightly modified): 'The extent to which doubt and the Cartesian Cogito are *punctuated* by this project of a singular and unprecedented excess – an excess in the direction of the nondetermined, Nothingness or Infinity, an excess which overflows the totality of that which can be thought, the totality of determined beings and meanings, the totality of factual history – is also the extent to which any effort to reduce this project, to enclose it within a determined historical structure, however comprehensive, risks missing the essential, risks dulling the *point* itself. Such an effort risks doing violence to this project in turn [...].' Derrida immediately identifies this violence, which is obviously the violence committed by Foucault against philosophical discourse, as the very origin of all factual violence: 'When I refer to the forced entry into the world of that which is not there and is supposed by the world, or when I state that the *compelle intrare* (epigraph of the chapter on "the great internment") becomes *violence itself* when it turns toward the hyperbole in order to make hyperbole reenter the world, or when I say that this reduction to intraworldliness is the origin and the very meaning of what is called violence, making possible all straitjackets, I am not invoking an *other world*, an alibi or an evasive transcendence' (ibid., p. 57, translation slightly modified).
49. Ibid., pp. 53–4 (translation slightly modified).
50. Ibid., p. 58 (translation slightly modified). See the pertinent analysis by Bernard Flynn in 'Derrida and Foucault: Madness and Writing', p. 208: 'Indeed Descartes has not interned madness in the manner claimed by Foucault, rather he has in fact interned, or excluded, it in another way – a way that is not specific to him but which is coextensive with language as such.'
51. Derrida, 'Cogito and the History of Madness', p. 58.
52. Ibid., p. 310, note 28.
53. As we will see, it is this same principle that – according to Derrida – condemns Foucault's project, insofar as the latter attempts to write a history of madness that integrates the experience of unreason.
54. Derrida, 'Cogito and the History of Madness', p. 56; ibid., p. 33.
55. At some point, the following hypothesis should be tested: the often excessive length of Derrida's writings and the way in which he regularly returns to the same texts or the same words are part of an interpretive strategy that consists in patiently and systematically erasing the distinction between the manifest meaning of his object of analysis and its conceptual architectonic framework, which is supposed to be consubstantial with it.
56. Derrida, 'Cogito and the History of Madness', p. 55 (translation slightly modified).

57. Ibid., p. 309, note 26 (translation slightly modified).
58. It is extremely revealing of Derrida's strategy when he finds the missing textual support for his reading of Descartes in one of Hegel's writings: 'Hegel also interprets madness as a certain Evil Genius (*der böse Genius*) taking control in man' (Derrida, 'To Do Justice to Freud', p. 98). When it is a question of shedding light on the *de jure* text, any factual textual evidence will do.
59. Derrida, 'Cogito and the History of Madness', p. 51. With respect to the philosophical repatriation of the term *extravagance*, I refer the reader to the following passage: 'This hypothesis [the one formulated with respect to dreams] above all will not run from the possibility of extravagances – of an epistemological nature – much more serious than madness' (ibid., p. 51, translation slightly modified). The term *God*, along with several other words, succumbs to the same fate in Derrida's hands. Instead of concerning himself with the diverse definitions proposed by Descartes, Derrida proposes a definition based on principle: 'But God is the other name of the absolute of reason itself' (ibid., p. 310, note 28).
60. Ibid., p. 308, note 15 (translation slightly modified). It is interesting to note that deconstructionist discourse is always susceptible to being deconstructed in turn, which assures it a strange parasitic vitality. As a good deconstructionist, I could examine the meaning of madness 'itself' that is not present in the text, I could question the attempt to ascertain the limits of madness or presence, or consider the way in which madness is never 'itself' except insofar as it exceeds its limits on all fronts (madness is only itself by not being itself, and so on). Derrida himself undertook this type of conceptual problematisation with respect to the 'madness' that constitutes the object of investigation in Foucault's work (see ibid., pp. 42–4).
61. Ibid., p. 58 (translation slightly modified). The entire reflection concerning the instant and temporal originarity aims at reinforcing the same distinction, that is, that which separates temporal facts, linguistic division, factual differences, and so forth from the archi-originary instant, the atemporal order of law, *différance*, and so on.
62. Foucault described with precision the way in which Derrida systematically detaches himself from the Cartesian text: 'For such an interpretation, Derrida needed first of all to deny that madness was in question in the place where it was named (and in specific terms, carefully differentiated), then he needed to demonstrate that it is in question in the place in which it is not named' ('My Body, This Paper, This Fire', in *History of Madness*, p. 571). I also refer the reader, in the same passage, to the list of 'two series of semantic derivations' that allows Derrida to transform the evil genius and the Cogito into 'the true scene of the confrontation with madness' (ibid., p. 571).

The Right of Philosophy and the Facts of History   93

63. Cited by Derrida, 'Cogito and the History of Madness', p. 39; ibid., p. 40 (translation slightly modified).
64. Around twenty pages further on and in an entirely different context, he makes a comparison between the Cartesian project of 'exceeding the totality of the world' and the Socratic project of surpassing 'the totality of beings, planting us in the light of a hidden sun which is *epekeina tes ousias*' (ibid., p. 57).
65. Ibid., p. 40.
66. Ibid., pp. 40–1.
67. Here one sees the dividing line that is supposed to separate, in Derrida's eyes, the historical exemplarity in Foucault from his own philosophical approach. Whereas Foucault chooses factual historical signs that refer to the discursive structures of an epoch, Derrida declares principles of law that do not require factual proof (be it historical or textual). This is why the questions brought up earlier concerning exemplarity in Derrida still lack precision. The latter can claim to find the totality of the project of Descartes or Foucault in a few pages of their writings precisely because he proceeds in an a priori manner, rather than in an a posteriori fashion. This amounts to saying that he undertakes a philosophical and not a historical reading of them. The question that imposes itself – and, speaking in Derrida's terms, this is the fundamental question for the entire Derridean corpus – is whether an a priori reading flattens every factual text beneath the juggernaut of the *de jure* Text. Whether it is Foucault, Plato, Mallarmé, Lévinas or others, is it not the same Text that lies at the bottom of all texts?
68. Derrida, 'Cogito and the History of Madness', pp. 41–2.
69. In *Of Grammatology*, Derrida edges close to Heidegger when he speaks of an 'internal modification' of the history of logocentrism in Descartes (p. 97).
70. Derrida, 'Cogito and the History of Madness', p. 62 (translation slightly modified). Jean-Paul Margot has proposed a long defence of Derrida's position: 'My conclusion is that the force of rationalism has to do with the fact that it shows the limits of human reason through a mad exercise of this same reason. But, given the history of Western thought, I believe that this conclusion can be applied to the entire history of philosophy [...]. In other words, all discourse, including that of the "insane", must, if it claims to be intelligible, carry normality within itself. Far from being excluded by a historical determination of thought, madness thus functions in the history of thought as a methodological recourse – a fiction that allows limits to be placed on thought which appears excessive vis-à-vis another, dominant way of thinking. To be mad is to dare to think difference at a moment in which coherent and

sufficient thought of the world reigns. To be mad is to think against a closed system of thought … in order to replace it with another system no less coherent and sufficient' ('La Lecture foucaldienne de Descartes', p. 37; my translation). Like Dalia Judovitz ('Derrida and Descartes: Economising Thought'), Margot makes a link between madness and fiction that seems very debatable to me. The analogy that they rely on is the following: reason is to madness what the discourse on truth is to fiction.

71. This explains in part why Gianni Vattimo condemns Derrida's position as fundamentally metaphysical: '*Différance* as archstructure is not in history, it never comes to pass, but then again constitutes a return to the most classic qualification of metaphysical Being, eternity' (*The Adventure of Difference*, p. 144). Defenders of deconstruction will be quick to point out that *différance* is, on the contrary, the condition of possibility for the very distinction between time and eternity (Derrida will say as much himself on page 54 of his article on Foucault). Strictly speaking, *différance* is what one can always redirect to an anterior plane. More than a term or an identifiable concept, it is the designation, always reformulated, of an operation of continual displacement between fact and law, between the said and the unsaid, between history and historicity, between delimitation and what delimits, and so on. The properly hyperbolic moment of deconstruction is the moment when one submits the series of terms that I have just enumerated to the same operation, by recalling that *différance* is not truly speaking in a simple *de jure* relation to factual differences, but is the condition of possibility of the very distinction between law and fact, and so forth. This is why it seems to me that *différance* is better defined as a transcendental operation constantly renewed rather than a simple transcendental. That being said, there is no factual definition or concept that serves to correctly name that which is a product of the order of law, or rather of the order of that which delimits law and fact, and so on (it is thereby necessary, obviously, to continue deconstructing since the naming of *différance* can always be resubjected to the transcendental operation).

72. Derrida, 'Cogito and the History of Madness', p. 43 (translation slightly modified). Derrida often employs this strategy, which consists in discovering in the author he studies a trace that contradicts their entire project while also serving as its profound truth. In the case of Foucault, this is done with the following sentence: 'The necessity of madness […] is linked to the possibility of history' (ibid., p. 42). The most extreme example is perhaps the sentence in *History of Madness* that could have – or should have, according to Derrida – 'spared us such a long and dramatic debate': 'It is true that the cogito is the absolute beginning but one

must not forget that the evil genius is anterior to it' (see Derrida, 'To Do Justice to Freud', p. 86, p. 87, translation slightly modified).
73. Foucault, 'My Body, This Paper, This Fire', p. 559.
74. Foucault, 'Reply to Derrida', p. 583; Foucault, 'My Body, This Paper, This Fire', p. 559.
75. Derrida, 'Cogito and the History of Madness', p. 37.
76. See ibid., p. 308, note 4: 'That all history can only be, in the last analysis, the history of meaning, that is, of Reason *in general*, is what Foucault could not fail to experience.' Alan Sheridan provides an insightful analysis of the relationship between Foucault's project and the process of rationalisation inherent in certain forms of history (see 'Madness, Death, and the Birth of Reason', pp. 13–16).
77. Derrida, 'Cogito and the History of Madness', p. 54 (translation slightly modified).
78. One wonders how Derrida has access to Descartes's true philosophical intention, even though it is precisely this intention that is obscured by language. By what right can he claim to unveil the spirit at the bottom of words, the inexpressible essence of Descartes's thought, all the while insisting on a supposed return to the manifest meaning of the text? This is the most fundamental right of philosophy: the right to speak the truth of mind, essence, totality, the absolute and everything that surpasses simple facts. Derrida's textualism is ultimately a textualism *of principle* founded on the absolute Text – that is, the Text of concepts where the philosopher claims to discover the conditions of possibility of all texts – and not at all a *factual* textualism.
79. See Derrida, 'Cogito and the History of Madness', p. 54: 'So that, to come back to Descartes, any philosopher or speaking subject (and the philosopher is but the speaking subject par excellence) who must evoke madness from the *interior* of thought (and not only from within the body or some other extrinsic agency), can do so only in the realm of the *possible* and in the language of fiction or the fiction of language.'
80. Ibid., p. 62 (translation slightly modified).
81. Derrida often refers to Foucault's preferred authors when he discusses the resistance to metaphysics by certain 'literary' writings: 'Yes, it is incontestable that certain writings classified as "literary" have seemed to me to produce spawnings or infractions at the most advanced points: Artaud, Bataille, Mallarmé, Sollers. [...] These texts carry out, in their very movement, the manifestation and practical deconstruction of the *representation* that was being made of literature' (*Positions*, p. 69, translation slightly modified).
82. Derrida, 'Cogito and the History of Madness', p. 35.
83. Ibid., p. 35 (Derrida's emphasis; translation slightly modified).

84. Ibid., p. 36 (translation slightly modified).
85. This elimination is all the more systematic, and all the more surprising, in 'To Do Justice to Freud', where Derrida cites long passages in Foucault on literary and artistic mediators of madness without ever directly addressing the question, without ever saying, to my knowledge, the word 'literature'.
86. The expressions *archaeology of silence* and *absence of work* bear the trace of some of Foucault's writers of reference (notably Mallarmé and Blanchot). When an interviewer asked him in 1961 about the influences on his project, he responded: 'Most of all, literary works ... Maurice Blanchot, Raymond Roussel. What interested me and guided me was a certain presence of madness in literature' ('Madness only Exists in Society', in *Foucault Live*, p. 7). During his thesis defence on 20 May 1961, he affirmed without ambiguity: 'To speak of madness one must have the talent of a poet' (cited by Eribon, *Michel Foucault*, p. 108). 'But you, sir, have it' was Georges Canguilhem's response (ibid., p. 108).
87. Derrida, 'Cogito and the History of Madness', pp. 54–5.
88. This is not the place for judging the success or failure of the literary dimension of Foucault's historical language. I merely wanted to highlight its existence. On this point, see the study by Frédéric Gros, 'Délire de l'insensé ou écriture littéraire', in *Foucault et la folie*, pp. 86–111.
89. It is interesting to note in this respect that Derrida and Foucault both seek to situate themselves on the good side of the dividing line between reason and madness, and that they compete with each other for the more radical conception of the latter, one which is better at resisting the evils of reason. Despite the various subjects of the debate, they thus share the general valorisation of madness against reason, of otherness against sameness, of the outside against the inside, and so on. It would be interesting, in another context, to study the influence of this metaphilosophical normative logic on post-war French thought. In the present case it will suffice to say that an unshakeable system of values underpins the arguments of Derrida and Foucault, which should be put into relation with what is largely perceived as the collapse of Western reason in the twentieth century (two world wars, the Cold War, the wars of decolonisation, and so forth). To quote François Dosse: 'The West was beginning to examine its nether side, the ways of being of the other scene, which was invisible, a place of a presence revealed by its very absence' (*History of Structuralism*, p. 352, translation slightly modified).
90. Derrida, 'Cogito and the History of Madness', p. 62; ibid., p. 56 (translations slightly modified).
91. Ibid., p. 56 (translation slightly modified).
92. Ibid., p. 56.

93. These terms, I remind the reader, are Derrida's own: 'If philosophy has taken place – which can always be contested – it is only in the extent to which it has formulated the aim of thinking beyond the finite shelter. By describing the historical constitution of these finite protective barriers against madness within the movement of individuals, societies and all finite totalities in general – a legitimate, immense, and necessary task – one can finally describe everything except the philosophical project itself. And except the project of this description itself' (ibid., p. 310, note 28). One finds here again the determining dividing line that distinguishes, on the one hand, philosophy and the project of thinking beyond the finite world, and, on the other, the taking-place of historical events and the finite constitution of forms of knowledge. The relationship of determination, and even the epistemological hierarchy, is also perfectly described: it is the philosophical project that underpins and surpasses all historical projects.
94. Ibid., p. 308, note 4; ibid., p. 36 (translation slightly modified); ibid., p. 36; ibid., p. 43; ibid., p. 54; ibid., p. 54 (translation slightly modified).
95. Ibid., p. 57 (translation slightly modified).
96. What is called Derrida's 'post-structuralism' could just as well be called a 'pre-structuralism' since he seeks, by a project exceeding the totality of facts, which he qualifies as 'insane', to return, stopping short of factual structures, to the principles of law that determine them. The 'opening' of structure in Derrida, that is, the fact that structural elements can continually replace or succeed one another in an unlimited sequence of movements, should not deceive us about the way in which it functions. Ultimately, it is a question of determining the principles that govern the very development of structures. For this reason, one could say that the totalising operation of deconstruction is even more all-encompassing than that of structuralism: while the latter only surveys closed structures, deconstruction struggles to bring out the foundational systematics that determines not only all structures but also the logic of their movement and displacement. Thus, it is henceforth the systematic displacement of structures that makes the system, and it is all the more totalising insofar as there is no longer any fact or event that would be exterior to it. Just as in metaphysics, nothing can rightfully escape deconstruction. Its totalising operation consists precisely in inscribing the departure from structure into the general systematics that determines all structures, be they static or dynamic.
97. It would be interesting to reread the Derridean critique of Lévi-Strauss, who claims that he 'became an anthropologist […] to get out of philosophy', in light of the philosophical call to order addressed to Foucault (Lévi-Strauss, *Myth and Meaning*, p. 11). One finds the same opposition

between the order of right and the order of fact (at the point where Derrida maintains that the ethnocentrism of the ethnologist is an irreducible necessity and not at all a historical contingency) and the same denunciation of certain forms of totalisation in the name of the excessive gesture of philosophy (see 'Structure, Sign, and Play in the Discourse of the Human Sciences', in *Writing and Difference*, pp. 278–93). This gesture is perfectly described in *Of Grammatology*: 'To exceed the metaphysical orb is an attempt to get out of the orbit (*orbita*), to think the entirety of the classical conceptual oppositions, particularly the one within which the value of empiricism is held: the opposition of philosophy and non-philosophy, another name for empiricism [...]' (p. 162). The apparent change of vocabulary in his 1966 lecture on Lévi-Strauss should not deceive us: the passage beyond philosophy, in the metaphysical sense of the term, does not at all amount to the abandonment of the philosophical gesture of deconstruction: 'the passage beyond philosophy does not consist in turning the page of philosophy (which usually amounts to philosophising badly), but in continuing to read philosophers *in a certain way*' ('Structure, Sign, and Play', p. 288). As is often the case with Derrida, each term – in this case 'philosophy' – is imbued with two opposed significations, which will frequently be brought together by revealing their point of indiscernibility: a metaphysical meaning and a deconstructionist meaning.
98. Foucault, 'Reply to Derrida', p. 577; ibid., p. 575.
99. Ibid., pp. 575–6.
100. Ibid., p. 576.
101. Ibid., pp. 576–7. On this subject, the rest of this passage is pertinent, as are Foucault's comments in an interview 'Prisons et asiles dans le mécanisme du pouvoir': 'If someone says to me "philosophy in general", I reply that when a philosopher affirms that he is speaking of nothing in particular, but of experience in general, he is really speaking about something extremely particular, that is, about his own historically determined experience, one which, however, he has transformed and valorised as a general experience. To discuss being means speaking from within a closed historical tradition such as is the case for the vision of philosophical teaching beginning in the 15th century. These sort of objects bore me' (*Dits et écrits*, vol. 1: 1954–1975, p. 1390; my translation).
102. Foucault, 'My Body, This Paper, This Fire', p. 573. I will take the liberty of citing Foucault's description of this pedagogy, which intersects with what I was saying above: 'A pedagogy which teaches the student that there is nothing outside the text, but that in it, in its interstices, in its blanks and silences, the reserve of the origin reigns; that it is never necessary to look beyond it, but that here, not in the words of course, but in words as

crossings-out, in their *lattice*, what is said is "the meaning of being". A pedagogy that inversely gives to the voice of the masters that unlimited sovereignty that allows it indefinitely to re-say the text' (ibid., p. 573).
103. This analysis is found on pages 45–57 of Derrida's article ('Cogito and the History of Madness').
104. Foucault, 'My Body, This Paper, This Fire', p. 563.
105. Ibid., p. 566.
106. Ibid., p. 566.
107. Ibid., p. 567 (translation slightly modified).
108. The relation between micro-analysis and macro-analysis should not be confused with the opposition between internal analysis and external analysis, or textualism and contextualism. It functions rather as a change of scale and perspective, and not at all as a mode of analysis founded on substantialist, atomist, ontological or metaphysical limits.

Chapter 3

AESTHETIC REVOLUTION AND MODERN DEMOCRACY: RANCIÈRE'S HISTORIOGRAPHY*

It has now been some fifteen years that Jacques Rancière has been developing his meticulous research on the aesthetic revolution that has deeply marked the last two centuries. His work testifies to a remarkable originality insofar as it opposes the modernist discourse that obstinately dominates debates on art history by trafficking in simple and reductive conceptual schemes: classical art and modern art, art theory and artistic practice, art for art's sake and committed art, the non- or anti-representative rupture, the intransitive turning point, and so on. Rancière's method, moreover, consists in integrating all of those who have been seduced by these schematic representations into his own historical project, turning them into pieces on his chessboard, via what I propose to call explanatory and synthetic polemics. His work also has the particularity of breaking with the dominant categories for thinking the relationship between art and politics, whether those of the Marxist tradition, those of the sociology of art, or those of the post-structuralists. In proposing the notion of a *distribution of the sensible* common to art and politics, he masterfully analyses their consubstantiality by showing that art, to the extent that it distributes and redistributes the categories of the sensible world (the visible and the invisible, the expressible and the inexpressible, the possible and the impossible, etc.), is already political.[1] In the case of the aesthetic regime of art, he foregrounds, moreover, the proximity between the aesthetic revolution of the last two centuries and the egalitarian politics of democracy, without however confusing the two.[2]

Given the unequalled rigour of Rancière's research, the originality

---

* This chapter was translated by Sabine Aoun and Sean Bray in close consultation with the author. Thanks to Daniel Cunningham for his work on the references and citations.

of the positions he takes, and all of the methodological innovations that he introduces, his reader cannot but be surprised that he only rarely broaches a question that nonetheless appears essential to his project, namely that of historical causality: why did the aesthetic revolution, in the specific form that it takes in Rancière's work, begin near the end of the eighteenth century? Why did it develop in such an intimate, but often conflictual, relationship with modern democracy? Rancière sometimes refers to a few key events of the modern age, be it the French Revolution, the revival of Christianity, the emergence of the social sciences, the democratic surge of the nineteenth century, or sometimes the birth of the museum and the circulation of novels.[3] But he hardly goes any further and seems to distrust in general the search for causes, to the point, in fact, that one might be led to believe that the project he initiated at the beginning of the 1990s currently remains only half-finished. If he has succeeded in proposing a persuasive historical description, the virtues of which are as numerous as its innovations, he has not yet undertaken a veritable genealogy of the aesthetico-political revolution by studying in detail the factors that favoured such changes. The fact that the aesthetic regime of art is the only regime that has not been present in European culture since the time of the Greeks (as opposed to the ethical regime of images and the representative regime of arts) only makes this genealogy that much more essential to his project. If all of the regimes of visibility are historical through and through, as illustrated, for example, by the codification of the representative regime of the arts during the classical age, the aesthetic regime of art has the particularity of being the only truly novel regime. The question that I would therefore like to submit to Jacques Rancière can be expressed with surprising concision: why?

Before further developing, if only slightly, this question, it should be acknowledged that Rancière has excellent reasons for avoiding certain forms of causal explanation. First of all, he follows Michel Foucault in his distrust of the search for origins and of everything that such searching presupposes historiographically: that every historical moment is endowed with an ideal essence present in each of its constituent parts; that facts generate each other through a necessary and uninterrupted chain from cause to effect; that a great continuity reconciles all the accidents and all the displacements of the past in a single system of truth; that the historian situates him or herself at the point of view of the eternal and the immortal by casting a supra-historical gaze over bygone centuries.⁴ Secondly, Rancière would like to keep at a distance the transcendental project, which consists in searching for the conditions of possibility determining a set of historical practices as a homogeneous and well-delimited totality. He rejects such a position of mastery in favour of an immanent analysis of spaces of possibilities that, in principle, does not fear perspectival knowledge.⁵ This is not only to distance himself from certain aspects of the work of Foucault; it is also a critique of what we could call, in the largest sense of the term, the structuralist project – namely the search for laws hidden behind appearances – if not of the social sciences as a whole. Thirdly, Rancière does not want to reduce every act and every utterance to external determinants by means of a reductive sociologism or historicism. He has an appetite for the singular and his analyses testify to an attempt to make works truly speak for themselves, instead of making them fit in the preconceived categories of a monolithic system.

The notion of a regime of visibility and of thought carries the trace of this distrust with respect to certain forms of historical causality. Neither an era, nor an *episteme*, neither a school, nor a movement, this notion opposes the periodisation of history while also countering any grouping of the social world under categories.⁶ Let us recall that although the aesthetic regime of art is a recent phenomenon, Rancière already finds traces of it in Cervantes and Vico. The general system of dating that he proposes does not correspond, therefore, to a clean break in the cultural and intellectual development of Europe. Furthermore, the aesthetic regime of art does not succeed the representative regime of the arts; rather, they exist simultaneously in a historical space shared with the ethical regime of images.⁷ Each regime, moreover, is constituted by autonomous axioms that variously combine according to the circumstances and which can link themselves to axioms of other regimes. In fact, no regime is absolutely pure, and the forms of hybridisation are as numerous as the various types of interlocking and interweaving. The methodological gain is considerable, not only in terms of conceptual flexibility, but also in terms of overcoming the antimony opposing the specific to the general and fact to principle. Instead of proposing a series of postulates that he indefatigably strives to discover in all of the works of art stemming from the same regime, Rancière examines each artistic practice as a unique combination of autonomous axioms. The work in question thereby becomes the crucible in which a singular alchemy of general principles is produced.⁸

Aesthetic Revolution and Modern Democracy

If the distance maintained by Rancière from certain types of historical causality is entirely understandable, the question concerning the onset of the aesthetico-political revolution does not lead him to a methodological reflection on other forms of causality, which might eventually allow him to find an answer to this question. Such an undertaking would not only serve to complement his research by adding a veritable genealogy to his impressive historical description. Without a genealogy, in fact, his project would be exposed to the most serious dangers. By leaving aside the transformations undergone by artistic practices in the modern age in the name of an analysis of the internal organisation of works of art, Rancière risks detaching artistic production from its anchoring points in the social world, and thus situating it within a community of disembodied minds where ideas freely circulate between all of those who are more or less caught in the same regimes of thought. From there it is just a small step to a reductive conceptualism capable of finding the same concepts everywhere. All the more so since Rancière's predilection for tripartite classifications (the ethical regime of images, the representative regime of the arts, the aesthetic regime of art; archi-politics, para-politics, meta-politics) cannot but recall grand dialectical histories while simultaneously falling in step with the recent celebration of a negative dialectic that perpetually engenders contradictions and paradoxes without resolution. Is not the 'positive contradiction' between incorporation and disincorporation the 'galvanising tension' at work in almost all of the artistic production of the last two centuries?[9]

In order to bypass these dangers, one must begin by insisting on the purely heuristic aspect of the notions used by Rancière while affirming that these are operative concepts whose consistency comes less from an ideal essence than from their concrete explanatory power. It is thus appropriate to refer here to one of the methodological aspects of François Hartog's work, namely the status of what he calls a 'regime of historicity', that is, the way in which 'a society treats its past and what it treats it as' or, in a larger sense, 'the modality of self-consciousness of a human community'.[10] A regime of historicity is a conceptual tool that one must avoid hypostasising: 'the notion of a regime of historicity is an instrument; it does not exist in reality: you will never come across a regime of historicity on your path! It is an instrument, as is Weber's ideal type.'[11] I personally would not hesitate to compare this heuristic method to the pragmatist tradition where, as William James says, theories become 'instruments, not answers to enigmas, in which we can rest'.[12]

In order to extend Rancière's reflections in the direction that seems the most promising to me, I would like to propose in the second part of this chapter some general indications concerning historical causality before underscoring factors that seem to have played a rather decisive role in the emergence of the aesthetic regime of art. In what follows, there is no claim to being exhaustive, and the analysis aims above all at opening up a field of investigation. It is much more of an interrogative propaedeutic than a theory of artistic practices in the modern age.

Concerning historical causality, to begin with it should be recognised that no social reality is the result of only one cause, even if a principal catalyst was at work in the production of a particular phenomenon. It would, in fact, be more appropriate to speak of *causal circumstances* insomuch as the arrival of an event depends on a circumstantial situation, which it is futile to try to reduce to a single determinant.[13] It would be useful at some point to enumerate the types and modes of historical causality, by defining their forms of effectivity and the ways in which they combine with one another. Let it suffice to say here that historical causes modify each other and adapt to one another in over-determined circumstances, and that the same cause can be polyvalent in the same situation or produce divergent effects in different situations. Finally, let us add that we should not understand by 'historical cause' a determination in the last instance. It is rather a decisive factor in the production of a dynamic space of possibilities. In what follows, it will not therefore be a question of clarifying the causes of the aesthetic revolution, if we understand by this the essential determinants that produced the aesthetic regime of art according to a necessary chain of events. Rather, it will be a matter of underscoring certain socio-historical factors that combine differently according to circumstances, and whose modalities vary based on the other factors acting in the same situation.

The Public Sphere. The place of art and literature in society has undergone important transformations over the last few centuries. Let us take as an example Jürgen Habermas's thesis in *The Structural Transformation of the Public Sphere*. Following the main lines of his analysis, we could say that the art of the seventeenth and the beginning of the eighteenth centuries essentially served a social function and was bound up with the ruling powers that framed it: the church and the court. The value of the artistic object derived from papal or governmental authority and was not therefore a public affair. Art detached itself from its functions in the service of social representation through the course of the eighteenth century and progressively extricated itself from the system of patronage. With the desacralisation and commercialisation of artistic products, art became a function of taste and personal choice. The birth of literary and artistic criticism was an integral part of this change insofar as the assessment of the arts, relieved of the weight of political and religious authority, became more and more entrusted to those who were capable of formulating the best arguments in the public sphere. Habermas affirms that toward the middle of the eighteenth century: 'philosophy was no longer possible except as critical philosophy, literature and art no longer except in connection with literary and art criticism. What the works of art themselves criticised simply reached its proper end in the "critical journals".'[14] Even if several elements in Habermas's study remain debatable,[15] there are still grounds for asking if the appearance of the aesthetic regime of art is not connected to the emergence of the public sphere in the course of the eighteenth century, or at least to the new place occupied by art in the social edifice. It is true that Rancière draws a parallel between the overthrow of the principle of genericity, founded on the hierarchy of represented subjects, and the transition from a strongly hierarchical society to one restructured by democratic struggles for equality. But the other aspects of the relation between the aesthetic revolution and the transformation of social structures in the modern age remain largely implicit. To take but one example, it seems absolutely necessary to link the suspension of the principle of fiction by the aesthetic regime, namely the principle that supposes 'a specific space-time in which fiction is offered and appreciated as such', to the displacement of art within society, and notably to its departure from spaces consecrated by the authority of the king and the church.[16]

Institutions. The place of art in society cannot be dissociated from modern institutions. The first case to note with respect to the plastic and visual arts is surely that of the modern museum. Theodore Ziolkowski identifies its prototype in an example that could not be closer to Rancière's field of investigation. It is the Altes Museum in Berlin, built based on the designs by Karl Friedrich Schinkel, a friend of Hegel, between 1823 and 1829, when the latter was giving his lectures on aesthetics at the University of Berlin.[17] Ziolkowski writes:

Schinkel's museum in the Lustgarten embodied an institution that had never before existed: a museum dedicated exclusively to art (and specifically including painting as well as sculpture), intended primarily for the education of the nation, located in such a manner as to make a statement about the equality of art vis-à-vis church and state, designed in such a manner as to suggest the religious power of art, displayed in such a manner as to emphasise the autonomous integrity of the work of art, and organised in such a manner as to reveal the historical development of art as a central phenomenon of human culture.[18]

André Malraux also dates the museum, in its modern sense, from the nineteenth century and sees in it the imposition of a new relation between the spectator, the work and the past:

The role of museums in our relation with works of art is so important that we have trouble conceiving of the fact that they do not exist, that they never existed, where modern European civilisation is or was unknown (and that they have only existed for us for less than two centuries). The 19th century lived off of them; we still do, and we forget that they imposed on the spectator an entirely new relation with the work of art. They have contributed to freeing – from their function – the works of art that they reunited, and they contributed to a metamorphosis into scenes [*tableaux*], all the way to portraits.[19]

To take a final example, Michel Foucault situates the museum at the heart of the preoccupations of the modern age and sees in the project of archiving the past the common root that it shares with the library. In a lecture in 1967, the publication of which he would not authorise until 1984, he claims:

The idea of accumulating everything, of establishing a sort of general archive, the will to enclose in one place all times, all epochs, all forms, all tastes, the idea of constituting a place of all times that is itself outside of time and inaccessible to its ravages, the project of organising in this way a sort of perpetual and indefinite accumulation of time in an immobile place, this whole idea belongs to our modernity. The museum and the library are heterotopias that are proper to western culture of the nineteenth century.[20]

In another text from the same period, he draws the same parallel between the museum and the library by insisting on their common archival task. A thesis on modern art and literature – or at least on a certain form of aesthetic modernity – results from this:

> It is very possible that *Déjeuner sur l'herbe* and the *Olympia* were the first 'museum' paintings: for the first time in European art, canvases were painted – not exactly to reply to Giorgione, Raphaël and Velázquez, but to testify, sheltered from this singular and visible relation and below the decodable reference, to a new [and substantial] relation of painting to itself, in order to manifest the existence of museums, and the mode of being and of kinship that paintings acquire in them. During the same period, *La Tentation* is the first literary work that takes into account these leafy-green institutions where books are accumulated and where the nit grows softly, the certain vegetation of their knowledge. Flaubert is to the library what Manet is to the museum. They write, they paint, in a fundamental relation to what was painted, to what was written – or rather to what remains indefinitely open in painting and writing. Their art constructs and edifies itself where the archive is formed.[21]

Rancière would no doubt contest the idea of a clean break between classical and modern art, but this does not negate the fact that the museum and the library seem directly connected – as is also the case for the modern university[22] – to the new regime of historicity in the aesthetic age. 'The aesthetic regime of the arts', Rancière writes, 'is first of all a new regime for relating to the past.'[23] In addition to these three institutions, one would of course have to examine, in a more detailed study, the nation-state (cultural heritage, national language, the culture of a people, and so on), artistic establishments (the theatre, the opera, and so forth), if not urban space (architecture, public spaces, transportation, and so on).[24] A study of institutions could, moreover, lead us back to the contradiction characteristic of the art and literature of the aesthetic age, namely that art only exists in the singular from the moment in time at which it dissolves itself into the prose of the world by losing everything that is specifically 'artistic' about it and by merging with the commonplace. Is it not the institution – be it the museum or publishing houses, bookstores or libraries – that ultimately takes a stance in these cases by determining what pertains to art and to non-art, and by resolving, at the social level, a conceptual contradiction?

The Media. The eighteenth century has often been called the age of the press, and the nineteenth century has more than once been baptised the age of the triumphant success of the book. Without entering into the numerous controversies concerning literacy rates and the circulation of printed publications, it should be noted that the modern age has been profoundly marked by the fact that the written word became a feature of everyday life. The overthrow of the ideal of speech as act by the model of writing, which is one of the traits of the aesthetic regime of art, seems indissociable from the significant development in the circulation of the printed word. Rancière affirms that 'the preferred site of representation is the theatre', where orators, generals, princes, preachers or magistrates learned the efficacy of the spoken word.[25] Modern literature is, by contrast, founded on the model of writing and on the genre without genre of the novel. If Rancière maintains that this model conveys 'the powers of the mute and loquacious letter since antiquity', one must add straightaway that the circulation of novels increased significantly in the nineteenth century thanks, in particular, to easier distribution, new readers and a new relationship between the author, the work and the public.[26] Outlining only the most general features, we could say that the transition from the spoken word of the stage, as the consecrated place of art, to the loquacious silence of the page, which circulated more or less freely through everyone's hands, seems to have been absolutely decisive for the emergence of the aesthetic regime of art.

Historical Consciousness. Reinhart Koselleck pinpointed a reconfiguration of historical time in the modern age where the model of *historia magistra vitae*, founded on the repetition of the past as a dispenser of examples, was replaced by a philosophy of history oriented around a future that is no longer the cyclical reiteration of the past, but a linear time made of discrete events.[27] The precursory signs of such a change go back to the emergence of 'politics' as of the fifteenth century, since politicians were concerned with the temporal instead of the eternal and attempted to anticipate the future through rational calculation. Although their diagnoses nonetheless reintroduced the past into the future, the notion of progress opened, in the eighteenth century, a new future cut off from the cycles of the past. The modern notion of revolution, and thus of aesthetic or political revolution, is founded on this new historicity insofar as the cyclical conception of revolution, as a return to a previous state of affairs, yields to a concept of revolution as an event opening on to an unknown future.[28] François Hartog studied this transition between the ancient regime and the modern regime of historicity by examining the works of a few authors who were situated between these two regimes (Chateaubriand, Volney, Tocqueville).[29] Although they were still partially under the influence of the ancient regime of historicity, in which the past exercised its role of *exemplum* by clarifying the future, they discovered that it was no longer operative and that the past had withdrawn in the face of the unpredictable future of the modern regime of historicity.[30] According to Tocqueville: 'I survey century after century back to remotest antiquity and I can see nothing resembling what I perceive before my very eyes. The past no longer casts light upon the future; our minds advance in darkness.'[31] Without being overly schematic, we can ask if what Rancière calls 'mute speech', which seems sometimes to be a somewhat abstract poetic figure, is not linked to the relation between a regime of historicity where the traces of the past announce the future and a regime of historicity where the vestiges of elapsed time fall silent before an unknown future.[32]

The public sphere, institutions, media and historical consciousness are obviously not the only factors to take into consideration in a genealogy of the aesthetic regime of art.[33] It must be recalled, moreover, that if Rancière has not yet dedicated a separate work to them, he is far from having ignored them. In fact, in one of his latest books, they play a larger role. In a revealing passage, he makes one of his *lexical references* (taking up the vocabulary of an author instead of directly citing him or her) to the work of André Malraux on museums and, short of a few nuances, takes up – without a doubt involuntarily – the main lines of Habermas's argument in *The Structural Transformation of the Public Sphere*:

> On the one hand, the discoveries of archaeology restore Greek antiquities to their place, and reinstate their distance by casting doubt on the classical age's conception of civilised Greece. With these discoveries, a new historicity comes to frame works, one made of proximities, of ruptures and of reprises, and which

contrasted sharply with the normative and evolutionary model governing the classical relation of the Ancients to the Moderns. At the same time, however, paintings and sculptures were severed from their functions of religious illustration and of decorating seigniorial and monarchic grandeurs by a revolutionary rupture which isolated them in the space of the – real or imaginary – museum. [...] The effect of these displacements was to accentuate the sensible singularity of works and to undermine not only their representative value but also the hierarchy of subjects and genres according to which they were classified and judged.[34]

By inviting Rancière to further develop the properly genealogical dimension of his project, it has simultaneously been a question here of indicating some of the rich paths of inquiry opened by his work. If he had explained everything, he would have been, according to his own analysis, a poor master.[35] However, if we were to ask him to explain everything, we would be even worse students.

NOTES

1. The adjective 'political' (*politique*) is not always linked for Rancière to the precise meaning of the noun 'politics' (*la politique*), understood as the 'dissensual refiguration of the distribution of the sensible' (*Aux bords du politique*, p. 13). In affirming that art is already political, Rancière means that it distributes and redistributes the sensible world. It can therefore just as well reconfirm the consensual order of the police as open breaches in it by getting closer to politics in the precise sense of the term.
2. Let us recall in passing the tensions that Rancière emphasises between the art of the aesthetic regime, which he often closely associates with metapolitics, and democracy in the precise sense of the term, which is 'neither a form of government nor a social lifestyle', but 'the mode of subjectivisation by which political subjects exist' (*Aux bords du politique*, p. 12). If art is political from the outset, this does not at all mean that it necessarily contributes to political subjectivisation, that is, to the declassifying of the police order by dissensus.
3. For purely indicative purposes, we may refer to the following passages: *The Names of History*, pp. 8–9 and 35–6, *Mallarmé*, pp. 54–6 and 104–5, *Mute Speech*, pp. 68–70, and 'The Aesthetic Revolution and its Outcomes'.
4. See in particular Foucault, 'Nietzsche, Genealogy, History', in *Language, Counter-Memory, Practice*, pp. 139–64.

5. 'I always try to think in terms of horizontal distributions, combinations between systems of possibilities, not in terms of surface and substratum. Where one searches for the hidden beneath the apparent, a position of mastery is established. I have tried to conceive of a topography that does not presuppose this position of mastery. It is possible, from any given point, to try to reconstruct the conceptual network that makes it possible to conceive of a statement, that causes a painting or a piece of music to make an impression, that causes reality to appear transformable or inalterable. This is in a way the main theme of my research' (Rancière, 'The Janus-Face of Politicised Art', in *The Politics of Aesthetics*, pp. 49–50).
6. 'The "history of art" in this sense is something quite different from the succession of works and movements. It is the history of regimes of thinking about art, that is, of particular ways connecting practices to modes of making those practices visible and thinkable. In the end this means a history of ideas of thought itself' (Rancière, *The Aesthetic Unconscious*, p. 47).
7. See in particular Rancière, *The Politics of Aesthetics*, p. 50: 'Statements or forms of expression undoubtedly depend on historically constituted systems of possibilities that determine forms of visibility or criteria of evaluation, but this does not mean that we jump from one system to another in such a way that the possibility of the new system coincides with the impossibility of the former system. In this way, the aesthetic regime of art, for example, is a system of possibilities that is historically constituted but that does not abolish the representative regime, which was previously dominant. At a given point in time, several regimes coexist and intermingle in the works themselves.'
8. Among the best examples of this method, see 'The Contradictions of the Work of Literature' (in *Mute Speech*, pp. 101–66) and the book on Mallarmé, as well as the studies published in *The Flesh of Words* and in *Film Fables*. It is nevertheless regrettable that the method used in the analysis of artistic regimes did not lead Rancière to map their distribution in social space by elaborating a veritable historical geography of aesthetic revolution (which seems to have especially touched, judging from his privileged objects of analysis, France and Germany).
9. Rancière, *The Politics of Aesthetics*, p. 59. It is quite revealing that Rancière answers the question 'Are there authors who escape this logic that dominates the nineteenth century?' by saying 'Undoubtedly', before giving examples of some non-French authors of the twentieth century whose works depend precisely on the same logic (ibid., pp. 58–9).
10. Hartog, *Régimes d'historicité*, p. 19.
11. 'Régimes d'historicité: Entretien avec François Hartog'. See also *Régimes d'historicité*, p. 118: 'A regime of historicity has, moreover, never been a metaphysical entity, descended from the sky and of universal reach.'

12. James, *Pragmatism*, p. 21.
13. Rancière is definitely right to attack 'the deduction of the aesthetic and political properties of a form of art from its technical properties' (*The Politics of Aesthetics*, p. 46; see also 'An Interview with Jacques Rancière'). However, in declaring that the aesthetic revolution comes before the technological revolution, he abruptly sets aside the possibility of a co-determination or reciprocal influence by bringing everything back to a single determinant: the aesthetic regime of art. His predilection for singular causes and for polemical positions sometimes leads him to make categorical affirmations where one should instead allow for nuances.
14. Habermas, *The Structural Transformation of the Public Sphere*, p. 42.
15. See Calhoun (ed.), *Habermas and the Public Sphere*, and Chartier, 'The Public Sphere and Public Opinion', in *The Cultural Origins of the French Revolution*, pp. 20–37.
16. Rancière, *Mute Speech*, p. 44 (translation slightly modified).
17. Despite being very uneven, Tony Bennett's study *The Birth of the Museum* contains a few useful indications on the subject.
18. Ziolkowski, *German Romanticism and Its Institutions*, p. 320. On the relation between Schinkel and the philosophy of art among the Romantics, see especially pp. 321–9. For a study of the emergence of the modern museum in France, consult Poulot, *Musée, nation, patrimoine 1789–1815*.
19. Malraux, *Le Musée imaginaire*, pp. 11–12. The museum also contributed, according to Malraux, to an intellectualisation of the relationship to art: 'Our relation with art, for more than a century, has not ceased to be intellectualised' (ibid., p. 13).
20. Foucault, 'Of Other Spaces', p. 26.
21. Foucault, 'Postface à Flaubert', pp. 298–9.
22. On the new university model, which appeared in particular in Halle (1694) and in Göttingen (1737) before spreading elsewhere, see McClelland, *State, Society, and University in Germany 1700–1914*, and Ziolkowski, 'The University Model of the Mind', in *German Romanticism*, pp. 218–308. For a more general perspective, see Charle and Verger, *Histoire des universités*.
23. Rancière, *The Politics of Aesthetics*, p. 25. In the lines that follow this passage, he refers to the invention of the museum: 'The aesthetic regime of the arts invents its revolutions on the basis of the same idea that caused it to invent the museum and art history, the notion of classicism and new forms of reproduction [...] And it devotes itself to the invention of new forms of life on the basis of an idea of what art *was*, an idea of what art *would have been*' (ibid., p. 25). In *Mute Speech*, Rancière opposes the historical poetics of the aesthetic age to representative poetics: 'There are only two kinds of poetics: a representative poetics that determines the genre and generic perfection of poems on the basis of their invention of a fable;

and an expressive poetics that determines them as direct expressions of the poetic power. A normative poetics says how poems should be made; a historical poetics says how they are made, that is, in the end, how they express the state of things, language, and manners that gave them birth' (p. 67).
24. One of the major risks of an institutional analysis that one must avoid is the tendency to bring everything under monolithic categories – such as *the museum, the library, the university* – without taking into account the diversity of practices and the variability in these establishments' modes of operation.
25. *The Future of the Image*, p. 116. See also *Mute Speech*, pp. 43–50.
26. Rancière, *Mute Speech*, p. 98. On this subject, see Cavallo and Chartier (eds), *A History of Reading in the West*, and Chartier, *Cultural Origins*.
27. The brief analysis proposed by Koselleck of the distance separating the historical temporality present in Albrecht Altdorfer's *Alexanderschlacht (The Battle of Alexander)* and the one attested to by Friedrich Schlegel's interpretation a few centuries later presents us with more than one point of similarity with the work of Rancière on the German thinkers of the beginning of the nineteenth century: 'Schlegel was able to distinguish the painting from his own time, as well as from that of the Antiquity it strove to represent. For him, history had in this way gained a specifically temporal dimension, which is clearly absent for Altdorfer. Formulated schematically, there was for Schlegel, in the three hundred years separating him from Altdorfer, more time (or perhaps a different mode of time) than appeared to have passed for Altdorfer in the eighteen hundred years or so that lay between the Battle of Issus and his painting' (*Futures Past: On the Semantics of Historical Time*, p. 10).
28. See also Arendt, *Between Past and Future* and *On Revolution*.
29. Hartog says the following about Chateaubriand: 'he was someone who wrote *on* the breach of time and wrote to himself from this breach, someone who was between two regimes of historicity. He does not give up on parallels, while nonetheless knowing that they are no longer operative. He piles up the dates and scratches out the palimpsests' (*Régimes d'historicité*, p. 105).
30. Among the numerous differences between Hartog's regimes of historicity and Rancière's artistic regimes, it is important to note that if Hartog challenges the idea of an event-like break between time periods, he maintains to a certain extent the existence of a chronological succession between the ancient regime and the modern regime of historicity. In his analysis of Chateaubriand, Volney and Tocqueville, it is thus a matter of studying a short period of transition. Regarding Chateaubriand, he writes: 'By the relation to time that constitutes it and by the one that it

constitutes, the *Essai* translates this brief moment when, under the effect of the Revolution, the *topos* [of *historia magistra*] ceases to be operative and when doing without it is not yet possible. In this sense, it is a text between two centuries: between the Ancients and the Moderns or between the two shores of the river of time' (*Régimes d'historicité*, p. 99). This being said, Hartog nevertheless makes room for 'anachronistic' phenomena by sometimes insisting on the overlap between regimes of historicity: 'It is very clear that the ancient regime of historicity does not disappear in 1789 and that the new regime, or the modern regime, starts before 1789, and that there is overlap. Moreover, one must introduce differentiations in terms of social differentiations, since the same milieux do not strictly live in the same times, and *a fortiori* in societies of the ancient regime. All this must be specified in great detail if one wants to avoid caricature; but what interested me was to position the projector on moments of putting-into-question, of crisis, of "rifts" or "breaches" (taking up the expression used by Hannah Arendt, who speaks of a "gap" in time), and evoking them, these "breaches", while thinking about our present present: are we in such a situation?' ('Régimes d'historicité: Entretien avec François Hartog').

31. Tocqueville, *Democracy in America*, p. 819. Also see Hartog's commentary in *Régimes d'historicité*, pp. 105–7.
32. It is obviously out of the question here to reduce all of Rancière's work on 'mute speech' to the transition between the ancient and modern regimes of historicity. This is only one factor among others that should be taken into account in a genealogy of the aesthetic regime of art. In a more detailed study, it would be necessary to closely examine the new mode of relation to the past that is characteristic of the aesthetic regime (see in particular Rancière, *The Politics of Aesthetics*, pp. 20–30).
33. One could add, in particular, the evolution of the economy, the transformations of the church and the history of the sciences. On this last point, let us mention the parallel made by Foucault – to which Rancière would surely be sensitive – between the new regime of medical thought at the end of the eighteenth century and the lyrical experience that searches for its language in the modern age (see in particular Foucault, *The Birth of the Clinic*, pp. 195–9, and the explanations provided by Alan Sheridan in *Michel Foucault: The Will to Truth*, pp. 11–45).
34. Rancière, *Aesthetics and Its Discontents*, pp. 8–9. One might also consult the article published in 2002 under the title 'The Aesthetic Revolution and its Outcomes'.
35. See Rancière, *The Ignorant Schoolmaster: Five Lessons in Intellectual Emancipation*.

Section II: Politics

Chapter 4

IS DIFFERENCE A VALUE IN ITSELF? CRITIQUE OF A METAPHILOSOPHICAL AXIOLOGY*

> That delusive mode of reasoning which regards diversity alone, [...] I have elsewhere likened to an invalid recommended by the doctor to eat fruit, and who has cherries, plums or grapes, before him, but who pedantically refuses to take anything because no part of what is offered him is fruit, some of it being cherries, and the rest plums or grapes.
>
> (G. W. F. Hegel)

The more one practises philosophy, the more readily one forgets that it is a practice. And like any practice, it is accompanied by its own practical sense, that is a series of dispositions and theoretical and affective reflexes, as well as modes of perception, values, objectives and all the strategies necessary to 'play the game' and believe in its stakes. Strictly speaking, it is not here a question of so many theoretical presuppositions that could be made explicit by philosophical reflection. On the contrary, it is a matter of the unquestioned givens (*évidences*) of practice, which are so obvious that they are not even objects of reflection or critique. One cannot forget, in this regard, that the philosophic practice that consists in unveiling the presuppositions behind a certain intellectual posture is itself founded upon an entire series of unquestioned givens, notably the following: there is an opposition between thought and the unthought; a presupposition is a sign of theoretical weakness; one must attempt to think the unthought by getting rid of all presuppositions; and the philosophy with the fewest presuppositions is the most astute. The unveiling of presuppositions is thus precisely part of philosophic practice, or rather of a certain philosophic practice.[1] The

---

* This chapter was translated by Axelle Karera in close consultation with the author.

same cannot be said for the metaphilosophical analysis of unquestioned givens. For, within a practice (if it be philosophical or not), one hardly ever interrogates the unquestioned givens that constitute it for at least two reasons. First of all, this is generally of no interest for the practice itself, and practical sense directs us toward other objects of analysis. Secondly, the study of a practice's unquestioned givens would hinder one's full participation in it, because questioning the rules of the game interrupts the playing of the game.

However, it is sometimes necessary to take stock of a given practice by examining its unquestioned givens, in order to reorient it in another direction. In the case of philosophy, such an investigation is properly speaking metaphilosophical, for it is a matter of exposing the unquestioned givens that render such a practice possible. In what follows, I will concentrate on a specific theoretical practice, which is the one of my own philosophical training: the 'philosophy of difference'.[2] My objective is by no means to commit parricide or to condemn in one fell swoop a group of thinkers who have made a major contribution to twentieth-century philosophy. I aim at highlighting the tacit code of the philosophic discourse of difference[3] and, more specifically, its metaphilosophical axiology. By this I mean the network of values and normative dispositions inherent in the philosophical practice of a certain constellation of French thinkers.[4] Hence, far from wanting to gather together a group of philosophers in order to condemn them as a whole, I would like to formulate a question pertinent to those who, in one way or another, were educated by a group of very important thinkers: is difference a value in itself?

THE PRACTICAL PHILOSOPHEMES OF THE PHILOSOPHY OF DIFFERENCE

All of the followers of contemporary French philosophy, or rather a certain strand of it, know that the logic of identity and difference plays a major role in it. From Emmanuel Lévinas and Jean-Luc Nancy to Gilles Deleuze, Jean-François Lyotard, Jacques Derrida and many others, an entire intellectual constellation was formed around the problematic of difference and alterity. Lyotard proposed to summarise it by insisting on the role of incommensurability:

> As for what you call the French philosophy of recent years, if it has been postmodern in some way, this is because it has also stressed

incommensurabilities, through its reflexion on the deconstruction of writing (Derrida), on the disorder of discourse (Foucault), on the epistemological paradox (Serres), on alterity (Lévinas), on the effect of meaning by nomadic encounter (Deleuze).[5]

Although it would be naive to claim to discover, in each of these thinkers, the same concept of incommensurability (especially since the practical imperative of intellectual differentiation is at work in this constellation[6]), it is nevertheless obvious that difference is part of a common thematic and constitutes one of the concepts-in-struggle for this host of thinkers.

What interests me here is not the idiosyncratic philosophical lexicon of individual thinkers. I have examined elsewhere, and in diverse contexts, the cases of Derrida, Foucault, Lévinas, Deleuze, Lyotard and others.[7] Rather I am interested in the practical knowledge of 'thinkers of difference' and their most faithful interpreters, that is, the set of intellectual dispositions that underpin and render possible their specific theoretical practices. A traditional philosophical reading, which would be committed to examining the question of difference in each individual thinker, would exclude from the outset the object of analysis of this investigation. In its own practice, it would risk reaffirming one of the unquestioned givens inscribed in the practical sense of specialists: each of these philosophers is, in fact and in principle, different. It is precisely this practical knowledge that interests me, meaning that which structures the practice of the philosophy of difference as well as its most faithful interpretation.

Let us get right to the point then. What does everyone implicitly know in the milieu of the philosophy of difference? Let us recall this with simple language, with neither the spirit of seriousness that imposes itself nor all of the scare quotes and typographical games required by a supposedly sophisticated – meaning *differentialist* – reflection on difference. Everyone basically knows that difference is preferable to identity, that it is better to be on the side of alterity than on that of sameness. We also know that the outside is more prestigious than the inside, that we need heterogeneity rather than homogeneity. This equally holds true for an entire network of related concepts: singularity, foreignness (*l'étrangeté*), absence, madness, the interval (*l'écart*), discontinuity, multiplicity, becoming, indiscernibility, ambiguity, indetermination, incommensurability, paradox, aporia, contradiction, and so on.[8] Each thinker establishes and modifies his or her personal lexicon as they see fit, but the fundamental normative field remains the same. Moreover, the latter is so profoundly inscribed within the practical knowledge of the followers of the philosophy of difference that it has been naturalised, thereby becoming the source of the most appropriate philosophical intuitions. Thus exposed in its simplicity, this metaphilosophical axiology can, indeed, only surprise us: in their diverse struggles against the hierarchical dichotomies of the thinking of the same, philosophers of difference rely firmly on a binary normative logic that bestows an absolute privilege on one term of the dichotomy, which is the one located on the side of heterogeneity (even if it means attempting to dissolve or surpass the rigid identity of the dichotomy itself by means of the indiscernible or by a difference even more radical than any dichotomous – and hence identitarian – difference). This is the paradox of the philosophy of difference: a hierarchical normative opposition is used to struggle against a – if not *the* – binary and hierarchised normative logic, and the *same* logic is always relied upon, namely the one that runs counter to the logic of sameness (including when it is a matter of displacing binary logic itself as a supposed identity undermined by fundamental and irreducible differences).

However, things are not that simple. For this metaphilosophical axiology has also given birth to an entire series of operations aiming precisely at evading such a contradiction, at rendering things 'more complicated' and 'problematic', at differentiating the alleged 'logic' of difference from any logic *identifiable* as such. Like the axiology itself, these operations are part of the practical knowledge of philosophers of difference. They do not take the exact same form in the work for each thinker, and the emphasis will often change as one moves from one text or concept to another (alterity is not difference, multiplicity is not the plural, and so forth). Be that as it may, to truly play the game of difference, it is necessary to master these operations and to make them one's own. The first such operation is that of radicalising difference. For it goes without saying in this milieu that unveiling a more fundamental difference, assenting to a more radical alterity, is advancing in the right philosophical direction. The more heterogeneities proliferate, the more the other is wholly other and radically heterogeneous, the better it is. Each trace of identity must be effaced in the name of a difference worthy of its name. One could cite, as an example, Samuel Weber's Derridean critique of Lyotard, which consists in reminding the latter that all language games are always already undermined by irreducible differences.[9] We could also refer to Lyotard's self-criticism in *The Differend*, where he decides to abandon the notion of language games – still overly tied to the governing body of the same in the form of the person meant to 'play' with language – in favour of phrase regimens and genres of discourse. Derrida's numerous criticisms of his contemporaries, especially in his early writings, are equally emblematic of this trend, including his critique of the way in which Lévinas remains attached to the metaphysics of presence, or of the manner in which Foucault excludes in advance reason's outside by undertaking an ultimately Cartesian, and hence rationalist, history of madness.[10] The rules of the game are known by all of those who accept the normative coordinates of such debates: it is necessary to radicalise alterity by differentiating one's own concept of difference from that of all the others.

Yet the traces of sameness are not that easy to efface since they lay hold of the very notion of difference. This is why the reflexive operation of purification is necessary. In saying that the latter is the second operation, this does not mean that there is an order of succession. This is a purely heuristic enumeration. For one knows from the outset that the most sophisticated approach to difference is the one that undertakes to differentiate this notion itself. Whether it be the idea of pure difference in Deleuze, that of Derridean *différance*, or that of the *otherwise than being* in the later Lévinas (which 'is stated in a saying that must also be unsaid'), the fundamental normative logic is the same: the concept of difference must itself undergo a radical differentiation, even if it means deconstructing the word and the concept of 'difference', even if it becomes a force that incessantly displaces itself by evading any linguistic and theoretical capture.[11] As Derrida showed, for instance, by means of a strategy of dynamic transcendentalism, a *de jure* difference (*une différence de principe*) always already exceeds any *de facto* difference, whether it be a textual, discursive, ethical, political or conceptual difference. Insofar as it is the philosopher himself or herself who plays the role of the guardian of this mysterious, and nearly ungraspable, sovereign difference, of this immemorial archi-origin that one cannot name as such,[12] it is necessary to emphasise the way in which the alleged philosophical openness to difference can give free rein to the valorisation of *one's own* difference. Indeed, the controversies over the most radical concept of alterity hardly conceal the real issue that is most often at stake for each philosopher: it is a matter of promoting one's own difference, the singularity of one's own thought on heterogeneity, the distinction of one's own differentialist conceptualisation of difference. Such a reversal reveals, moreover, the reason why the philosophy of difference's normative logic is also a generative logic. Indeed, all of the connoisseurs of the philosophy of difference know full well what must be done in the future in order to accomplish the next important step in the history of philosophy (if they are not satisfied with merely defending the philosophical project of their spiritual progenitor[13]): it is necessary to think an even more radical heterogeneity, to liberate the outside from the identitarian mooring that inevitably corrupts all words and all concepts. In short, it is necessary to repeat what French thinkers have already done with their German predecessors by penetrating even further into the purifying differentiation of difference. This situation creates a veritable competition for intellectual distinction in which each individual seeks to showcase the heteroclite singularity of their own thought, or that of their intellectual master, as if the true difference were ultimately to be found in one's own philosophical identity.

The third operation is an analogical operation of ethico-political valorisation. According to an indubitable, unquestioned given, it is known that thinking difference is equivalent to participating in a primordial ethico-political battle.[14] Traditional political struggles are, in some way, doomed to failure because they do not attack the genuine source of problems: the philosophy of sameness in all of its guises. What we have here is a true logocentrism, which consists in reducing the totality of ethical and political reality to a theoretical and discursive core, to logos as the privileged domain of philosophy. If classical Marxism runs the risk of economic determinism, we can speak of a risk of theoretical determinism in the work of the thinkers of difference.[15] This does not mean that they necessarily distance themselves from practice,[16] but rather that any possible practice is inscribed in a theoretical foundation that serves as the determinant in the last instance, a discursive foundation that is structured by two poles: homogeneity on the one hand, and heterogeneity on the other.[17] Even in the case of Lévinas, who regularly insists on the way in which 'the face resists possession, resists my powers', one cannot forget that this is a discursive conceptualisation, by Lévinas himself, of the encounter with the other.[18] Moreover, this conceptualisation presents the encounter, even after the operation of unsaying, as always being *the same encounter* with *the same other*, namely the other such as it is valorised by Lévinas's own theoretical schemas and strategies (including the strategy of unsaying), which establish the model of all possible encounters with alterity.[19]

This operation of analogical valorisation is directly linked to a totalising historiographical operation: the entire history of philosophy is torn between differentialist forces and homogenising forms. In the name of heterogeneity, indeed, philosophers of difference provide us with one unique key for understanding the totality of Western history, because it is always the same history, namely the history of the perpetual struggle between the same and the other. This is what I propose to call the dead end of the totalising critique of totality: totalising thought is called into question by means of an even more totalising historical logic, which reduces all of the diversity of history to a single and unique schema. Putting it simply, and abandoning the philosophical shield of a sophisticated lexicon (that is, one that aims at undoing the supposed identitarian logic of language), there is a repetitive battle, which must always be renewed, between the forces of good (differentialist) and the forces of evil (identitarian). Obviously, it is necessary – according to the imperatives of differentiation and purification mentioned above – to dissimulate the simplicity of this historical logic by turning difference into a radical force breaking away from the thought of the same that claims *to identify* difference as the good opposed to the evil of sameness. Yet, for those aware of the unspoken code, this dissimulation has the effect of making that much more clear the real historical dividing lines between the small differences of identitarian thought and the sovereign Difference that surpasses them while rendering them possible. Such a logic of history is, moreover, often connected to the analogical operation of ethico-political valorisation since it is precisely the historical victory of the thought of the same that is supposed to be responsible for contemporary ethico-political problems, if not for the worst crime of the twentieth century.[20] Being itself the guardian of thought, and hence the defender of what is 'naturally' the most fundamental, philosophy has much more than a partial responsibility in such a victory. For the true source of historical events is not to be found in a banal sequence of facts, but in the – more originary – *Geschichte* of thought wherein homogenising structures and heterogeneous forces confront each other. And when it comes to the future, philosophy is thus our only hope. Rather than abandoning it because of its alleged complicity in the ethical and political crimes of the twentieth century, we must instead redouble our philosophical efforts. The convalescence of the human species – perhaps always *to come* – depends precisely on the salvation of thought.

In making explicit these four operations of the metaphilosophical axiology of the thinking of difference, we can say in summary that it is necessary to deepen and radicalise alterity in order to save the integrity of thought, and hence the most fundamental ethico-political values, by thereby assuming the enormous responsibility that weighs on philosophers as the guardians of the history of spirit. It is essential to note, moreover, that such operations also allow for the categorical valorisation of difference and its adjoining concepts to be called into question, at least in appearance.[21] Numerous strategies have been deployed, but this most often consists in situating the opposition between good and evil within the framework of identitarian thought. Insofar as difference breaks with the latter, it is therefore impossible to simply identify it with 'the good'. Rather than being better than identity, difference (as is notably the case for différance in Derrida's work) renders the very distinction between good and evil possible. What is more, as the condition of possibility for such a distinction, it is simultaneously its condition of impossibility because indiscernibility comes in the end to destabilise such oppositions. That being said, dismantling the antinomy of good and evil does not mask what is most essential for the followers of this discourse: it is a matter of changing the scale and redefining terms (the dichotomous thinking of good and evil being designated as identitarian thought) in order to valorise *otherwise* differentialist forces, which constantly displace themselves. If difference is not a good in itself, at least in the most extreme cases of this discourse, it is because it renders possible the production of meaning and values. It is because the distinction between good and evil originates in a more fundamental difference. The distinctive feature of the concept of difference is thus not simply that it is 'better' but, precisely, that it is different, that it differentiates itself, that it is incompatible with the identitarian thought of good and evil while rendering it possible (and impossible). Philosophers of difference thereby obey a tacit imperative of differentialist valorisation: even better than being a good in itself, difference is precisely *different* (from the identitarian opposition between good and evil). It is a matter of an absolute over-value (*survaleur*), which comes to work on the very structure of values, while mysteriously remaining short of or beyond – thus different from – all concepts and all values. It ultimately comes down to a master concept more sovereign than all other concepts

Is Difference a Value in Itself?

because it is capable of constantly displacing itself between the plane of facts and that of principles, thereby becoming the absolute condition of possibility – though ungraspable – of any conceptual understanding and of any value. This does not take the form of a static transcendental principle but rather that of a transcendental dynamism that is always susceptible to moving everything back to a different level, by passing from givens to their conceptual or axiological principle, or by identifying the very distinction between givens and their organising principle as 'the given' in order to transition to the principle of principles governing such a distinction (a principle capable of being reinscribed, in turn, at the level of givens in order to be displaced, once again, by an *other* principle in a transcendental play of infinite differentiation in which the stopping point is always *to come*).

Objectifying the operations of the metaphilosophical axiology characteristic of this constellation of thinkers will undoubtedly face resistance. People will attempt to show that one of the philosophers is an exception to the rule, that this or that concept is more singular and dons differently the holy halo of difference, in short, *differentiates itself* from 'the thought' of difference (whatever *that* is). In doing so, such criticisms will ultimately only tacitly defend – as is necessary – the practical sense of philosophers of difference. Given the vigour of practical sense and all of the professional, vocational, psychological, affective and libidinal investments linked to it,[22] this kind of reaction is probably structurally inevitable. This demonstrates, moreover, the extent to which this is a case of practical philosophemes – at once affective and effective – that are so deeply rooted in philosophers' practical sense that they are already operative prior to the onset of reflection.

This does not, however, mean that there are no variations. It is obvious, for instance, that the later Lyotard's discourse on history is more dramatic and oriented toward pathos than Deleuze's,[23] that the latter largely abandoned the term *difference* in his later work in favour of a reflection on becoming and multiplicity, that the later Derrida moves closer to Lévinas, and that the latter maintains a discourse that is more critical of Heidegger than Lacoue-Labarthe and Nancy, and so forth. The issue here is not at all one of reducing the thought of difference to a monolithic conceptual unit, since a common problematic does not imply that everyone shares a series of philosophical principles. Rather, it is a matter of a set of practical dispositions, which manifest themselves differently depending on individual cases. If all of these thinkers play the game of difference, and if they all participate in a common thematic, supported by a metaphilosophical axiology, we must insist on the fact that they do not all play in the same manner. According to an imperative inscribed in the game itself, it is necessary, moreover, that they play differently, that they differentiate themselves while playing, that their discourses operate simultaneously as reflections on difference and performances that display difference.

THE RISKS OF THE POLITICS OF DIFFERENCE

The philosophy of difference has been relatively well received by the politics of difference in the anglophone world. In this regard, it would be interesting to examine the way in which the metaphilosophical axiology of thinkers of difference can be translated into politics, by analysing point by point their reception in the Anglo-Saxon world, and particularly in the dominant trends in multiculturalism, identity politics and the politics of recognition. In the interests of space, I will limit myself to scrutinising some of the risks – and I insist on the word *risk*, since it is not always the case – of fetishising difference in politics.[24] For reasons of clarity, I will focus on the four operations of the thinking of difference by opposing to them four axioms.

1. *Difference is not a value in itself*. It is a purely relational concept that is neither better nor worse than the notion of identity. This is also the case for all of the dichotomies of the normative logic implicit in thinkers of incommensurability. It all depends on the manner in which they are used and the situations in which they take shape. In this regard, it is necessary to recall that what is 'different' or 'identical' changes according to a series of variables (the context, the definitions used, the points of view, and so forth). It is therefore necessary to definitively abandon the normative essentialism in the thinking of difference, as well as the highly metaphysical logic of the apotheosis of alterity, in the name of a historical, pragmatic and relational approach to words and concepts. For nothing guarantees that the absolutisation of 'difference' will result in desirable political consequences.

Let us pause to briefly consider one of the most blatant examples of suspicious uses of difference in politics, which will undoubtedly appear rather distant from the philosophy of difference. George W. Bush's administration has probably been the most multicultural, and hence 'differentialist', in the history of the United States.[25] But this diversity did not at all prevent the most severe political abuses. Colin Powell, for instance, was the first black Secretary of State (2001–2005). He notably promoted the war in Iraq before the UN Security Council by providing 'irrefutable evidence' of the existence of weapons of mass destruction by relying on, among other things, the testimony of tortured detainees and an article written by a PhD student in California (which had been plagiarised in a British government file, without even the correction of grammatical and typographical errors).[26] This occurred in spite of the fact that Powell had publicly declared, in February 2001, that the sanctions against Iraq had prevented Saddam Hussein from acquiring weapons of mass destruction. Condoleezza Rice was the first black woman to hold the position of Secretary of State, where she replaced Powell in 2005, after having worked as National Security Advisor. She attempted, in particular, to justify to the European Council the existence of a global network of CIA secret prisons, as well as the programme known under the extraordinary euphemism of 'extraordinary rendition', which allows the United States to kidnap, transfer, detain and torture (or have tortured) suspects irrespective of international law.[27] Alberto Gonzales became the highest-ranking Hispanic in an American administration when he was confirmed as Attorney General in 2005, following his service as White House Counsel since 2001. He notably drafted the 25 January 2002 memorandum aimed at establishing that members of 'Al-Qaeda' and 'the Taliban' do not fall under the protection of the Geneva Convention.[28] He also solicited the 1 August 2002 memorandum which redefined torture in such a way that it is more or less impossible for an American interrogator to be found guilty of it.[29] As Attorney General, he publicly lied, moreover, regarding his involvement in the political purge of federal prosecutors in 2006, and he was also implicated in a vast programme of illegal wiretapping. I will skip over the rest of George W. Bush's multicultural dream team by referring to an article published by *Time* magazine in early 2005. In 'The Benetton-Ad Presidency', Bush – who had been named *Time*'s 'person of the year' – was granted the extremely uncanny title of 'American Revolutionary'.[30]

This obviously does not mean that diversity is a bad thing in itself. We should not simply invert the normative logic of thinkers of difference. On the contrary, it is necessary to demonstrate that neither difference nor identity can absolutely guarantee a more just politics. Indeed, difference has no value in itself: it is a purely analytic and relational concept. Let us consider another concrete example by reminding ourselves of the way in which the logic of the radicalisation of difference perfectly serves the objectives of late capitalism and the so-called post-Fordist economy.[31] From the 1960s, but especially since the 1980s, there has been a radical differentiation of consumer products under the slogan 'long live difference!'. As Martin Davidson rightly points out: 'Capital has fallen in love with difference; advertising thrives on selling us things that will enhance our uniqueness and individuality. [...] From World Music to exotic holidays in Third-World locations, ethnic TV dinners to Peruvian knitted hats, cultural difference sells.'[32] The 'globalisation' of the capitalist market since the 1980s has only intensified this logic of the consuming sacralisation of difference. It is interesting to note, in this regard, that the concept of multiculturalism has roughly the same history as that of globalisation (in both the anglophone and the francophone worlds). If it is possible to find some uses of them in the 1970s and 1980s, it is especially since the 1990s that both terms have undergone a staggering inflation.[33] Naomi Klein appears to want to explain this at least partial historical synchrony when she describes the disturbing coincidence between the marketing of the 'global era' and the politics of difference: 'The need for greater diversity – the rallying cry of my university years – is now not only accepted by the culture industries, it is the mantra of global capital. And identity politics, as they were practiced in the nineties, weren't a threat, they were a gold mine.'[34] As Henry Giroux has brilliantly shown, Benetton's advertising campaigns between 1984 and the beginning of the 1990s are one of the best examples of this possible harmony between the politics of difference and the differentiation of consumer products. He insisted, in particular, on the way in which difference is depoliticised in the global marketing of diversity in order to become a playful game of heteroclite signifiers with no real referent: 'Within the logic of restructured global capital markets, cultural differences have to be both acknowledged and depoliticised in order to be contained.'[35] Let us note in passing, and without being able to develop the point further in the current setting, that it is precisely in this context of the commercialisation of cultural difference that there was a considerable expansion in the Anglo-Saxon reception of French thought.[36]

If one wishes to conclude that there are good and bad differences, and that it is merely a matter of valorising those that allow for an opening to alterity, rather than those that are manipulated for commercial or imperial ends, one risks missing the crux of the matter. For if there are good and bad differences, it is very precisely because the concept of difference is purely relational and is not at all a value in itself. Rather than holding on to this notion as if it were the conceptual messiah of the 'post-revolutionary' era, it is advisable that we abandon the attempt to fix it in the heaven of ideas as an absolute ethico-political anchoring point. To the normative or meta-normative use of the category of difference, we should oppose an analytic and heuristic use.

2. *The allegedly reflexive operation of thinkers of difference inevitably comes up against an internal limit: the identitarian logic of difference.* Philosophically, this means that the most radical difference will never lose its minimal constitutive identity as difference, without which it would simply be confused with identity. Similarly, no alterity can make the originary sameness of the logic of the same and the other disappear, since it is the latter that makes alterity recognisable, including the most radical alterity. Politically, the internal limit of the discourse on difference appears concretely in the refusal of the most heterophile thinkers to accept practices judged to be *truly* different, such as clitoridectomies, the repressive acts of 'the Taliban', suicide bombings or acts of 'terrorism'.[37] For, ultimately, there is in the differentialist discourse a good and bad alterity, the latter being that which calls into question the limits implicitly or explicitly established by the politics or the philosophy of difference. This shows quite clearly, moreover, that difference is by no means a value in itself, even for those who claim to adhere to it. It is a matter of a specific difference, a delimited difference, a difference *identified* – more or less implicitly – as *the good difference*.

By a reversal that recalls the contradiction of the competition for differentiation mentioned above (in which it is precisely a matter of making the value of difference felt by valorising *one's own conception* of difference), a patronising paternalism risks infiltrating the politics of recognition insofar as the existence of the other – the one identified as truly other – depends on *my own* benevolent view of things (the other always remaining *the same*, reduced to a fixed element in my experience or discourse). In the most extreme cases, such paternalism turns into a narcissistic voyeurism, in which one takes pleasure in scrutinising the details of the life of the oppressed, which subtly confirm and consolidate our privileged position. The success of the politics of difference depends, in these extreme cases, on my ability to be even more sensitive to alterity than others. Ultimately, it is I who distinguish myself from others by being even more attentive to differences, since the other always remains the same, except when she or he is graced with the singularity of my own reflection on her or him, except when *my own difference* comes to bear. In the name of being open to alterity, one risks then reducing politics to my own act of recognition and to my own sensitivity regarding difference. For the other would only have value if I recognise her or him as such, namely according to a fixed identity (ideal or otherwise) as 'other'. What can change, and what can therefore be judged positively or negatively, is only *my* reaction. All ethico-political activity, as well as the normative distinction between good and bad ethics or politics, would thus be situated on the side of the reactive subject, the genuine locus of praxis and ethico-political value judgements. What fundamentally matters is not what the other does, who is always other, always petrified in alterity like a fixed and absolute element of my lived experience. What counts is my reaction to the other, *my recognition* of the other, and especially – at least in philosophical discourses – the recognition of *my* other (which is, according to the logic of differentialist fundamentalism, more radical and more absolute than all of the others).

3. *Setting forth the value of difference is not equivalent to saving the world or the integrity of thought.* On the contrary, philosophy thereby gives free rein to a problematic hubris by posing as the healer of the Western world. This is rendered possible by means of a veiled essentialism and an utterly reductive normative logic, which end up bogging thought down in a bogus sophistication, paralysed by a long series of implicit instructions: it is necessary to liberate multiplicities, the aporias of Western thought must be foregrounded, we should unsay the inevitable thematisation of language, and so forth.[38] Even if such instructions are linked to philosophical projects worth taking seriously, they run the risk of preventing every act of thought that is not simply a 'critical' reflex, a differentialist intuition, which seems to go without saying. By way of a tacit discursive code, founded on a powerful metaphilosophical axiology, the philosophy of difference could easily serve to paralyse thought more than to open it to *something different*.

The politics of recognition, for its part, runs the risk of reducing political action to an individual, and more or less private, moral act entirely disconnected from the material transformations of the world, as well as from concrete and collective political actions.[39] It can easily give birth to the most disengaged politics that is satisfied with merely recognising minority identities while keeping them in their minority status, precisely in the interest of better recognising them![40] While it is true that some thinkers – including the likes of Nancy Fraser and Cornel West[41] – have insisted on the importance of a politics of redistribution, unfortunately the *Realpolitik* of the contemporary world and the question of power have at least partially been forgotten in favour of a discourse on rights and recognition,[42] as well as a more or less blind belief in the absolute value of 'democracy'. In an age when the supposed purveyor of democracy – the United States – has found a new justification for plutocratic imperialism in a so-called War on Terror (an expression that inadvertently reveals its deep truth, for it is indeed a matter of founding war *on* terror by spreading paranoia in order to justify wars without justification), such a position risks merging into a simple, feeble reformism, if not a blind apology for the systems in place.

Moreover, it is important to remind ourselves, in the face of differentialist essentialism, that there are as many oppressive differences as there are liberatory differences, and the same goes for identity. In spite of the wishes of certain philosophers, domination and emancipation do not comply with our own conceptual categories. In affirming that homogeneity and heterogeneity are relational terms without any a priori value, I am not however denying that specific uses of the concept of difference can have positive results in concrete struggles. Certain forms of the politics of difference have had, indeed, the merit of exposing various structures of oppression, ranging from Eurocentrism to misogyny, and including racism, anti-Semitism, homophobia and xenophobia.[43] But the concept of difference can just as well serve to support, openly or clandestinely, the most oppressive practices.[44] Contrary to what those who celebrate the 'ethical turn' in political thought sometimes think, alterity is by no means the panacea for the ethico-political evils of our age.[45]

4. *History is irreducible to a battle between identity and difference.* I studied in detail the rewriting of philosophic history by the 'thinkers of difference' in my book *Logique de l'histoire: Pour une analytique des pratiques philosophiques*. I will make do here with simply saying that the Manichean vision of history – as deconstructed as it might be – is largely insufficient. History is not reducible to a struggle between thinkers of identity and those of multiplicity, or to a battle between the forces of sameness and those of difference, even if they become 'indiscernible' at a certain level. When it comes to political history, it is absolutely vital

to recall the historicity of the discourse on difference instead of tacitly relying on, as is too often the case, a historical narrative of teleological progress,[46] according to which the openness to difference would constitute a major advance – if not the veritable end of history – in relation to previous modes of thought, and in particular the long history of Eurocentrism. According to Bernard McGrane's analysis in *Beyond Anthropology*, the discourse on the other as *different* rather than *primitive, uncivilised* or *pagan* is a phenomenon of the twentieth century. And if such a discourse distances itself from evolutionary schemas, it does not necessarily break with the universalist point of view of the privileged spectator, namely the one that sees the Other and establishes a discourse on the true nature of its difference. McGrane claims that it is a case of trivialising the encounter with the other, who is reduced to the passive object of our gaze and of our discourses, while we use it to flatter ourselves with having broken with all forms of Eurocentrism.[47] If we remind ourselves that the monological discourse of philosophy must open itself to the voice of the other instead of speaking in its place, we inevitably come up against the paradox of differentialist discourse: the only successful way of truly opening one's discourse to the other is by ending one's own monologue. Thus, the only legitimate discourse on alterity would be silence, which is not to be confused with a discourse on silence. The master of discourse, who will always have the privilege of saying what is different, or unsaying it in her or his own way, must ultimately fall silent.

CONCLUSION

My aim here has by no means been to condemn the philosophy and politics of difference as a whole. I am also not claiming to have summed up, with a few unifying principles, the totality of writings by the authors cited. On the contrary, I wanted to highlight the risks of fetishising alterity philosophically and practically by raising a question that could appear naive: is difference a value in itself? In searching for an answer, it was first and foremost necessary to show how a set of differentialist operations aims at complexifying the simplicity of the normative logic operative in the metaphilosophical axiology of the thinkers of difference. I then went on to show, by means of some concrete examples, that concepts do not have a priori value but are rather analytic tools entwined with various practices, which can be mobilised for divergent ends. Far from being a simple return to the thought of the same, this has been an attempt to call into question the normative or meta-normative use of concepts, if it be the notion of sameness or that of alterity. In the so-called age of the War on Terror, when there is a supposed clash between the forces of good (democracy) and the forces of evil (terrorists and tyrants),[48] it is insufficient to make do with the clumsy logic of identity and difference by holding on to the presumed intrinsic value of the latter, as if it were the theoretical messiah for the alleged age of the end of grand narratives.

NOTES

1. See, for instance, the analysis proposed by Hans-Georg Gadamer of the requirement to overcome all prejudices in *Truth and Method*, pp. 271–7.
2. I am using this expression purely heuristically. It does not refer to a school of thought, nor to an intellectual movement, but rather to a constellation of thinkers who, instead of laying claim to the same philosophic principles, share a problematic (*une problématique*) concerning difference and alterity. It should be noted that numerous thinkers have only participated partially or intermittently in this constellation. One finds in the work of Michel Foucault, for instance, and particularly in his early writings, a keen interest in discontinuity, differences, transgression, the outside, and so forth. Yet, he was also rather critical of the historical schemas used by the philosophers who thought of themselves as participating in an immemorial struggle between difference and the thinking of the same. Jacques Rancière, to take another example, explicitly attacks the logic of irreducible difference (see *Disagreement*, p. 43), while still having a penchant for paradox and contradiction.
3. On this topic, see the discursive analyses proposed by Louis Pinto in *Les Philosophes entre le lycée et l'avant-garde*. See, in particular, his discussion of Michel Serres: 'The opposition that structures his discourse is sure to be recognised, and unrecognised as such, by all of those who know the code, this cultured public that knows enough to grasp, via the sound of unheard-of words, that "difference" signifies freedom or liberation [...] and that "identity" is associated with the demand for order and control by "inspectors", "bureaucrats" of the "river police"' (p. 210).
4. It goes without saying that this constellation does not dominate the totality of the French intellectual scene, nor does it govern all of the theoretical production of the philosophical avant-garde. To take but a single example of one of the major philosophers to take issue with the consecration of difference, I refer the reader to Cornelius Castoriadis, 'Agora International

Interview' (1990): 'I don't know if what I am saying is clear: it's not a matter here of some process of mechanical standardisation, and not the "respecting difference" crap, all that nonsense people keep repeating all day long that it's enough to make you vomit. It's not a matter of respecting difference for the sake of respecting difference.'
5. Lyotard, *Political Writings*, p. 28.
6. See Derrida's discussion in '"We Other Greeks"': 'What these "thoughts of difference", as they have been called, paradoxically have in common is thus also that which resists, like difference, the analogy of a certain community or contemporaneity: whatever in the configuration cannot be configured, or whatever lends to the configuration the figure or face of the mask or of the simulacrum, one might even say of the lure (*leurre*)' (p. 23).
7. I take the liberty of referring the reader, in particular, to my book *Logique de l'histoire*.
8. Louis Pinto sees in this conceptual architectonic the 'philosophical quest of freedom': 'The blurring of classifications is a principle of the contemporary trend of "undecidables", "paradoxes", "singularities", and other "events", of this Bergsonism in practical form, to which one sometimes explicitly lays claim, that leads to structuring the thinkable according to an opposition between the pole of fixed identities, of closed identities, and the pole of "different", "multiple", "heterogeneous" things, where the philosophical quest of freedom can find a way of fulfilling itself' (*La Vocation et le métier de philosophe*, p. 168).
9. See Weber, 'Afterword: Literature – Just Making It'.
10. On this topic, I take the liberty of referring the reader to Chapter 2 of this book.
11. Lévinas, *Otherwise than Being or Beyond Being*, p. 7.
12. We touch here upon what I would call the metaphysical essentialism of the thinking of difference, which is founded on the philosophic faith in the existence of a Difference that is so pure and absolute that it escapes – in fact and in principle – all possible descriptions.
13. Since he had the messianic genius to predict the failure of his own discourse by affirming that it is in fact impossible to definitively escape metaphysics, Derrida lends himself particularly well to this type of sacralisation. For the alleged failure of his discourse, its glorious fall into metaphysics, transforms itself straightaway into success via an inescapable theoretical redemption.
14. I here refer the reader to Louis Pinto's excellent book *Les Philosophes entre le lycée et l'avant-garde*, particularly p. 119.
15. Derrida asserts in 'Force of Law: The "Mystical Foundation of Authority"': 'Deconstruction is justice' (p. 945). In *Spectres of Marx*, he writes: 'The necessary disjointure, the de-totalising condition of justice, is indeed here

that of the present – and by the same token the very condition of the present and of the presence of the present. This is where deconstruction would always begin to take shape as the thinking of the gift and of undeconstructible justice, the undeconstructible condition of any deconstruction, to be sure, but a condition that is itself *in deconstruction* and remains, and must remain (that is the injunction) in the disjointure of the *Un-Fug*' (p. 28).

16. On the question of keeping distance from practice, see the description of his generation provided by Michel Serres in his book with Bruno Latour, *Conversations on Science, Culture, and Time*, pp. 2–4.
17. It should be noted that this therapeutic logic, which consists in interpreting concrete ethico-political ills as so many symptoms of an illness of mind and spirit (*de l'esprit*), allows for – but does not necessitate – Martin Heidegger's 'political' recuperation. This is obviously not the place to enter into the debate on Heidegger and politics. I take the liberty of referring the reader to Louis Pinto's work, which provides an overview of the debate in France while also taking a clear and precise position (see *La Vocation et le métier de philosophe*, pp. 215–24).
18. Lévinas, *Totality and Infinity*, p. 197.
19. On this point, please refer to my article 'L'Écriture de l'histoire philosophique', as well as to my dialogue with Alfredo Gomez-Muller in *Politics of Culture and the Spirit of Critique*, pp. 1–24.
20. The historical narrative that Lyotard establishes in *Heidegger and 'the Jews'*, founded on the perennial antagonism between 'the Jews' and the West, is not only one of the best examples of this tendency. It is also a nearly perfect model of what he had previously called, in order to criticise it, a 'grand narrative'.
21. As an example, we can cite the first error regarding supple and molecular segmentarity according to Gilles Deleuze and Félix Guattari: 'The first is axiological and consists in believing that a little suppleness is enough to make things "better"' (*A Thousand Plateaus*, p. 215).
22. Randall Collins deserves credit for having foregrounded the role of 'emotional energy' in intellectual history (see *The Sociology of Philosophies*). The following passage by Deleuze is rather revealing in this regard: 'This intensive way of reading, in contact with what's outside the book, as a flow meeting other flows, one machine among others, as a series of experiments for each reader in the midst of events that have nothing to do with books, as tearing the book into pieces, getting it to interact with other things, absolutely anything [...] is reading with love' (*Negotiations*, pp. 8–9).
23. See Deleuze, *Negotiations*, p. 88: 'I've never been inspired by overcoming metaphysics or the death of philosophy, and I never made the

renunciation of the All, the One, the subject into a drama' (translation slightly modified).
24. To cite but one – at least partial – exception I refer the reader to the second interview in the book *For What Tomorrow ...*, where Derrida outlines a position that one could call pragmatic or contextualist (see Derrida and Roudinesco, *For What Tomorrow ...*, pp. 21–2).
25. Everything depends on the criteria of analysis, but it seems that the Bush administration was actually more 'multicultural' than the Obama administration, with at least one exception: Obama was elected the first black – or rather mixed-race – president of the United States. See Jonathan Stein's article in *Mother Jones*, 'Bush's Biggest Achievements', as well as his note on the journal's blog, 'The Best Part of Obama's Multicultural Cabinet: The Effortlessness of It'.
26. See the article 'UK Accused of Lifting Dossier Text', published on 7 February 2003 on CNN's website, and the article by Julian Rush, 'Downing St Dossier Plagiarised', published on 6 February 2003 on Channel 4 News's website.
27. We should also note the central role that she played in the CIA's use of torture. See, for instance, the article by Jan Crawford Greenburg, Howard L. Rosenberg and Arianne de Vogue, 'Bush Aware of Advisers' Interrogation Talks', published on ABC News's website on 11 April 2008.
28. See also the 22 January 2002 'Memorandum for Alberto R. Gonzales' by Jay S. Bybee. For a revealing genealogy of the term 'Al-Qaeda', which also calls into question its misuses, see Jason Burke, *Al-Qaeda: Casting a Shadow of Terror*, and Adam Curtis's television documentary series *The Power of Nightmares* (2004). For a critique of the overly generic expression 'the Taliban', I refer the reader in particular to the interviews with Rangina Hamidi (10 March 2009) and Juan Cole (17 March 2009) on *Democracy Now!*.
29. This is because it is not only necessary that the pain inflicted during the interrogation be equivalent to that of organ failure, but also that the interrogator have the *specific* intention of injuring the person interrogated (whereas the specific intention of interrogators is obviously to obtain information).
30. Klein, 'The Benetton-Ad Presidency'.
31. On this topic, see Hall, 'Brave New World', and Harvey, *The Condition of Postmodernity*, in particular p. 156.
32. Davidson, *The Consumerist Manifesto*, quoted in Giroux, *Disturbing Pleasures*, p. 12.
33. For purely indicative purposes, it is relatively revealing that there is not a single article in the *New York Times* on globalisation or multiculturalism before 1970. The statistics for the following decades attest, moreover, to a partial synchrony: one article on globalisation and two

on multiculturalism in the 1970s, 172 articles on globalisation and fifteen on multiculturalism in the 1980s, 911 articles on globalisation and 737 on multiculturalism in the 1990s, and 2,857 articles on globalisation and 369 on multiculturalism from 2000 to 2010. The results for the database LexisNexis Academic follow the same pattern for 'major U.S. and world publications', with one difference: the number of articles on multiculturalism continues to grow in the new millennium. We could also cite the number of books in the catalogues of the Library of Congress or the Bibliothèque Nationale de France, which shows a similar, although deferred, tendency in the book world, where there has been a very significant increase since 1990 in works devoted to globalisation and multiculturalism.

34. Klein, *No Logo*, p. 115. See also two television documentary series by Adam Curtis: *The Century of the Self* (2002) and *The Trap* (2007). In spite of an overly linear historical narrative and reductionist tendencies, Curtis clearly brings to light the way in which individual differences have been forcefully mobilised by the marketing world.
35. Giroux, *Disturbing Pleasures*, p. 12 (also see pp. 14–15).
36. See Cusset, *French Theory*.
37. I refer the reader, on this issue, to Žižek, 'Multiculturalism, or, the Cultural Logic of Multinational Capitalism', Shivani, 'A Left Critique of Multiculturalism', and Badiou, *Ethics: An Essay on the Understanding of Evil*, p. 24: 'As a matter of fact, this celebrated "other" is acceptable only if he is a *good* other – which is to say what, exactly, if not *the same as us*? Respect for differences, of course! But on condition that the different be parliamentary-democratic, pro free-market economics, in favour of freedom of opinion, feminism, the environment ... That is to say: I respect differences, but only, of course, in so far as that which differs also respects, just as I do, the said differences.'
38. On this topic, I recommend consulting François Laruelle's work, notably *Philosophies of Difference: A Critical Introduction to Non-Philosophy*. Also see *Philosophy and Non-Philosophy*, which states: 'Instead, it is necessary to suspend the *belief-in-philosophy* that supports these fairly massive slogans, the spontaneous belief according to which, for example, *there is* logos or logocentrism, and *there is* the Other or the Undecidable' (p. 9).
39. See the article by Pierre Bourdieu and Loïc Wacquant, 'NewLiberalSpeak: Notes on the New Planetary Vulgate'. This is a modified version of an article published in *Le Monde diplomatique* in May 2000.
40. On this point, I refer the reader to Aimé Césaire's severe criticism of a certain form of the politics of recognition in *Discourse on Colonialism*, pp. 58–9. It should be noted that Césaire does not, however, abandon the demand for recognition (see Césaire, *Discours sur le colonialisme*, p. 89).

41. See Fraser, *Justice Interruptus*, and West, *Democracy Matters* and *Race Matters*.
42. This general forgetting of the question of power has had devastating effects on the way in which the history of social movements has been written, as Jacquelyn Dowd Hall has brilliantly explained in the case of the Civil Rights Movement in 'The Long Civil Rights Movement and the Political Uses of the Past'.
43. I refer the reader, for instance, to a few very important works: Butler, *Gender Trouble*, Fraser, *Justice Interruptus*, Said, *Orientalism*, and West, *Democracy Matters*.
44. This is what Luce Irigaray perfectly demonstrated – while still remaining within differentialist logic – in her critique of Emmanuel Lévinas in *An Ethics of Sexual Difference*, pp. 185–217.
45. For concrete examples, I refer the reader to Pierre-André Taguieff's work on differentialist racism: 'The definitional reduction of racism to a dual process of rejecting difference and establishing a hierarchy makes us blind to any and all racialising discourse that would develop by centring on difference, and would treat the latter as an object of exaltation or respect. However, there is a racist praise of difference, a racism founded on the principle of difference, whose imperative can be formulated as such: act in such a way that the differences between human groups are preserved, whatever may be the desires or choices of the individuals inherent therein' ('Le Néo-racisme différentialiste', p. 72). Also see his book *Force of Prejudice*, and Étienne Balibar and Immanuel Wallerstein's *Race, Nation, Class*. Finally, I also recommend the critique of 'racial reasoning' in Cornel West's *Race Matters*, pp. 35–49.
46. It should be noted that the triumphant history of the other is teleological even if the telos is always *to come*, and thus *different* from any factual or attainable end.
47. See McGrane, *Beyond Anthropology*, particularly pp. 113–29. On this topic, I also refer the reader to David Scott's work, in particular 'Culture in Political Theory', 'Toleration and Historical Traditions of Difference' and 'Criticism and Culture'.
48. See in particular *The National Security Strategy of the United States of America*, September 2002.

Chapter 5

CASTORIADIS AND THE TRADITION OF RADICAL CRITIQUE

> In relation to animals, humans are sick beings, because they can't live without making sense of what is and what they do. Everything must have meaning; everything must make sense. As a consequence, it is a shock to discover that nothing makes sense of itself.
> (Cornelius Castoriadis)

Cornelius Castoriadis audaciously defined philosophy as the act of 'taking responsibility for the totality of the thinkable [*prise en charge de la totalité du pensable*]'.[1] His life and work attest to the intensity with which he dedicated himself to this project. If he sometimes lamented the lack of major philosophic voices in an era when academic interpretations of the past had come to dominate 'professional thinking', he almost single-handedly made up for it himself.[2] A quintessential iconoclast who admitted suffering from an *éros du savoir*, he broke through the ideological torpor of French academic and political circles, and he established one of the most original and comprehensive bodies of work in twentieth-century European philosophy.

Born in 1922 to a Greek family that had immigrated to Constantinople, Castoriadis grew up in pre-war Athens and moved to Paris in 1945 to study philosophy. In Paris, he co-founded, with Claude Lefort, the revolutionary group and journal *Socialisme ou barbarie* (published from 1949 to 1965). The journal distanced itself from Trotskyism and broke in more or less fundamental ways with Marxism. It provided a radical critique of bureaucracy, arguing in favour of a revolutionary socialism founded on workers' management, and many have argued that it had a direct impact on the events of 1968.[3] Castoriadis wrote under pseudonyms until the 1970s, once he had been naturalised as a French citizen. From 1948 until 1970, he worked as an economist at the Organisation for Economic Co-operation and Development.[4] In 1973, he began working as a trained psychoanalyst, and he was named Directeur d'études at the École des Hautes Études en Sciences Sociales in 1981. He passed away in Paris in 1997.

The quintessential dissident, Castoriadis cut across the rigid structures of academic life and stalwartly refused the simple dividing lines between theoretical endeavours and practical engagements. His work impressively spans across the fields of philosophy, political theory, sociology, history, economics, psychoanalysis and the philosophy of science. However, he did not aim to establish a system or unify the sciences under a single logic. On the contrary, he was keenly aware of the precarious and limited nature of the attempt to think the world:

> Theory as such is a doing, the always uncertain attempt to carry out the project of elucidating the world. And this is also the case for the supreme or extreme form of theory that is philosophy, i.e. the attempt to think the world without knowing, in advance or afterwards, whether the world is really thinkable, or even what thinking actually means.[5]

Philosophy, as the extreme form of theory, is neither a founding gesture nor a conceptual system of all systems. It is a form of total and absolute interrogation with no a priori limit, which simultaneously recognises that there are things that we do not know and will never know. Moreover, philosophy, like all theoretical undertakings, is never the work of an isolated individual (Castoriadis was very critical of what he refers to as the egological tradition of modern philosophy). It is a specific type of social-historical activity that happened to be invented by the Greeks and, as we will see, is linked to the promotion of a new imaginary social signification: autonomy.

The autonomy exercised by Castoriadis himself in the elaboration of a unique theoretical enterprise has produced a singular project that cannot be comfortably situated within the standard models used to schematise twentieth-century francophone philosophy. Although there are striking similarities between some of his claims and the work of Jean-Paul Sartre, there are also significant divergences, particularly in their respective relationships to the Marxist tradition. Although Sartre is rumoured to have claimed 'Castoriadis was right, but at the wrong time', Castoriadis's quip succinctly sums up their political disagreements: 'Sartre had the honour of being wrong at the right time!'⁶ Regarding structuralism, which many perceive as the next major theoretical movement after the phenomenological existentialism promoted by Sartre and others, Castoriadis could not have been clearer in his condemnation. In attacking what he calls inherited ontologies, he highlights two essential types. The first is labelled 'physicalist', and it consists in reducing society and history to nature, and particularly to the biological nature of man. Functionalism, he argues, is the best representative of this point of view since it posits a set of fixed human needs and explains social organisation as the series of functions aiming to satisfy these needs. The second type of inherited ontology is called 'logicist', and the poorest form of logicism is structuralism. It is based on the assumption that:

> The same logical operation, repeated a certain number of times, would [...] account for the totality of human history and the different forms of society, which would only be the different possible combinations of a finite number of the same discreet elements.⁷

He not only lambasts structuralism's pseudo-scientific naivety,⁸ but he also impugns the political orientation of the thinkers affiliated to a greater or lesser degree with the diverse avatars of structuralism (including what is called, in the anglophone world, 'post-structuralism'). In particular, he attacks the thesis formulated by Luc Ferry and Alain Renaut concerning *la pensée '68* on the grounds that the major thinkers affiliated with it came into vogue after the failure of May '68, and they 'played no role even in the vaguest "sociological" preparation of the movement, at once because their ideas were totally unknown to the participants and because these ideas were diametrically opposed to the participants' implicit and explicit aspirations'.⁹ He also eschews and derides the valorisation of difference, which clearly demarcates him from a number of his French contemporaries:

> It is quite obvious that, in defiance of the hardly enticing rose water being amply sprinkled about everywhere today, I do not respect others' difference simply as difference and without regard to what they are and what they do. I do not respect the difference of the sadist, of Eichmann, or Beria – any more than of those who cut off people's heads, or even their hands, even if they are not

threatening me directly. Nothing in what I have said or written commits me to 'respect differences' *for the sake of* respecting differences.[10]

Finally, he identifies deconstruction as one of the symptoms of the current social crisis because it limits critique to the pedantic dissection of historical texts.[11] He similarly assails the reduction of history to the endless proliferation of metaphysics as well as the theological turn of many of the post-Heideggerians.[12] Against the recognised movements and intellectual fashions of his day, Castoriadis unflinchingly asserted that he wanted to be part of

> a tradition of radical critique, which also entails [a tradition] of responsibility (we cannot put the blame on God Almighty, etc.) and self-limitation (we cannot invoke any extra-historical norm to regulate our modes of action [*normer notre agir*], which nevertheless must be regulated).[13]

In what follows, I would like to provide a brief aperçu of Castoriadis's key philosophical and ontological claims before examining, with a critical eye, the primary facets of his expansive work on politics, art, psychoanalysis and the philosophy of science.[14]

HISTORICAL ONTOLOGY

Let us begin with one of Castoriadis's most general claims: 'being is creation'.[15] As he explains in *Figures of the Thinkable*, 'creation means, above all, discontinuity, emergence of the radically new and stratification of what exists.'[16] Rather than the perpetual repetition of the same fundamental elements or structures, being attests to the appearance of the unprecedented. This is, in part, because being is temporal, or rather – in Castoriadis's dauntless formulation – 'being is time (and not "in the horizon" of time)'.[17] In short, 'creation, being, time go together: being means to-be [*être signifie à-être*], time and creation require one another.'[18]

'The imaginary and the imagination', Castoriadis writes, 'are the mode of being that this *vis formandi* of Being in general takes in this offspring of overall Being-being [*l'être-étant global*] that is humanity.'[19] The imaginary and the imagination are not simply reproductive or combinatory faculties. The imaginary is an 'incessant and essentially *undetermined* (social-historical and psychical) creation of figures/forms/ images', and the imagination is 'the capacity to give rise [*faire surgir*] to something that is not the "real"'.[20] Castoriadis tends to use the vocabulary of the imagination to refer to the creative capacity of the psyche, which he describes more specifically as a 'radical imagination' because it is neither determined nor reproductive but is actually capable of producing 'reality'. The terminology of the imaginary is commonly used to refer to the social imaginary and the 'creative capacity of the anonymous collective'.[21] Castoriadis uses these two poles of the *vis formandi* to dismantle the simplistic opposition between individual and society, thereby demonstrating that individuals are, and must be, social: 'There is no "human individual". There is a psyche that is socialised and, in this socialisation, in the final result, there is almost nothing individual in the true sense of the term.'[22] Moreover, since society only exists qua self-alteration, Castoriadis introduces the notion of the social-historical – defined as the 'self-creation [*autocréation*] of society as such and of the historical field as such' – to emphasise the extent to which society and history are consubstantial in the creative production of social institutions:

> The social makes itself and can only make itself as history; the social makes itself as temporality; and it makes itself in every instance as a specific mode of actual temporality, it establishes itself [*s'institue*] implicitly as a singular quality of temporality. [...] The historical *is* this very thing – the self-alteration of this specific mode of 'coexistence' that is the social, and is nothing apart from this. The historical makes itself and can only make itself as social; the historical is, in an exemplary and pre-eminent manner, the emergence of the institution and the emergence of *another* institution [*une* autre *institution*].[23]

Castoriadis further divides the social imaginary into the instituting social imaginary and the instituted social imaginary. The former refers to the creation of social imaginary significations by the anonymous collective and, more generally, the social-historical field. Once these are created, they solidify into the instituted social imaginary, which guarantees the continuation of society and the perpetuation of its forms. Every society is self-instituted, for Castoriadis, but most societies attempt to guarantee their own proper institution by *instituting* an extra-social origin of the social order itself. There are two important ramifications of this position. On the one hand, it means that history is understood as creation and is therefore undetermined (which does *not* mean that it is unconditioned):

> History is creation: the creation of total forms of human life. Social-historical forms are not 'determined' by natural or historical 'laws'. Society is self-creation. 'That which' creates society and history is the instituting society, as opposed to the instituted society. The instituting society is the social imaginary in the radical sense.[24]

On the other hand, since there is ultimately no guarantee to social institutions outside of the powers that created them, then societies can be separated according to whether they are heteronomous or autonomous. The former are founded on the belief that their institutions were not created by them but were instead bestowed upon them by someone else (spirits, ancestors, Gods, nature, etc.). Autonomous societies, which are relatively rare, recognise and assume responsibility for the creation of their institutions; they consciously and explicitly establish their own laws.

THE VICISSITUDES OF POLITICAL AUTONOMY

Castoriadis regularly invokes two prime examples of autonomous societies: ancient Greece and Europe as of the 'first Renaissance' around the eleventh or twelfth century.[25] Greece is the social-historical locus in which both democracy and philosophy appear for the first time, and it is therefore the origin of modern Europe according to Castoriadis. These dual projects share a common interrogative orientation, a common critical stance. Philosophy, as we have seen, is not a systematic conceptual enterprise but is, instead, the passionate investigation of all things with no pre-established limits. Similarly, democracy is not the rule of law or the rights of man; it is rather the collective act of putting the law in question. Both philosophy and democracy are projects of autonomy insofar as they seek to create laws for themselves rather than accepting entrenched rules; they aim at deliberately investing and reflexively clarifying the instituting power of the imagination. Their simultaneous appearance in ancient Greece therefore constituted a rupture that 'inaugurated the explicit questioning by society of its own instituted imaginary'.[26] The West attests to a powerful re-emergence of the Greek project of autonomy as of approximately the twelfth century, and the 'modern' era, beginning in the eighteenth century, is characterised by the mutual contamination of two imaginary significations: autonomy and 'rational mastery'.[27] Since approximately the middle of the twentieth century, Castoriadis claims that the heteronomous forces of insignificance have been seriously encroaching on the project of autonomy.[28] Before taking a closer look at his analysis of the contemporary era of conformism, we should briefly discuss his overall conception of politics.

Politics, in the strict sense of the term, is not reducible to the various battles over governmental power, the multifarious plots of manipulation and control, or the motley attempts to defend the interests of groups or individuals. It is 'a collective activity whose object is the institution of society as such'.[29] It therefore belongs to the human domain of creative production. There is no final form of politics or ultimate structure that can be determined once and for all, meaning that there is no end to the activity of politics itself. Moreover, there is no *episteme* or scientific knowledge of politics for Castoriadis; it exists in the realm of *doxa* or opinion.[30] And he has gone to great lengths to dismantle the various determinist forms of history, teleology and theodicy found in the Marxist and liberal traditions.[31] Thus, it is not only impossible to deduce a particular type of politics from a specific form of theoretical expertise, but it is equally impossible to sanction political structures based on the supposed fatality of history.

In the contemporary era, politics has been taken over by self-proclaimed specialists. What is inappropriately called democracy is actually a liberal oligarchy in which the ruling elite maintains 'democracy' as a propitious prop. The close correlation between democracy and the education of the citizenry has been replaced by a rampant stultification of the masses, and true socio-political tensions and struggles have given way to the fragmentation of lobbies and interest groups, not to mention the false opposition between the 'right' and the 'left'. Compared to the direct democracy of ancient Athens, the representative pseudo-democracy of the contemporary world has turned *rule of the people*, in the sense of *rule by the people*, into *rule over the people*. The public/public sphere, which Castoriadis identifies as the 'first condition for the existence of an autonomous society – of a democratic society', has been *de facto* privatised.[32] Although citizens are not legally barred from participating in what the Greeks called the *ecclesia*, the latter is almost exclusively dominated by private interests:

> On the factual level the essential features of public affairs are still the private affair of various groups and clans that share effective power, decisions are made behind closed doors, the little that is brought onto the public stage is masked, prefabricated, and belated to the point of irrelevancy.[33]

In short, the autonomous political project of democracy, as it was once understood, has been gutted of its true content, leaving only the abject carcass of pseudo-democratic oligarchy.

The demise of the project of autonomy at a political level is closely tied to an overall crisis in social imaginary significations, that is, the significations that determine the prevailing representations, affects and intentions of a society. The capitalist imaginary of unlimited expansion of production and consumption has become the 'dominant, and nearly exclusive, imaginary signification of contemporary society'.[34] The consumer, who is content to cast votes on the political marketplace every few years, has more or less entirely replaced the citizen, once defined by Aristotle as 'one who shares in governing and being governed'.[35] The unlimited world of endless consumption tends to engulf all other social significations in a sinister abyss where money – or its avatars, such as media notoriety and power – is the only value. Far from having the 'freedom' naively presupposed by the apologists of neoliberal ideology, the unchecked consumer is plunged into a world of unbridled conformism and actually ends up thinking and acting in strict accordance with what the institution calls for. Heteronomy thereby establishes its hegemony in the heart of the supposed freedom of unlimited consumerism. Moreover, the dominant imaginary signification of unlimited expansion becomes a vortex in which other significations disappear, leading to an overall atrophy of the imagination and a retreat of creativity in all fields (philosophy, art, science, and so forth). Insignificance comes to saturate almost everything in a determined world of blind narcissism and hedonism orchestrated by the Eleatic fatalities of neoliberalism. And the project of autonomy – a distinctive feature of the West – is relegated to the margins. Nevertheless, far from being a cynical and acquiescent condemnation of the present,

Castoriadis and the Tradition of Radical Critique

Castoriadis's truculent criticisms of his historical conjuncture are one example among others of his defiant repudiation of the dominant imaginary signification in the name of revolutionary praxis and the struggle to demonstrate that history is not a fatality because a 'break' is always possible.

POETIC WINDOWS ONTO THE ABYSS

The institution of society has always aimed at covering over what Castoriadis calls Chaos, the Groundless, the Abyss, by producing a powerful and compelling web of meaning.[36] The core social imaginary significations, those produced by religion, present the Abyss at the same time that they occlude it. Art, on the contrary, particularly when it is honed into a masterpiece, is nothing short of the 'presentation of the Abyss (of Chaos, of the Groundless) [*présentation de l'Abîme (du Chaos, du Sans-Fond)*]'.[37] In creatively giving form to chaos, which Castoriadis carefully distinguishes from the act of 'imitation', it is closely related to both philosophy and science:

> Not only does one see the creative imagination at work in all of them, but art, as well as philosophy and science, attempts to give form to chaos – to the chaos underlying the *cosmos*, the world, the chaos that is behind the successive strata of appearances.[38]

The difference between these three ways of giving form to chaos is that – unlike philosophy and science, which attempt to elucidate the world that is given to us – art actually 'creates a world and new worlds, and it does so relatively freely'.[39]

By giving form to chaos, the artist reminds society that it is living on the abyss:

> Tomorrow, and tomorrow, and tomorrow
> Creeps in this petty pace from day to day
> To the last syllable of recorded time,
> And all our yesterdays have lighted fools
> The way to dusty death. Out, out, brief candle.
> Life's but a walking shadow, a poor player
> That struts and frets his hour upon the stage
> And then is heard no more. It is a tale

Told by an idiot, full of sound and fury,
Signifying nothing.⁴⁰

These notable lines from Shakespeare's *Macbeth* instantiate the essential gesture of all art by opening a window on to chaos, thereby reminding society that the only true salvation is deliverance from the very idea of salvation itself. It is for this reason that art can and does play a critical role and is closely linked, for Castoriadis, to the project of autonomy. By opening on to and giving form to chaos, art 'calls into question the established significations, even the meaning [*signification*] of human life and its most indisputable contents'.⁴¹ Indeed, the modern European era, from 1800 to 1950, is characterised by a series of artists for whom 'there is no pre-given meaning'.⁴² Castoriadis highlights, moreover, the historical specificity of the avant-garde as a rupture between creative artists and established society dating from the mid-nineteenth century.⁴³ As of the 1950s, however, the critical role of art has sharply declined, replaced by a pseudo-avant-garde that artificially produces the new and the 'subversive' for their own sake, all the while sinking into an insipid conformism that quiescently accompanies the mummification of culture and the reduction of past icons to funerary monuments.⁴⁴

Although Castoriadis recognises the socio-historical specificity of cultural production as well as of certain 'figures' of the art world ('pure art', avant-garde art, the accursed artist, the misunderstood genius, etc.), he nonetheless identifies a universal and transhistorical nature of art itself as a window on to the chaos of being.⁴⁵ In fact, unlike the project of autonomy, art extends well beyond the Western world and includes popular forms of creative production. From the caves of Lascaux to African masks, Mayan statues and *The Art of the Fugue*, art has always sought to bring humanity to the border of the abyss from which it comes: 'every culture [...] creates its own path toward the Abyss.'⁴⁶ Moreover, Castoriadis believes in 'great art' as the singular, unexplainable, timeless creation of an individual genius capable of halting the world and perching us on a novel precipice over the chasm of non-meaning. This is precisely why art is 'intemporal' for him: great works of art act as timeless monuments demonstrating the autonomous ability to accept mortality and create signification while inhabiting the border of Chaos.⁴⁷ In short, art is not only universal and transhistorical in the sense of extending across the histories of all human cultures, but it is 'intemporal' insofar as it bears witness to the dauntless creative power of humanity.

AUTONOMY OF THE PSYCHE

'The aim of psychoanalysis', Castoriadis claims, 'is consubstantial with the project of autonomy.'[48] Psychoanalysis ultimately belongs to the same emancipatory project as democracy and philosophy since it aims at helping the social individual become a creative source of possibilities who, instead of being trapped within the fatalities of a psychic life, is an active participant in the construction of his or her own story (*histoire*). This does not amount to the victory of reason over the instincts or the conquest of the unconscious by the conscious mind, but rather the establishment of a new relationship between the conscious I and the unconscious in which the former opens itself up to the latter. Castoriadis jettisons, moreover, the more or less resolute individualism that has plagued much of the psychoanalytic tradition, and he insists on the central role played by society, institutions and imaginary significations in the formation of the psyche.[49] As mentioned above, he rejects the reification of the distinction between individual and society in the name of thinking through the diverse ways in which the psychic and the social are 'radically irreducible to one another and absolutely indissociable, impossible without one another'.[50]

This is evident in his account of the developmental trajectory of the psyche. Initially, we can postulate that it is in a monadic state of indifferentiation between self and other, as well as between affects, representations and desires. This state, characterised by a conatus of perpetual identity, is prior to the mother – prior to any distinction with the mother as well as any fusion with the mother – and precedes the existence of the partial object. There is, strictly speaking, no differentiation: 'I am everything, I am being itself, being is me, and I am pleasure, pleasure is me.'[51] This is what Freud meant, according to Castoriadis, by the expression 'I am the breast [*Ich bin die Brust*]'. The 'object' is not separate since I am the source of pleasure and the immediate satisfaction of all desire. This is, moreover, the root of the absolute egocentrism that will remain with the psyche and of what Freud called the 'magical omnipotence of thought'. In Castoriadis's interpretation, the newborn at the stage of the psychic monad expresses the radical imagination because even when the breast is not there, the baby imagines its existence, sometimes in conjunction with thumb sucking. This illustrates his distinction between *organ pleasure* and the *pleasure of representation* insofar as human beings are capable of feeling pleasure simply through the representations of their imagination. Indeed, he affirms that 'the human is defined by the predominance of the pleasure of representation over organ pleasure, over the simple satisfaction of drives'.[52] It is not sexuality per se that characterises human beings, for Castoriadis, but rather 'the *distortion of sexuality*', which includes this parting of ways between biological pleasure and imaginary pleasure.[53]

The other ruptures the closed circuit of the psychic monad. In what Castoriadis calls the *triadic phase*, a new relation is established between the infant, the mother and the partial object, the breast. The newborn, who believed that he or she was all powerful, discovers the truth and transfers this omnipotence to the mother. This is the beginning of the process of socialisation. However, the exit from monadic life is in fact a false exit because the originary omnipotence is simply transferred to the mother. The child, in 'normal' development, must overcome the mother's all-powerfulness in recognising it as incomplete, engaged with the other of the father. Yet the father is not omnipotent either because he is a father among other fathers; instead of being the source of the Law, he himself is subservient to the Law of society.

It is important to note that, for Castoriadis, the process of socialisation is not simply a negative process of repression. By being socialised, the psyche enters into the instituted magma of social significations, for society itself is a magma of imaginary significations that gives meaning to collective and individual life. Society is therefore not simply repressive or prohibitive, but it provides a framework of meaning to the psyche. In fact, Castoriadis asserts that if the psyche does not emerge into a social space of meaning that replaces its originary, monadic meaning, it cannot survive. As he regularly claims, society can make almost anything out of the psyche (a Christian, a bourgeois, a Nazi, and so forth), but it cannot *not* provide the psyche with meaning.[54] The psychic monad, through a series of ruptures, thus eventually develops into the social individual, that is, the subject split between a monadic pole tending toward self-enclosure and the pole of imposed social significations, which have been gradually integrated through a succession of syntheses.

The psychoanalytic cure does not lead to an end of analysis, nor does it provide the subject with a definitive understanding of the meaning of life. Castoriadis writes:

> The practical essence of psychoanalytic treatment is that the individual rediscovers himself as the partial origin of his history [*histoire*], freely experiences the act of making himself, which was not initially recognised as such the first time around [*fait gratuitement l'expérience du se faire non su comme tel la première fois*], and becomes once again the origin of possibilities, as having had a history [*histoire*] that was a history [*histoire*] and not a fatality.[55]

In fostering the autonomy of the social individual, psychoanalysis is simultaneously a *praxis*, that is, an action that encourages the autonomy of others, and a form of *poiesis* insofar as it aims at liberating the creative potential of the radical imagination.[56] Ultimately, psychoanalysis allows the subject to live 'on the border of the abyss' by constructing a cosmos on the edge of chaos as a response to the double imperative: 'live as a mortal, live as if you were immortal.'[57]

A PHILOSOPHICAL PASSION FOR THE SCIENCES

Castoriadis proclaims that 'science is, should be, contrary to what has happened since Hegel, an object of passion for the philosopher'.[58] Yet he goes on to explain in the same passage that he does not have in mind a fetishisation of the supposed certainties of scientific discourse. On the contrary, science should be an object of philosophical passion because it is an 'endless fount of enigmas, an inextricable mixture of light and darkness, bearing witness to an incomprehensible meeting – always secured and always fleeting – between our imaginary creations and what is'.[59] Furthermore, science should be of central concern to philosophers because it is a glaring example of autonomy, that is, of the rejection of inherited beliefs in the name of our ability to create something new and transform ourselves.

Castoriadis lambasts the myths of scientific progress on numerous occasions. The evolution of the sciences is not cumulative in any sense of the term, be it the gradual addition, the spread or the progressive perfection of scientific knowledge.[60] Instead, the historical stages of science correspond to so many ruptures and breaks. However, Castoriadis distances himself from Kuhnian paradigms and Foucauldian *epistemes* – as well as epistemic breaks – on the grounds that they ignore the problem of the relationship between the 'contents' of scientific knowledge at different stages. This problem, he claims, has come to the forefront in the twentieth century since the macroscopic world is still explained within the framework of classic Newtonian physics, and it is unclear exactly how this relates to the microscopic world of quantum mechanics.[61] Moreover, he asserts that the Newtonian model is not a purely arbitrary construction but actually 'corresponds' to an important class of elements and has been able to make predictions beyond what was originally in its purview when it was established.[62] This does not, however, mean that he believes that there is a world of identifiable facts independent of scientific interpretation. Quite to the contrary, he insists on the ways in which experiential 'facts' are rendered identifiable and observable by scientific theories:

> We cannot therefore pretend to believe that there exists a world of facts in themselves, which are what they are prior to all scientific interpretation, and independently of it, with which we compare theories in order to see whether or not they are falsified by it. To be sure, a scientific theory cannot behave in an entirely arbitrary fashion, nor can it forego all empirical content; but this empirical content has always undergone an enormous degree of conceptual elaboration, precisely at the hands of the theory in which it is presented.[63]

One of the major lessons of contemporary science is precisely that the separation between philosophy and science, between a conceptual base and empirical results, is absolutely untenable. Castoriadis refers to this situation as 'the end of scientific tranquility'.[64] Henceforth, philosophy and science must proceed in concert with one another.

Castoriadis's work is a testament to just such an orientation, but this is unfortunately not the place to explore the various positions he has taken on the different sciences. For our current purposes, let us concentrate on two fundamental claims related to his engagements with mathematics and biology. Concerning the former, set theory serves as an essential reference point for his ontology insofar as he distinguishes between two dimensions of being. One dimension he refers to as 'set-theoretical or ensemblistic [*ensembliste*]', that is, based on the logic of set theory (*la théorie des ensembles*). He also calls this dimension 'identitary' and abbreviates these two adjectives in the neologism 'ensidic [*ensidique*]'. This dimension, which is an essential aspect of all language, life and social activity, is characterised by 'the logic of the principle of identity, of contradiction, and of the excluded third, the logic that is at the basis of arithmetic and mathematics in general and that is formally and effectively realised in set theory and its interminable ramifications'.[65] According to Castoriadis, ensidic logic corresponds to an organisable stratum of being (the 'first natural stratum'), and it deploys itself in social institutions via what he calls the *legein* (language as a purportedly univocal code) and the *teukhein* (practice in the functional and instrumental sense). This ensidic dimension does not exhaust being. There are what Castoriadis calls 'magmas', which are irreducible to the formalisation of ensidic logic. Indeed, the activity of formalisation itself, insofar as *it* cannot be formalised, is a preliminary indication of the existence of magmas. More germane to our discussion here, we can take the example of society. For if there is an ensidic dimension of society, as we have just seen, society itself 'is neither a set, nor a system or hierarchy of sets (or of structures); it is a magma and a magma of magmas'.[66] Similarly, the psyche rebels against ensidic logic as radical imagination and undetermined creation.[67]

Turning to Castoriadis's engagement with biology, we can begin with his description of living beings (*des vivants*) as those who support themselves on the ensidic being of non-living nature and create a world for themselves. More specifically, a living being is a self-constituting for-itself characterised by self-finality (conservation, reproduction, and so forth) and the creation of a proper world of representations, affects and intentions.[68] Autonomy, properly speaking, appears to be a characteristic of humanity alone. 'Man is the only animal', Castoriadis writes, 'capable of breaking the closure in and through which every other living being *is*.'[69] He also emphasises the extent to which one of the major differences between humanity and the rest of the natural world is that the imagination of other living beings is 'subservient to functionality and given once and for all', whereas for human beings 'it is defunctionalised and perpetually creative'.[70] Indeed, this is one of the reasons that the human species, at a biological and psychological level, is incapable of life and probably would have disappeared if it wasn't for the invention of something without precedent in the natural world: the self-creation of society.[71]

NOTHING IF NOT CRITICAL

It would be a twofold contradiction to remain at the level of pure exegetical commentary. On the one hand, it would contradict my own work, where I have called into question the limitations of *exegetical thought* (where thinking is reduced to thinking within and through the canonised figures of the past) and charted out its historical emergence as the dominant modus operandi of professional philosophers in the 'continental' tradition.[72] On the other hand, it would contradict Castoriadis's work insofar as he criticises the philosophic cannibalism of the tradition of pure commentary and asserts that 'for a philosopher, there *can* only be a critical history of philosophy'.[73] In the name of pursuing the tradition of radical critique that Castoriadis himself identifies with, it is therefore necessary to discuss some of the limitations and problems inherent in his project.

First of all, he deploys a strategy that has now become commonplace among those philosophers seeking to accentuate the originality of their work. This strategy might be called *personal apotheosis via selective history*, and it consists in claiming that no one in the past – barring, perhaps, a few soothsayers – has thought what the philosopher in question has been able to think, and that all other philosophers have been trapped to a greater or lesser extent in an illusory mode of thinking. In Castoriadis's case, he regularly states that the quasi-totality of Western philosophy – which is philosophy proper for him[74] – has thought being in terms of *déterminité* (determinacy) and ignored the radical imaginary. He therefore purports to be the first thinker to truly break with what he calls *inherited thought* by elucidating the creative imagination and asserting that being is undetermined.[75] He sometimes suggests at least partial exceptions,[76] and it is obviously necessary to examine his general claim as it plays itself out in the various interpretations he provides of individual philosophers. Since this is not the place for such an undertaking, let us simply state that it is highly unlikely that nearly the entire Western world would think in one way and a single individual would suddenly think differently. It is much more likely that Castoriadis is reproducing an element of his own social world, and more specifically of the philosophical habitus that he shares with many of his compatriots. The professed singularity of his project would thereby actually confirm its conformity to an unoriginal strategy of personal apotheosis through historical promotion. The recognition of this conformity at a strategic level does not, of course, invalidate *in toto* his claims to originality, but it does relativise his self-promotional strategies and the crude logic of history they produce.

This is not the only strategy that Castoriadis shares with many twentieth-century European philosophers. He also employs the chiaroscuro technique for delineating history by contrasting the light and shadow of two fundamental tendencies: autonomy and heteronomy, the instituting imaginary and instituted social significations, the magmatic dimension and the ensidic dimension, and so on. In spite of a partial attempt to avoid a categorical valorisation of one term over the other, and despite the insistence that both dimensions are necessary or inevitable (at least for certain terms), it is nonetheless a patent verity that Castoriadis is more enamoured with the imaginative acts of creation than with the fixity and determinedness of what has already been instituted. Moreover, he runs the risk of treating these notions and values as transhistorical, as if there was a perennial conceptual and normative vocabulary allowing us to discuss *any* socio-historical configuration. Indeed, he tends to assume that his conceptual arsenal – the imaginary, institution, heteronomy, and so forth – is valid for any and all social and historical milieus, as if categories such as *the imagination, creation* or *art* could have the same purchase on the ancient Greeks, the Aztecs, Buddhists in the third century BC, Eskimos in the eleventh century AD and ourselves.[77] Any differences that are recognised tend to be superficial differences situated at the level of varying definitions, misunderstandings or unadulterated ignorance of the *same basic categories and values*, which therefore appear to *determine* the totality of phenomena. Insofar as these absolute categories seem to preclude the possibility of practices *undetermined* by his binary normative and conceptual edifice (that is, that are neither simply autonomous nor heteronomous, neither 'creative' nor determined, neither 'art' nor 'non-art', and so on[78]), Castoriadis risks slipping into an ontology of determinacy *through the back door*, so to speak, that is to say through the systematic valorisation of creative indetermination. Of course, he historicises autonomy and its various avatars in a certain sense by restricting them to the Greco-Western world, but this does not change the fact that the entire history of humanity can be conceived of with the categories of autonomy and heteronomy. His work thereby approximates a form of *selective socio-historicism* since he chooses what is part of society and history, as well as what escapes socio-historical specificity in the strong sense of the term (his own systematic vocabulary). As a final note in this regard, it cannot go unnoticed that Castoriadis's conceptual and normative framework is largely, if not entirely, dependent on a modern European sensibility. The valorisation of creation, novelty and the imagination, in spite of occasional counter-claims, bears the indelible mark of the modern glorification of creativity (not to mention the rediscovery of the Greeks as of the late eighteenth century).[79] Furthermore, the identification of Greece as the politico-philosophic origin of Europe is a relatively recent trope rooted in a new codification of philosophic history that emerged at the end of the eighteenth and the beginning of the nineteenth century.[80]

To his credit, Castoriadis recognises that his schematisation of history is situated *within* history:

> When we speak of history, *who* is speaking? It is someone of a given period, society and class – in short, it is a historical being. And yet the very thing that founds the possibility of historical knowledge [*une connaissance historique*] (for only a historical being can have an experience of history and talk about it) prevents this knowledge [*connaissance*] from ever being able to acquire the status of complete and transparent knowledge [*savoir*] – since it is itself, in its essence, a historical phenomenon that demands to be apprehended and interpreted as such. The discourse on history is included within history.[81]

This opens the door for a more generous reading of his work in terms of an attempt to lucidly and explicitly formulate a creative intervention from within a particular socio-historical conjuncture.[82] On this reading, for which there is textual evidence, Castoriadis's appeal to certain universals would be a situated and reflexive appeal that attempts to overcome the risks of cultural relativism by proposing transcultural reference points. Instead of indiscriminately positing transhistorical concepts, he would be suggesting heuristic tools for making sense of socio-historical developments while at the same time remaining open and transparent about his presuppositions.

While I certainly hope that this is the case, Castoriadis nevertheless regularly makes sweeping statements about the history of humanity that would need to be qualified. For instance, the claim that the entire history of the human race has been dominated by heteronomy and that there are only two 'moments' of autonomy – Greece and the West – is a moot point at many levels.[83] To begin with, it presupposes the ability to know the inner workings of all cultures that have ever existed, or at least all of those that have ever been known to exist.[84] This not only poses serious hermeneutic problems, but it is also structurally impossible from our current position because there are cultures that have partially or totally disappeared, and to which we have little or no access. So the claim itself can only be advanced on hypothetical grounds. Moreover, there is something slightly patronising, self-aggrandising and unduly simplistic about a Greek living in modern Europe who affirms that the only two moments of autonomy occurred in ancient Greece and Europe. Of course, Castoriadis claims that he does not want to elevate Greece to the status of a model, and he is extremely critical of his own socio-historical conjuncture and the crisis of autonomy. However, it is nevertheless clear that he valorises the Greco-Western project of autonomy and believes that no other cultures in the world are on a par with it: 'Before Greece and outside the Greco-Western tradition, societies are instituted on the principle of a strict closure: our view of the world is the only one that is meaningful and true, the "others" are bizarre, inferior, perverse, bad, disloyal, etc.'[85] It is rather ironic, in this regard, that the Greco-Western break with the closure of 'traditional societies' purportedly means a true openness to other cultures, for this 'openness' actually implies, among other things, the ability to recognise the universal closure – and, hence, relative inferiority – of all other cultures.[86] In fact, the closure of traditional societies is a trait that the members of these societies share with the animal world, whereas the autonomy of the Greco-Western world is defined as a properly *human* invention.[87] When Castoriadis asserts that 'the true interest in others was born with the Greeks' (a debatable claim in its own right[88]), he means, moreover, that Greece is the privileged origin not only of philosophy, democracy and politics proper, but also of true history and ethnology, as well as of what he calls 'judging and choosing, in a radical sense'.[89] When confronted with the criticism that he affirms and defends the superiority of Western culture, he retorts that he is actually only asserting the superiority of one dimension of this culture over another dimension of the same culture.[90] Even if this point is granted, it is nonetheless the case that the West is apparently the only place where the closure of instituted societies was ruptured by a creative project of critical inquiry aiming at taking on the task of the autonomous institution of society. Indeed, Castoriadis unabashedly declares – in perfect conformity with the colonial historiography of the *mission civilisatrice* – that 'Western humanity' is 'the most advanced' part of humanity.[91] This not only casts a long shadow over the rest of humanity and the deep history of cultures, but it also raises the question of his contribution to the perpetuation of colonial narratives, as well as the issue of the desire to spread the project of autonomy and the simplicity of its implicit historiography: do other cultures have any choice other than to either remain in their arcane and archaic ways or recognise and embrace the superiority of one dimension of European culture?[92] Even if the project of autonomy could end up taking on different iterations in various cultures (if it spreads), it is rather unfortunate that Castoriadis – who clearly has broad interests in other cultures – does not make ample room for the emergence of alternative cultural projects.[93]

CONCLUDING REMARKS

When driven by an intense eros of inquiry that knows no a priori bounds, it is perhaps inevitable that you will occasionally falter. In the case of Castoriadis, there are plenty of aspects of his work that invite critical reflection. Nevertheless, the breadth, depth and originality of his project need to be recognised in their own right. It is extremely rare, particularly in an era of increasing academic specialisation, that a single thinker is able to span the fields of philosophy, politics, psychoanalysis, art theory, economics, sociology, history and the philosophy of science. It is much more rare that he or she can do so while establishing a unique and expansive philosophical project that does not fit comfortably within the dominant models and intellectual fashions of the times. It is a testament to the intensity of Castoriadis's eros of inquiry that his passion for critical reflection broke through the strictures of his intellectual milieu in order to establish a novel, unique and wide-ranging philosophical project. His passion for independent elucidation should serve as an open invitation to all of us to fervently pursue the tradition of radical critique.

NOTES

1. *The Castoriadis Reader*, p. 362/*Fait et à faire*, p. 11 (translation slightly modified).
2. See *Figures of the Thinkable*, p. 81/*Figures du pensable*, p. 104.

3. On *Socialisme ou barbarie*, see *The Castoriadis Reader*, pp. 1–39.
4. Since there is significant fluctuation in the biographical information available regarding Castoriadis, I have decided to rely on the Association Castoriadis, whose members include many of his close friends and family members: <http://www.castoriadis.org> (last accessed 11 December 2015). However, I decided to follow the bio-bibliography provided by Éditions du Seuil for the date of employment at the OECD because 1945 (the date found on the Association Castoriadis website) seemed premature due to the fact that Castoriadis had just arrived in Paris on a scholarship for a *doctorat d'État* in philosophy (which he never finished).
5. *The Imaginary Institution of Society*, p. 74/*L'Institution imaginaire de la société*, pp. 110–11 (translation slightly modified).
6. This rumoured exchange is referred to in the Agora International obituary 'Cornelius Castoriadis Dies at 75'.
7. *The Imaginary Institution of Society*, p. 171/*L'Institution imaginaire de la société*, pp. 256–7 (translation slightly modified).
8. 'It [structuralism] has nothing to say about the sets of elements it manipulates, about the reasons for their being-such, about their modifications in time' (ibid., p. 171/p. 257). On the 'pseudo-scientific ideology' of structuralism, see *World in Fragments*, p. 51/*La Montée de l'insignifiance*, p. 35.
9. *World in Fragments*, pp. 50–1/*La Montée de l'insignifiance*, p. 34 (translation slightly modified).
10. *The Castoriadis Reader*, p. 398/*Fait et à faire*, p. 63. Also see the 'Agora International Interview'.
11. See *La Montée de l'insignifiance*, pp. 90–2 and *Philosophy, Politics, Autonomy*, p. 14/*Le Monde morcelé*, p. 282.
12. See *Philosophy, Politics, Autonomy*, pp. 16–17/*Le Monde morcelé*, pp. 285–6.
13. Ibid., p. 4/p. 128 (translation slightly modified).
14. Since the interviews are all from the 1990s, I have primarily concentrated on Castoriadis's later work, from approximately *The Imaginary Institution of Society* (1975) until the end of his life.
15. *Fait et à faire*, p. 253 (all translations, unless otherwise indicated, are my own). The entire quote reads: 'being is creation, *vis formandi*: not the creation of "matter-energy", but the creation of forms.' Castoriadis also asserts that 'being is creation/destruction' (*Figures of the Thinkable*, p. 190/*Figures du pensable*, p. 223).
16. *Figures of the Thinkable*, p. 190/*Figures du pensable*, p. 223 (translation slightly modified).
17. *Fait et à faire*, p. 258.
18. *Domaines de l'homme*, p. 9.
19. *World in Fragments*, p. 184/*Fait et à faire*, p. 116 (translation slightly modified). For reasons of clarity, I have exceptionally translated *l'être* as Being

(in general) in order to distinguish it from *l'étant* (being in the sense of a specific thing or phenomenon).
20. *The Imaginary Institution of Society*, p. 3/*L'Institution imaginaire de la société*, p. 8 (translation slightly modified); *World in Fragments*, p. 181/*Fait et à faire*, p. 113 (also see *Domaines de l'homme*, p. 48).
21. *World in Fragments*, p. 131/*Le Monde morcelé*, p. 182.
22. *World in Fragments*, p. 190/*Fait et à faire*, p. 124 (translation slightly modified). Also see ibid., p. 187/p. 120; *Philosophy, Politics, Autonomy*, p. 145/*Le Monde morcelé*, p. 139, p. 187; *The Castoriadis Reader*, p. 332.
23. *Domaines de l'homme*, p. 12; *The Imaginary Institution of Society*, p. 215/*L'Institution imaginaire de la société*, pp. 319–20.
24. *The Castoriadis Reader*, p. 269/*Domaines de l'homme*, p. 329.
25. *World in Fragments*, p. 86/*La Montée de l'insignifiance*, p. 194. Castoriadis has provided variable dates for this 'first Renaissance', ranging from about the eleventh to the fourteenth century.
26. *The Imaginary Institution of Society*, p. 215/*L'Institution imaginaire de la société*, p. 319.
27. See *Le Monde morcelé*, pp. 18–22.
28. See ibid., pp. 22–4.
29. *The Castoriadis Reader*, p. 272/*Domaines de l'homme*, p. 353.
30. See, for instance, *A Society Adrift*, p. 125; *Domaines de l'homme*, p. 356; *Figures du pensable*, p. 155.
31. See *The Imaginary Institution of Society*, pp. 9–70/*L'Institution imaginaire de la société*, pp. 13–104.
32. *The Castoriadis Reader*, p. 407/*Fait et à faire*, p. 76.
33. Ibid., p. 407/p. 76.
34. *Le Monde morcelé*, p. 210.
35. Politics in *The Complete Works of Aristotle*, vol. 2, p. 2037 (1283b40–1284a1).
36. See *The Castoriadis Reader*, p. 315/*Domaines de l'homme*, p. 521 and *Figures of the Thinkable*, p. 171/*Figures du pensable*, p. 203: 'The chaos/abyss/groundless [*chaos/abîme/sans-fond*] is what is behind or under every concrete existent, and at the same time it is the creative force – what we would call the *vis formandi* in Latin – that causes the upsurge of forms, organised beings. The singular human being is a fragment of that chaos, and at the same time a fragment or an agency of that *vis formandi*, of that force or that creativity of being as such' (translation slightly modified).
37. *Domaines de l'homme*, p. 347.
38. *Figures of the Thinkable*, p. 80/*Figures du pensable*, p. 102 (translation slightly modified). On the issue of imitation, see *Fenêtre sur le chaos*, particularly pp. 152–3.
39. *Figures of the Thinkable*, p. 80/*Figures du pensable*, p. 103 (translation slightly modified).

40. *The Tragedy of Macbeth* (Act V, scene v), in *The Norton Shakespeare*, p. 2613. For Castoriadis's discussion of Shakespeare and *Macbeth*, see *Fenêtre sur le chaos*, pp. 104–5, p. 155.
41. *La Montée de l'insignifiance*, p. 75.
42. Ibid., p. 75.
43. See *Figures of the Thinkable*, p. 84/*Figures du pensable*, p. 107 (*l'avant-garde* should clearly be translated as 'the avant-garde' instead of 'the vanguard').
44. See ibid., pp. 84–5/pp. 107–8 and *Fenêtre sur le chaos*, p. 17.
45. See *Domaines de l'homme*, p. 344 and *Fenêtre sur le chaos*, p. 25.
46. *Domaines de l'homme*, p. 347.
47. See *La Montée de l'insignifiance*, p. 76 and *Fenêtre sur le chaos*, p. 47.
48. *World in Fragments*, p. 129/*Le Monde morcelé*, p. 178 (translation slightly modified).
49. See, for instance, *Crossroads in the Labyrinth*, p. 103/*Les Carrefours du labyrinthe 1*, p. 157; *Figures of the Thinkable*, p. 89, pp. 197–8/*Figures du pensable*, pp. 112–13, p. 232.
50. *The Castoriadis Reader*, p. 291/*Domaines de l'homme*, p. 482 (translation slightly modified).
51. *Figures of the Thinkable*, p. 170/*Figures du pensable*, p. 202.
52. Ibid., p. 217/p. 254 (translation slightly modified).
53. *World in Fragments*, p. 150/*Le Monde morcelé*, p. 250 (for a more detailed description of the various aspects of the distortion of sexuality, see the ensuing pages).
54. See *Figures of the Thinkable*, p. 217/*Figures du pensable*, p. 254 and *Domaines de l'homme*, p. 125.
55. *Crossroads in the Labyrinth*, p. 26/*Les Carrefours du labyrinthe 1*, pp. 61–2 (translation slightly modified).
56. Human beings, for Castoriadis, are not defined essentially by their rationality, but rather by 'the continuous, uncontrolled and uncontrollable surge of our creative radical imagination in and through the flux of representations, affects, and desires' (*World in Fragments*, pp. 127–8/*Le Monde morcelé*, p. 177, translation slightly modified).
57. Ibid., p. 136/p. 189.
58. *Philosophy, Politics, Autonomy*, p. 270/*Le Monde morcelé*, p. 119 (translation slightly modified).
59. Ibid., p. 270/p. 119 (translation slightly modified).
60. See *Crossroads in the Labyrinth*, p. 167/*Les Carrefours du labyrinthe 1*, p. 218.
61. Ibid., p. 168/p. 219.
62. Ibid., p. 171/p. 223.
63. Ibid., p. 176/pp. 228–9 (translation slightly modified).
64. Ibid., p. 178/p. 231 (translation slightly modified).

65. *The Castoriadis Reader*, p. 352/*Fait et à faire*, p. 174. Also see *The Castoriadis Reader*, p. 328: 'Everything that is must contain an ensemblistic-identitary ("logical", in the largest sense possible) dimension; otherwise it would be *absolutely* indeterminate, and (at least for us) nonexistent.'
66. *The Imaginary Institution of Society*, p. 228/*L'Institution imaginaire de la société*, p. 336 (translation slightly modified). In *Fait et à faire*, Castoriadis asserts that 'being is magmatic because it is creation and temporality' (p. 258).
67. See *Crossroads in the Labyrinth*, p. 97/*Les Carrefours du labyrinthe 1*, p. 149.
68. *World in Fragments*, pp. 145–50/*Le Monde morcelé*, pp. 243–9.
69. *The Castoriadis Reader*, p. 314/*Domaines de l'homme*, p. 520.
70. *World in Fragments*, p. 178/*Fait et à faire*, p. 109 (translation slightly modified; also see *Fait et à faire*, p. 16, pp. 179–81/*The Castoriadis Reader*, pp. 356–7). This is one of the reasons Castoriadis derides the definition of human beings as rational animals: 'he [man] is much less reasonable than animals' (*World in Fragments*, p. 177/*Fait et à faire*, p. 108). 'Man', he states in an interview, 'is a living, but monstrous, totally dysfunctional being' (Rotzer, *Conversations with French Philosophers*, p. 33).
71. See *Domaines de l'homme*, pp. 48–9, p. 542/*World in Fragments*, p. 354; also see *The Castoriadis Reader*, p. 331.
72. See *Logique de l'histoire: Pour une analytique des pratiques philosophiques*.
73. *Philosophy, Politics, Autonomy*, p. 17/*Le Monde morcelé*, p. 287; also see p. 23 and *Figures of the Thinkable*, p. 81/*Figures du pensable*, p. 104.
74. This stance gives rise to a series of important questions: why – and on what grounds – does Castoriadis classify all philosophic developments outside of the Greco-Western world as heteronomous, and therefore not true philosophy? Why does he accept as a more or less natural given the history of Western philosophy as it has been codified since approximately the early nineteenth century (with its supposed origin in Greece and the sequence of its canonical figures)? Why doesn't he recognise that philosophy, far from having a proper nature supposedly invented by the Greeks, is a variable socio-historical construct, a concept-in-struggle with no inherent essence (even a historical essence)? Isn't he ultimately naturalising the contingent, contemporary edifice of the history of Western philosophy? Isn't he acting as if the instituted significations of the Western tradition as of only approximately 200 years were actually more or less *natural* significations stretching back to the Greeks? On these and related issues, see my *Logique de l'histoire*.
75. See, for example, *Crossroads in the Labyrinth*, pp. 209–10/*Les Carrefours du labyrinthe 1*, pp. 268–9; *Fait et à faire*, p. 270; *Figures of the Thinkable*, p. 73/*Figures du pensable*, p. 95.
76. See, for instance, *The Castoriadis Reader*, pp. 371–2/*Fait et à faire*, pp. 23–4.

77. Here is one example among others: 'Of this abyss, of this chaos, humanity has always had at once a sharp and confused perception. It has always felt its intolerable and insurmountable nature, and it responded to it by social institutions and above all by the institution that, almost everywhere, almost always, was its nuclear element: religion' (*Fenêtre sur le chaos*, pp. 99–100).
78. To take the flagrant example of the category of 'art' (and, therefore, 'non-art' as well as 'great art'), which is culturally ubiquitous for Castoriadis, there is excellent research that has demonstrated the extent to which it is a modern, European category that cannot and should not be applied to all time periods and all cultures. See, for instance, Rancière, *The Politics of Aesthetics* and Shiner, *The Invention of Art*.
79. On this issue, see Nathalie Heinich's work on the novel social imaginary that emerged around the turn of the nineteenth century, particularly *L'Élite artiste: Excellence et singularité en régime démocratique* and *Être artiste: Les Transformations du statut des peintres et des sculpteurs*.
80. I have explored this issue in *Logique de l'histoire*.
81. *The Imaginary Institution of Society*, pp. 32–3/*L'Institution imaginaire de la société*, pp. 48–9 (translation slightly modified).
82. Along these lines, Castoriadis writes that 'we have to understand [...] that *there is* truth – and that *it is to be made*, that in order to *attain* it, we must *create* it, which means, first and foremost, to *imagine* it' (*World in Fragments*, p. 373/*Domaines de l'homme*, p. 570, translation slightly modified).
83. It should be noted that Castoriadis occasionally suggests that there are *perhaps* other moments by using phrases such as 'at least two moments'.
84. 'The human domain appears, at the start, as a highly heteronomous domain [...]. Archaic societies, like traditional societies, are very highly closed societies informationally, cognitively, and organisationally. In fact, this is the state of almost all societies we know of, almost everywhere, almost always' (*The Castoriadis Reader*, p. 311/*Domaines de l'homme*, p. 514).
85. Ibid., p. 268/pp. 326–7 (translation slightly modified).
86. It is worth noting that Castoriadis has nonetheless suggested, in *Philosophy, Politics, Autonomy*, that it is impossible to establish a hierarchy of the multiple social-historical worlds (p. 66/*Le Monde morcelé*, p. 69).
87. As we saw above: 'Man is the only animal capable of breaking the closure in and through which every other living being *is*' (*The Castoriadis Reader*, p. 314/*Domaines de l'homme*, p. 520). However, some men are apparently not capable of this, so they remain within the closure of the animal world.
88. Castoriadis tends to downplay the central role of slavery and imperialism in ancient Athens in favour of a relatively halcyon image of autonomous democracy. On the centrality and importance of slavery, imperialism and

various forms of rigid social hierarchy in Athenian society, see Finley, *Ancient Slavery and Modern Ideology* and *Democracy Ancient and Modern*, as well as Lévy, *La Grèce au Ve siècle*.
89. *The Castoriadis Reader*, p. 268/*Domaines de l'homme*, p. 327 (translation slightly modified); ibid., p. 272/p. 353.
90. See *The Castoriadis Reader*, pp. 397–8/*Fait et à faire*, p. 63.
91. *Le Monde morcelé*, p. 212.
92. In an interview with *Esprit*, Castoriadis claims that other cultures need to extricate themselves from their religious closure and accept Western universalism, and he bemoans the fact that the West is not currently able to have an emancipatory influence on these closed societies (see *La Montée de l'insignifiance*, pp. 70–1).
93. For a debate on this and related issues, see Castoriadis, Escobar, Gondicas and Vernay, *Démocratie et relativisme: Débats avec le MAUSS*.

Chapter 6

THE HATRED OF RANCIÈRE: DEMOCRACY IN THE HISTORY OF POLITICAL CULTURES*

THE HATRED OF RANCIÈRE

Jacques Rancière is not known for lacking polemical verve. When he is not engaged in controversies with his contemporaries – whether explicit or implicit – he describes, with a thinly veiled contempt, their scorn for his own manner of thinking. One of his recent works, *Hatred of Democracy*, has the apparent advantage of being situated at the intersection of these two tendencies, as it is at once a description of the hatred of others and a polemical intervention against them. Published in 2005 as a circumstantial piece, the book is an acerbic critique of what Rancière perceives as the present hostility toward democracy. It is true that he affirms on the book's first page that the hatred of democracy 'is as old as democracy itself for a simple reason: the word itself is an expression of hatred'.[1] However, his own object of analysis in this little book is the new form taken by this perennial hatred in the contemporary world. It is in this light that he examines the modes of questioning democracy recently formulated by citizens of democratic countries. For these authors, democracy is understood not as a series of institutional mechanisms, but as a set of customs: 'For them democracy is not a corrupt form of government; it is a crisis of civilisation afflicting society and through it the State.'[2] Rancière thus relies on an implicit distinction between *political democracy*, or the state institution of democracy, and *cultural democracy*, or the civilisational practice of democracy. The principal thesis of the detractors of cultural democracy in our time is summarised in the following way: 'there is only one good democracy, the one that represses the catastrophe of democratic civilisation.'[3]

* Translated by Jared C. Bly in close consultation with the author.

In order to pay homage to Rancière's polemical verve, I would like to engage in a polemic myself. So that it might truly be an homage, it is indeed necessary to follow him on this perilous path that leads beyond intellectual appropriateness and to the heart of matters, the path that led him to break radically with Althusser, to call into question Deleuze's entire aesthetic project, to lash out violently against Lyotard's reflection on the sublime, to criticise Badiou's aesthetic incompetence, and so forth. Hence, it is not worth recalling the extent to which I esteem Rancière's work by providing an inventory of everything that I have learned by reading his works and by dialoguing with him on diverse occasions, inasmuch as such a reminder would risk attenuating my polemic. Neither would it be necessary to slip into autobiography in explicating how the discovery of Rancière's works was among the most important in my intellectual itinerary, notably by helping me to find my own path, since such a reminder would give the impression that I am merely satisfied with offering a sterile pseudo-polemic like those that characterise the intellectual life of schools of thought. Therefore, let us forget these brief remarks I could not help making due to my profound respect for one of the most important intellectuals of our time, and let us move on to what is essential.

First of all, it is necessary to note that the overwhelming majority of the references in *Hatred of Democracy* refer to French publications, which are cited three times more than books written in other languages (which themselves come in particular from the Anglo-Saxon world). Judging from these references, the new hatred of democracy that constitutes Rancière's principal object of analysis is an antipathy specific to a sector of the French intelligentsia (that of the 'new reactionaries' like Alain Finkielkraut and Jean-Claude Milner), with a few traces in the work of Anglo-Saxon authors such as Daniel Bell.[4] If Rancière's critique is limited to this group of entrenched conservatives, it is largely legitimate and constitutes an important intervention against the republicanist political imaginary that presently dominates France.[5] This being said, Rancière sometimes recognises that these authors tend to call into question one conception of democracy in the name of another, judged to be positive, instead of condemning categorically all forms of democracy in a pure and simple hatred. Furthermore, it is obvious that Rancière does not have the slightest desire to limit his concerns to a handful of contemporary French authors. As we will see in a moment, he wishes to advance a thesis on the more or less ahistorical nature of democracy and of its detractors.

Before proceeding, we should therefore cite the specific definition that Rancière gives to democracy:

> Democracy is not a political regime. Insofar as it is a rupture in the logic of *arche* – that is, in the anticipation of rule in the disposition for it – democracy is *the* regime of politics in the form of a relationship defining a specific subject. [...] Democracy is *the* institution of politics – the institution of both its subject and its mode of relating.[6]

Strictly speaking, 'democracy' refers to a type of action rather than a state of society. In other words, Rancière abandons the *substantialist conception* of democracy as a political system or a state of society in the name of a *militant* and *generative conception* understood as an act of rupture that reconfigures a given system. Conceptually, it is a question of a displacement from being to event, from democracy as a *state* to democracy as *act*.[7] This theoretical displacement constitutes one of the principal means of parting ways with the Marxist paradigm in the second half of the twentieth century. If Marxism – or at least a certain form of Marxism – was founded on history's true being and the hypothetical arrival at the end of a historical trajectory via the establishment of a final state of equality, certain 'post-Marxists' like Rancière have rethought politics as a type of intermittent action that needs to be perpetually renewed. What Jean-François Lyotard called 'permanent revolution', or later 'politics without end' – and what Rancière names acts of democratic subjectivisation that are constantly renewed – goes hand in hand with a constant recuperation, to use the Marxist term, or an inevitable and immediate return to the police order in Rancière's language.[8] The work of the negative, which is supposed to lead teleologically to a moment of final synthesis, is replaced by a recurrent conflict between democracy and the police, a struggle that itself becomes the norm governing the totality of political history, or at least the totality of the history of the common's forms of symbolisation: there can only be the police, and possibly politics.[9] This implies an almost complete eradication of the properly historical dimension of politics.[10] From Plato to Milner, the entirety of political history – or at least everything that deserves to be analysed in political history in Rancière's opinion – is summed up in the establishment of police orders and intermittent political incursions aiming, as much as possible, at displacing or reconfiguring them.[11] The formal concepts of politics and the police are fixed beyond time. The only thing that changes in the course of history is the specific content of these concepts, as illustrated by the differences between the hatred of democracy in Plato and the disdain for democracy in Milner.[12] Rancière falls here into what I call *selective historicism*: he chooses himself what escapes history, which happens indeed to be his own concepts.

Let us pause briefly to consider the case of the concept of the police, which is very revealing. In *Disagreement*, Rancière explains his use of this term by referring to a late text by Foucault. The identification of the police with the petty police, he explains, is completely contingent since:

> Michel Foucault has shown that, as a mode of government, the police described by the writers of the seventeenth and eighteenth centuries covered everything relating to 'man' and his 'happiness'. The petty police is just a particular form of a more general order that arranges the sensory world in which bodies are distributed in community.[13]

In distancing himself from the contemporary use of the term *police*, Rancière does not only refer to the concept of the police studied by Foucault, but *he endeavours to generalise it*:

> So from now on I will use the word *police* or *policing* as a noun and adjective in this broad sense that is also 'neutral', non-pejorative. [...] The police is, essentially, the law, generally implicit, that defines the party's share or lack of it.[14]

The undertaking is quite remarkable. Initially, he shows that the present-day concept of the police is contingent by relying on the Foucauldian analysis of the use of the term *police* in the seventeenth and eighteenth centuries. Let us note in passing that, for Foucault, the police plays a major role in the specifically modern art of governing, that broke with a certain Christian and judiciary tradition: '"the police" is the term covering the whole new field in which centralised political and administrative power can intervene.'[15] It is from this historical definition of the police that Rancière establishes his broadened concept of the police by a slight displacement of emphasis, since he insists on the sensible distribution of bodies rather than on the specific practices and technologies of people's shared lives.[16] Finally, he generalises this concept, which is based on a notion *just as contingent as the present-day concept of the police*. The historicity of the notion of police, which in fact allows him to underscore the contingency of the idea that we have of it today, does not prevent him in any way from generalising another concept of the police which is every bit as contingent.

Is it a question of a purely pragmatic definition of the police? Does Rancière simply rely on Foucault in order to show that there are several conceptions of the police and in order to propose one which would be, in his opinion, particularly promising? If this were the case, it would perhaps be possible for him to carefully avoid this problem. Yet he regularly insists on the importance of the historical use of terms, as if he were looking not so much to propose pragmatic or heuristic definitions as to underscore the true meaning of a word in a precise historical conjuncture. For example, in his brilliant introduction to *Mute Speech*, he explains in detail the difference between the use of the word *littérature* in Racine's era and the modern sense of the term. In an interview concerning his political writings, he affirms:

> I am not Heideggerian. This means: I do not reason beginning from the etymology of words – an approach whose effect is to refer to certain primitive Indo-European roots and to institute in the end a grand synonymy summed up in the identity of *legein* as speaking/gathering. I construct arguments from the use of languages. In classical Greece, '*to sumpheron*' is a common word that means: the useful, what is in one's interest. It is in this sense that it is used by Aristotle, whom I discuss.[17]

Nevertheless, as we have just seen, this is not at all the case for the concept of the police since he uses *one* historical – and therefore contingent – usage to show the contingency of another historical use while establishing, based on this, a concept of a purportedly transhistorical scope. He therefore ends up projecting a contingent conception of the police on to the entire history of political practices, as if there were only one formal structure of *the* police.

In order to return to the concept of democracy, a concept which undergoes – as we shall see – the same operation of hegemonic generalisation, it is important to underscore at the outset that Rancière *does not need* this notion in his conceptual artillery. In truth, this term only complicates things. Given that it is a synonym for *politics* and for *subjectivisation*, it is difficult, indeed impossible, to discern its analytic function (at least the term *subjectivisation* allows Rancière to insist on the dynamic aspect of politics and the central role of subjects). One might think, trusting common sense, that Rancière employs the word *democracy* in order to underscore the specificity of democratic developments in the modern world, following, for example, the analyses of Claude Lefort. However, this is not at all the case. He goes to a lot of trouble in order to show, in fact, that his own definition of democracy is in no way to be confounded with the common understanding of democracy as a political or social system proper to the modern age:

> Democracy is not the parliamentary system or the rule of law. It is not a state of the social either, the reign of individualism or of the masses. Democracy is, in general, politics' mode of subjectivisation, if, by politics, we mean something other than the organisation of bodies as a community and the management of places, powers, and functions. Democracy is more precisely the name of a singular interruption of this order of distribution of bodies in a community that we proposed to conceptualise with the broadened concept of the police. It is the name of what comes and interrupts the smooth working of this order through a singular mechanism of subjectivisation.[18]

We must not misunderstand the details either. It is not as if democracy were *a* 'mode of subjectivisation' among others. Democracy is *the* mode of subjectivisation of politics. But given that politics manifests itself precisely in subjectivisation, the exact function of the concept of democracy is far from being obvious. Rancière sometimes describes it as 'the institution of politics', but we know that politics doesn't institute itself for him, or rather that it can only be instituted as a rupture: 'politics is the outline of a vanishing difference, with the distribution of social parts and shares'.[19] Democracy, as an ephemeral manifestation of politics, is nothing less than politics itself.[20]

Rancière draws the same conclusion many times over. Consider for example his detailed description of democracy in *Disagreement*, where he underscores its ternary apparatus:

> The *forms* of democracy are nothing other than the forms in which this ternary mechanism manifests itself. There is democracy

The Hatred of Rancière

if there is a specific sphere where the people appear. There is democracy if there are specific political actors who are neither agents of the state apparatus nor parts of society, if there are collectives that displace the modes of identification in terms of parts of the state or of society. Lastly, there is democracy if there is a dispute conducted by a nonidentary subject on the stage where the people emerge.[21]

The sphere of the people's appearance, the intervention of political subjects, and the enactment of a political dispute: this is the apparatus of democracy. Yet this apparatus, as Rancière affirms himself a few pages later, is precisely that of politics:

The ternary apparatus of democracy – *that is, of politics* – is strictly opposed by the proposition of a world in which everything is on show, in which parties are counted with none left over and in which everything can be resolved by objectifying problems.[22]

Why then use a term that is structurally identical to others and one that produces confusion above all?[23] The response to this question is to be found in the massive valorisation of democracy in the contemporary world, or what one could call *the love of democracy* (I will return to this point later): it is a question of exploiting the approving resonance attached to the name *democracy* in order to adorn his own reflection on politics with a sacred halo. In other words, the term *democracy* functions for him less as a denotative signifier indicating a distinct signified (he already has the terms *politics* and *subjectivisation* at his disposal) than as a connotative signifier indirectly signalling the positive and progressive value of his own political discourse.

Moreover, this suspect rhetorical procedure is linked to a general strategy of *conceptual transcendentalism*, which consists in detaching concepts from their concrete usage and specific political situations in an attempt to distil their abstract essences (which are supposed to manifest themselves precisely in concrete situations). This is the case not only for the notion of democracy but also for Rancière's other master concepts in the domain of politics: the police, subjectivisation, equality, politics, the people. He distances himself from the methodology of his own work in aesthetics and comes dangerously close to the orientation of his former colleague at the University of Paris VIII, Alain Badiou, by postulating formal ideas that stand above and overlook the social and historical world. The only person to have authority over these ideas is, moreover, the Philosopher himself. Strictly speaking, and in a rather undemocratic fashion (in the banal sense of the term *democracy*), Rancière is the only one capable of knowing for a fact if this or that act is really and truly democratic, political or egalitarian. Furthermore, this goes against the ideal of the ignorant and emancipatory master highly praised by Rancière in *The Ignorant Schoolmaster* because the master of master concepts is the only one capable of correctly using them and verifying their accurate implementation.

Let us take the case of *Hatred of Democracy*. To all appearances, this book uses the conceptual architectonic established in *Disagreement* and *On the Shores of Politics* in order to intervene in the present. In principle, *anyone* could do this, *anyone* could – in Rancière's vocabulary – verify the presupposition of equality by taking the place of the master, or rather by dismantling the hierarchy of knowledge in the name of equality. Nevertheless, only the master proves to be up to such a task. For there is almost no possibility of theory exportation, if one understands by this the use of Rancière's political concepts according to relatively objective criteria in order to be able to say with a minimum of certainty – and without the explicit consent of Rancière himself – if a specific phenomenon derives from politics or from the police. Such distinctions, rooted as they are in a strategy of conceptual transcendentalism, depend in the end on the whims of the master. Even though the infatuation with democracy in the present age has been well documented (I will return to this), he has instead sensed an intense animosity, to the point of adding to the list of democracy's denigrators those who incessantly proclaim their love for it. Fundamentally, the hatred in question is not the hatred of democracy as we normally understand it, rather it is a disdain for the term appropriated by Rancière – for its positive connotative qualities – as a synonym for politics. Finally, democracy's imprecators are those who, in Rancière's view, favour his concept of the police and denigrate his own notion of politics. Yet only the master of concepts can judge with precision who respects and who does not respect his own concepts. Given that they are not rooted in a concrete world open to the analysis of *anyone*, it is necessary to await the judgement of the master, the only one capable of saying with certainty whether a particular phenomenon inscribes itself in the framework of one of his formal concepts. Let us add, furthermore, that a vague usage of the term *democracy* allows Rancière to operate at two levels at once by oscillating without any apparent distinction between words and things: at times he references the use of the term *democracy*, at others he refers to the proper concept of democracy (and the use of the term is not always a trustworthy index thereof). Independently of the words employed and despite diverse uses of the concept of democracy, it is always a question of cultivating respect for the proper meaning of democracy, namely the meaning of democracy as it is understood by the master.[24]

One of the most revealing examples of the impossibility of theory exportation is the bewildering interview published in *Libération* concerning the events that took place in autumn 2005, which were classified by the media under the all-too-suspicious heading of 'the crisis of the *banlieues*'. Rancière affirms here that the participants in the revolts were not true political subjects:

> The problem is not one of knowing whether people are treated badly or feel unhappy. It is about knowing if they count as political subjects, endowed with a common voice. The meaning of the revolt is also linked to their own capacity to consider themselves as such. Apparently, this movement of revolt did not find a political form, such as I understand it, of the constitution of a scene of interlocution that recognises the enemy as being part of the same community as you. The reaction to a situation of inequality is one thing. Equality, for its part, manifests itself politically whenever the excluded declare themselves as included in their very manner of denouncing exclusion. In order to exit a medical schema of the expert treatment of symptoms, it is necessary that a form of subjectivisation emerges, traversing all of the social, cultural, and religious mediations in order to become the speech of a 'we' that constructs a material scene where speech becomes act.[25]

Rancière seems to anticipate here, in this interview from December 2005, the media parade of spring 2006 that beat the francophone public over the head with the quasi-systematic opposition between the barbarism of the 'hooligans of the *banlieues*' in their revolt against the *République* and the properly republican[26] protests organised with spokespeople by the French students against the CPE, and supported by unions and political parties (protests which, moreover, cannot be separated from the deep complicity between the media machine and the government's machinations, which appeared as clearly as ever in the staging of the power struggles – this would be the last one – between Dominique de Villepin and Nicolas Sarkozy[27]). Independently of the value judgements made regarding this contract, the fundamental message was clear: there are republicans on one side and hooligans on the other; there is a true act of speaking out in the republican tradition and 'violent' reactions that do not go through the established channels of 'revolts' (but which sometimes disrupt republican protests).[28] By philosophical decree, Rancière inscribes the same dividing line as the majority of journalists and politicians, namely that which distinguishes true politics from apolitical events.

This consensus between Rancière and the French oligarchy is all the more surprising because he refers in this interview to his early works linking politics to 'the constitution of a scene of interlocution which recognises the enemy as taking part in the same community as yourself'.[29] He seems to be thinking of his analysis of the manner in which Ballanche repeated, in 1829, Livy's narrative regarding the secession of Roman plebeians on the Aventine Hill. According to Ballanche, it was a matter of politically reconfiguring – to employ Rancière's vocabulary – the distribution of the sensible. Although the plebeians, from the point of view of the intransigent patricians, were deprived of logos, 'they established another order, another distribution of the sensible [...] as speaking beings sharing the same properties as those who deny them these. They thereby execute a series of speech acts that mimic those of the patricians.'[30] Is this to say that every political act must necessarily – in order to be recognised as such – institute a scene of speech imitating those who are already counted among speaking beings? Is politics for Rancière, in the end, a case of speaking out?[31] Moreover, is it necessary that every political act play the game of the police order by imitating those who are already accounted for within it so that it can constitute itself as a properly political act? Is this not a way of excluding in advance every act which would radically break the distribution of the sensible by 'a disidentification, a removal from the naturalness of place'?[32] Is not the proper of politics reduced to what is *properly political* according to the police order, namely what is recognisable as a political act according to the distribution of the sensible of the police, such as for instance a political protest in the republican tradition? Is it necessary to draw the conclusion that Rancière's lesson is ultimately one of political philosophy, that is to say, a lesson that reminds us that, actually, *politics is nothing other than the police*? Yet does not Rancière's lesson consist in reminding us that the proper of politics is to be *improper*, that is, to break with the police definition of politics, with the *proper* concept of politics, by reconfiguring the distribution of the sensible intended to distinguish *politics proper* from what is *apolitical* or *pre-political*?

TOWARDS AN OTHER HISTORY OF DEMOCRACY

Rancière's remarks on the perennial hatred of democracy and his decision to write a work on the present form of this contempt are that much more surprising since it is precisely in our era, contrary to all of the other phases of Euro-American history, that one finds a massive valorisation of democracy. Historically, this means that the *hatred of democracy* is in no way a key feature of our age, but rather there is a *love of democracy*. If Rancière decided to publish a work on a largely anachronistic subject, it is probably because a book on the love of democracy today would have required several volumes, whereas an analysis of the hatred of democracy only required a 106-page pamphlet.

In order to push forward in the polemic that I am initiating with him here, I would like to insist on the necessity of resisting his largely transcendental and ahistorical approach to politics. Instead of studying the actual history of the concept and term *democracy*, as well as the material transformation of democratic practices, he isolates a rarefied conception – itself dependent on modern democracy – and projects it on to the totality of history after having largely purified it of all concrete historical elements. This is one sign among others of his philosophical habitus and of his clandestine use of the Heideggerian distinction between *Geschichte* and *Historie*, or, more simply, of the separation between the intuitive history of fundamental concepts and the empirical history of facts.

Before sketching the broad lines of an entirely different approach to the history of democracy, I would like to briefly call attention to the major contribution of an author who is also called, by a surprising homology, Jacques Rancière. Contrary to his counterpart in politics, this Jacques Rancière, in working on aesthetics, refuses selective historicism and conceptual transcendentalism in the name of a radical historicism in which *everything is historicised*, including the very concepts of the historian. The most obvious example of this is the displacement effectuated by Rancière from the history of art or of literature, in which one presupposes the existence of a transhistorical object – art or literature – that undergoes metamorphoses through the years, towards a genealogy of the regimes of identification of the arts wherein art itself is taken as a properly historical phenomenon linked to what Rancière calls the aesthetic regime of art. Contrary to the transitive history of most of his predecessors, who took a supposedly natural object as their point of departure, Rancière proposes an intransitive history of the arts whereby one does not suppose in advance the existence of transhistorical objects like *art* or *literature in themselves*.

In a frank and sharp opposition to the intuitive history of monolithic philosophical concepts, I willingly follow this Rancière – the one working on aesthetics – by demanding an analytic of practices and an intransitive approach to history. In what follows, I would like to sketch, in broad strokes, four phases of 'democracy' with the aim of laying the groundwork for an analytic of democratic practice and, more broadly, for a history of political cultures, that is, a history of the modes of practical intelligibility of politics. I use the word *phases* instead of *epochs* because history does not cleanly divide itself into conceptual categories, and the transitions between phases take the form of *metastatic transformations* rather than *events*. As I explain in *Logique de l'histoire*, it is necessary to provide an account of the three dimensions of history (the vertical dimension of time, the horizontal dimension of space, and the stratigraphic dimension of practices) in order to definitively dismiss the illusion that there exist cataclysmic changes or that everything dramatically shifts everywhere in the world at a single, precise moment.

Dēmokratia

We should first recall the historical specificity of democracy in ancient Greece by following Anthony H. Birch's valuable insights, among others: 'The Greeks gave us the word, but did not provide us with a model. The assumptions and practices of the Greeks were very different from those of modern democrats.'[33] Let us briefly note that Athenian democracy was a direct democracy, and the Assembly was open to all citizens; it was limited to a *polis* of around 42,000 to 43,000 citizens;[34] there was no state in the sense of an autonomous apparatus distinct from the collective; there were not any political experts or professional politicians in the modern sense of the term; there were not political parties; religion and mythology played a central role; there was a rigid distinction between citizens (adult males) and non-citizens (women, children, slaves, metics), and the latter groups did not participate in politics; the concept of democracy was new, apparently an offshoot of the notion of isonomy;[35] the individualism of modern democracy was absent, and political activity was strongly centred on the collective or groups of individuals formed by *paideia*; political liberalism did not exist; and a properly universal dimension was missing from political activity.[36]

Moreover, it is within this very precise historical conjuncture that it is necessary to situate the numerous critiques of democracy among the Greeks. To take only a single example, when Plato (427–347 BC), through the medium of his presumed mouthpieces, calls the democratic regime into question, he is not thinking in any way of representational democracy. On the contrary, he is thinking of a regime like the one that lost the Peloponnesian War against Sparta, an oligarchic and conservative power, and that – four years after its restoration – put to death his teacher, Socrates. If Plato was against democracy, it was not at all a question of a hatred of democracy *itself* in all of its possible historical forms (including those which did not yet exist and which were properly unimaginable). Rather, he had a profound antipathy toward political regimes such as the one which had lost the most important war of his generation and had killed his master. Unfortunately, Rancière is hardly attentive to the historical specificity of *dēmokratia* in ancient Greece and to the particular disdain that it aroused among Greek philosophers. Through an attitude that could ironically qualify as Platonic, he runs the risk of a conflation by acting as if Plato was against democracy *itself* in all its imaginable forms rather than being against *dēmokratia*, that is to say, democracy as it was conceived and practised in Greece during his time.

Years in the Desert

In speaking of a perennial hatred of democracy, Rancière acts as if the latter were something more or less constant across history, at least since ancient Greece. Yet the reference to democracy as a contemporary practice largely disappeared between the end of antiquity and the beginning of the seventeenth, and especially the eighteenth, century:

'One can say that during the middle ages and up until the 17th century, the word "democracy" remained a scholarly word whose usage was generally reserved for designating a very specific form of ancient constitution.'[37] The term, when it was employed by the few specialists who made use of it, especially made reference to a practice which was no longer operative: 'for a long time the word democracy only designated an obsolete political form. In the 18th century, the word democracy was only used in reference to the world of antiquity.'[38]

Among the examples of this general disappearance and timid return of the word *democracy*, let us call attention to the striking case of John Locke (1632–1704). Even though one identifies him most often as one of the initiators of modern democracy in connecting him with the American founding fathers, there are only a small handful of references to democracy in his entire corpus. Moreover, in the principal passage in which he invokes it, it is in part to distinguish democracy from the *commonwealth*, which constitutes his true object of analysis:

> By commonwealth, I must be understood all along to mean, not a democracy or any form of government, but any independent community which the Latins signified by the word *civitas*, to which the word which best answers in our language is 'commonwealth'.[39]

Contrary to what is sometimes claimed, there is no theory or argued defence of democracy to be found in Locke.

The Power of the Rabble

When the term and the concept slowly began to spread beginning with the Enlightenment, or slightly earlier, the values attached to it were generally negative. As Raymond Williams recalls, democracy meant approximately mob rule, and, according to Bertlinde Laniel, this negative image persisted:

> During at least the first quarter of the 19th century, these words [democracy and democratic] still smelled of sulphur, revolution and anarchy, and their usage for numerous Americans still implied a strong disapproval. In Europe, it was necessary to await the 20th century before the word 'democratic', for example, became respectable, expressing favourable judgement in general.[40]

Let us take some examples of authors often associated today with the 'democratic tradition'. Jean-Jacques Rousseau (1712–1778), like Montesquieu (1689–1755) before him, was not a simple defender of democracy for at least three reasons.[41] First, he affirmed that the best form of government always depends on the situation and there is no general rule in this domain. Secondly, he declared that democracy, in the strict sense of the term, never existed and never will exist. This is because, thirdly:

> It is contrary to the natural order that the majority governs and the minority is governed. It is unimaginable that the people would remain constantly assembled to handle public affairs; and it is readily apparent that it could not establish commissions for this purpose without changing the form of administration.[42]

Immanuel Kant (1724–1804) in turn formulated an incisive critique of democracy in 'Toward Perpetual Peace'. There he identifies three forms of sovereignty (autocracy, aristocracy and democracy) by juxtaposing them with two forms of government: republicanism, founded on the principle of the separation of executive and legislative power, and despotism, which ignores such a principle. From these distinctions, Kant draws the following conclusion:

> Of the three forms of state, that of democracy in the strict sense of the word is necessarily a *despotism* because it establishes an executive power in which all decide for and, if need be, against one (who does not agree), so that all, who are nevertheless not all, decide; and this is a contradiction of the general will with itself and with freedom.[43]

It is possible, in his opinion, to combine the other forms of sovereignty with republicanism, and it turns out that monarchy is best suited for a republican constitution. It suffices to recall the first definitive article with a view to perpetual peace ('The civil constitution of every State shall be republican') in order to see the extent to which democracy is, for Kant, the form of sovereignty that is the least favourable to perpetual peace.[44]

Such distrust with regard to democracy was quite widespread in the United States during the time of the founding fathers. To cite only a few examples, Alexander Hamilton demanded the unification of states into a 'confederative republic' rather than in a democracy.[45] James Madison contrasted the qualities of republics, which were founded on representation and better suited to large states, with the flaws of democracies, which were incapable of extending across vast territories and of protecting themselves against pernicious factions.[46] The American constitution adheres to this general principle in guaranteeing each state a 'republican' form of government (section 4, article IV), and George Washington's first inaugural address, on 30 April 1789, makes reference to a republican model without even evoking democracy. Contrary to what certain contemporary ideologues would have us believe, the United States of America was founded as a *republic* and not at all as a *democracy*.[47]

Democratophilia

The last phase of democracy's history is that of an unprecedented valorisation. Even if there were a few traces of this change in Thomas Paine (1737–1809) and Maximilien de Robespierre (1758–94),[48] it was not until the 1830s that it became widespread. This began in the United States with Andrew Jackson, the first 'democrat' president and the symbol of the average American (who put an end to the long reign of patricians from Virginia and Massachusetts). In his meticulous study *Le Mot 'democracy' et son histoire aux États-Unis de 1780 à 1856*, Bertlinde Laniel writes: 'Liberated from the stigma of chronic political instability (democracy does not mean anarchy), democracy is not only interpreted in a political and social sense as a form of regime implying the people's natural right to political participation in its own interest, but as an ideal, and even an ideology.'[49] Pierre Rosanvallon situates the semantic turning point in French in the 1830s, while specifying: 'It was not in fact until 1848 that the word democracy truly imposed itself in political language in France.'[50]

From Moses Finley to Robert Dahl, and including R. R. Palmer, Bertlinde Laniel, Pierre Rosanvallon, Raymond Williams and many others, the historians of democracy agree that our era is unique insofar as it is the first time in the history of the Western world that there exists a nearly unanimous endorsement of democracy. For example, let us cite a few of the authors who have analysed this present-day democratophilia:

The Hatred of Rancière

In antiquity, intellectuals in the overwhelming majority disapproved of popular government, and they produced a variety of explanations for their attitude and a variety of alternative proposals. Today their counterparts, especially but not only in the west, are agreed, in probably the same overwhelming majority, that democracy is the best form of government, the best known and the best imaginable.[51]

Today, the word 'democracy/*démocratie*' evokes everywhere favourable sentiments for the majority of people and too often regardless of the context in which it is used.[52]

No one now contests that democracy constitutes the most desirable type of political regime. This hasn't always been the case.[53]

The word 'democracy' has today become a general symbol of broadly shared personal and political values.[54]

'Democracy' and 'democratic' have become in the 20th century words which imply the endorsement of the society or institution which is thereby described.[55]

Rancière's work on democracy is situated very precisely within the political culture of democratophilia. Yet his conceptual transcendentalism in the domain of politics prevents him from recognising the historical anchoring of his own discourse. He thus merely succumbs to its effects. This does not mean that it is simply necessary to choose between a strictly historical use of concepts and a transcendental usage. Rancière could have presented his concepts as pragmatic interventions, that is, as attempts to present new concepts while recognising that ideas inevitably circulate in a socio-historical field that is already established.[56] It is possible to recognise the historicity of practices and concepts while also striving to modify them. I would say, for my part, that it is precisely in recognising and understanding their historicity that we can better intervene in order to reconfigure them.

To conclude, I will return to my principal objective: to initiate a polemic with Rancière concerning his broadly ahistorical approach to politics. To this end, I called into question his strategy of hegemonic generalisation, which consists in generalising a concept from out of its specific historical usage, whether it be the notion of the police in the seventeenth and eighteenth centuries or the contemporary idea of democracy. I also showed to what extent the notion of democracy plays no significant conceptual role in his work, and that it is primarily invoked as a value-concept in order to adorn his own discourse with a sacred halo in the era of the *love of democracy*. This led me, next, to cast doubt over the master discourse that subtends his conceptual transcendentalism insofar as he is the only one capable of establishing the link between his master concepts in politics (politics, democracy, subject, people, police, equality) and specific phenomena. I relied in particular on the striking example of his analysis of the events in the autumn of 2005, where he purports to inscribe – like the French oligarchy that he, moreover, continually criticises – a definitive limit between the proper of politics and what is not properly political. Finally, I appealed to the *other* Rancière, the one who works on aesthetics, in sketching the broad contours of another approach to political history. This approach would allow us, although this is not the place for such an undertaking, to take back up, in an entirely different way, the question of the relationship between democracy – in its specifically modern form – and the emergence of the aesthetic regime of art.

NOTES

1. Rancière, *Hatred of Democracy*, p. 2.
2. Ibid., p. 3.
3. Ibid., p. 4.
4. On this subject see Maurice T. Maschino's article 'Les Nouveaux Réactionnaires'. It is surprising in this context that Rancière fails to closely examine the work of Leo Strauss. Moreover, we should note that, at the very end of his book, Rancière says that anti-democratic fury 'is particularly intense in France, where a self-proclaimed group of intellectuals has a place in the media that gives it power quite unheard-of in other countries in the day to day interpretation of contemporary phenomena and the formation of dominant opinion. We know just how this power was confirmed after 1968 [...]' (*Hatred of Democracy*, p. 85). It is also worth consulting a striking article published in March 2004, which has the advantage of being more circumspect than *Hatred of Democracy*: 'Criminal Democracy?', in *Chronicles of Consensual Time*, pp. 120–4.
5. On this subject, see my article 'Vers une critique historique de l'imaginaire politique contemporaine en France'. Another aspect of Rancière's

argument should be emphasised in passing insofar as it is absolutely accurate as long as it remains circumscribed within a precise sphere of intervention. We find in *Hatred of Democracy* traces of an argument fully developed in *Disagreement*. Rancière explains there that today we proclaim the triumph of a form of democracy that he calls consensual democracy. He brilliantly underscores the paradoxes of the democratic wisdom that imposes itself in this new form: 'At the very moment when Marxism's use-by date is being declared along with the failure of politics' bowing down to economics, we see regimes said to be liberal democracies take up, off their own bat, a sort of rampant Marxism according to which politics is the expression of a certain state of the social and it is the development of the forces of production that make up the bulk of its forms' (*Disagreement*, p. 97).

6. Rancière, 'Ten Theses on Politics', pp. 10–11. Rancière's definition comes close in more than one way to Cornelius Castoriadis's definition. See, notably, *La Montée de l'insignifiance* (p. 268): 'To discuss democracy is to discuss politics (*la politique*). Yet, politics itself does not exist everywhere and always; true politics results from a rare and fragile socio-historical creation. What necessarily exists in every society is *the political* (*le politique*).' Rancière discusses his relationship to Castoriadis with Nicolas Poirier in 'Entretien avec Jacques Rancière'.

7. For Rancière, 'democracy is neither a form of government nor a style of social life; it is the mode of subjectivisation by which political subjects exist' (*Aux bords du politique*, p. 12).

8. 'We should not forget either that if politics implements a logic entirely heterogeneous to that of the police, it is always bound up with the latter. The reason for this is simple: politics has no objects or issues of its own' (Rancière, *Disagreement*, p. 31).

9. Probably in order to respond to critics of his monolithic approach, Rancière proposes in an interview to distinguish between the police and domination (without, however, furnishing a conceptualisation of domination comparable to the theorisation of politics and the police that he has already offered): 'the police/politics opposition does not cover the entire field of human relations. It opposes two forms of symbolisation of the common of the community as such [...] The police is not domination in general; it is the domination that is exercised as the account of the community, the deployment of the internal law that constitutes "communality". Politics is the reconfiguration of this form of domination. This means that it is not everywhere but also that it is capable of being everywhere' (Arrous and Costanzo, 'Questions à Jacques Rancière', p. 16). A few pages further on, he adds: 'For me, there isn't politics on one side and the police on the other, but rather stagings of their relation' (ibid., p. 18).

10. On this point, Rancière distances himself from Claude Lefort, who proposed a definition of democracy that is not completely foreign to his own (despite the criticisms of the logic of the king's 'double body' formulated by Rancière): 'in my opinion, it is essential that democracy is instituted and maintained in the *dissolution of the benchmarks of certainty*. It inaugurates a history in which men challenge a final indetermination regarding the founding of Power, the Law and Knowledge, and the founding of the relation *with one another* in all the registers of social life' (Lefort, *Essais sur le politique: XIXe–XXe siècles*, p. 30).
11. It is true that Rancière affirms: 'Of course, this does not prevent there from being historical forms of politics, and it does not exclude the fact that the forms of political subjectivisation that make up modern democracy are of an entirely different complexity than the people in Greek democratic cities' (*The Politics of Aesthetics*, p. 51). Nevertheless, he has never put forward an examination of these historical differences, at least in the domain of politics, and it remains to be seen whether it is a question of fundamental differences or completely superficial ones.
12. It is revealing in this regard that Rancière advances a purely formal definition of politics: 'What makes an action political is not its object or the place where it is carried out, but only its form, the form that inscribes the verification of equality in the establishment of a dispute, of a community existing solely through division' (*Disagreement*, p. 32, translation slightly modified).
13. Ibid., p. 28.
14. Ibid., p. 29. Here is what follows: 'But to define this, you must first define the configuration of the perceptible in which one or the other is inscribed. The police is thus first an order of bodies that defines distributions between ways of doing and making, ways of being, and ways of saying, and sees that particular bodies are assigned by name to a specific place and task; it is an order of the visible and the sayable that makes it such that a particular activity is visible and another is not, that this speech is understood as discourse and another as noise' (ibid., p. 29, translation slightly modified).
15. Foucault, 'Omnes et Singulatim: Toward a Critique of Political Reason', in *Power: The Essential Works of Foucault, 1954–1984*, vol. 3, p. 320.
16. See the discussion of police in Foucault's *Security, Territory, Population* (p. 326): 'Generally speaking, what police has to govern, its fundamental object, is all the forms of, let's say, men's coexistence with each other. It is the fact that they live together, reproduce, and that each of them needs a certain amount of food and air to live, to subsist; it is the fact that they work alongside each other at different or similar professions, and also that they exist in a space of circulation; to use a word that is anachronistic in

relation to the speculations of the time, police must take responsibility for all this kind of sociality.'
17. Arrous and Costanzo, 'Questions à Jacques Rancière', p. 18.
18. Rancière, *Disagreement*, p. 99 (translation slightly modified).
19. Rancière, 'Ten Theses on Politics', p. 17. See also *Disagreement*, p. 101 (translation slightly modified): 'Democracy is not a regime or a social way of life. It is the institution of politics itself, the system of forms of subjectivisation through which any order of distribution of bodies into functions corresponding to their "nature" and places corresponding to their functions is called into question, rendered contingent.'
20. This is why he affirms that 'every politics is democratic in this precise sense: not in the sense of a set of institutions, but in the sense of forms of expression that confront the logic of equality with the logic of the police order' (*Disagreement*, p. 101).
21. Ibid., p. 100 (translation slightly modified).
22. Ibid., p. 102 (my emphasis).
23. This confusion is augmented by Rancière's suggestion that the common usage of the term *democracy* is itself affected by a confusion.
24. It is possible that Rancière has an interventionist or pragmatic conception of the use of concepts, which would allow him, if he were much more explicit in this regard, to emerge unscathed from these criticisms. Although he does not identify with the pragmatist tradition, he often suggests that his writings are, properly speaking, interventions that aim at displacing common sense. Could we not draw the conclusion from this that his proposed definitions of his master concepts do not seek in the least to encompass the distinctive feature of each notion by correcting bad students of philosophy, but rather that they are interventions – sometimes quite vigorous – into the conceptual battlefield? I admit that I would personally like to see Rancière's work evolve in this direction.
25. 'Le Scandale démocratique', 15 December 2005. Rancière repeats the same idea in 'Entretien avec Jacques Rancière' (pp. 38–9): 'What characterises our present is not a "loss of the symbolic". It is the withdrawal of certain forms of symbolising the other and violence. Thus, racism develops according to new forms against the immigrant, who does not fall within worker or proletarian political subjectivisation but appears solely in her or his ethnic difference. This develops in an inverted way among young "immigrants" who no longer identify the bourgeoisie as the enemy but simply the society that excludes them. The activity of a group of adolescents who attack a bus or greet the police with a hail of stones does not fall within the "loss of the symbolic". It falls within a symbolising of identity and of alterity that is regressive with respect to political symbolisation. Yet what is "pre-political" is not for that matter "extra-symbolic".'

26. This is apart from a few deviations whose responsibility was largely attributed to 'vandals' from the suburbs and an anarchic spirit from another time: May '68.
27. On this subject, I refer the reader to Étienne Balibar's excellent article 'Uprisings in the Banlieues': 'we have to ask if he [Interior Minister Sarkozy] did not in fact seek to touch off an episode of "criminal" violence to boost its [the government's] own legitimacy and law-and-order propaganda. When speaking of the government, let us not forget that it was riven at the time by an implacable rivalry between its two heads, Prime Minister Villepin and Interior Minister Sarkozy' (in *Egaliberty: Political Essays*, p. 235).
28. The future president of the Republic presented himself and was presented as the one who knows this fundamental difference, the one who, contrary to his rival, does not impose – with a violence unworthy of a head of state – reforms relating to the economic interests of republicans, but who concentrates on the security of the state when faced with savage violence coming from 'elsewhere'. Apparently, this staging worked, and it worked in spite of the quite remarkable 'passive organisation' of the riots of autumn 2005: without prior planning, the violence – as spectacular as it was – only claimed three victims (including the two young people killed indirectly by the police) and resulted in very few personal attacks. The violence was almost exclusively directed toward objects, vehicles and symbolic locations.
29. Rancière is not attentive enough, in the case of the riots, to the problematic of 'the constitution of a scene of interlocution'. Taking into account the – largely justified – mistrust of the media and politicians, how can he ask rioters to establish a scene of interlocution through the recognition that the enemy is part of the same community, even though the wrong – to use Rancière's vocabulary – that they express is rightly linked to their exclusion from the republican community that pretends to include them? Isn't this a perfect example of what Rancière calls disagreement? 'Disagreement', he writes, 'clearly does not have to do with words alone. It generally bears on the very situation of those who speak. In this, disagreement distinguishes itself from what Jean-François Lyotard has conceptualised under the name of differend' (*Disagreement*, p. xi). If the situation of those who express themselves – if only through phatic gestures of violence that seem to mean: *here we are, the un-seen, the un-heard!* – is such that only noise is heard, is it not necessary to wonder if the fault is not only their own, as if they only needed to 'clearly' express their propos?
30. Rancière, *Disagreement*, p. 24.
31. Sometimes Rancière suggests – as he clearly affirmed on 30 April 2008 during the conference 'Politiques de l'esthétique: Autour de l'œuvre de

Jacques Rancière' – that politics requires an act of speaking out and a reconfiguration of logos: 'Politics exists because those who have no right to be counted as speaking beings make themselves of some account, setting up a community by the fact of placing in common a wrong that is nothing more than this very confrontation, the contradiction of two worlds in a single world: the world where they are and the world where they are not, the world where there is something "between" them and those who do not acknowledge them as speaking beings who count and the world where there is nothing' (*Disagreement*, p. 27); 'Politics exists because the logos is never simply speech, because it is always indissolubly the *account* that is made of this speech: the account by which a sonorous emission is understood as speech, capable of enunciating what is just, whereas some other emission is merely perceived as a noise signalling pleasure or pain, consent or revolt' (ibid., pp. 22–3). At other times, he suggests political activity is not in any way limited to discourse: 'I now propose to reserve the term *politics* for an extremely determined activity antagonistic to policing: whatever breaks with the sensory configuration whereby parties and parts or lack of them are defined by a presupposition that, by definition, has no place in that configuration – that of the part of those who have no part. This break manifests itself in a series of actions that reconfigure the space where parties, parts or lack of parts have been defined' (ibid., pp. 29–30, translation slightly modified); 'Political subjectivisation redefines the field of experience that gave to each their identity within their lot. It decomposes and recomposes the relationships between the ways of *doing*, of *being*, of *saying* that define the sensory organisation of the community, the relationships between the places one does one thing and those where one does something else, the capacities associated with this *doing* and those required for another' (ibid., p. 40, translation slightly modified).
32. See *Disagreement*, p. 36: 'Any subjectivisation is a disidentification, removal from the naturalness of a place, the opening up of a subject space where anyone can be counted since it is the space where those of no account are counted, where a connection is made between having a part and having no part.'
33. Birch, *The Concepts and Theories of Modern Democracy*, p. 45. He continues: 'The Greeks had little or no idea of the rights of the individual, an idea that is tied up with the modern concept of democracy. Greek practice granted the right of political participation to only a small minority of the adult inhabitants of the city. When those granted this right were able to take political decisions, they did so by a direct vote on issues, which is very different from the system of representative government that has developed in the west in the past two centuries.'
34. Lévy, *La Grèce au Ve siècle*, p. 128.

35. See Lévêque and Vidal-Naquet, *Clisthène l'athénien*: 'It was above all necessary to attempt to extricate, something Herodotus was unable to do, the exact signification of this isonomy that appears at the end of the 6th century at once as the rallying point for certain aristocrats opposed to tyranny and as the watchword for those who we would later call democrats' (p. 11); 'The notion of isonomy thus seems to go back to a time when the "oligarchs" had not yet completely distinguished themselves from the "democrats", to the close of the 6th century that marks in so many ways a turning point' (pp. 30–1). See also Lévy, *La Grèce au Ve siècle*, p. 196.
36. On the differences between Athenian democracy and modern democracy, I refer the reader to the following works: Castoriadis, *La Montée de l'insignifiance*; Finley, *Democracy Ancient and Modern* and *Ancient Slavery and Modern Ideology*; Lévy, *La Grèce au Ve siècle*; Vidal-Naquet, *Le Chasseur noir*.
37. Laniel, *Le Mot 'democracy' et son histoire aux États-Unis de 1780 à 1856*, p. 47. See also Finley, *Democracy Ancient and Modern*, p. 9; Graubard, 'Democracy'; Palmer, 'Notes on the Use of the Word "Democracy" 1789–1799', p. 204. The counter-example that is most frequently cited – the exception which confirms the rule – is that of the *Landsgemeinde* of the rural cantons in Switzerland (see the *Dictionnaire historique de la Suisse*).
38. Rosanvallon, 'L'histoire du mot démocratie', in Gauchet, Manent and Rosanvallon (eds), *Situations de la démocratie*, p. 11. See also Dahl, *On Democracy*, pp. 7–9: 'As everyone acquainted with European history knows, after its early centuries in Greece and Rome the rise of popular government turned into its decline and disappearance. Even if we were to allow ourselves considerable latitude in deciding what governments we would count as "popular", "democratic", or "republican", their rise and decline could not be portrayed as a steady upward climb to the distant summit, punctuated only by brief descents here and there. Instead the course of democratic history would look like the path of a traveller crossing a flat and almost endless desert broken by only a few hills, until the path finally begins the long climb to its present heights.'
39. Locke, *The Second Treatise on Government*, p. 74. We should note in passing that the constitution of North Carolina, whose writing was overseen by Locke, calls for avoiding democracy.
40. Laniel, *Le Mot 'democracy'*, p. 31.
41. In his discussion of democracy, Montesquieu writes: 'The principle of democracy is corrupted not only when the spirit of equality is lost but also when the spirit of extreme equality is taken up and each one wants to be the equal of those chosen to command' (*The Spirit of the Laws*, p. 112). The true spirit of equality is neatly distinguished for him from the spirit of extreme equality: 'As far as the sky is from earth, so far is the true spirit of

equality from the spirit of extreme equality' (ibid., p. 114). This is because the representatives, contrary to the people, are capable of discussing political and social matters: 'The great advantage of the representatives is that they are able to discuss public business. The people are not at all appropriate for such discussions; this forms one of the great drawbacks of democracy' (ibid., p. 159). In the end, Montesquieu thus presupposes the existence of a social hierarchy that it is necessary to maintain in the organisation of the government: 'In a state there are always some people who are distinguished by birth, wealth, or honours; but if they were mixed among the people and if they had only one voice like the others, the common liberty would be their enslavement and they would have no interest in defending it, because most of the resolutions would be against them' (ibid., p. 160).

42. Rousseau, 'On the Social Contract', in *The Basic Political Writings*, p. 180. 'Montesquieu and Rousseau's democracy', writes Pierre Rosanvallon, 'is at once an ideal-type that can enter into a typology of political regimes in the manner of Aristotle and a historical model put to work in rare republics of antiquity with austere customs. Yet neither of these two authors imagine that democracy could be suitable for the modern world' ('L'histoire du mot démocratie', p. 13).
43. Kant, 'Toward Perpetual Peace', in *Practical Philosophy*, p. 324.
44. Ibid., p. 322.
45. Rossiter (ed.), *The Federalist Papers*, pp. 66–71.
46. Ibid., p. 76.
47. It is obviously the same for the French Republic. Regarding the use of the term *democracy* in the language of the Revolution, see Rosanvallon, 'L'histoire du mot démocratie', p. 15: 'The antiquated and almost technical connotation of the word "democracy" in the 18th century allows us to understand why it was also absent from the language of 1789. The idea of a regime in which the people would straightaway be legislators and magistrates does not effectively mobilise anyone as much as it seems to refer to a distant and bygone past, corresponding to an archaic and instable stage of political life.'
48. See the writings of Thomas Paine in *Common Sense, Rights of Man, and Other Essential Writings*. Regarding Robespierre, see *Textes choisis* and Rosanvallon's article 'L'histoire du mot démocratie'.
49. Laniel, *Le Mot 'democracy'*, p. 205. Also see further on the same page: 'In the course of the 19th century, the political, constitutional meaning of democracy as a political regime among others loses out more and more against significations both social (the reign of the majority) and ideological (*democratic* justice and virtue are the ultimate objectives of political life).'
50. Rosanvallon, 'L'histoire du mot démocratie', p. 12.

51. Finley, *Democracy Ancient and Modern*, pp. 8–9.
52. Laniel, *Le Mot 'democracy'*, p. 31.
53. Rosanvallon, 'L'histoire du mot démocratie', p. 11.
54. Palmer, 'Notes on the Use of the Word "Democracy"', p. 203.
55. Parry, *Political Elites*, p. 141.
56. Regarding this subject, see note 24.

Section III: Aesthetics

Chapter 7

THE ART OF TALKING PAST ONE ANOTHER: THE BADIOU–RANCIÈRE DEBATE*

Alain Badiou (1937–) and Jacques Rancière (1940–) have come to occupy two of the most prominent positions in contemporary theoretical debates. As the junior faculty members at the University of Paris VIII (Vincennes-St. Denis), they were for a long time in the shadow of the founder of the philosophy department, Michel Foucault (1926–84), and prestigious faculty members like Jean-François Lyotard (1924–98) and Gilles Deleuze (1925–95).[1] Although they are not far in age from Jacques Derrida (1930–2004) and are of the same generation as Jean-Luc Nancy (1940–), Philippe Lacoue-Labarthe (1940–2007) and Étienne Balibar (1942–), the massive importation of 'post-structuralist theory' into the anglophone world – often at the expense of other intellectual developments – created the unfortunate illusion, founded on a veritable parallax in transatlantic visibility, that nothing else of great importance had been going on in France since the 1960s. With the passing away of an older generation and the changing fads of the intellectual world, Badiou and Rancière have now increasingly come into the limelight, often as a pair.

However, in spite of the fact that they have worked for years together in very close proximity and have written on one another's work, their

---

* As noted at the beginning of the book, this essay was not updated to include the most recent writings by these two thinkers, primarily because their positions on the topics analysed have not significantly changed. This is clear, for instance, in the following discussion, which nonetheless has the advantage of elucidating some of their important political differences: 'Contre-courant: Le Face-à-face Badiou-Rancière' (20 May 2014). For relatively recent restatements of their respective positions on the issues studied here, see also Badiou with Fabien Tarby, *La Philosophie et l'événement*, pp. 81–107; Badiou, *Second Manifesto for Philosophy*; and Rancière, *Aisthesis: Scenes from the Aesthetic Regime of Art*.

interactions have generally been decidedly one-sided. Badiou's major essays on Rancière all deal with the question of politics (with only a few passing comments on aesthetics), but the latter has not – to my knowledge – published an extensive reply to Badiou's account of their fundamental dissensus in this area.[2] Instead, he has written articles berating Badiou for his work on aesthetics, and the latter has graced him with the same silent rejoinder, as far as I know.[3] As illuminating as these polemical writings are, one cannot help but wonder why they have not led to responses and to the development of a veritable intellectual exchange and debate.[4] As things stand, it is as if they have cultivated, perhaps unwittingly, the art of talking past one another. They send salvos from two privileged citadels – politics (Badiou) and aesthetics (Rancière) – with little or no reaction from their apparent adversary. In what follows, I would therefore like to try to stage one part of this debate – which is precisely not a debate – by outlining their respective positions on art, while simultaneously considering some of the important political and historical stakes. This will allow us to identify where their paths cross, as well as where they definitively part ways. It will also afford us the opportunity to raise a series of critical questions with an eye to alternative approaches to the question of aesthetic practice and its relationship to politics and history.

ALAIN BADIOU

Unlike many of his French compatriots, Alain Badiou is a self-proclaimed systematic thinker. Although his position on aesthetics has developed since his early writings, I will focus on the more detailed description and systematised account of art he has provided since *Being and Event* (1988) and particularly *Manifesto for Philosophy* (1989).[5] In these works, art, and more precisely 'the poem', is identified as one of the four truth procedures that – along with science, politics and love – constitute the conditions of philosophy. Truth procedures are *not*, according to Badiou, founded on the encyclopaedic accumulation of knowledge. Properly speaking, knowledge (*le savoir*) exists when correct statements are made about a given state of affairs, and nothing occurs that is not in conformity with the rules that regulate this state of affairs. Knowledge can therefore allow us to make veridical (*véridique*) statements through a process of discernment and classification, but it cannot attain truth (*la vérité*), which means that knowledge is fundamentally about 'situations'. Truth for Badiou is a 'post-evental' process dependent on a pure event that supplements the situation, an event that can be neither named nor represented by the resources available in the situation. As a process or procedure, truth introduces an immanent break by tracking the effects of the supplementary event within the situation itself.

Badiou's examples of events include the following: the various instances of what he calls 'modern poetry', Galileo's scientific revolution, the French Revolution and Plato's theorisation of love in the *Symposium*. For each of these events, the same basic process occurs: an undecidable event arises at the edge of the situation; a subject proclaims its existence and decides to relate to the situation from the point of view of the supplemental event; the truth procedure undertaken by the subject attempts to reconfigure the situation in relationship to the truth of the event, which requires resisting the *doxa* or 'knowledge of the situation' in the name of the evental truth of the Idea.[6] This means that, at least at one level, Badiou has an interventionist, process-oriented conception of truth: 'There is only authentic truth under the condition that we can choose truth.'[7]

If truth is an evental hole in our situational knowledge produced via poetry, science, politics or love, what, then, is philosophy? First of all, Badiou rejects what he takes great pleasure in castigating as modern sophism and historicist philosophising. Against the modern sophists, which include the vast majority of his French predecessors, he maintains that there is indeed a definition of philosophy that is a historical invariant (since its inception in ancient Greece). 'Philosophy', he writes, 'is a construction of thought in which it is proclaimed, *against the art of the sophists*, that there are truths.'[8] It is important to add, however, that philosophy is not itself a truth procedure, which means that it does not produce truths. The role of philosophy is to track down and stake out truth procedures in order to group them together in a unified conceptual space. It provides a systematic framework – a 'shelter' – for the protection of artistic, scientific, political and amorous truths. There is, moreover, always the danger of suturing philosophy to one of these truths and putting at risk its role as the neutral guardian of truth procedures. According to Badiou, this has been the case in recent history: philosophy was sutured to science under the reign of positivism; it was sutured to politics in Marxism; and it has been sutured to poetry since the time of Nietzsche.[9] For the philosophic renaissance advocated by

Badiou to be successful, philosophy has to be de-sutured from the four truth procedures.

In relationship to his immediate predecessors in France, Badiou's most notable difference is his stalwart emphasis on Platonism. In the realm of aesthetics, this means that art for him does indeed have an essence that is a historical invariant: it is a singular thought process of Ideas that traces the ephemeral event in the real.[10] This is illustrated by the art form that Badiou openly identifies, in rather Heideggerian fashion, with the very essence of art: the poem. At its core, a poem is an act of naming, for all time, an undecidable evental presence at the limit of the situation.[11] Moreover, as an act of naming the disappearance of that which is presented, 'every poem is an interruption of language, conceived as a simple tool of communication.'[12] In short, a poem is a nominal trace of the event in the sensible that displaces the parameters of the given aesthetic situation.[13] This is precisely what distinguishes true art from false art: the former introduces an immanent break by bringing Ideas into the situation, whereas the latter simply capitalises on possibilities already inventoried within the situation. Art is only true art, and truly acts on an event, if it is an event of thought.[14]

It is important to highlight in this regard that Badiou rigorously maintains the 'principle of genericity',[15] which he inherited in part from Sartre's *What Is Literature?*, and ultimately from Aristotle's *Poetics*. The opening sentence of the latter work clearly announces the first two axioms of this principle. Aristotle proposes to discuss 'both poetic art in itself and its forms [*peri poiētikēs autēs te kai tōn eidōn autēs*]'. This means that: (1) art – more specifically *poiētikē* – exists as a distinct entity in and of itself, and (2) art or *poiētikē* is naturally divided into a set of distinct forms or genres. A third axiom is added later that, in the case of Badiou, has only been partially systematised: (3) the forms or genres of art are arranged according to a natural hierarchy. As we have seen, the essence of art in general is defined by Badiou as 'a thought whose works are the real'.[16] He believes, moreover, in the universality of great works of art, which in striving toward the infinite bear eternal witness to the existence of events.[17] Regarding the delimitation of the arts, Badiou states that 'there is in reality no way to move from one art to another. The arts are closed. No painting will ever change into music, no dance into a poem.'[18] We have already seen, concerning the hierarchical organisation of the arts, that the poem is the acme of art because it names the undecidable event in a language that extracts itself from the standard situation of language. Dance, to take an example from the opposite end of the spectrum, is not even properly speaking an art. Since it lacks words, and therefore the possibility of naming the event, it is only 'the sign of the possibility of art, such as it is inscribed in the body'.[19] Theatre, while not occupying the imperial place of the poem, is nonetheless the positive obverse of dance: it is the arrangement of a near physical presentation of an Idea, which *does* have recourse to words. To return to the lower end of the spectrum, film is classified as the lowest art form because it is 'an impure art'.[20] Whereas painting is the art of donation that provides an integral presentation of the Idea, and music invents the pure time of the Idea by exploring the configurations of the movement of the thinkable, film combines allusions to the more mimetic arts and can only serve, at best, as an art of visitation where Ideas pass by but are never fully embodied.[21] For film to properly act as an art, it therefore only appears to have one path open to it: it has to show that it is *only* film and that 'its images only bear witness to the real insofar as they are *manifestly* images'.[22] The principle regulating the hierarchy of the arts is the Platonic principle of the proximity to the Idea. The poem is closest to the Idea and therefore comes first, followed apparently by theatre (Badiou has yet to systematise these relations). Painting and music seem to be the median arts, whereas film is clearly the lowest and dance is excluded (the precise position of some of the other arts remains unclear). The delimitation of the arts is not strictly speaking based on their media or empirical characteristics but on the very being of each individual art. This is why Badiou delimits his claims regarding the principles of dance in the following way (a delimitation that could be generalised to all art forms): 'Not [the principles] of dance thought out of itself, its technique and its history, but dance such as philosophy receives and protects it.'[23] Ultimately, just as the distinction between art and non-art is founded on the existence or non-existence of thought, the arts are themselves delimited philosophically according to an aesthetic ontology, and they are placed in a hierarchy based on their proximity to the Idea.[24]

In the opening essay of his major work on aesthetics to date, *Handbook of Inaesthetics* (1998), Badiou provides an account of the relationship between his own project and what he sees as the three pre-existing schemas for thinking the connection between art and philosophy. According to the didactic schema, to begin with, 'art is incapable of truth, [...] all truth is exterior to it'.[25] As 'the charm of a semblance of truth', art must, therefore, either be condemned or used in a purely instrumental fashion.[26] The romantic schema takes the opposite approach by asserting that art *alone* is capable of truth. Finally, the classical schema follows the didacticians in maintaining that art is incapable of truth, but it redefines the essence of art as mimetic. Art's distance from truth is thereby no longer worrisome precisely because its destination is *not* truth. On the contrary, art qua mimetic semblance has a therapeutic function, and the rules of art are to be deduced from this function. When Badiou inquires into recent developments in the arts and art theory, he concludes that the twentieth century has not introduced any new schemas. Identifying the three major dispositions of twentieth-century thought as Marxism, psychoanalysis and hermeneutics, he asserts that 'Marxism is didactic, psychoanalysis is classical, and Heideggerian hermeneutics is romantic'.[27] The avant-garde movements (from Dadaism to the Situationists) only added a mediating schema, the didactico-romantic schema. It is against the backdrop of this account that Badiou proposes a new, fourth schema for thinking the relationship between art and philosophy. What is lacking in all prior work, according to him, is a way of thinking art's relationship to truth as being both immanent *and* singular: truth is immanent in art and art is a singular form of truth irreducible to other such forms. It is this very simultaneity that Badiou wants to defend in claiming that art is in and of itself a singular truth procedure. He baptises this new schema 'inaesthetics'.

Badiou has developed his account of contemporary art in *The Century* (2005).[28] Throughout this book, artwork from the twentieth century is marshalled to bear witness to the subjective nature of the century, which Badiou defines as the 'passion for the real [*passion du réel*]'.[29] The works cited are not used, properly speaking, as historical documents, but rather as forms of testimony (*témoignage*) that attest to the subjective commitments of the century. Badiou thus remains faithful to the idea that art *thinks* in and of itself, and he is primarily interested in how the century has thought itself through art and the three other truth procedures. His central claim is that all four truth procedures became impassioned with the real in the twentieth century. They attempted to bring the Idea – qua *real* – into reality by radical acts of foundation aimed at new beginnings, which were disjunctively synthesised with acts of destruction. The entire century, he argues, was structured by non-dialectical battles, which manifested themselves in the art world through the constant avant-garde struggles to overcome pre-existent, classical forms in the name of an Idea. At the very end of the book, Badiou gives 'less esoteric' names to the war of the century, which the reader will easily recognise as a battle between Badiou's major philosophic concepts: the Idea and reality, the event and the situational state of affairs, truth and opinions, and so forth.[30]

It is therefore not difficult to reconcile Badiou's references to historical developments with his more systematic, ahistorical work on aesthetics: even though circumstances might change with time, the very essence of art nevertheless remains the same.[31] This central idea is perhaps best illustrated in the preface to *Logics of Worlds* (2006), where Badiou claims that in spite of all of the circumstantial differences separating Picasso from the authors of the cave paintings at Chauvet-Pont-d'Arc, their respective renderings of horses nonetheless attest to the same fundamental truth: the eternal Idea of a horse. The multiplicity of worlds does not preclude, according to Badiou, the existence of universal truths.

JACQUES RANCIÈRE

While it is true that Jacques Rancière's early work on politics and history shows signs of a longstanding interest in aesthetics, it is primarily since the 1990s that he has presented what has become a general account of the arts.[32] Unlike Badiou, who has written relatively few books dedicated exclusively to art, Rancière's publication record constitutes a veritable tour de force in the field of aesthetics. It might be said that whereas Badiou is more interested in establishing a totalising philosophic system in which aesthetics plays a significant role, Rancière has dedicated his intellectual energies to making a singular intervention in the field of aesthetics, in much the same way as he has done in the fields of history and politics. He obviously does not share Badiou's penchant for grand theories, and his philosophic strategies owe more to guerrilla warfare than to epic frontal offensives à la Badiou.

This difference in scope and strategy is at least one of the reasons why the Badiou/Rancière debate has largely been a *dialogue de sourds*, that is to say, an exchange in which they talk past one another. In one of the rare passages where Badiou explicitly engages with Rancière's aesthetics, he tries to situate him within what he calls the 'subjectivity of the century' by suggesting that some of his work is a 'sophisticated echo' of what he sees as the *Tel Quel* thesis, that is, that the formal mutations of art are more political than politics itself.[33] Whether or not one agrees with the orientation Rancière has taken in his recent writings, it is important to avoid restricting his work – as Badiou appears to be doing in this passage – to the opposition in post-war France between content-based commitment and formal commitment. Successful or unsuccessful, Rancière clearly wants to take a decisive step in aesthetics by breaking with both the Sartrean notion of prosaic commitment and the *Tel Quel* claims regarding the political potential of aesthetic form. To take but two representative publications, it might be said that what Rancière wants to reject is the simplistic choice between following Sartre's work in *What Is Literature?* (1948) and Barthes's formalist reworking of Sartre's thesis in *The Degree Zero of Writing* (1953). Rather than looking for the political dimension of art in the content of prose or in the third dimension of form (what Barthes calls *l'écriture*, distinct from both *la langue* and *le style*), Rancière wants to shift the conceptual tectonic plates upon which this opposition is based. The very notion of 'politicised art' presupposes that art and politics are distinct entities that can be joined, either by prosaic content (Sartre) or through writing as a social function (Barthes). However, it is precisely this presupposition that Rancière wants to reject. Art and politics, he claims, are in fact consanguineous insofar as they are both distributions of the sensible (*partages du sensible*), that is, ways of organising the field of sensory experience by determining what is visible and audible, as well as what can be said, thought, made or done. As a distribution of the sensible, art is inherently political precisely insofar as it presents a common world of experience (replete with a set of shared objects and recognised subjects), which distinguishes what is possible from what is impossible.

Rather than the *Tel Quel* group, the most obvious predecessor to Rancière's work is Michel Foucault. Although Foucault was occasionally close to the *Tel Quel* group, his understanding of literature in his early writings goes beyond the framework of formal commitment. Literature was seen as a unique discourse born with the emergence of the modern *episteme* and the appearance of the human sciences around the end of the eighteenth century. In negating the existence of man and resisting the instrumentalisation of language, it was properly speaking a 'counter-discourse' aimed at bringing language back to its brute being, which had been buried since the Renaissance. The historical appearance of literature is thus structurally equivalent to the return of the repressed at the end of the classical age: the brute being of non-representational language in its open relationship to madness (and after the 'death of God'). When all is said and done, literature 'compensates' European culture for its repression of madness by abandoning the strict Cartesian delimitation between reason and unreason, thereby allowing language to escape from the imperial mastery of the rational human subject.[34]

Although Rancière does not share Foucault's preoccupation with madness and collective repression, the latter's historical approach to literature is essential to Rancière's project: 'The genealogy of the concept of literature that I have attempted in *La Parole muette* [*Mute Speech*], or in my current work on the systems of art, could be expressed in terms close to Foucault's concept of *episteme*.'[35] Like Foucault, Rancière takes art to be a historically constituted practice that is always situated within a framework of possibility. This framework, which Rancière calls a *regime* instead of an *episteme*, has undergone significant transformations through the course of history. These changes vaguely follow the historical delimitation outlined by Foucault in his early work between the classical age and the modern age. However, Rancière's regimes differ from Foucault's *epistemes* in a few important ways. First of all, regimes are not mutually exclusive chronological blocks. Unlike *epistemes*, the chronology of regimes conforms to Augustine's description of the temporality of human souls in *The City of God*: although they are created in time, they will apparently never perish in time. The ethical regime of images, which was born in ancient Greece, and the representative regime of arts, which dominated the classical age, both persist in the modern age, that is to say, the age that has been marked by the emergence of the third major regime: the aesthetic regime of art. Rancière thereby rejects the idea that structural blocks hegemonically dominate a given epoch until being cataclysmically replaced, through a discontinuous event, by another structural block. Although Foucault's position was more nuanced than this since he did allow for the possibility of a 'counter-discourse' like literature, it is nonetheless clear that, for Rancière, the 'modern' era is characterised by conflicting regimes and that there are no tragic events separating historical epochs. To borrow from one of André Robinet's criticisms of Foucault, which perfectly encapsulates Rancière's reworking of Foucauldian *epistemes*, the conflict is not simply *between* time periods but *within* them.[36]

These differences in historical methodology lead to a divergence in hermeneutic practice. At least in his early work, Foucault tended to interpret individual works of art as signs of their times that reveal structural conditions of possibility. Rancière is more interested in showing how individual works of art make choices within and between conflicting regimes by actualising certain potentialities and ignoring others. Works of art can still be held up as indices of their historical conjuncture, but Rancière tends to focus on the ways in which each work carves out a unique space between the axioms of various regimes. He wants to avoid monolithic accounts of art-historical epochs in favour of a more detailed analysis of the specificity of individual works. In methodological terms, this amounts to saying that Rancière resists one of the working assumptions of what's called 'structuralism', namely that there is a single set of determinants behind the totality – or a given set – of phenomena. At the same time, he is generally allergic to the 'post-structuralist' reflex that consists in claiming that *every* structure is fissured and de-centred.[37] In short, Rancière rejects the simplistic choice between a totalising structure and a de-centred structure by postulating that competing frameworks and axioms are at work within the same time period.

This being said, the backdrop to all of Rancière's recent studies in aesthetics is never difficult to discern: the three regimes of art, which are so many 'distributions of the sensible'. The ethical regime of images, to begin with, is best exemplified in the work of Plato. Within this regime, images are arranged and distributed according to their origin and their telos, based on how they can best educate the citizenry and contribute to the ethos of the community. The representative regime of arts, rooted in Aristotle's critique of Plato, liberated 'the arts' from the communal ethos by redefining them as fictional imitations of action. This amounted to isolating an autonomous domain of fiction founded on a series of axioms of representation: the hierarchy of subject matter and genres, the principle of appropriateness by which modes of expression and action are to conform to the subject matter and genre, and the privileging of speech over action. The aesthetic regime of art abolishes the autonomous domain of fiction by blurring the lines between art and life. It also dismantles the axioms of representation by dissolving the hierarchy of subject matter and genres, promoting the indifference of style with regard to content, and privileging writing over the present truth of speech.

Since Rancière's work concentrates primarily on the contradiction between – and within – the representative and aesthetic regimes of art, it will be helpful to elucidate one extended example of this conflict. In the representative regime, which dominated the classical age, there was a strict hierarchical distinction between subject matter worthy of representation and subject matter that was best left outside of the artistic frame. Since around the end of the eighteenth century, this hierarchy has been widely contested in the name of the egalitarian principle that anything can become an object of art. Rancière cites the example of Flaubert's decision to write an entire novel on the adulterous affairs of a promiscuous, bourgeois woman prone to novelistic fantasy: *Madame Bovary*. However, he traces this 'aesthetic revolution' back to the later Kant and German Romanticism, where he finds an attempt to overcome the representative hierarchy between intelligent form and sensible matter (which is perhaps most visible in Schiller's concept of *Spiel*).

It is precisely this egalitarian principle of the aesthetic regime that would later allow for the emergence of the mechanical arts of photography and film. Rancière argues, against Walter Benjamin, that in order for these to be recognised as arts, it was first necessary that it be recognised that *anything* could become the subject matter of art, including the recording of brute reality devoid – in principle – of all aesthetic hierarchies. In other words, photography and film became possible only after the artistic revolution that introduced the aesthetic regime of art. The technological revolution, for Rancière, came after the artistic revolution.[38] He makes a very similar argument concerning the historical emergence of psychoanalysis, which only became possible after the breakdown of the representative hierarchy between consciousness and the unconscious, logos and pathos.

Rancière refers to art within the aesthetic regime in much the same way as his American counterpart, Arthur Danto: the art of the commonplace (*l'art du quelconque*). Since there is no longer any hierarchy of subject matter in the aesthetic regime, anything – any commonplace object or occurrence – can in principle become art. This is, of course, what Danto argued in his more recent analyses of the art world since Andy Warhol's 1964 *Brillo Box* project.[39] In producing objects that were visually identical to industrially produced Brillo boxes and lacked the artist's signature, Warhol definitively dissolved the borderlines between art and commonplace objects. Although the Danto/Rancière debate never occurred, it is nonetheless easy enough to underscore one inevitable point of contention. For Rancière, unlike for Danto, the postmodern era is not a separate historical sequence; it is only the unfolding of possibilities inherent in the aesthetic regime of art since approximately the late eighteenth century. In other words, Warhol's *Brillo Box* project is nothing more than a contemporary variation on a theme going back to Flaubert, Schiller and other artists of the aesthetic regime. As with Foucault's discontinuous events, Rancière rejects the idea of a 'postmodern break'.

In spite of this difference in historical analysis and in historiographical method, Rancière and Danto at least partially agree on the fundamental contradiction of the art of the commonplace. We can take as an example here Joseph Beuys's *7000 Eichen* project, which he began in 1982 for Documenta 7 by planting oak trees in Kassel, Germany, and which he hoped would be extended throughout the world as a global mission to effect social and environmental change. In Rancière's terms, the contradiction of such art of the commonplace can be expressed in two ways: (1) 'Art of the *commonplace*' is only *commonplace* by losing its status as art (in the case of Beuys, the artist is confounded with the urban planner or forester); (2) '*Art* of the commonplace' must not be entirely commonplace in order to remain *art* (the *artistic* gesture of planting trees is only maintained by its link to Beuys's name as an artist, implicitly manifest in the columnar basalt markers accompanying the trees). Danto privileged the first formulation of this contradiction by arguing that the distinction between art and non-art is no longer guaranteed by a systematic historical narrative: 'Today there is no longer any pale of history. Everything is permitted.'[40] In the contradictory era of the 'end of art', it is up to the philosopher to distinguish between what is properly art and what is not. Rancière emphasises both formulations of this contradiction and maintains that there is no way of resolving it. In fact, he views it as a 'productive contradiction' insofar as the search for solutions has been the driving force behind two centuries of artistic production.

CONCLUDING QUESTIONS

Although there is much more that could be said about Badiou and Rancière, it should at least be clear to what extent their positions on aesthetics differ. First of all, Rancière rejects Badiou's Platonic essentialism in favour of a historical approach to artistic regimes. It is not surprising, therefore, to see him castigate Badiou for talking about Plato's theory of art, reminding him that for Plato and the ethical regime of images, 'art' in the singular did not exist, only images properly distributed for the good of the ethos. According to Rancière, there is no art in general, there are only aesthetic practices and theories within historical regimes. In conformity with his explanatory and synthetic polemics, by which his criticisms of authors simultaneously serve to situate these same authors within his own theory, Rancière perceives behind Badiou's anti-aestheticism a convoluted conflict between different regimes of art. On the one hand, Badiou aligns himself with the modernism born out of the aesthetic regime, meaning the attempt to embrace the singularity of art while refusing its forms of disidentification (where the limits between art and non-art dissipate). On the other hand, Badiou's 'ultra-Platonism' – which is ultimately indebted to the romantic Platonism of the aesthetic age – reveals his adherence to one of the axioms of the ethical regime, which he maintains via a *mimetic* division of the arts: the poem is of value only insofar as it serves to instruct us on the Idea. These two positions have a common goal, which is to construct a philosophic bulwark against the aesthetic regime's dissolution of the 'proper' of art. If this bulwark is destined to fail, it is precisely because the proper of 'modern' art, according to Rancière, is to be improper, to disturb and unsettle hierarchical distributions of the sensible such as the one that elevates art above the commonplace.

We can add to Rancière's primary criticism of Badiou a list of additional problems that are visible in his work on aesthetics. To begin with, his theorisation of art is largely dependent on a historically specific conception of aesthetics that is unique to the modern age. By assuming that art is an iconoclastic gesture refusing the norms of the day in order to venture beyond the givens of the situation, Badiou's working understanding of art is clearly rooted in a romantic ideal proper to the modern age.[41] However, this historical specificity is not recognised and assumed as such, and the iconoclastic conception of art is hegemonically imposed as a universal on the entire history of 'art'. Secondly, Badiou relies on a simplistic distinction between true art and entertainment that he unquestioningly inherits from a hierarchy operative in the social field, which has been analysed in detail, for instance, by Pierre Bourdieu in *Distinction*. Thirdly, Badiou – much like Sartre – doggedly adheres to the principle of genericity while focusing on an era (the last two centuries) in which the distinctions between the arts have been regularly called into question, both in theory and in practice. Finally, Badiou's approach to art is largely dependent on what might be called *illustrative hermeneutics*.[42] Like many of his fellow admirers of Lacan, he tends to 'discover' in art an illustration of his own philosophic concepts. It is true, of course, that he has gone to great lengths to try and show that this is not the case. He repeatedly affirms, for instance, that art *thinks for itself* and that the philosopher cannot think in its place. However, if we follow Badiou's logic through to the end, we cannot help but wonder if he has done anything other than philosophically colonise the art world. As we have already seen, the distinction between art and non-art, as well as the delimitation and hierarchisation of the arts, are all based on defining art strictly in terms of thought and reifying the Platonic distinction between Ideas and opinions. In claiming that art *thinks*, hasn't Badiou already commandeered the very essence of art by making it coterminous with the privileged material of philosophy (thought)? Isn't the apparent elevation of art (art *thinks* like philosophy) simply a disguised denigration (art is only of value, and therefore only truly art, if it is elevated – by the philosopher's act of recognition – to a supposedly superior level by thinking)? Isn't art always secondary to philosophy since artistic practice is only of value and interest insofar as it produces thoughts, which are then humbly welcomed by philosophers into the palace of Ideas? Isn't this why assiduous readers such as Rancière cannot help but recognise which artistic 'thoughts' actually make it into the realm of Ideas, which are always more or less subtle translations of Badiou's *own* ideas?[43] If these questions are answered in the affirmative, then Badiou can be legitimately criticised, like his fellow traveller Slavoj Žižek, for using art as an illustration of his own concepts while feigning an illuminating process of discovery.[44] It is important to remind ourselves in this regard that the illustration of a philosophic idea in a work of art no more explains the work of art than it proves the philosophic idea; it simply extends a pre-existent theory through a rhetorical logic of transubstantiation by which philosophic ideas are translated more or less cunningly into artistic practices.

Rancière's project is equally open to a series of criticisms. To begin with, his description of the regimes of art is thus far devoid of any developed genetic account that explains why these regimes emerged.[45] Part of this is due to his allergy to the social sciences and to 'externalist' accounts of the arts that directly engage with the transformation of institutions and artistic practices in the modern era.[46] Secondly, the scope of Rancière's description of the three major artistic regimes needs to be qualified. From the Greeks down to the present, these are apparently the only regimes that have existed, and yet Rancière has still not provided any detailed study of the Middle Ages or the Renaissance. Moreover, although he occasionally makes reference to the 'Western tradition' (a very problematic notion), it is unclear to what extent these regimes are unique to a particular geographic or cultural region. Thirdly, his affirmation of the consubstantiality of art and politics is only justified as a historical claim demonstrated through the analysis of specific artistic and intellectual communities. When this assertion is transformed into an ontological constant, it is in dire need of proof in order to be validated. It is arguable that, as things stand, the ontological affirmation of the consanguinity of art and politics is simply based on defining them tautologically as distributions of the sensible. If this is the case, nothing can preclude anyone else from defining art and politics in different ways and drawing alternative conclusions.

This last problem in Rancière's work points to one of the fundamental issues – and problems, I would argue – that links Rancière and Badiou: the ontologisation, or meta-ontologisation, of aesthetics. Although Rancière goes to great lengths to show that art is a thoroughly historical phenomenon, his readers cannot help but be struck by at least one level of ontologisation. He affirms that works of art have a politics inherent in their very being, which is independent of any explicit political intention on the part of the artist and distinct from the gradual constitution of a work of art through its circulation in the social field. Works of art are produced as a combination of the various 'objective politics' inscribed in the distribution of the sensible and manifest in the plastic and narrative field of possibilities at a given moment.[47] As a philosopher of art, Rancière appears to be the only one who has access to this objective political being of art. While it is true that he highlights the historical formation of this political being, there is little or no room for a veritable account of the circulation and reception of works of art and how this social dimension relates to their political potential. The very being of art is fixed in relationship to the possibilities inherent in the regimes of art. Since Badiou lacks Rancière's historical sensibilities, his theorisation of art is founded on a much more explicit aesthetic ontology. As we have seen, the very being of art is defined in terms of an unchanging structural relationship between situations and events: art is a truth procedure that bears the trace of the passage of the event and interrupts the representational situation in which it occurs by naming 'the un-nameable'. This mode of being of art is precisely what qualifies it – and what has ostensibly always qualified it – as art proper. The discrepancy between these respective forms of aesthetic ontology allows us to conclude by returning to one of the most fundamental differences between Rancière and Badiou: whereas the latter disdains historicism as a sophistic flight from the mighty heights of essentialism, the former insists on the need to situate art theory and practice within the flow of time, including the theory and practice of his Platonist colleague.[48]

NOTES

1. On the history of the philosophy department at the University of Paris VIII, see Charles Soulié's article 'Le Destin d'une institution d'avant-garde'.
2. See Badiou's two chapters on Rancière in *Abrégé de métapolitique/Metapolitics* and his article in Cornu and Vermeren (eds), *La Philosophie déplacée*, which is available in English in Rockhill and Watts (eds), *Jacques Rancière: History, Politics, Aesthetics*.
3. See Rancière's articles in Ramond (ed.), *Alain Badiou: Penser le multiple* and in *Politique de la littérature*. The first article is available in English in Hallward (ed.), *Think Again: Alain Badiou and the Future of Philosophy*.
4. There are some minor exceptions to this general tendency, particularly in the case of conferences and public debates such as those organised at the Collège international de philosophie (some of which have been published). See, for instance, Badiou, Lacoue-Labarthe, Lyotard and Rancière, 'Liminaire sur l'ouvrage d'Alain Badiou *L'Être et l'événement*', and Badiou, Bellour, Martin and Rancière, 'Autour de *La parole muette* de Jacques Rancière'.
5. For reasons of space, the current analysis focuses on Badiou's theoretical – as opposed to his literary – writings.
6. For the purposes of concision, I am primarily drawing on Badiou's more schematic account of events in books like *Manifesto for Philosophy* and *Ethics*. For a more detailed account, which introduces the important distinction between the 'situation' and the 'state of the situation' (as well as between presentation and representation, count-as-one and the count of the count, structure and metastructure, and so forth), see *Being and Event*.
7. Badiou, *Petit Manuel d'inesthétique*, p. 86/*Handbook of Inaesthetics*, p. 54 (all translations are my own). Badiou rejects, however, what he calls 'speculative leftism', which imagines that interventions are founded solely on their own iconoclastic desire for new beginnings instead of being temporally

inscribed in the circulation of events that have already been decided upon. Strictly speaking, it is the event that founds the possibility of an intervention, for Badiou, even though it is only through an intervention that an event 'exists' by circulating in the situation.
8. Badiou, *Conditions*, p. 65; see also pp. 79–82.
9. See Badiou, *Manifeste pour la philosophie*, p. 59/*Manifesto for Philosophy*, p. 79.
10. It is, of course, open to debate whether this is Plato's own view of art or, more precisely, *poiēsis*.
11. The influence of Heidegger is readily visible in Badiou's work on aesthetics. However, it would be a mistake to hastily identify their positions without being attentive to the points on which they diverge. Although a detailed comparison of their work goes well beyond the framework of the current analysis, it is nonetheless possible to highlight a series of similarities and differences. Regarding the points of convergence, both Heidegger and Badiou agree that: (1) art has an essence; (2) the essence of art is the becoming or occurrence of truth; (3) art can be distinguished from non-art based on its relationship – or lack thereof – to truth; (4) great art, which is the only true art, is clearly distinguishable from entertainment and other forms of non-art; (5) poetry constitutes the very essence of art. Among their points of divergence, the following list can serve as a starting point: (1) art is only one truth procedure among four according to Badiou, whereas it becomes one of the central, privileged avenues for truth in Heidegger; (2) truth is defined as an eventual hole in the situation for Badiou, whereas it is understood as *alētheia* or unconcealedness by Heidegger; (3) Badiou explicitly rejects Heidegger as a Romantic and accuses him of suturing philosophy to poetry. At a more general level, one of the clear dividing lines between Badiou and Heidegger is their interpretation and evaluation of Platonism. Badiou repudiates what he labels as Heidegger's 'poetic ontology' and the latter's critique of the Platonic retreat from poetic *alētheia* due to his interpretation of Being as *idea*. Against Heidegger's conception of the history of metaphysics, Badiou valorises Platonism as an essential part of the originary moment of philosophy insofar as it participates in the birth of 'mathematical ontology'.
12. Badiou, *Petit Manuel d'inesthétique*, p. 124/*Handbook of Inaesthetics*, p. 80.
13. Badiou spurns the 'Christly [*christique*]' vision of truth inherent in the idea that the work of art is *both* a truth *and* an event (ibid., p. 24/p. 11). However, he nonetheless states: 'Since the poem is an operation, it is also an event' (ibid., p. 51/p. 29).
14. Badiou appears to be remarkably close to Gilles Deleuze on this point and, in particular, to the position outlined in his two-volume analysis of film. Among his numerous objectives, Deleuze wanted to demonstrate

that the great film directors had thought with images in much the same way as great thinkers (see *Cinéma 1. L'Image-mouvement*, p. 7/*Cinema 1: The Movement-Image*, p. xiv). This explains, moreover, the centrality in his analysis of Bergson, whose philosophical thinking on movement and time is strictly coextensive with the thinking of movement and time within the history of filmic images (this is made extremely explicit in the recordings of his seminar entitled *Gilles Deleuze: Cinéma*). However, this proximity between Badiou and Deleuze is only partial. As we will see, film is for Badiou the impure art par excellence, which constantly runs the risk of slipping into simple entertainment or dissolving the strict limits that structure the relationship between the arts.

15. Although I am borrowing this expression from Rancière, I am not using it in exactly the same sense as he does in *Mute Speech*.
16. Badiou, *Petit Manuel d'inesthétique*, p. 21/*Handbook of Inaesthetics*, p. 9. See also 'Fifteen Theses on Contemporary Art': 'an artistic truth is a happening of *l'Idée* in the sensible itself' (p. 106).
17. See Badiou, *Petit Manuel d'inesthétique*, p. 75/*Handbook of Inaesthetics*, p. 46. A similar idea is developed in 'Fifteen Theses on Contemporary Art': 'Art is not the sublime descent of the infinite into the finite abjection of the body and sexuality. It is the production of an infinite subjective series through the finite means of a material subtraction' (pp. 103–4).
18. Badiou, *Petit Manuel d'inesthétique*, p. 127/*Handbook of Inaesthetics*, p. 82.
19. Ibid., p. 109/p. 69 (see also p. 97/p. 61 and p. 107/pp. 67–8). Seven years later, in *Le Siècle*, Badiou writes that dance is, since the Russian ballets of Isadora Duncan, 'a major art [*un art capital*]' (p. 224/*The Century*, p. 159). As with the example in the note above of the relationship between Badiou's stance on truth and his critical comment regarding the Christly vision of truth, it is unclear whether this is an oversight on his part, a contradiction in his work, an element easily clarified within his system, or, in this particular case, the sign of an evolution in his thinking.
20. Badiou, *Petit Manuel d'inesthétique*, p. 128/*Handbook of Inaesthetics*, p. 83.
21. See ibid., p. 134/p. 87 and pp. 126–7/p. 82.
22. Badiou, 'Dialectiques de la fable', in Badiou et al., *Matrix*, p. 120. While it is true that all art forms, according to Badiou, have their own limit where they alienate themselves from 'true art', it is clear that film is the lowest of the arts because it is the most susceptible to this danger, especially when compared, for instance, to literature: 'Film, that great impurifier, always runs the risk of pleasing too much, of being a figure of debasement. True literature, which is rigorous purification, runs the risk of getting lost in a proximity to the concept in which the effect of art is exhausted itself and prose (or poetry) is sutured to philosophy' (*Petit Manuel d'inesthétique*, p. 135/*Handbook of Inaesthetics*, p. 88).

23. Badiou, *Petit Manuel d'inesthétique*, p. 99/*Handbook of Inaesthetics*, pp. 62–3. In another statement that could be generalised for all of the arts, Badiou asserts, regarding film, that formal elements must only be invoked to the extent that they contribute to the passing of the Idea (ibid., p. 131/p. 85).
24. Strictly speaking, Badiou claims that his delimitation of the arts is based not on genres but on 'configurations'. A configuration is an identifiable sequence that produces a truth for a particular art, and it is philosophy's role to outline such configurations. As examples, Badiou cites 'Greek tragedy', 'classical music' and 'the novel' (ibid., pp. 26–7/p. 13). His rejection of the term 'genre' for these art forms is an additional indication that the delimitation of the arts is of a deeply philosophic nature.
25. Ibid., p. 10/p. 2.
26. Ibid., p. 11/p. 2.
27. Ibid., p. 15/p. 5.
28. 'Fifteen Theses on Contemporary Art' is an equally good example that focuses on art in the era of 'globalisation'.
29. In addition to the criticisms of Badiou's work that will be highlighted in the conclusion, it is worth noting that his personification of 'the century' is rife with historiographical problems, including those poignantly described by Henri Focillon: 'We have trouble not conceiving a century like a living being, refusing it a resemblance with man himself. Each century shows itself to us with its colour, its physiognomy, and projects the shadow of a certain silhouette' (*Vie des formes*, pp. 84–5).
30. *Le Siècle*, p. 231/*The Century*, p. 164.
31. One way of understanding Badiou's references to history is in relationship to his appropriation of the Hegelian notion of 'concrete universality' (see 'The Adventure of French Philosophy') and his definition of 'historical ages' as 'epochal situations of philosophy' (see Badiou, 'L'Age des poètes', in Rancière (ed.), *La Politique des poètes*.
32. For an instructive account of Rancière's early work in light of his most recent interests in aesthetics, see his 'The Method of Equality' in Rockhill and Watts (eds), *Jacques Rancière: History, Politics, Aesthetics*.
33. Badiou, *Le Siècle*, p. 210/*The Century*, p. 148.
34. Literature also acts as the rabbit hole that allows Foucault to go through the looking glass of the modern *episteme*, as is evident most notably in the role played by Borges in the preface to *The Order of Things*.
35. Rancière, 'Literature, Politics, Aesthetics', p. 13.
36. See Robinet, *Le Langage à l'âge classique*. An excellent example of Rancière's rejection of discontinuist historiography can be found in his criticisms of Deleuze's work on film, most notably in *La Fable cinématographique* (*Film Fables*) and 'Les Écarts du cinéma'. Unfortunately, Rancière has not

sufficiently taken into account Deleuze's conception of becoming and its effects on his historical methodology (compare 'Les Écarts du cinéma', p. 165, and *Cinéma 2. L'Image-temps*, p. 59/*Cinema 2: The Time-Image*, p. 41).
37. I use the categories 'structuralism' and 'post-structuralism' as purely heuristic tools. Since this is not the place to assess their explanatory power, let it suffice to say that I think they should be used with the utmost caution in discussing developments in post-war French thought.
38. For a critical evaluation of the positions taken by Rancière and Benjamin, see my 'Le Cinéma n'est jamais né' in Déotte (ed.), *Le Milieu des appareils*, pp. 187–211.
39. See Danto, *Beyond the Brillo Box* and *After the End of Art*.
40. Danto, *After the End of Art*, p. 12.
41. On this topic, see the work of Nathalie Heinich, most notably *L'Élite artiste* and *Être artiste*.
42. Another essential question for Badiou is whether his work in *The Century* has served to supplement his illustrative hermeneutics with a form of illustrative historiography: is the supposed 'passion for the real' simply a projected illustration of Badiou's concepts in terms of a century-long battle over them? For an extremely pertinent sociological analysis of these illustrative strategies in philosophic discourse, see Louis Pinto's *Les Philosophes entre le lycée et l'avant-garde*.
43. In 'Esthétique, inesthétique, anti-esthétique', Rancière writes, concerning Badiou: 'The poem only says what philosophy needs it to say and what it feigns to discover in the surprise of the poem' (in Ramond (ed.), *Alain Badiou: Penser le multiple*, p. 491).
44. For an excellent critique of Žižek's illustrative hermeneutics, see David Bordwell's 'Slavoj Žižek: Say Anything' (April 2005). Also see Judith Butler's comments in Butler, Laclau and Žižek, *Contingency, Hegemony, Universality*, most notably p. 26 and pp. 156–7.
45. For a detailed critique of Rancière on this point, see my contribution to Cornu and Vermeren (eds), *La Philosophie déplacée*, which has been translated into English as Chapter 3 of this book.
46. Foucault's break with his early position on literature is enlightening in this regard (see Droit, *Michel Foucault, entretiens*).
47. See Rancière, 'The Janus-Face of Politicised Art', in *The Politics of Aesthetics*, p. 60: 'Commitment is not a category of art. This does not mean that art is apolitical. It means that aesthetics has its own politics, or its own meta-politics. That is what I was saying earlier regarding Flaubert and microscopic equality. There are politics of aesthetics, forms of community laid out by the very regime of identification in which we perceive art (hence pure art as well as committed art). Moreover, a "committed" work of art is always made as a kind of combination between these objective

politics that are inscribed in the field of possibility for writing, objective politics that are inscribed as plastic or narrative possibilities.'
48. See Badiou's revealing comments on his relationship to Rancière at the end of *Logiques des mondes* (pp. 586–7), where he claims that they share a common philosophic fidelity to the 'red' sequence (1965–80) in spite of their different relationship to History.

Chapter 8

THE HERMENEUTICS OF ART AND POLITICAL HISTORY IN RANCIÈRE

RANCIÈRE'S POLITICS OF AESTHETICS AND THE RECENT HISTORY OF POLITICISED ART

In the recent history of politicised art, two forms are readily identifiable. The first might be called content-based commitment and is founded on the representation of politicised subject matter. The second, which might be referred to as formal commitment, locates the political dimension of works of art in their mode of representation or expression rather than in the subject matter represented. In the post-war era in France, content-based commitment is often identified with the work of Jean-Paul Sartre. Roland Barthes's *The Degree Zero of Writing* (1953), a critical re-appropriation of Sartre's *What Is Literature?* (1948), can be seen as one of the pivotal publications in the turn toward more formal concerns, which eventually led to the work of what are now called the French structuralists and post-structuralists, the *Tel Quel* group, the *nouveau roman* circles, and certain members of the French New Wave.

There is, however, a notable difference between these two socially recognised positions on the question of artistic commitment and the specific arguments formulated by the authors and artists who purportedly defended them. It is worth recalling, for instance, the following features of Sartre's position in *What Is Literature?* and other publications from the same time period: he generally restricted the notion of commitment to prose; he affirmed that the very act of writing leads to an inevitable form of commitment independent of the author's intentions; he insisted on the importance of the literary and stylistic dimension of committed prose; he formulated a distinct conception of poetic *engagement*; he made explicit reference to a type of reader's commitment based on the social nature of writing; and he considered that *engagement* was always bound to a specific situation.[1] Concerning the work of Roland Barthes, it should be remembered that the history of *l'écriture* he proposes in *The Degree Zero of Writing* is not a history of style or language (*la langue*) but a history of the formal signs used by an author to situate his or her writing in relationship to society. In other words, when he claims that Form remains 'the first and last instance of [literary] responsibility', he is not referring to an author's style or to language in general but to a third formal reality, writing, that links literary production to the larger social order.[2] Writing is what he calls an act of historical solidarity by which an author, through a general choice of tone and of an 'ethos', commits herself or himself to a particular conception of language and its relationship to various sectors of society. Barthes's work in *Mythologies* (1957) extended this reflection on the social function of signs – irreducible to the standard form/content distinction – outside the domain of literature to include the entire field of cultural production.

It is partially in response to these two positions on commitment and the intellectual communities within which they emerged that Jacques Rancière has formulated an alternative conception of the relationship between art and politics. Instead of searching for the definitive solution to the longstanding problem of the connection between these two realms, he attacks the guiding assumption upon which this problem is based: that art and politics are separate domains in need of being linked together.[3] The notion of the 'distribution of the sensible [*partage du sensible*]' succinctly sums up Rancière's unique position: art and politics are consubstantial insofar as they organise a common world of self-evident facts of sense perception.[4] In fact, the very delimitation and definition of what is called 'art' and 'politics' is itself dependent upon a distribution of the sensible or a regime of thought and perception that identifies them as such.[5] Rancière has thus far outlined three principle regimes of identification for the arts (the ethical regime of images, the representative regime of the arts, and the aesthetic regime of art), which very loosely correspond to three regimes of politics (archi-politics, para-politics and meta-politics). In other words, he not only rejects the idea that there is an a priori separation between art and politics, but he also argues that these are 'contingent notions': 'The fact that there are always forms of power does not mean that there is always such a thing as politics, and the fact that there is music or sculpture in a society does not mean that art is constituted as an independent category.'[6]

Rancière's criticisms of his contemporaries never compel him to simply discard their theories as incorrect. On the contrary, he goes to great lengths to show that their mistaken assumptions are the result of certain structural conditions produced by a regime of thought. In other words, his polemics are always explanatory or synthetic polemics insofar as he insists on providing a genealogical account of the theories he attempts to refute. In this way, he not only purports to disprove the theories he is arguing against, but he simultaneously co-opts them as elements in his own system of explanation. For example, he calls into question Sartre's distinction between the transitivity of prose writing and the intransitivity of poetry by highlighting the difficulty he had explaining why prose writers such as Flaubert used language intransitively like poets. He then relates Sartre's assessment of Flaubert's 'petrification of language' to similar critiques that had been formulated in the nineteenth century (most notably by Charles de Rémusat, Barbey d'Aurevilly and Léon Bloy) and claims that Sartre's work participates in the same interpretive regime.[7] This means that Sartre's mistaken position is in fact the result of a new set of interpretive possibilities introduced by the aesthetic regime of art, which reconfigured the function of meaning ('a relationship between signs and other signs' rather than a 'relation of address from one will to another'), the interpretation of writing (which was no longer considered to be the imposition of one will on another but rather an act of presenting and deciphering symptoms), and the role of politics in interpretation (which became centred on the investigation of the underbelly of society through the symptoms of history instead of on the conflict of wills and interests sharing a common stage of struggle).[8] Rancière refers to this new interpretive model, which attempts to tell the truth about literary discourse by deciphering its hidden political message, as the '"political" or "scientific" explanation of literature'.[9] Although Sartre criticised Flaubert's 'aristocratic assault against the democratic nature of prose language', he shared the same interpretive framework as the nineteenth-century critics who condemned Flaubert's disregard for the distinction between high and low subject matter as a symptom of democracy.[10] In both cases, it is a matter of interpreting literary discourse as the symptom of a latent political meaning. This symptomatological approach to literature is in fact part of a longstanding tradition that emerged within the aesthetic regime and has spanned at least the last 150 years, from Marx and Freud to Benjamin and Bourdieu.[11] In rejecting its account of the relationship between art and politics, Rancière simultaneously integrates it into his own system of historical explanation.

Roland Barthes's early work, most notably *Mythologies* (1957), was heavily indebted to the tradition that held meaning to be latent in works themselves and in need of interpretation. According to the terms he would later use in *Camera Lucida* (1980), he concentrated solely on the *studium* at the expense of the *punctum*. Whereas the former is a set of decipherable meanings and significations, the latter is an affective force that resists all forms of explanation. The evolution of Barthes's corpus, according to Rancière, attests to an attempt to atone for his early sins as a mythologist who purported to have transformed the spectacle of the sensible into a system of symptoms. He did this by privileging the *punctum* that escapes all mythological interpretation and remains an insurmountable obstacle to the exchange of meaning. This decision is not unrelated to a conception of art that Rancière has identified most notably with the work of Adorno and Lyotard. Art in this tradition is no longer the symptom of a political meaning, but rather art is political precisely insofar as it resists the communicational flow of meaning and the exchange economy of signs. Art, it might be said, is political because it is an obstacle to interpretation rather than a symptom of latent meanings.

In rejecting this second conception of the relationship between art and politics, Rancière once again integrates it into his own system of explanation. Barthes's primary mistake consisted in the fact that he did not recognise that both of these approaches – the symptomatological and the asymptomatological – are based on 'a reversible principle of equivalence between the muteness of images and their speech'.[12] In other words, these two conceptions of the political potential of art correspond to the two sides of what Rancière has theorised under the heading of 'mute speech [*la parole muette*]'. This expression refers to the contradictory dialectic of signification in the aesthetic regime of art. On the one hand, meaning is a hieroglyph in need of interpretation, that is, a mute sign requiring an interpreter who speaks in its place and reveals its inner truth. On the other hand, meaning is immanent in the things themselves and resists all external voices to the point of sinking into an irretrievable silence. Barthes's attempt to maintain a strict opposition between *studium* and *punctum* not only tries – unsuccessfully – to resolve this contradiction, but it also has the unfortunate consequence of foreclosing the genealogy of this very opposition.[13]

It would be a grave mistake to confuse Rancière's position on the consubstantiality of art and politics with either the notion of committed art or – a slightly more understandable confusion – the conception of art that affirms its innate political force as a form of resistance to the status quo. In order to further elucidate his own position, it is first necessary to dissipate a dangerous and perhaps unnecessary ambiguity. Rancière has recourse to at least two different definitions of politics.[14] More often than not, he refers to politics as the 'dissensual reconfiguration of the distribution of the sensible' by intermittent acts of subjectivisation that disturb the police order.[15] In his most recent work, however, he has increasingly referred to politics as itself a distribution of the sensible:

> What really deserves the name of politics is the cluster of perceptions and practices that shape this common world. Politics is first of all a way of framing, among sensory data, a specific sphere of experience. It is a partition of the sensible, of the visible and the sayable, which allows (or does not allow) some specific data to appear; which allows or does not allow some specific subjects to designate them and speak about them. It is a specific intertwining of ways of being, ways of doing and ways of speaking.[16]

The readers of *Disagreement* and *On the Shores of Politics* will have little difficulty understanding this definition of politics because it is strictly equivalent to what Rancière had earlier called the 'police':

> The police is thus first an order of bodies that defines the allocation of ways of doing, ways of being, and ways of saying, and sees that those bodies are assigned by name to a particular place and task; it is an order of the visible and the sayable that sees that a particular activity is visible and another is not, that this speech is understood as discourse and another as noise.[17]

As is well known, Rancière maintained in principle a rather rigorous distinction between the police and politics: 'political activity is always a mode of expression that undoes the perceptible divisions of the police order [*les partages sensibles de l'ordre policier*] by implementing a basically heterogenous assumption, that of a part of those who have no part [...]'.[18] Has Rancière abandoned or reformulated this earlier distinction in his most recent work? Is the separation between politics and the police order not as strict as he once claimed it to be?

Eliminating these apparent ambiguities is essential to understanding Rancière's most recent work. To begin with, the primary link between art and politics is clearly the fact that they are both distributions of the sensible: 'Art and politics are not two permanent and separate realities about which it might be asked if they *must* be put in relationship to one another. They are two forms of distribution of the sensible tied to a specific regime of identification.'[19] On numerous occasions, he reminds his reader that art is not in and of itself an act of political subjectivisation. On the contrary, art as a distribution of the sensible often acts as a police order that inhibits political subjectivisation, as is the case with the meta-political art of the aesthetic regime. This being said, it is equally clear that Rancière does not simply want to identify art as a police distribution of the sensible that excludes political dissensus. It seems that art is inherently political for him insofar as it acts as a potential meeting ground between a configuration of the sensible world and possible reconfigurations thereof. In other words, the epithet 'political' would be better understood neither in terms of what Rancière earlier defined as politics qua subjectivisation (*la politique*) nor in terms of the police order (*la police*), but according to what he sometimes calls 'the political' (*le politique*), that is, the meeting ground between *la politique* and *la police*. However, this solution does not eliminate all of the difficulties highlighted above.

In an attempt to clear up the remaining ambiguities, it is important to remind ourselves that Rancière's earlier work on politics (*Disagreement* and *On the Shores of Politics*) often maintains a rather strict opposition between a consensual order and acts of political dissensus. In spite of his criticisms of his former colleagues Deleuze and Lyotard, his work from this period nonetheless shares with them the logic of identity and difference, which continues to dominate one large sector of contemporary political theory. The limitations inherent in this logic are numerous, but there are at least four that should be highlighted: (1) it reduces the dynamism of the social world and the complexity of history to monolithic conceptual constructs that purport to explain the totality of events; (2) it is anchored in an implicit value system that is never justified or questioned, which consists in everywhere privileging the concept of difference over the notion of identity as if difference was an innate ethico-political good;[20] (3) since identity and difference are purely relational terms, it freely – if not arbitrarily – fixes the threshold between what is 'the same' and what is 'different' based on the needs of the situation; and (4) anything *truly different* from the binary of identity and difference remains unthinkable, and this polarisation becomes a universal lens for interpreting the world. Although Rancière is clearly indebted to the logic of identity and difference, it is arguable that some of his most recent work has led to a slightly more nuanced position, perhaps by foregrounding elements that remained somewhat peripheral in his earlier work.[21] Instead of simply opposing a consensual distribution of the sensible to dissensual acts of political subjectivisation, Rancière increasingly uses the terms *politics* and *art* to refer to both distributions *and* redistributions of the sensible order. In other words, in providing a more detailed account of the conjunction of art and politics, Rancière has been led – at times – to break down the rather strict opposition between an established order and intermittent moments of destabilisation. In *Aesthetics and Its Discontents* (2004), the distribution of the sensible clearly refers to both of these elements: 'This distribution and redistribution of places and identities, this delimitation and re-delimitation of spaces and times, of the visible and the invisible, of noise and speech constitutes what I call the distribution of the sensible.'[22] The note at the end of this sentence refers the reader to *The Politics of Aesthetics* (2000). However, the primary definition Rancière gives to the distribution of the sensible in this work focuses on only one of the two features highlighted in *Aesthetics and Its Discontents*: 'I call the distribution of the sensible the system of self-evident facts of sense perception that simultaneously discloses the existence of something in common and the delimitations that define the respective parts and positions within it.'[23] A similar change in vocabulary is visible in his use of the term *politics*, which he defines in *Aesthetics and Its Discontents* as 'the configuration of a specific space, the delimitation of a particular sphere of experience, of objects established in common and coming from a common decision, of subjects recognised as capable of designating these objects and arguing about them'.[24] As mentioned above, this definition differs considerably from the description of politics he provided in *Disagreement* (1995) and *On the Shores of Politics* (1992/1998), and seems much closer to what he had earlier called *the police*.[25] In emphasising – at least implicitly – the police process in politics and the dissensual elements in the distribution of the sensible, Rancière breaks down the rigid opposition between stable structures and intermittent acts of reconfiguration. Politics in *Aesthetics and Its Discontents* is a distribution of the sensible insofar as every distribution presupposes at least the potential for a redistribution. If art is consubstantial with politics, it is not simply because it is a meeting ground between a police distribution of the sensible and political subjectivisation. It seems that it is primarily because it is, like politics (*la politique*), at once a distribution and a potential redistribution of the sensible.

POLITICAL HISTORY AND AESTHETIC HERMENEUTICS

I have thus far made a concerted effort to remain within Rancière's conceptual framework in order to emphasise significant recent developments in his work, point to a specific set of problems, suggest solutions to these problems that appear feasible within this framework, and urge him in a certain direction (namely away from the logic of identity and difference). In the remainder of this chapter, I will jettison this heuristically constructed internal perspective in favour of a critical evaluation of his project from the outside. In doing so, I will concentrate primarily – but not exclusively – on the more schematic account of the relationship between politics and aesthetics that I have been edging him away from with the help of certain passages in his most recent work.

I would first like to call into question the near absolute lack of any historical approach to politics. Rancière argues that his decision to avoid the historicisation of politics is based on a strategic choice complicit with his historical analysis of art. In both cases, he claims, it is a matter of showing that '*art* and *politics* are contingent notions'.[26] This is done through a historical dismantling of the idea of an eternal essence of art, on the one hand, and through a decoupling of the link between specific historical developments and the notion of politics on the other. The latter move requires a 'dehistoricisation' of politics and a transhistorical definition thereof: 'Politics exists when the figure of a specific subject is constituted, a supernumerary subject in relation to the calculated number of groups, places, and functions in a society. This is summed up in the concept of the *dēmos*.'[27] It is interesting to note that, in the same passage, he is quick to add: 'Of course, this does not prevent there from being historical forms of politics, and it does not exclude the fact that the forms of political subjectivisation that make up modern democracy are of an entirely different complexity than the people in Greek democratic cities.'[28] Implicit in these statements is the philosophic distinction between empirical history and conceptual history, or what we might call, following Heidegger, *Historie* and *Geschichte*. While there can be differences in the banal factual configuration of politics through the course of empirical time, the conceptual nature of politics nonetheless remains unchanged. Showing that politics is a contingent notion therefore amounts to de-suturing the proper nature of politics from any specific historical conjuncture. Strictly speaking, however, this does not make the notion of politics 'contingent'. It simply makes all historically specific definitions of politics contingent if and when they do not live up to the transhistorical concept of politics proper. Since it is this concept that Rancière himself purports to have access to, this amounts to saying that every definition of politics is contingent if and when it is not identical with his own.[29]

Rancière's transhistorical approach to politics has reached its zenith in one of his recent works: *Hatred of Democracy* (2005). His bête noire throughout the entire book is democratophobia: the perennial fear and hatred of democracy – understood as politics proper – insofar as it disturbs the established police order. Although this hatred has changed forms through the course of history, as he illustrates with his analysis of a handful of contemporary books criticising recent forms of cultural democracy, he clearly takes democratophobia to be a historical constant: 'The hatred of democracy is certainly not something new. It is as old as democracy for one simple reason: the word itself is an expression of hatred.'[30]

Rancière's account of democracy suffers from what I propose to call 'transitive history': the object of historical analysis (democracy, in this case) is assumed to be a historical constant that simply takes on different external forms through the course of time. Historical transitivity of this sort loses sight of the fact that there is no 'democracy in general', but only specific socio-historical practices like 'democracy in ancient Greece', 'democracy in modern Europe', and so forth. It succumbs to a form of teleological archaeology by which the final historical phase of an idea or a practice is retroactively projected back on to its entire history as a unifying form. It is only by overcoming such historical myopia that it is possible to bring to light the fundamental structural differences, for example, between *dēmokratia* in ancient Greece and modern democracy, be it at the level of representation, citizenship, the separation of powers, rights, elections, political expertise, or the relationship between the individual and the community.[31] It is important to recall, in this regard, the general disappearance of the word *democracy* from popular vocabulary between antiquity and the eighteenth century (a period during which it remained a term for specialists and the practice itself more or less vanished).[32] When the word reappeared during the eighteenth century, it was still very distant from its contemporary meaning and was primarily used as a pejorative synonym for 'Jacobin'.[33] It is only very recently that the concept of democracy has met with near-universal acclaim.[34]

Rancière's own book is, in fact, a direct product of this historically specific democratophilia. It is a perfect illustration of the way in which 'democracy' has become, especially over the last few decades, a value-concept whose analytic content has been siphoned out and replaced by an inchoate mass of positive moral connotations.[35] *Democracy* has largely become a signal – to use Barthes's term – used to indicate what is morally condoned by the author using the word.[36] In Rancière's own case, this is quite obvious because he actually has no need for the term *democracy* in his conceptual arsenal. In fact, if this word does anything, it introduces unnecessary confusion. Since it is more or less an exact synonym for politics (*la politique*) understood as subjectivisation (*la subjectivation*), it is questionable whether it plays any analytic role whatsoever.[37] One might assume, following common sense, that Rancière uses it to pinpoint the specificity of democratic developments, particularly within the modern world. However, such commonsense assumptions would be misguided because Rancière goes to great lengths to show that his own personal definition of democracy is extremely far from – and often incompatible with – the common understanding of democracy.[38] Why, then, does he insist on using a term that has little or no analytic purchase and which, on the contrary, only seems to introduce confusion? The answer is to be found in the widespread valorisation of democracy in the contemporary world: he wants to imbue his own stance on politics with the positive and progressive connotations attached to the term *democracy*. In other words, he uses the term less as a denotative signifier to refer to a distinct referent (which is arguably the case for synonyms such as *politics* and *subjectivisation*) than as a connotative signifier indicating the positive value of his own discourse on politics.

This detour into the question of democracy shows to what extent it is necessary to resist Rancière's political ahistoricism in the name of a socio-historical analysis of political cultures. Contrary to what Rancière affirms, there is no 'politics in general', and certainly no 'politics proper' (even if the *properness* of politics is to *be improper*); there are only political cultures – understood as practical modes of intelligibility of politics – that change through the course of history and are variably distributed through social space. As we have seen in the case of his faulty universalist claims regarding democracy, Rancière's own discourse is dependent upon a socially and historically specific political culture.

Now let us consider Rancière's work on aesthetics. I have had the opportunity elsewhere to discuss some of the shortcomings of his project, including his negative dialectic of modern history, the lack of a genetic explanation that accounts for why the aesthetic regime has emerged, his restricted focus on the modern European world, his unqualified disdain for the social sciences, his tautological definition of art and politics, and his underlying aesthetic ontology.[39] In what follows, I will therefore restrict myself to one central problem in his work: the relationship between art and politics.

The first thing to note is that Rancière jettisons the notion of committed art as being vacuous and undetermined. Since there is 'no criterion for establishing a correspondence between aesthetic virtue and political virtue', artists will use different means at various points in time to try and 'politicise' their work.[40] The art that results from their choices can, however, be interpreted as being politically progressive just as well as it can be judged politically reactionary or nihilistic. Citing the example of American films on the Vietnam War from the 1970s and 1980s, such as *The Deer Hunter*, Rancière affirms that: 'It can be said that the message is the derisory nature of the war. It can just as well be said that the message is the derisory nature of the struggle against the war.'[41] Since there are no criteria for properly politicising art, it is generally the 'state of politics' that decides if a work of art is interpreted as harbouring a political critique or encouraging an apolitical outlook.[42] Given this lack of absolute criteria, Rancière wants to step back from the social battle over the political meaning of works of art in order to elucidate their inherent politicity. It is thereby presumed that each work of art, in spite of whatever motivations might be behind its creation or how it may be received by a public, has an objective political being.[43] This is what I propose to call Rancière's hermeneutic epoché: by bracketing the realm of the political 'experience' of art, he purports to isolate its pure political being. It might be said that he is fundamentally interested in the politics of art (understood as the politics ontologically inscribed in works of art), and that he therefore excludes the politicisation of art (the social struggle over the political dimension of art, be it at the level of production, distribution or reception).

I would argue that Rancière here suffers from the ontological illusion. What he perceives as the 'politics of art' is in fact only the sedimentation of the 'politicisation of art', in much the same way as what Sartre calls the practico-inert is a sedimentation of praxis. Works of art have no political being; there are only socio-historical struggles over the political dimension of artwork, some of which have led to recognisable formulas of politicised art. Rancière's own claims regarding the objective political being of art are in fact only one more contribution to the ongoing battle over art and politics. By overstating his case and acting as if his own politicisation of art is in fact coextensive with the true politics of art, he of course wants to convince his readership that he has provided the definitive account of the politics of aesthetics.[44] However, he has in fact only made one more contribution to an ongoing debate. In resisting these claims, it is important not only to remind ourselves of Rancière's rhetorical strategies but also to provide an alternative account of the politicisation of art.

Let us therefore take a specific example. The film *Lili Marleen* (1981) demonstrates at more than one level the way in which works of art are always social works in progress. The focal point of the film is the unique history of the famous song 'Lili Marleen'. After being exposed to the complex motives and circumstances behind the song's production, the spectator is led through the story of its singular distribution and reception. The first time it is sung by Willie, the main character, it is in a music hall where a group of Brits get in a fight with a band of German soldiers because they won't keep quiet. The image of Willie singing as the brawl breaks out and envelops the entire music hall visually sums up the future of the song: it gave birth to a battlefield with shifting allegiances. After being largely forgotten, the song rises to fame when it is played over the radio and is cherished by the German troops at the front. Through the course of the film, the song is: listened to approvingly by Robert Mendelssohn, a classical music aficionado and Willie's lover across the border; judged macabre by Goebbels; admired by Hitler; used by the Nazis to torture Robert, discovered to be a Jewish resistance fighter; blacklisted by the German government; sung by a mass of German soldiers when they see Willie, in spite of the fact that '*Das Lied ist verboten!*'; sung by Willie during a major Nazi spectacle organised after her attempted suicide, where her shadow – as in the song 'Lili Marleen' – bears the trace of Robert's fedora and trench coat; and heard at the front by Willie's former pianist, who assumes he has stumbled upon allies, only to be shot by the Russians, who were apparently also admirers of 'Lili Marleen'.

It is commonly assumed that there is an ontological opposition between the work of art in and of itself and the appropriation of the work for certain interpretive ends (hence the idea that the song was simply co-opted by various listeners). However, this opposition is founded on a fundamental misapprehension, which is undoubtedly rooted in the practical habituation to 'individual objects' through physical experience and language use. In spite of what its delimited physical nature and title might suggest, a work of art is a social object; it is a site of collective meaning production. The creator of a work of art is not an isolated subjective will that arbitrarily organises the world according to his or her personal whims. An artist is a participant in socially recognised rituals and institutions that sculpt what is artistically possible.[45] This is one of the reasons why the controversy about authors' intentions is a false debate. Contrary to what the 'anti-intentionalists' claim, it is possible to tap into the production logic of a particular work of art by understanding the historical time period, the social setting, the institutional framework, the poetic norms of the time, the artist's habitus, the operative modes of distribution and circulation, and the spectators' or readers' 'horizon of expectation' (the system of objectifiable references).[46] However, this does *not* amount to reducing a work of art to its 'context' as if there were some external monolithic construct determining the totality of artistic production.

The fundamental problem with Rancière's approach is that he wants to be able to judge the constituent political forms of a work of art outside of the social struggle over such forms. Like Robert Mendelssohn in *Lili Marleen*, who says to Willie 'I must know what side you are on', Rancière wants to know once and for all where things stand. Willie's response to Robert can here be taken as a hint for how we should reply to Rancière: 'on your side, as long as I live. [...] But one cannot always choose how to live when one wants to survive.' Fassbinder's psycho-politics, here as elsewhere, reveal to what extent decisions are always made within a conjuncture of circumstances that preclude simple binary value judgements from the outside. The title of the film can be taken as a synecdoche summing up this grey-zone politics of survival. Just as the song – which is named after two women – has many different social lives, Willie has at least two different sides to her: she is at once Willie, Robert's lover, and Lili Marleen, the singer of a famous song under the Third Reich. As the film shows, it would be short-sighted to wholeheartedly condemn her for being Lili Marleen, since it is as Willie that she makes the majority of her choices.[47]

Rather than having a single fixed political valence that can be determined once and for all by ontological deduction, works of art are sites of contestation and negotiation in which meaning is dynamically produced and reproduced. To use the vocabulary I've just introduced, we can be more or less successful in tapping into a work of art's production logic. This means that we can, without appealing to the 'political being' of a work of art, provide better or worse arguments for understanding the political issues at stake.[48] With this in mind, I'd like to turn to Rancière's interpretation of three films released in 2003: *Dogville*, *Mystic River* and *Elephant*.[49] According to his argument, by presenting average Americans as evil-doers equivalent to America's 'enemies' throughout the world, these films reflect the flip-side of the global American crusade against the 'axis of evil'. In both cases, there is the same basic logic at work: finite evil can only be overcome – domestically or internationally – by recourse to an irreducible, infinite evil. The political dimension of these films is thus found in the ways in which they reflect a new era of evil, replete with a novel understanding of good deeds as deeds to be punished (*Dogville*), a new definition of humanism as the acceptance of the impossibility of justice (*Mystic River*), and a unique brand of neo-hippy nihilism where the naive solution 'make love, not war' is replaced by the utterly inane solution 'make films, not war' (*Elephant*).[50]

Although Rancière is a careful interpreter who always sheds an interesting light on the works of art he analyses, there are grounds for believing that his particular account of the supposedly objective political being of these films masks as much as it reveals. In the case of *Mystic River*, for instance, he has neglected the absolutely essential role of religion, community and family values. As the very title of the film suggests, there is a mystic river linking the cycles of crime and punishment. The entire story takes its root in an event that would forever bind together three childhood friends: Jimmy Markum (Sean Penn), Sean Devine (Kevin Bacon) and Dave Boyle (Tim Robbins). Upon Jimmy's instigation, the boys decide to write their names in a patch of freshly poured concrete in their neighbourhood. When they are apprehended by two men claiming to be undercover policemen, the one boy who doesn't live in the immediate vicinity, Dave, is escorted back to his home. However, he never arrives at home and is instead sequestered in an isolated location and sexually abused by the two men. Although he finally escapes from 'the wolves' and makes it home, he would never be the same again, as symbolised by his unfinished name forever etched in the neighbourhood concrete ('DA') and his inability to ever really be at home again with himself, his family or the rest of the community.[51]

Years later, Sean Devine, who has since become the 'good cop', is called in on a murder case in 'the old neighbourhood'. When he recognises the victim to be the cherished daughter of his old friend Jimmy Markum, he murmurs half out-loud: 'What the fuck am I gonna tell him? "Hey Jimmy, God said you owed another marker. He came to collect."'[52] And when Jimmy does learn the news, a sea of policemen hold him in a position of near-crucifixion as he screams 'Oh, God, no!' beneath a vertical crane shot retracting into heaven, followed by a second crane shot of his dead daughter in the old bear cage that swoops up to an image of the beyond. The message should be unequivocal: the mystic river linking sin to retribution has caught up with Jimmy. In case it wasn't clear, Jimmy later mutters to himself in a moment of private rumination on his porch, and prior to yet another helicopter shot of the Mystic, 'I know in my soul I contributed to your death. But I don't know how.' And when he eventually becomes convinced that it was Dave who murdered his daughter and decides to finish him off, he declares, prior to hurling his bloody knife into the waters of the Mystic, 'We bury our sins here, Dave. We wash them clean.'

The only catch is that Jimmy apparently kills the wrong man. It wasn't Dave who murdered his daughter but Ray Harris, the mute brother of the boy dating Jimmy's daughter. However, this is not a simple remake of Fritz Lang's *You Only Live Once* (1937) or Alfred Hitchcock's *The Wrong Man* (1956), nor is it, as Rancière claims, a script based on the promised victim in which Eastwood and his collaborators are calling for us to accept the slipshod – and unjust – work of justice in much the same way as the discourse on the axis of evil.[53] On the contrary, the message is that the Mystic River is doing its work of higher justice above and beyond the free will of the individuals involved (hence all of the helicopter shots of the river and neighbourhood). Even though Ray Harris – along with his friend – apparently killed Katie to prevent her from taking his brother away from him, he was unknowingly paying Jimmy back not only for having contributed to Dave's demise,[54] but also for having killed his own father, whose body he had thrown into the Mystic years ago: Just Ray Harris was the *just* man who had sent Jimmy away to prison and then looked after his family. Jimmy half recognises this higher truth when he explains how he felt when he killed Just Ray Harris, who had himself admitted that Jimmy was 'a good man': 'I could feel God watching me, shaking his head, not angry, but like you do if a puppy shat on a rug.' And even though Jimmy apparently killed an innocent man, Dave actually deserved to die – according to the mysterious logic of the Mystic River – for at least three reasons: (1) he was guilty of the murder of a paedophile (described, but not portrayed, as a violent 'wolf'); (2) his wife had sinned by turning him in for a crime he did not commit, and she thereby deserved to lose her husband and be exiled from the community; and (3) Dave had in fact died years ago and was, based on his own description, a vampire, a werewolf in the neighbourhood. These are the reasons why Dave's sacrifice, as the final shots of the movie illustrate, is for the 'good' of the neighbourhood.[55]

The moral of the film is that a mystic river holds us in its sway in spite of our intentions and that it is only through the – voluntary or involuntary – sacrifice for past crimes that a community survives. At the end of the movie, this is made clear at three different levels: (1) 'the old neighbourhood' where the boys grew up has been 'cleansed' of its past crimes; (2) the solidity of the family unit is reaffirmed in the juxtaposition between Jimmy's 'royal' family reunion and Celeste's bewildered wanderings; and (3) the *Devine* couple is reunited since Sean, after recognising and implicitly condoning Jimmy's act of higher justice, apologises to his wife for past sins, an act undoubtedly provoked by his growing awareness of the 'mystic river'.

Dogville also has a deeply religious dimension. Grace, the main character, wanders into a small town of 'good, honest folks' while trying to escape from her past life as a gangster. After she is apprehended stealing a bone from the dog, Moses, she decides to follow the advice of the town luminary, Thomas Edison Junior, and tries to be accepted into the town as a refuge from her past life (thereby acting for Edison as the perfect moral illustration of the acceptance of a gift). In offering her services to the townspeople in order to be integrated and atone for her past sins, she at first meets with resistance because they do not need her help. However, she soon gets her foot in the door, and the vacuum from the lack of need is filled by a growing desire. After a springtime filled with a relative balance between the gift – Grace – and its acceptance, things slowly turn sour. As the police search for Grace intensifies, the town democratically decides that from a 'business perspective' it is more and more expensive to keep Grace. Therefore, they ask her to work more to fulfil their non-existent needs. Through a long series of events, including several acts of rape and a failed escape, she is eventually transformed into a modern-day masochistic Christ who becomes the benevolent pin-cushion for the community's psycho-social problems. She is turned into the unseen dog from which the town takes its name, replete with Moses' collar around her neck and unbridled bestial abuse of her person.[56] Given the paradigmatic nature of this democratic town of 'good, honest folks' (which is intensified by the film's theatrical minimalism and its debt to Brecht), the larger commentary on the twisted and corrupt nature of American democracy in the early twenty-first century is not difficult to discern: the gift of *grace*, the manifestation of *God*, is 'accepted' as a *dog* to be sadistically abused – partially from a business perspective – in order to cathartically alleviate the 'suffering' of a community that has no dire needs.[57]

However, in a cabalistic *deus ex machina*, the *dog* of the community is given the powers of *God* with the return of the Father.[58] Following a change in the light, Grace's masochistic phase comes to a close, and the vengeful power of the God of the Old Testament is released through fire-power on to the town.[59] The *dog* become *god*, seated at the right hand of the Father, gives the town what it deserves for how it treated the arrival of grace: it merits the same rigorous moral judgement that Grace had inflicted on herself. The moral of the story is not simply, as Rancière claims, that it is impossible to be good in an evil world. It is also not – as Luis Buñuel suggests in *Viridiana* (1961) – that a soft but constant perversion undergirds and withers away the supposed 'good' of religious devotion and social facades. On the contrary, it is that those who don't recognise grace for what she is, and particularly those who mistake the gift of God for a pitiful dog to be democratically abused from a 'business perspective', those who, in short, act like this good little American town, will be mercilessly punished on judgement day.[60]

Rancière's interpretation of *Elephant* is the most egregious. He claims, to begin with, that it situates itself 'outside of all considerations of justice and all causal perspectives'.[61] It portrays the world of adolescents as being innocently devoid of reasons, law and authority,[62] to such an extent that normality and monstrosity become equivalent. The final shot reminds us, according to his interpretation, that this is all only a film, and the underlying message in this naive and nihilistic movie is 'make films, not massacres'.[63]

As an explicit reaction to the 1999 Columbine shootings and an implicit response to Michael Moore's *Bowling for Columbine* (2002), Gus Van Sant's entire film is constructed on the logic of false leads in order to resist the monocausal determinism that runs rampant in documentaries like Moore's.[64] The problem with such films is not only that they tend to drastically reduce the complexity of the socio-political world by attempting to single out a unique cause behind an entire series of events, but also that they aim primarily at edifying the viewer: by identifying the source of evil and locating it in the external world, spectators are bequeathed with an all-too-welcome dose of self-righteous moral superiority.[65] As Van Sant himself says, 'It's in our interest to identify the reason why so that we can feel safe, [...] so that we can feel that we're not part of it, [...] it's demonised and [...] it's identified and controlled.'[66] It is precisely this moralistic approach to political films that he wants to avoid. This does not, however, mean that he simply takes a headlong plunge into the abysmal pool of nihilism.

It is worth reminding ourselves, to begin with, how carefully and systematically Van Sant has constructed a network of false leads, set as so many traps for those viewers craving the cathartic identification of evil outside of themselves: (1) the opening shots with John's father drunk-driving him to school and then talking about going hunting with the gun 'grandpa' brought back from the South Pacific after WWII; (2) Nathan's lifeguard sweatshirt, suggesting that he is going to save someone; (3) John crying alone, only to be discovered by an apathetic Acadia; (4) Alex grabbing and shaking his head, as if one could simply say 'he is crazy'; (5) the kitchen help smoking pot; (6) the elephant drawing in Alex's room; (7) Alex's frustration at not being able to master Beethoven's 'Moonlight' Sonata; (8) the rapid weather changes and the storm coming in, as if one could say 'maybe it's the weather'; (9) the Nazis on television; (10) the 'homosexual' relationship between the boys in the shower; (11) Alex's recitation of Macbeth's first lines in the eponymous play: 'So foul and fair a day I have not seen.' Some of these false leads are clearly revealed as such: John is very thoughtful and protective, the 'lifeguard's' cross becomes the cross-hairs for Alex's gun as Nathan is apparently unsuccessful in saving his girlfriend or himself, Alex and Eric are uninformed and dismissive of the Nazis, and Eric has never kissed anyone before and doesn't really know what his sexual orientation might be. Others are left more or less hanging, like the passing reference to insanity, the elephant drawing, Alex's piano playing, the kitchen help, the weather and the reference to *Macbeth*. Finally, this long chain of false leads allows Van Sant to introduce what might be *false* false leads: (1) the discussion of electrons at 'Watt High School' and the statement that the electrons furthest from the nucleus – like Alex at the back of the classroom – are 'high energy' and can be kicked out of the atom when energy is added; (2) the spit wads thrown at Alex; (3) the *Gerry*-style video game in Alex's room; (4) the website 'Guns USA'; (5) the general lack of parental presence at Alex's house. In any case, there is *never* the identification of a single cause, and the aim of the film is to show that multiple determinants participate in the production of any event. This logic of false leads is combined with a *huis clos* aesthetic: there is generally one plane of focus with slow semi-subjective tracking shots in which characters are 'stalked' as if from a zero-point of visibility, a technique borrowed from scenes in Stanley Kubrick's *The Shining* (1980) as well as Alan Clarke's *Elephant* (1989). Moreover, there are no establishment shots by which the viewer can grasp all of the spatial relations in the school (there is only Alex's map, which is part of his 'plan', his exit strategy from the labyrinth of adolescent life), and time doubles back on itself through multiple perspectives on the same event, making film time shorter than real time just prior to the moment the shooting begins.[67]

This does not add up to nihilistic relativism. It amounts to replacing the determinist monocausality of self-edifying, moralistic political films by a set of overdetermined causal concatenations and chance relations that don't allow us to identify a single cause behind each event. Instead of being placed on a moral throne, viewers are forced into the *huis clos* existence of the labyrinthine and prison-like hallways of American high schools, where cliques and personas trap everyone in a complex network of social forces beyond their control. In refusing to isolate a single identifiable cause for high school violence, the film forces us to think for ourselves in trying to grapple with the ways in which an overdetermined sequence of events can produce the most extreme forms of violence.[68]

This radical change in perspective, which is not – as Rancière claims – a turn toward nihilism, is clearly illustrated by the Buddhist tale that is one of the sources of the film's title.[69] According to the tale, three blind men examine different parts of an elephant, and each one of them thinks he knows its true nature. The one who touches a leg thinks it's a tree trunk. The one who touches an ear thinks it's a fan. And the one who touches its trunk thinks it's a snake. However, none of them realise, from their limited point of view, that it is an elephant. The problem Van Sant is pointing to in a popular brand of political films is the tendency to mistake elephants for trees, fans or snakes. Instead of trying to reduce the complexity of events to a single edifying cause, he urges his viewers to let the enormity of events stand on their own, even if it's at the price of our own rational and moral mastery of these events.

At the beginning of this chapter, I situated Rancière's account of the politics of aesthetics in relationship to his immediate predecessors and emphasised significant developments in his most recent work. In an attempt to clear up certain ambiguities in his project, I presented what I take to be the most feasible – and textually justified – way of shoring up his account, which is largely based on distancing his work from the *franco-française* logic of identity and difference. I then went on to examine and evaluate Rancière's project from an external perspective, and I indicated two central points where our paths diverge. First of all, I questioned his ahistorical approach to politics and his ever-present political ontology.[70] In emphasising the limitations inherent in Rancière's schematic account of democracy and his fondness for 'transitive history' in the realm of politics, I advocated a truly historical analysis of political cultures. Secondly, I called into question his hermeneutic epoché in the realm of aesthetics and his attempt to philosophically bracket the socio-historical struggle over the politics of art. In light of this critique, I argued that works of art are never fixed objects that can be judged once and for all from the privileged position of the philosopher of art. Artistic production is a dynamic process that is part of a socio-historical world. This means that there is no permanent politics of art; there are only various modes of politicisation. And these take place in different dimensions: not only the dimension of historical regimes (Rancière), but also the dimensions of production, circulation and reception. In order to provide concrete examples of my divergence with Rancière on the politics of aesthetics, I concluded my analysis with a critical evaluation of his interpretation of three recent films. This critique was not simply based on an appeal to the 'facts'. It was fundamentally methodological in nature insofar as it broke with the reference to the political being of works of art in the name of an interpretive intervention founded on the production logic of these films and aimed at directly participating in the ongoing battle of the politicisation of art.

NOTES

1. Sartre's stance on commitment evolved very quickly through the course of the late 1940s and into the 1950s, as evidenced perhaps most notably by his discussion of the functional and committed aspects of 'black poetry' in 'Orphée noir' (originally published in 1948 and reprinted in *Situations, III*).
2. *Le Degré zéro de l'écriture*, in *Œuvres complètes*, vol. 1 (1942–65), p. 183 (also see p. 147). Unless otherwise noted, all translations are my own.
3. See *Malaise dans l'esthétique*, p. 40.
4. See most notably 'The Distribution of the Sensible: Politics and Aesthetics', in *The Politics of Aesthetics*, pp. 12–19.
5. Rancière provides at least three different definitions of politics: (1) the act of political subjectivisation that breaks with the police order; (2) the meeting ground between police procedures and the process of equality; and (3) the overall distribution of the sensible. It is primarily this last meaning that is being discussed here.
6. Rancière, *The Politics of Aesthetics*, p. 51.
7. See *La Parole muette*, pp. 17–18, and 'The Politics of Literature'. The essay 'The Politics of Literature' was reworked and published in French as the opening chapter in *Politique de la littérature*.
8. Rancière, 'The Politics of Literature', pp. 16, 17, 18, 19.
9. Ibid., p. 20.
10. Ibid., p. 11. Rancière writes on page 20 of the same article: 'Sartre's flawed argument about Flaubert is not a personal and casual mistake.'
11. According to Rancière: 'The patterns of their critical explanation of "what literature says" relied on the same system of meaning that underpinned the practice of literature itself. Not surprisingly, they very often came upon the same problem as Sartre. In the same way, they endorsed as new critical insights on literature the "social" and "political" interpretations of nineteenth-century conservatives. Further, the patterns they had to use to reveal the truth on literature are the patterns framed by literature itself. Explaining close-to-hand realities as phantasmagorias bearing witness to the hidden truth of a society, this pattern of intelligibility was the invention of literature itself. Telling the truth on the surface by travelling in the

underground, spelling out the unconscious social text lying underneath – that also was a plot invented by literature itself' ('The Politics of Literature', p. 20).
12. Rancière, *Le Destin des images*, p. 19.
13. Rancière has provided this genealogy most notably in *La Parole muette* and, more recently, in *Le Destin des images*.
14. As mentioned in note 5, there is at least one additional sense in which he uses the term.
15. Rancière, *Aux bords du politique*, p. 13. The 1998 French edition of *Aux bords du politique* includes a number of articles that are not available in the 1995 English translation (*On the Shores of Politics*) that appeared in 1992.
16. Rancière, 'The Politics of Literature', p. 10.
17. Rancière, *Disagreement*, p. 29.
18. Ibid., p. 30; *La Mésentente*, p. 53.
19. Rancière, *Malaise dans l'esthétique*, pp. 39–40.
20. Although Chantal Mouffe's work is squarely situated in the logic of identity and difference, she nonetheless indicates one of the dangers inherent in this logic: 'I consider that, despite its claim to be more democratic, such a perspective [extreme pluralism] prevents us from recognising how certain differences are constructed as relations of subordination and should therefore be challenged by a radical democratic politics' (*The Democratic Paradox*, p. 20). Nancy Fraser puts her finger on this problem in her critique of what she calls deconstructive antiessentialism: 'Deconstructive antiessentialists appraise identity claims on ontological grounds alone. They do not ask, in contrast, how a given identity or difference is related to social structures of domination and to social relations of inequality' (*Justice Interruptus*, p. 183). She also rejects the pluralist version of multiculturalism where 'difference is viewed as intrinsically positive and inherently cultural': 'This perspective accordingly celebrates difference uncritically while failing to interrogate its relation to inequality' (ibid., p. 185).
21. As we will see in the next section, *La Haine de la démocratie* nonetheless remains largely within the logic of identity and difference.
22. Rancière, *Malaise dans l'esthétique*, p. 38.
23. Rancière, *The Politics of Aesthetics*, p. 12.
24. Rancière, *Malaise dans l'esthétique*, p. 37.
25. Rancière himself seems to recognise this (see ibid., p. 37).
26. Rancière, *The Politics of Aesthetics*, p. 51.
27. Ibid., p. 51.
28. Ibid., p. 51.
29. It is likely that Rancière would reply to this criticism by reminding us that the 'proper' of politics is to be 'improper' by constantly stirring up the sediments of the police order. However, we should not be distracted by

what has become a common deconstructivist strategy: politics will *never* be so improper that it will throw off its proper harness of *being* improper.
30. Rancière, *Hatred of Democracy*, p. 7. Rancière's earlier article, 'La démocratie criminelle?' (March 2004), remains far superior to the book that eventually grew out of it precisely because he focused on the reconfiguration of the French political imaginary since the dissolution of the Soviet Union rather than venturing into historical generalisations regarding the perpetual disdain for democracy (see *Chroniques des temps consensuels*).
31. See Moses I. Finley's revised edition of *Democracy Ancient and Modern* and his *Politics in the Ancient World*, Anthony H. Birch's *The Concepts and Theories of Modern Democracy*, and Cornelius Castoriadis's 'Imaginaire politique grec et moderne' and 'La démocratie athénienne: fausses et varies questions' in *La Montée de l'insignifiance*.
32. See Finley, *Democracy Ancient and Modern*, p. 9, Graubard, 'Democracy', Palmer, 'Notes on the Use of the Word "Democracy" 1789–1799', and Dahl, *On Democracy*, pp. 7–9.
33. See Raymond Williams's *Keywords*, p. 14, and Palmer, 'Notes on the Use …', p. 205: 'It is rare, even among the *philosophes* of France before the Revolution, to find anyone using the word "democracy" in a favorable sense in any practical connection.' To take a few poignant examples, Montesquieu and Rousseau both suggest that democracy is against the natural order (see *The Spirit of the Laws*, I, XI, vi; *The Social Contract*, III, iv). Anthony Birch asserts that: 'The founders of the American constitution shared in the generally poor view of democratic government. […] The Founding Fathers talked of creating a republic, based on representative institutions, not a democracy; the leaders of the French Revolution talked of a republic also; and in Britain people described their system as one of representative and responsible government' (*The Concepts and Theories of Modern Democracy*, pp. 45–6). As an example thereof, see the critique of 'pure democracy' in Rossiter (ed.), *The Federalist Papers* (most notably nos. 9 and 10). The writings of Alexis de Tocqueville, although far from being unequivocal, can be taken as signs of important conceptual and terminological changes, whereby 'democracy' was partially revalorised: 'To want to stop democracy thus appears to be to struggle against God himself, and nations would but have to accommodate themselves with the social state imposed upon them by Providence' (*De la démocratie en Amérique I*, p. 61).
34. Moses Finley's historical analysis clearly points to one of the fundamental problems with Rancière's schematic account of the perennial hatred of democracy: 'In antiquity, intellectuals in the overwhelming majority disapproved of popular government, and they produced a variety of explanations for their attitude and a variety of alternative proposals. Today their counterparts, especially but not only in the west, are agreed, in probably

the same overwhelming majority, that democracy is the best form of government, the best known and the best imaginable' (*Democracy Ancient and Modern*, pp. 8–9; see also Palmer, 'Notes on the Use …', p. 203, and Laniel, *Le Mot 'democracy' et son histoire aux États-Unis de 1780 à 1856*, p. 31).

35. To say that one is in favour of democracy today, at least within the majority of cultural matrices, is a moral given structurally equivalent to statements like 'I am for peace' or 'I am against child abuse'. Such statements are generally devoid of any analytic content and primarily function as social signs, whose message can be literally translated as 'I am a good person like all other good people'. The relatively small group of conservatives Rancière attacks is in fact playing off this moralisation of political categories and sardonically reversing the values by condemning democracy as a form of cultural corruption.
36. We could therefore say the same thing about democracy that Paul Valéry says about freedom: 'It's one of those detestable words that have more value than meaning, that sing more than they speak [*C'est un de ces détestables mots qui ont plus de valeur que de sens; qui chantent plus qu'ils ne parlent*]' (quoted in Kerbrat-Orecchioni, *La Connotation*, p. 6).
37. 'Subjectivisation', at the very least, allows Rancière to underscore the dynamic aspect of politics (see the three definitions of politics in note 5), and it emphasises the role of subjects in the political process.
38. This confusion is exacerbated by Rancière's tendency to claim that the commonsense use of the term is 'confused' (*La Haine de la démocratie*, p. 101).
39. See, for instance, Chapters 3 and 7, as well as my book *Radical History and the Politics of Art*.
40. Rancière, *The Politics of Aesthetics*, p. 61.
41. Ibid., p. 61.
42. Ibid., p. 62.
43. There is at least one important qualification to make: Rancière *does* provide a fascinating account of the ways in which art is re-appropriated by various regimes (see most notably *L'Inconscient esthétique*). This might be interpreted as suggesting that the political being of art always depends on its regime. However, even if this is the case, Rancière nonetheless purports to have access to the 'political being of art' within each regime rather than recognising that the politicity of art is a concept in struggle, a site of social negotiation.
44. Paraphrasing his own terminology, we might say that he suffers from a *meta-politics of art*.
45. It is interesting in this regard that the story of the film *Lili Marleen* is not significantly different from the story of the song. The project had its origins in the work of two representatives of Papa's Kino. The producer,

Luggi Waldleitner, was known for being a conventional member of the establishment, and the screenwriter, Manfred Purzer, had a reputation as a conservative. In agreeing to direct the film, R. W. Fassbinder appears to have concluded a devil's pact. However, he states in one of his interviews, echoing the theme of the 'right to survival' in *Lili Marleen* and many of his other films: 'If someone objects, as some of my friends do, that you shouldn't make films with the money of rightists, all I can say is that Visconti made almost all his films with money from rightists. And always justified it with similar arguments: that they gave him more leeway than the leftists' (*The Anarchy of the Imagination*, p. 61).

46. Some useful reference points in the elucidation of 'logics of production' include the work of Pierre Bourdieu and his followers, H. R. Jauss's aesthetics of reception and Anthony Giddens's theory of the 'duality of structure'.

47. The same thing could be said about Robert. Although he is portrayed as a Jewish resistance fighter deserving of all of the obligatory social credit, he is also depicted as Mr Mendelssohn, the cowardly pawn and eventual perpetuator of patriarchal power. On this and other related issues, see the chapter on *Lili Marleen* in Thomas Elsaesser's *Fassbinder's Germany: History, Identity, Subject*.

48. Since there are no transhistorical, objective criteria in hermeneutics, the distinction between better and worse arguments can only be based on various forms of legitimation through social negotiation. Although this is not the place to develop such an argument, it is important to note that the position I am taking on this issue should not be unduly identified with relativism.

49. See 'Les Nouvelles Fictions du mal' (in *Cahiers du cinéma* and also reprinted in *Chroniques des temps consensuels*, pp. 169–75) and 'Le tournant éthique de l'esthétique et de la politique' in *Malaise dans l'esthétique*, pp. 143–73.

50. In 'Le tournant éthique de l'esthétique et de la politique', the reference to *Elephant* is dropped, and the other two films are used as illustrations of the ethical turn in contemporary politics and aesthetics. Juxtaposed with the work of Brecht, Hitchcock and Lang, these films are taken to be signs of a new 'consensual' age in which facts and principles are rendered indistinct in a morass of unbridled wickedness: evil is used to battle evil in a world in which the difference between the innocent and the guilty has dissipated against the backdrop of an original 'trauma' shared by all (the link between 11 September 2001 and the war parade against the 'axis of evil' should be clear). It is interesting that Rancière, in what is otherwise one of his most intriguing recent articles, insists on there being two 'eras' of cinema, whereas he dedicated a large portion of *Film Fables* to proving

that Deleuze's division of film history into two periods was a mistake. Although this is not the place to analyse the relationship between these two claims, it should be noted that his argument in *Film Fables* focuses on perceived changes in film between the early and the mid- to late twentieth century, whereas his claims in 'Le tournant éthique' – which are also made in passing in 'Les Nouvelles Fictions du mal' – concentrate on the differences between cinema in the mid-twentieth century and in the early twenty-first century.

51. There are a number of interesting elements in this film that are situated at the limit of justifiable interpretation. For instance, the 'DA' in the concrete immediately recalls Freud's analysis of a child's *'fort ... da ...'* game in *Beyond the Pleasure Principle* and suggests that Dave's childhood game with Jimmy and Sean, unlike the little boy's game described by Freud, was marked by a 'Da' that trapped him forever 'there' at his last moment of happiness. Although it is difficult to know with certainty, it seems like this kind of reference, which was not present in Dennis Lehane's novel, would be within the reach of a screenwriter like Brian Helgeland. The references to 'the wolves' recalls, moreover, Freud's paraphrase of Plautus in *Civilisation and Its Discontents*: '*Homo homini lupus* [Man is a wolf to man]' (p. 58).

52. Jimmy's last name is Markum, and he bears the mark of his debt on his shoulders in the form of a tattooed cross, which recalls the cross in Katie's mother's name: Marita, or Maria bearing a cross. The other names in the film are equally symbolic, as should be clear from the 'good' cop who knows when divine law trumps the rules of the here-and-now (Sean *Devine*) and the phantom-like wanderer who cannot keep his deep-seated rage from overflowing (Dave *Boyle*).

53. In uncritically accepting the auteur policy with all of its limitations, Rancière has placed undue emphasis on the role of the director. He doesn't even mention the fact that the screenplay was based on a novel by Dennis Lehane that was published in 2001, and therefore written prior to the discourse on the 'axis of evil'.

54. It is significant that Jimmy's daughter was murdered in 'the old bear cage', just as Dave had been tortured as a boy in a 'wolf's' den.

55. Like Rancière, I refuse to condone this conception of 'justice'. However, I do think it's important to understand its inner logic and its mystical underpinnings.

56. The only time the dog is seen is at the very end of the film, when Grace decides to spare him his life since he is justifiably angry at her for having stolen his bone. A vertical tracking shot receding into the heavens, which echoes the final shot in *Breaking the Waves*, reveals Moses barking toward the sky.

57. It is, of course, important that this was the first film in Lars von Trier's trilogy *USA – Land of Opportunities*, since followed by *Manderlay* (2005).
58. Grace mentions that (like Christ) she doesn't have a family, only a father.
59. The end of *Dogville* recalls Augustine's account of the earthly city: 'But the earthly city will not be everlasting; for when it is condemned to that punishment which is its end, it will no longer be a city' (*The City of God against the Pagans*, p. 638). It would certainly be a mistake, however, to identify the life of the gangsters with the 'City of God'.
60. In addition to its religious dimension, there are many other aspects to this film, as visible in the proliferation of references to the Greek world (Jason and the rest of his family), famous fairy tales (*Snow White*), theatre (Brecht) and the 'birth' of film (Thomas Edison). However, the spiritual themes developed in *Dogville* are clearly part of a larger project, which includes both *Breaking the Waves* (1996) and *Dancer in the Dark* (2000). In the former film, von Trier weaves together a comparable story of perverted yet authentic spiritual devotion based on very similar themes: the divine gift, its acceptance, exile and excommunication, the proof of love, the logic of sacrifice, the battle between dogma and truth, and the struggle between the life of the flesh and the life of the spirit. *Dancer in the Dark* is also based on a story of misunderstood devotional sacrifice in which an outsider (Selma, a young Czech working in an American factory) dedicates herself to saving her son from blindness with a level of commitment (including her devotion to protecting the police officer's secret) that is scarcely understandable to those around her. She finds 'salvation' in a parallel world of musicals that allows her to face hardship and eventually capital punishment. The final shot of the film is structurally equivalent to the final shots in *Breaking the Waves* and *Dogville*: a vertical tracking shot ascending into heaven is doubled by the providential statement 'it's only the last song if we let it be'.
61. Rancière, 'Les Nouvelles Fictions du mal', p. 96.
62. Rancière seems to have overlooked the important role played by the high school principal, who punishes John at the beginning and is gunned down by Eric toward the end of the film.
63. Rancière, 'Les Nouvelles Fictions du mal', p. 96.
64. Diane Keaton, one of the executive producers of *Elephant*, responded to a question about her immediate reaction to the shootings at Columbine with the following description: 'My immediate reaction is, why? That's it. Why why why why why why why? I think this movie [*Elephant*], as well as *Bowling for Columbine*, actually tries to deal with the whys of it in its own way. What's interesting to me about Gus's movie is that he's not trying to say, "It's because of *this*!" He forces you to sit there and watch it unfold before you in this amazing way, and you have the responsibility of your

own thoughts. You have to sit there with your own fucking thoughts and think about it. That was astonishing, because for me it was something, for Bill [presumably excecutive producer Bill Robinson] it was something else, for Gus it was something else. For me, it was about being a parent, because I'm a parent' (Keaton and Van Sant, 'Elephant: Interview with Gus Van Sant and Diane Keaton').

65. A similar psycho-social pattern is to be found in the demonisation of individual politicians: a single, external cause is isolated as the unique root of all evil. The belligerent and repetitive vilification of Mahmoud Ahmadinejad in the mainstream Western media is an excellent example of the extreme shortcomings of political monocausality: a president elected by universal suffrage for a four-year term who had no direct control over the armed forces, military intelligence, security operations or foreign policy (these are all the prerogative of the supreme leader, Ayatollah Ali Khamenei) was transformed into an evil 'dictator' anxious to use nuclear weapons to wage war (even though Iran is still several years away from having nuclear power, and the Iranian president does not even have the right to declare war). It is clear that such political monocausality is directly linked to the drumbeat for more war in the Middle East and has been part of the 'perfect' exit strategy for the debacle in Iraq: it 'explains' the failure of the American military in Iraq (it's Iran's fault); it is capable of distracting public opinion from Iraq, which is old news, in the same way that Iraq threw a blanket over almost all major media coverage of Afghanistan; it provides a clearly identified diabolic enemy to fill the shoes of Saddam Hussein; it perpetuates a faulty image of Iran as unjustifiably hostile to the United States and contributes to American amnesia regarding the recent history of Iran (marked perhaps most notably by the 1953 coup organised by the CIA to replace a democratically elected regime by the autocratic Shah). In the case of military action, such ideologically generated monocausality could serve to fuel America's pluto-imperial military-industrial complex. It could also help prevent the emergence of any robust form of democracy in Iraq (which would allow for a Shia majority, most probably with leanings toward Iran), and it could further the cause of the fundamentalists in Iran by providing them with a justification for repressive policies while fanning the nationalist flames of a people under attack.
66. 'Rencontre avec Gus Van Sant'.
67. These aesthetic choices recall the work of another great portraitist of American life and social violence, who was equally fond of referencing *Macbeth* and avoiding facile, one-sided explanations: William Faulkner. The six different trailers for *Elephant*, which are guided by the name intertitles in the film, emphasise the connections to novels such as *The Sound and the Fury* and *As I Lay Dying*.

68. See Van Sant's answer to the question concerning kids' reactions to his film in Keaton and Van Sant, 'Elephant: Interview': 'I think that kids will probably be the best audience, because I think that they recognise the quote-unquote answers as scapegoats or red herrings. They know, since they live in this situation, that the answer is way more unpredictable. You can say, "Well, you know, these are the signs to look for. If you look for these signs, you will be safe. Or, if you look for these signs, you can fix it before it happens." They're smarter than that, I think. They already know they have to do a little more thinking, and that it's less curable than just [watching for] the warning signs. And they live with it. Since they're in high school, they live with this day to day; they live inside of it. When you talk to them, they can play the part of the student who is just playing up to the adult, pretending they know all the things they should be saying about school shootings, or they can be themselves, and they can just tell you that they're sick of the whole thing – adults don't get it, and it's their own world, and leave them alone, basically.'
69. Interview with Gus Van Sant in *Repérages*, 42:9–10, 2003, p. 33. This reference is borrowed from Roei Amit's article 'Trauma-Image: The Elephant Experience'. Unfortunately, I have not been able to obtain the original interview.
70. It remains to be seen whether Rancière's more recent rejection of ontology and essentialism – see for instance his contribution to Rockhill and Watts (eds), *Jacques Rancière: History, Politics, Aesthetics* – constitutes a significant shift in his work or is simply an authoritative rejection of certain criticisms of his stance on politics. In assessing his interestingly pragmatic stance at the end of 'The Method of Equality', it is important to remember that claiming that something is the case does not necessarily make it so.

Chapter 9

THE FORGOTTEN POLITICAL ART PAR EXCELLENCE? ARCHITECTURE, DESIGN AND THE SOCIAL SCULPTING OF THE BODY POLITIC

To the maestro of hand and mind

The social fact is sometimes so far materialised as to become an element of the external world. For instance, a definite type of architecture is a social phenomenon but it is partially embodied in houses and buildings of all sorts which, once constructed, become autonomous realities, independent of individuals.

(Émile Durkheim)

ABANDONED BUILDINGS

Through the course of the long twentieth century, an expansive and robust philosophical debate developed on the relationship between art and radical politics, ranging from the work of the Frankfurt School to post-war French theory and contemporary discussions in the anglophone world. Although there are a few important exceptions, this debate has evinced a decidedly disproportionate interest in the literary and visual arts at the expense of architecture and public art. The theorists who have participated in it – including such prominent figures as Theodor Adorno, Max Horkheimer, Herbert Marcuse, Georg Lukács, Jean-Paul Sartre, Jean-François Lyotard, Jacques Rancière and many others – have primarily been concerned with the relationship between literature and the fine arts (occasionally music), on the one hand, and more or less radical forms of politics on the other. There are, of course, a few intermittent and partial reflections by these theorists and their major interlocutors on various types of architecture and design, many of which have been meticulously collected by Neil Leach in *Rethinking Architecture: A Reader in Cultural Theory*.[1] However, these authors' voluminous writings on the literary and visual arts far outweigh the handful of texts that have been collected in this anthology or elsewhere.

We must not confound this tendency with a general law or fall into simplistic schematisations that lose sight of the fine-grained nuances of historical dynamics. Let us insist at the outset, therefore, on the exceptions to this trend by briefly spotlighting some of the thinkers to have significantly engaged with the politics of architecture: Walter Benjamin, Michel Foucault, Henri Lefebvre and Paul Virilio in continental Europe, as well as David Harvey and Frederic Jameson in the anglophone world.[2] As we will see with some specific examples below, architecture has clearly not been completely ignored. Nevertheless, it is still far from functioning as a lodestone in the dominant critical theory debates on art and radical politics in the long twentieth century, which have tended to gravitate around literature and the fine arts to the detriment of architecture, building, design, decorative art, public monuments, sculpture and urban planning.[3] Three of the more prominent and lengthy collections of essays on contemporary architectural theory appear to corroborate this observation, at least insofar as it concerns critical philosophic engagements with the art of building. In spite of the fact that they are all over 600 pages in length, they only include a handful of pieces by prominent philosophers, and some of them only approach the issue of architecture rather obliquely.[4] This is probably one of the reasons why Hubert Tonka has forcibly proclaimed, in a recent interview that critically reflects on Jean Baudrillard's *Vérité ou radicalité de l'architecture?*: 'Architecture is a domain that interests almost no one from a philosophic point of view. There are very few texts, especially contemporary texts, on contemporary architecture.'[5]

Architectural practice did not wait, of course, for its intellectual – and material – encounter with politics. Indeed, many of the political experiments of the long twentieth century cast their claims in concrete forms. The history of the modern world could, in fact, be written in terms of the battle of buildings, and the urban landscape is one of the privileged sites of ideological and social struggle. Kenneth Frampton provides an interesting account of these clashes in his now-canonical work *Modern Architecture: A Critical History*. In Chapter 24, to take one poignant example, he revisits many of the central tensions of the period 1914–1943 and recasts them in terms of the general opposition between the Modern Movement and the New Tradition. Analysing a number of the significant fronts in the architectural skirmishes of the period – from India and the Soviet Union to Italy, Germany and the United States – he charts out the shifting confrontations between monumental state powers and forces of change. The former ultimately triumphed, according to him, during the interwar period:

> That aspect of the New Tradition which took the form of a stripped Classical style emerged as the ruling taste in the 1930s, wherever power wished to represent itself in a positive and progressive light. [...] This taste for Neo-Classical monumentality was not restricted [...] to totalitarian states, but could be seen in Paris [...]. It also made itself manifest in the United States.[6]

It was around the time of World War II that this tendency was reversed, he argues, and 'after the war the general ideological climate of the West was hostile to any kind of monumentality'.[7]

This is not to suggest that we can thereby isolate architecture and focus simply on the confrontation between individual edifices. To begin with, there is no essential or natural dividing line between architecture and the other arts. The concept and practice of architecture itself has a complex history, and it is only in the modern era that individual architects have come to be recognised as the responsible agents behind particular designs. The majority of what is built today is still constructed without a proper architect per se. Moreover, the art of building is very often part of a larger constructed environment, and it frequently includes sculptural elements, as well as drawing, painting and aspects of scenography. Architects have sought, at times, to foreground and enhance this potential for architectural designs to function as *Gesamtkunstwerke*, or total works of art that integrate all or most of the other arts. Walter Gropius's 1927 Total Theatre project is a remarkable incorporation not only of the theatre with its biomechanical stage (based on the model of Meyerhold's October Theatre in Moscow) but also of film and the performing arts since it included a cinema screen and an aerial stage.

It is also important to note that many of the other arts have what could be heuristically referred to as architectural elements. This is readily apparent in a significant portion of contemporary installation art, as evidenced by the aesthetic ecosystems produced by artists such as Matthew Barney, Thomas Hirschhorn, Ugo Rondinone and many others. Public art in the form of happenings, graffiti, outside projections, public performances and so forth obviously also has an architectural and urban dimension. Alex Villar's project 'Temporary Occupations', for instance, is an excellent example of the intertwining of performance art and architecture since he ignores city codes and social regulations by occupying non-functional and unused spaces in the urban environment. Creators such as Leandro Erlich and Sophie Ernst weave together the art of building and the construction of art to such an extent that the borders between the two become porous, if not obsolete. It is also arguable, to take what might be considered a more extreme example, that there are prominent architectural elements in Victor Hugo's writings, both stylistically and in content, as well as in Charles Baudelaire's work. 'With Baudelaire,' Walter Benjamin writes, 'Paris becomes for the first time the subject of lyric poetry. This poetry of place is the opposite of all poetry of the soil. The gaze which the allegorical genius turns on the city betrays, instead, a profound alienation.'[8] Architectural designs have also been reciprocally influenced by other arts, and Kenneth Frampton has suggested, for instance, that Albert Speer was so marked by Leni Riefenstahl's film *Triumph des Willens* that henceforth his 'designs for stadia at Nuremberg were determined as much by camera angles as by architectural criteria'.[9] For all of these reasons, and many more, we should avoid reifying architecture as a distinct entity with an identifiable nature and instead understand it as a negotiated social practice bound up in various and complex ways with other artistic – as well as social and political – practices.

With these important provisos in mind, it is now possible to nuance the structural frame of my argument. Rather than seeking to establish a massive historical generalisation according to which philosophy missed its encounter with architecture in the twentieth century, my working hypothesis is much more specific: theoretical debates on the relationship between art and radical politics, particularly within the field of Euro-American critical theory broadly construed, have evinced a disproportionate interest in literature, the visual arts and sometimes music (which is also a special case) at the expense of what is commonly recognised as a distinct field of practices, namely those of architecture, building, design, urban planning and public art.

THE SOCIAL ART PAR EXCELLENCE?

> As the practice of imagining and building a new world, architecture will always be political.
>
> (Kim Dovey and Scott Dickson)

> It is a question of building which is at the root of the social unrest of today; architecture or revolution.
>
> (Le Corbusier)

The lack of gravitational pull exercised by architecture and design over core theoretical debates on art and politics in the contemporary era is particularly remarkable due to the patent ways in which the art of building is intimately interlaced with numerous social and political struggles. This is particularly apparent when we consider the social politicity of the built environment, meaning the various political aspects of its social life, including those operative in its design and production, its concrete materialisations and its assorted appropriations.

Regarding design and production, to begin with, architecture and public art almost always take place, in our day and age, in a constructed milieu, or at the very least within the charted territories of traversed landscapes. They cannot, therefore, be easily isolated from their immediate inscription in a larger socio-political space, as the fetishisation of individual buildings and architects is apt to do. National laws, local ordinances, building codes, zoning rules and urban planning influence the practices of architecture, as well as such things as non-codified regulations, building and design technologies, transportation routes, pressure from clients and investors, economic exigencies, media representations and cultural values.[10] The fact that built architecture tends overwhelmingly to be anchored in a functional setting brings with it a series of more or less immediate social and political concerns.[11] Moreover, since production costs are often exorbitant, some authors have argued that 'architects are reliant on their clients' patronage in ways that other cultural producers are not'.[12] Whatever the case may be, it is clear that contemporary architectural design and production is very often the result of collective negotiations between multiple sources and types of agency. 'The actions of architects and other agents involved in the production of the built environment', write Rob Imrie and Emma Street, 'are entwined in complex ways with a panoply of state, non-state and civil organisations, associations and relations.'[13] It is in this force field of agencies that important socio-political battles are fought regarding what can be built, how it is constructed, what materials are used, where it is assembled, who erects it, how it interacts with its immediate environment, who has access to it, and so forth. Louis Sullivan's brief summary of the emergence of the high-rise building points to some of these 'extra-architectural' pressures and socio-political struggles over production that led to a novel type of building: 'The tall commercial building arose from the pressure of land prices, the land prices from pressure of population, the pressure of population from external pressure.'[14]

Once they are built, the materialised products of architecture and design often stand as powerful and lasting symbols of cultural values and systems of meaning. This is quite obvious in the case of the five types of urban shrines identified by Maria Kaika and Korinna Thielen:

> Pre-modern monuments – deference to state and church authority; public cathedrals of technology and money power – tributes to a new era of secularisation and industrialisation; private secular shrines – homage to individual achievement under capitalism; social housing projects – pa[la]tially inscribed bold statements of the post-war welfare state; and private-public shrines – temptresses for global finance.[15]

Above and beyond these forms of iconic symbolism, the built environment serves as the revealing agent of social structure, a powerful force of naturalisation and a potential site of contestation. It demonstrates the fundamental values of a cultural world order, which materially manifests itself in such elements – depending on the location – as prominent financial districts, cheap structures propping up corporate signage, highly accessible tourist sites, the structural privileging of vehicles over pedestrians and public transportation, the destruction or sequestering of the natural environment, and so forth. The constructed milieu simultaneously naturalises this cultural system as well as its dominant social relations by creating an ingrained sense of 'normal' relationships, as is the case not only with the examples just cited but also with such things as the ample use of individual as opposed to collective living units, or the isolation and ghettoisation of certain social groups.[16] In all of these ways, architectural forms tend to both manifest and accentuate socio-political structures and norms, while at the same time being the site of ongoing struggles over the collective formation – and potential reconfiguration – of the social order.

Architecture and public arts also play a central role in sculpting the body politic by canalising movement, structuring perception, forming social agents, conveying political imaginaries and codifying collective and individual behaviour in various ways. Walter Benjamin has cogently analysed, for instance, how the phantasmagorias of the marketplace took on architectural and urban forms in the transmogrification of the everyday aesthetics of modern Paris. From the world exhibitions and the proliferation of arcades to the rituals of fashion, the hypnotic meanderings of the *flâneur*, the development of private interiors and Haussmann's muscular rending of the urban fabric, the entire cityscape came to be saturated with 'the pomp and the splendour with which commodity-producing society surrounds itself, as well as its illusory sense of security'.[17] In addition to examining the various ways in which the city became an expansive and intricate shrine to commodity fetishism, he notoriously insisted on the direct political implications of Haussmann's project of slicing wide, long boulevards into the dense urban environment:

> The true goal of Haussmann's projects was to secure the city against civil war. He wanted to make the erection of barricades in the streets of Paris impossible for all time. With the same end in mind, Louis Philippe had already introduced wooden paving. Nevertheless, barricades had played a considerable role in the February Revolution. Engels studied the tactics of barricade fighting. Haussmann seeks to forestall such combat in two ways. Widening the streets will make the erection of barricades impossible, and new streets will connect the barracks in straight lines with the workers' districts. Contemporaries christened the operation 'strategic embellishment'.[18]

This final expression appropriately summarises one of Benjamin's chief concerns in his posthumously published *Arcades Project*: the ways in which the everyday aesthetic environment of the built world functions as a more or less discreet vehicle for socio-political and economic forces.

To take another example, Michel Foucault has poignantly argued that architecture plays an important role in the complex of power relations that shape and form subjects. In *Discipline and Punish*, he partially juxtaposed the classic schema of *le grand renfermement*, which erects strict boundaries between two spaces, with the modern model of disciplinary power, in which there are manifold divisions, individualising distributions and multiple levels of surveillance. The emergence of disciplinary power produces, according to him, a specific set of architectural problems and concerns:

> A whole problematic then develops: that of an architecture that is no longer built simply to be seen (as with the ostentation of palaces), or to observe the external space (cf. the geometry of fortresses), but to permit an internal, articulated and detailed control – to render visible those who are inside it; in more general terms, an architecture that would operate to transform individuals: to act on those it shelters, to provide a hold on their conduct, to carry the effects of power right to them, to make it possible to know them, to alter them. Stones can make people docile and knowable. The old simple schema of confinement and enclosure – thick walls, a heavy gate that prevents entering or leaving – began to be replaced by the calculation of openings, of filled and empty spaces, passages and transparencies.[19]

Although the spatial orders of closure and disciplinary distribution are distinct, and Foucault identifies a partial sequential development from one to the other, they are by no means irreconcilable. In fact, he claims that disciplinary schemas are grafted on to exclusionary models in the nineteenth century:

> They are different projects, then, but not incompatible ones. We see them coming slowly together, and it is the peculiarity of the nineteenth century that it applied to the space of exclusion of which the leper was the symbolic inhabitant (beggars, vagabonds, madmen and the disorderly formed the real population) the technique of power proper to disciplinary partitioning. Treat 'lepers' as 'plague victims', project the subtle segmentations of discipline onto the confused space of internment, combine it with the methods of analytical distribution proper to power, individualise the excluded, but use procedures of individualisation to mark exclusion – this is what was operated regularly by disciplinary

power from the beginning of the nineteenth century in the psychiatric asylum, the penitentiary, the reformatory, the approved school and, to some extent, the hospital.[20]

Furthermore, Foucault emphasises the variable practical uses of spaces, as we will see below, and he rejects the idea that they simply have an inherent politics that is established at the moment of their creation. When Paul Rabinow asks him in an interview if certain architectural projects appear to represent forces of liberation or resistance, he retorts: 'I do not think that there is anything that is functionally – by its very nature – absolutely liberating. Liberty is a *practice*.'[21]

The social politicity of public arts includes, in addition to the Byzantine struggles over their production and the diverse social effects of their materialisations, their reception and appropriation by various agents. The proposed symbolism or signification of a building is not equivalent, of course, to its actual import or significance. As Paul Knox has argued, 'there is an important distinction between the *intended* meaning of specific groups or individuals and the *perceived* meaning of the built environment as seen by others. [...] Another important point is that the social meaning of the built environment is *not static*.'[22] The same is true for the projected purpose or use of a public construction, as poignantly emphasised by Louis Aragon in his significant ruminations on urban space in *Le Paysan de Paris*: 'No one is suggesting that the architect foresaw the use that would be made of these fittings: could the engineer who drew up the plans for the Pont de Solférino have had an inkling of the debaucheries that his arches would one day shelter?'[23] Michel Foucault has similarly argued, using the example of Jean-Baptiste Godin's Familistère in Guise, that architectural spaces lend themselves to a myriad of possible appropriations rather than having a single political valence:

> Godin's architecture was clearly aimed at freedom. Here was something that manifested the power of ordinary workers to participate in the exercise of their trade. [...] Yet no one could enter or leave the *familistère* without being seen by everyone else – an aspect of the architecture that could be totally oppressive. But it could only be oppressive if people were prepared to use their own presence in order to watch over others. Let's imagine a community that might be established there, which would indulge in

unlimited sexual practices. It would once again become a place of freedom. I think it is somewhat arbitrary to try to dissociate the effective practice of freedom, the practice of social relations, and spatial distributions.[24]

There are various socio-political dimensions to the reception of public works of art as they take on a life of their own in the hands of their users. The re-appropriation of buildings or public spaces, for instance, can be an important part of political struggles, as the history of occupations clearly illustrates, as well as such catalysing moments as the Paris Commune or the recent occupations of Tahrir Square in Cairo, the Pearl Roundabout in Manama, the Puerta del Sol in Madrid, Zuccotti Park in New York, Taksim Square in Istanbul, and so many other occupations elsewhere. Paul Virilio has argued, in this light, that the re-appropriation of functionalised spaces was key to the uprisings of May 1968 in France:

> The amazing phenomenon that abruptly emptied the streets and filled the monuments shattered the airtight compartments of our society. It revealed the alienation hidden beneath the most ordinary everyday habits. By forgetting prohibitions, for a time, and inhabiting the uninhabitable, the populace committed their very first adultery vis-à-vis the spatial appropriation that desocialises them, isolates them, and sequesters them.[25]

These types of communal struggles over the built environment and public spaces are a crucial aspect of the social politicity of architecture and urban planning.

REFLECTIONS ON A MISSED ENCOUNTER BETWEEN THEORY AND PRACTICE

Any etiological account of complex social phenomena requires a methodological framework that discards the structuralist assumption – which stretches well beyond structuralism in the strict sense of the term – that there is a single cause, a sole plane of determination or a unique scaffold behind social circumstances. In the socio-historical world, there are always multiple factors that are operative, and they form shifting constellations of pressure that change in each particular conjuncture. It is thereby necessary to eschew the search for single causes or determinants in favour of a multivariate analysis of dynamic complexes of force.

Without pretending to propose an exhaustive analysis, let us underscore some of the significant elements at work in the network of factors that has contributed to the largely missed encounter between radical politics and architecture in the broad critical theory tradition (with the exception of figures like Benjamin, Foucault and Virilio). To begin with, it is arguable that much of the contemporary debate on art and politics has grown out of the intellectual and cultural crucible of the late eighteenth and early nineteenth century. This is obviously not the place for a detailed investigation of this historical conjuncture, but it is worth highlighting the near-simultaneous emergence of art – in the modern sense of the term – and revolutionary politics. Beginning with the former, we should note that the modern notion of fine art developed in part by distinguishing itself more stringently from crafts as well as from the work of the sciences, and it consolidated itself in new institutions such as the public museum. At the same time, the artist and the work of art were further individualised and more strongly affiliated with the creative powers of exceptional forms of imagination. The modern concept of literature also appeared at this time, and the term came to refer to a canonical group of writings that embody a specific experience of language.[26] These changes did not occur, of course, as a swift sea change, and we must not imagine these complex and shifting reconfigurations in terms of the simple dropping and raising of a curtain allowing for a near-instantaneous change in the set design of the historical stage. What happened in this gradual and intermittent alteration of social practices was that a relatively new problematic emerged, in certain foyers of transformation, in which a gulf appeared between the immediate functionalism of the manual arts and crafts, on the one hand, and the supposedly higher calling of the fine arts on the other. Multiple positions emerged on this issue, and there was no overwhelming consensus across society as a whole. In fact, one of the fundamental concerns that has continued to plague much of what is generically labelled modern art is precisely the overcoming of this divide, as evidenced by the Arts and Crafts movement, the Bauhaus, and so many other endeavours to unite hand and mind. This being said, the emergence of the modern institutions of art and literature, as well as of art history and literary history, has led to the development and sedimentation of parallel institutional worlds. At times, this has favoured an increasing separation between the manual arts, which are often affiliated with the lowly domain of crafts, and the lofty realm of art in the restricted sense of the term.

Revolutionary politics in the strict sense is also a modern phenomenon. As thinkers like Hannah Arendt, Félix Gilbert, Reinhart Koselleck and Raymond Williams have argued, it is only in approximately the last third of the eighteenth century that the notion and practice of social revolution appears. As in the case of the modern concept of art, fine methodological footwork would be necessary to avoid schematic accounts of the history of revolutionary practice. For our current concerns, let it suffice to say that there is ample evidence to suggest that radical social revolutions, which stretch beyond institutional and political changes in order to reconfigure the very structure of society, are relatively novel phenomena that began to appear around the end of the Enlightenment. It is not surprising, then, that one of the philosophical concerns that emerged at this point in time had to do with the relationship between the newly institutionalised fine arts, on the one hand, and the relatively recent appearance of revolutionary politics on the other. In fact, one of the unique features of much of the debate on art and politics in the modern world is that the question 'what is the relationship between art and politics?' actually tends to mean 'what is the relation between high art and revolutionary politics?'.

One of the reasons for this, at least in the twentieth century but perhaps earlier, is surely that many of the leading figures in German critical theory and contemporary French thought are members of the middle-class, white, male, intellectual elite. They are largely part of the *Bildungsbürgertum*, and they tend to incarnate the bourgeois liberal ideals of education. This means that they were usually well versed in the history of art, instructed implicitly or explicitly to appreciate the high arts, and trained to varying degrees to reproduce the social hierarchies inherent in the theoretical distinction between the lofty culture of the urbane elite and the lowly crafts and entertaining amusements of the uncouth masses. When they sought to break with the bourgeois tradition in order to engage in radical politics of various ilks, one of the pressing – but sometimes implicit – questions became: what is the relationship between the bourgeois art of our past and the political transformation that we aspire to in the future? Moreover, given the fact that many of these authors clearly continued to appreciate the high art on which they had been weaned, there was a general concern with how the art and literature of their bourgeois upbringing could contribute to the political struggle that they hoped to instigate or support.

This preoccupation with the radical political implications of high art is particularly interesting given the number of architects in the long twentieth century who were dedicated to destroying the very opposition between high and low art. The Bauhaus could again be cited for its unique capacity to bring together architects, designers, painters, photographers and so on in an effort to unify the spiritual and the material, the artistic and the technical, mind and hand. In fact, this concern cuts across many of the important architectural movements of the twentieth century, and it is perhaps Le Corbusier who provided the most concise summary of this agenda by defining architecture as the 'esthetics of the engineer', which unites the technical precision of building with the creative powers of art.[27]

This corrective on the part of certain architects does not mean, of course, that the distinction between high and low art has dissipated, or that these hierarchies have stopped having social effects and implications. In fact, they continue to haunt the work of those architects and theorists who redeploy the very same hierarchy of high and low art within the built environment by juxtaposing true architecture (high art) to average building (low art). If we remain blind to such iterations of the distinction between high and low art, which is still obviously an important feature of much of the constructed milieu, then we run the risk of ignoring crucial socio-political aspects of the entire built environment. For this distinction creates, at least potentially, a social and often economic line of demarcation between the prestigious architect-designed buildings and the less than glamorous constructions of the everyday world. Diane Ghirardo has discerningly highlighted this problem in critical discussions of architecture:

> To the degree nonarchitect or builder designs enter into the architectural discussion, it is as the objects of thoroughgoing condemnation: from subdivisions, to mini-malls, to tract houses. In the current orthodoxy, such building production lacks the virtue of design [...] that is to say, the buildings lack the artistic qualities associated with architect-designed structures. Whereas fervent debate animates discussions about most architect-designed buildings [...] there is tacit and often explicit professional

agreement that nonarchitect-designed buildings cannot be considered Architecture. Such a view refers back to a general belief that Architecture is an art, and that art in turn has a high moral purpose in the formation and transmission of culture.[28]

It is with this in mind that she judiciously asserts that 'Whatever problems, flaws, or weaknesses one might discern in nonarchitectural building – or "low art" – ignoring them, dismissing them out of hand, or failing to analyse the relationship between high and low art in effect means that one is not engaging in the act of criticism, but rather acting to preserve a particular status quo.'[29]

Two other important factors that have contributed to prescinding the built environment from major theoretical discussions of art and politics are what I propose to call the talisman complex and the social epoché, which have beleaguered a significant portion of contemporary debates.[30] Much of the current controversy tends to focus on individual works of high art and their ability or inability to directly produce political effects. This has the unfortunate consequence of reducing the politics of art to the talisman-like power of isolated aesthetic artefacts (talisman complex), which are largely sequestered from the various dimensions of their complex social existence (social epoché). Such an approach tends to lead, moreover, to an impasse insofar as the politics of art, far from being a force magically inherent – or not – in certain privileged objects, plays itself out in the ongoing social battles over the production, circulation and reception of collectively negotiated works. It is not surprising, given this isolation of aesthetic products and the general bracketing of the social world, that works of art strongly rooted in a functional environment of everyday social use have tended to be ignored.

Finally, we should note that architectural history does not fit well with many of the standard accounts of art history, and more specifically those that seek to establish certain political narratives. Consider, to begin with, the widespread description of artistic and literary history in terms of a classical age of mimesis, characterised in part by its conservative preservation of the status quo, which was supposedly followed by a modern era of anti-mimetic art and an iconoclastic assault on good form. Leaving aside the crucial question of the viability of such a schematisation for the fine arts, it is far from obvious that classical architecture sought – at least in any straightforward sense – to imitate nature or that modern architecture merely repudiated such imitation. In fact, Gaudi's cavernous constructions, like the sinuous forms of art nouveau, could be considered closer to nature than many of the buildings of the seventeenth and eighteenth centuries. Furthermore, the other customary accounts of artistic modernism largely fail to capture what is commonly referred to as modern architecture. For instance, it is unclear how the supposed autonomisation of art, the emergence of abstraction, the appearance of the 'aesthetics of the commonplace', or the development of what is called intransitive art and literature could help make sense of significant changes in building practices in the early part of the twentieth century. Many of these were bound up with the relatively new embedded technologies of concrete and steel (as well as novel uses of glass), but also with the social and economic pressures of the contemporary urban environment and capitalist expansion. These overlapped in many ways, moreover, with what is often called avant-garde architecture, which, once again, cannot be easily aligned with the now-standard historical narratives regarding the development of avant-garde art and literature. Perhaps the most widespread thesis is still that of Peter Bürger, who vigorously argued that the historical avant-garde – understood above all as the avant-garde in the fine arts – ultimately failed in its socio-political aspirations because it was not able to truly link art with life. Yet it could easily be claimed that this is precisely what avant-garde architecture and design accomplished. To begin with, most architecture, whether it be identified as avant-garde or not, does not have to join art with life because its very existence presupposes just such a connection. Secondly, it might be argued that the architectural avant-garde – if this term makes sense – succeeded in developing and spreading new forms of design that have now become more or less ubiquitous in the 'high modernism' of the contemporary urban landscape. Once again, we see that the case of architecture cannot be comfortably situated within the dominant historical schematisations of artistic and literary history, and more specifically within those that are premised on a certain political interpretation of historical developments (where modernism and avant-gardism are often linked to the iconoclastic rejection of established conventions). For these and other reasons, many theorists have conveniently sidelined or ignored architecture, public art and urban design.

This list of factors is surely not exhaustive, and the individual elements vary in intensity and form depending on the specific socio-historical intersection. However, it does provide us with at least partial indications regarding the conjuncture of factors that have contributed to the tendency to turn a blind eye to the social politicity of the built world in critical theories of art and politics.

CONCLUSION

The built environment forms and shapes our daily lives even if we do not go to museums or galleries, attend public performances, frequent the cinema, or even read books and periodicals. It delivers to us an implicit sense of our collective cosmos as a naturalised world, often inconspicuously enchanted with value and meaning. It is the art that sculpts our social existence and creates a physical field of possibility, punctuated by symbolic icons, as well as a structured realm of experience that forms us as social beings and codifies our behaviour and thought in multiple ways. 'Building is the art we live in,' writes Robert Hughes, 'it is the social art *par excellence*, the carapace of political fantasy, the exoskeleton of one's economic dreams. It is also the one art nobody can escape.'[31]

The social politicity of architecture and the built environment includes, in addition to the material forms that directly shape daily social interaction, the complicated battles and debates that go into the production of buildings. In the contemporary world, it would be naive to separate architectural practice from its inscription in a larger politico-economic space and a general struggle over a common world. This is not only because individual edifices are almost always part of a larger built milieu, or at the very least a charted territory, but also because the entire sphere of construction is bound up with the political stakes inherent in establishing and negotiating a material domain of shared existence.

A third aspect of the social politicity of public art is the way in which it is appropriated and used by the general population, which often includes significant clashes over the meaning and role of constructed spaces. Once a structure is erected (and even before, for that matter), it takes on a social life of its own and becomes a site that can be appropriated and re-appropriated to various ends. The politics of constructed spaces does not end, therefore, with the erection of buildings. This is, one might say, only its beginning.

Ignoring or bracketing these assorted aspects of the social politicity of architectural practices has the unfortunate consequence of excluding from debates on art and politics what might be considered – at least from a certain point of view, for this is not the position that I am advocating across the board – the political art par excellence. Much of contemporary critical philosophy, marked by the inheritance of the historical problematic of the relationship between high art and revolutionary politics, has indeed turned a blind eye to architecture in favour of meditating on the potential for the grand art of the bourgeoisie – and particularly individual works of fine art and literature – to contribute to radical social and political transformation. It thereby runs the risk of reproducing, at least implicitly or to a certain degree, one of the very same social hierarchies that radical politics aims at overcoming and that many architects have sought to destroy, in part by creating buildings that cannot be easily inscribed within schematic historical narratives concerning the politics of art.

The overall objective of this analysis has, therefore, been threefold: to highlight a fundamental problem and limitation in critical theoretical debates on art and politics, to explore the conjuncture of factors that have contributed to this predicament, and to propose an alternative methodology that allows us to abandon a restricted understanding of the politics of art in favour of a broad-based analysis of the social politicity of aesthetic practices. The ultimate goal has thus been to open space for a renewed interrogation into the political stakes of the built environment and the diverse ways in which the collective building and negotiating of a shared material and symbolic world is also the forging – and potential re-forging – of a people.

NOTES

1. Since Rancière has written a number of important works after the publication of Leach's book, it is worth signalling at least two chapters that constitute a partial but minor exception to his tendency to accord a considerable privilege to the visual arts, and especially to literature. He reflects on the question of design in a text in *The Future of the Image* (pp. 91–107), and he pursues certain aspects of this reflection in a chapter in *Aisthesis* that also discusses issues related to architecture (pp. 133–53).
2. Ernst Bloch, Guy Debord, Jürgen Habermas and Siegfried Kracauer (who studied architecture and worked as an architect) have also written pieces on architecture and urban planning. There are surely other examples that could be cited, ranging from the important work of the Situationist

International to the relatively short writings on architecture by thinkers like Antonio Negri and Slavoj Žižek, or the rather brief musings by philosophers who were less dedicated to critical social theory, such as Martin Heidegger and Jacques Derrida.
3. Dance, both as a performing art and as a social practice, could probably be added to this list.
4. See Nesbitt (ed.), *Theorising a New Agenda for Architecture*, Hays (ed.), *Architecture Theory since 1968*, and Contandriopoulos and Mallgrave (eds), *Architectural Theory, Vol. II*.
5. Tonka, 'Vérité ou radicalité de l'architecture? de Jean Baudrillard'.
6. Frampton, *Modern Architecture*, p. 219.
7. Ibid., p. 222.
8. Benjamin, *The Arcades Project*, p. 21.
9. Frampton, *Modern Architecture*, p. 218. In 'Reflexions on the Autonomy of Architecture', Frampton discusses the dissolution of contemporary architecture into an endless proliferation of images, and he claims that 'this is a situation in which buildings tend to be increasingly designed for their photogenic effect rather than their experiential potential' (in Ghirardo (ed.), *Out of Site: A Social Criticism of Architecture*, p. 26).
10. On this topic, see the special issue of *Urban Studies* on the regulation of design (46:12, November 2009).
11. See, for instance, Ghirardo (ed.), *Out of Site*, pp. 17–26. In a longer analysis, it would be interesting to explore the important role and status of theoretical designs, meaning the significant number of architectural plans that are never actually materialised in concrete forms. For reasons of concision, I am here concentrating on built architecture.
12. Jones, 'Putting Architecture in Its Social Place', p. 2521. This is a statement by Paul Jones, summarising the work of Magali Safuri Larson.
13. Imrie and Street, 'Regulating Design: The Practices of Architecture, Governance and Control', p. 2508.
14. Sullivan, *The Autobiography of an Idea*, p. 310.
15. Kaika and Thielen, 'Form Follows Power: A Genealogy of Urban Shrines', p. 67.
16. On the latter issue see, for instance, Michel Kokoreff's work.
17. Benjamin, *The Arcades Project*, p. 15.
18. Ibid., p. 23. Also see Frampton's discussion of Haussmann in *Modern Architecture* (pp. 23–4).
19. Foucault, *Discipline and Punish*, p. 172.
20. Ibid., p. 199. The rest of the quotation reads: 'Generally speaking, all the authorities exercising individual control function according to a double mode; that of binary division and branding (mad/sane; dangerous/harmless; normal/abnormal); and that of coercive assignment, of differen-

tial distribution (who he is; where he must be; how he is to be characterised; how he is to be recognised; how a constant surveillance is to be exercised over him in an individual way, etc.).'
21. Foucault, 'Space, Knowledge, and Power', p. 245.
22. Knox, 'Symbolism, Styles and Settings', p. 112.
23. Aragon, *Paris Peasant*, p. 57.
24. Foucault, 'Space, Knowledge, and Power', p. 246 (translation slightly modified; see Foucault, *Dits et écrits*, vol. 4: 1980–1988, pp. 276–7).
25. Virilio, 'Critical Space', p. 31.
26. See Rancière, *Mute Speech*.
27. Le Corbusier, *Vers une architecture*, p. xvii.
28. Ghirardo (ed.), *Out of Site*, p. 11.
29. Ibid., p. 13.
30. I develop both of these ideas in *Radical History and the Politics of Art*.
31. Hughes, *The Shock of the New: The Hundred-Year History of Modern Art*, p. 164.

BIBLIOGRAPHY

Agamben, Giorgio, *What Is an Apparatus?*, trans. David Kishik and Stefan Pedatella (Stanford: Stanford University Press, 2009).

Agora International, 'Cornelius Castoriadis Dies at 75', <http://www.agora international.org/about.html> (last accessed 11 January 2016).

Alcoff, Linda Martín, 'A Call for Climate Change for Women in Philosophy', <http://alcoff.com/articles/call-climate-change-women-philosophy> (last accessed 11 January 2016).

Alcoff, Linda Martín, 'Philosophy's Civil Wars', Presidential Address to the APA Eastern, 2012, <http://alcoff.com/2012-american-philosophical-association-presidential-address> (last accessed 11 January 2016).

Alpert, Avram, 'Practices of the Global Self: Idealism, Transcendentalism, and Buddhist Modernism in the Era of Colonisation', dissertation defended at the University of Pennsylvania, Department of Comparative Literature, 2014.

Amit, Roei, 'Trauma-Image: The Elephant Experience', in Austin Sarat, Nadav Davidovitch and Michal Alberstein (eds), *Trauma and Memory: Reading, Healing, and Making Law* (Stanford: Stanford University Press, 2008), pp. 78–94.

Aragon, Louis, *Paris Peasant*, trans. Simon Watson Taylor (Boston: Exact Change, 1994).

Arendt, Hannah, *Between Past and Future: Six Exercises in Political Thought* (New York: Viking, 1961).

Arendt, Hannah, *On Revolution* (New York: Viking, 1963).

Aristotle, *The Complete Works of Aristotle*, vol. 2, ed. Jonathan Barnes (Princeton: Princeton University Press, 1984).

Arrous, Adrien and Alexandre Costanzo, 'Questions à Jacques Rancière', *Drôle d'époque*, 14, Spring 2004, pp. 15–29.

Asad, Talal, *Anthropology and the Colonial Encounter* (Amherst, NY: Humanity Books, 1998).

Augustine, *The City of God against the Pagans*, trans. R. W. Dyson (Cambridge: Cambridge University Press, 1998).

Azouvi, François, *Descartes et la France* (Paris: Fayard, 2002).
Badiou, Alain, *Abrégé de métapolitique* (Paris: Éditions du Seuil, 1998).
Badiou, Alain, 'The Adventure of French Philosophy', *New Left Review*, 35, September–October 2005, pp. 67–77.
Badiou, Alain, *Being and Event*, trans. Oliver Feltham (London: Continuum, 2005).
Badiou, Alain, *The Century*, trans. Alberto Toscano (Cambridge: Polity Press, 2007).
Badiou, Alain, *Conditions* (Paris: Éditions du Seuil, 1992).
Badiou, Alain, *Ethics: An Essay on the Understanding of Evil*, trans. with an introduction by Peter Hallward (London: Verso Books, 2001).
Badiou, Alain, 'Fifteen Theses on Contemporary Art', *Lacanian Ink*, 23, 2004, pp. 103–19.
Badiou, Alain, *Handbook of Inaesthetics*, trans. Alberto Toscano (Stanford: Stanford University Press, 2004).
Badiou, Alain, *Logiques des mondes* (Paris: Éditions du Seuil, 2006).
Badiou, Alain, *Manifeste pour la philosophie* (Paris: Éditions du Seuil, 1989).
Badiou, Alain, *Manifesto for Philosophy*, ed. and trans. Norman Madarasz (Albany: State University of New York Press, 1999).
Badiou, Alain, *Metapolitics*, trans. Jason Barker (London: Verso Books, 2006).
Badiou, Alain, *Petit Manuel d'inesthétique* (Paris: Éditions du Seuil, 1998).
Badiou, Alain, *Second Manifesto for Philosophy*, trans. Louise Burchill (Cambridge: Polity Press, 2011).
Badiou, Alain, *Le Siècle* (Paris: Éditions du Seuil, 2005).
Badiou, Alain et al., *Matrix: Machine philosophique* (Paris: Ellipses, 2013).
Badiou, Alain, Raymond Bellour, Jean-Clet Martin and Jacques Rancière, 'Autour de *La parole muette* de Jacques Rancière', *Horlieu-(X)*, 18, 2000, pp. 60–98.
Badiou, Alain, Philippe Lacoue-Labarthe, Jean-François Lyotard and Jacques Rancière, 'Liminaire sur l'ouvrage d'Alain Badiou *L'Être et l'événement*', *Le Cahier* (Collège international de philosophie), 8, October 1989, pp. 201–25, 227– 45, 247–68.
Badiou, Alain and Jacques Rancière, 'Contre-courant: Le Face-à-face Badiou-Rancière', 20 May 2014, <http://www.dailymotion.com/video/x1vssyi_contre-courant-le-face-a-face-badiou-ranciere_news> (last accessed 11 January 2016).
Badiou, Alain with Fabien Tarby, *La Philosophie et l'événement: Entretiens* (Meaux: Éditions Germina, 2010).
Balibar, Étienne, *Egaliberty: Political Essays*, trans. James Ingram (Durham, NC: Duke University Press, 2014).
Balibar, Étienne and Immanuel Wallerstein, *Race, Nation, Class: Ambiguous Identities* (London: Verso Books, 1991).

Barthes, Roland, *Critical Essays*, trans. Richard Howard (Evanston: Northwestern University Press, 1972).
Barthes, Roland, *Œuvres complètes*, vol. 1 (1942–65) (Paris: Éditions du Seuil, 1993).
Benjamin, Walter, *The Arcades Project*, trans. H. Eiland and K. McLaughlin (Cambridge, MA: The Belknap Press of Harvard University Press, 1999).
Bennett, Tony, *The Birth of the Museum* (London and New York: Routledge, 1995).
Bernasconi, Robert, 'Philosophy's Paradoxical Parochialism: The Reinvention of Philosophy as Greek', in Keith Ansell-Pearson, Benita Parry and Judith Squires (eds), *Cultural Readings of Imperialism* (New York: St. Martin's Press, 1997), pp. 212–26.
Birch, Anthony H., *The Concepts and Theories of Modern Democracy* (London and New York: Routledge, 1993).
Bordwell, David, 'Slavoj Žižek: Say Anything', April 2005, <http://www.davidbordwell.net/essays/zizek.php> (last accessed 11 January 2016).
Borges, Jorge Luis, *Other Inquisitions, 1937–1952*, trans. Ruth L. C. Simms (Austin: University of Texas Press, 1964).
Boschetti, Anna, *The Intellectual Enterprise: Sartre and 'Les Temps Modernes'*, trans. Richard C. McCleary (Evanston: Northwestern University Press, 1988).
Bourdieu, Pierre, *Distinction: A Social Critique of the Judgement of Taste*, trans. Richard Nice (Cambridge, MA: Harvard University Press, 1984).
Bourdieu, Pierre, *Pascalian Meditations* (London: Polity Press, 2000).
Bourdieu, Pierre, 'The Philosophical Institution', in Alan Montefiore (ed.), *Philosophy in France Today* (Cambridge: Cambridge University Press, 1983), pp. 1–8.
Bourdieu, Pierre, *Sociology in Question* (London: Sage Publications Ltd, 1993).
Bourdieu, Pierre and Jean-Claude Passeron, 'Sociology and Philosophy in France since 1945: Death and Resurrection of a Philosophy without Subject', *Social Research*, 34:1, Spring 1967, pp. 162–212.
Bourdieu, Pierre and Loïc Wacquant, 'NewLiberalSpeak: Notes on the New Planetary Vulgate', trans. D. Macey, *Radical Philosophy*, 105, January–February 2001, pp. 2–5.
Buñuel, Luis (dir.), *Viridiana* [film], 1961.
Burke, Jason, *Al-Qaeda: Casting a Shadow of Terror* (London and New York: I.B. Tauris, 2003).
Butler, Judith, *Gender Trouble: Feminism and the Subversion of Identity* (New York: Routledge, 2006).
Butler, Judith, Ernesto Laclau and Slavoj Žižek, *Contingency, Hegemony, Universality* (London: Verso, 2000).

Bybee, Jay S., 'Memorandum for Alberto R. Gonzales', 22 January 2002, <http://www.gwu.edu/~nsarchiv/NSAEBB/NSAEBB127/02.01.22.pdf> (last accessed 11 January 2016).
Calhoun, Craig (ed.), *Habermas and the Public Sphere* (Cambridge, MA: The MIT Press, 1992).
Cassirer, Ernst, *The Philosophy of the Enlightenment* (Princeton: Princeton University Press, 2009).
Castoriadis, Cornelius, 'Agora International Interview', 1990, <http://www.agorainternational.org/enccaiint.pdf> (last accessed 11 January 2016).
Castoriadis, Cornelius, *Les Carrefours du labyrinthe 1* (Paris: Éditions du Seuil, 1978).
Castoriadis, Cornelius, *The Castoriadis Reader*, ed. and trans. David Ames Curtis (Oxford: Blackwell Publishers Ltd, 1997).
Castoriadis, Cornelius, *Crossroads in the Labyrinth*, trans. Kate Soper and Martin H. Ryle (Cambridge, MA: The MIT Press, 1984).
Castoriadis, Cornelius, *Domaines de l'homme* (Paris: Éditions du Seuil, 1986).
Castoriadis, Cornelius, *Fait et à faire* (Paris: Éditions du Seuil, 1997).
Castoriadis, Cornelius, *Fenêtre sur le chaos* (Paris: Éditions du Seuil, 2007).
Castoriadis, Cornelius, *Figures du pensable* (Paris: Éditions du Seuil, 1999).
Castoriadis, Cornelius, *Figures of the Thinkable*, trans. Helen Arnold (Stanford: Stanford University Press, 2007).
Castoriadis, Cornelius, *The Imaginary Institution of Society*, trans. Kathleen Blamey (Cambridge, MA: The MIT Press, 1987).
Castoriadis, Cornelius, *L'Institution imaginaire de la société* (Paris: Éditions du Seuil, 1975).
Castoriadis, Cornelius, *Le Monde morcelé* (Paris: Éditions du Seuil, 1990).
Castoriadis, Cornelius, *La Montée de l'insignifiance* (Paris: Éditions du Seuil, 1996).
Castoriadis, Cornelius, *Philosophy, Politics, Autonomy: Essays in Political Philosophy*, ed. David Ames Curtis (Oxford: Oxford University Press, 1991).
Castoriadis, Cornelius, *A Society Adrift: Interviews and Debates 1974–1997*, ed. Enrique Escobar, Myrto Gondicas and Pascal Vernay, trans. Helen Arnold (New York: Fordham University Press, 2010).
Castoriadis, Cornelius, *World in Fragments: Writings on Politics, Society, Psychoanalysis, and the Imagination*, ed. and trans. David Ames Curtis (Stanford: Stanford University Press, 1997).
Castoriadis, Cornelius, Enrique Escobar, Myrto Gondicas and Pascal Vernay, *Démocratie et relativisme: Débats avec le MAUSS* (Paris: Mille et une nuits, 2010).
Castro, Eduardo Viveiros de, *Cannibal Metaphysics*, ed. and trans. Peter Skafish (Minneapolis: Univocal Publishing, 2014).

Cavallo, Guglielmo and Roger Chartier (eds), *A History of Reading in the West* (Cambridge: Polity, 1999).

Césaire, Aimé, *Discours sur le colonialisme, suivi du Discours sur la Négritude* (Paris: Présence Africaine, 2004).

Césaire, Aimé, *Discourse on Colonialism*, trans. Joan Pinkham (New York: Monthly Review Press, 2000).

Chakrabarty, Dipesh, *Provincialising Europe: Postcolonial Thought and Historical Difference* (Princeton: Princeton University Press, 2007).

Chardel, Pierre-Antoine, 'Socio-philosophie de la technique et de l'internet', 14 November 2013, <http://savoirs.ens.fr/expose.php?id=1548> (last accessed 11 January 2016).

Charle, Christophe and Jacques Verger, *Histoire des universités* (Paris: Presses Universitaires de France, 1994).

Chartier, Roger, *Au bord de la falaise: L'Histoire entre certitudes et inquiétude* (Paris: Éditions Albin Michel, 1998).

Chartier, Roger, *The Cultural Origins of the French Revolution*, trans. Lydia Cochrane (Durham, NC: Duke University Press, 1999).

Clarke, Alan (dir.), *Elephant* [film], 1989.

CNN, 'UK Accused of Lifting Dossier Text', 7 February 2003, <http://www.cnn.com/2003/WORLD/meast/02/07/sprj.irq.uk.dossier/index.html> (last accessed 11 January 2016).

Collins, Randall, *The Sociology of Philosophies: A Global Theory of Intellectual Change* (Cambridge, MA: The Belknap Press of Harvard University Press, 2000).

Contandriopoulos, Christina and Harry Francis Mallgrave (eds), *Architectural Theory, Vol. II: An Anthology from 1871–2005* (Malden, MA: Blackwell Publishing, 2008).

Cornu, Laurence and Patrice Vermeren (eds), *La Philosophie déplacée: Autour de Jacques Rancière* (Paris: Horlieu Éditions, 2006).

Curtis, Adam (dir.), *The Century of the Self* [TV documentary series], 2002.

Curtis, Adam (dir.), *The Power of Nightmares* [TV documentary series], 2004.

Curtis, Adam (dir.), *The Trap* [TV documentary series], 2007.

Cusset, François, *French Theory: How Foucault, Derrida, Deleuze, & Co. Transformed the Intellectual Life of the United States*, trans. Jeff Fort (Minneapolis: University of Minnesota Press, 2008).

Dahl, Robert A., *On Democracy* (New Haven and London: Yale University Press, 1998).

Danto, Arthur, *After the End of Art: Contemporary Art and the Pale of History* (Princeton: Princeton University Press, 1997).

Danto, Arthur, *Beyond the Brillo Box: The Visual Arts in Post-Historical Perspective* (Berkeley: University of California Press, 1992).

Darlu, Alphonse, 'Introduction', *Revue de métaphysique et de morale*, 1, 1893.

Bibliography

Deleuze, Gilles, *Cinéma 1. L'Image-mouvement* (Paris: Les Éditions de Minuit, 1983).
Deleuze, Gilles, *Cinema 1: The Movement-Image*, trans. Hugh Tomlinson and Barbara Habberjam (London: The Athlone Press, 2001).
Deleuze, Gilles, *Cinéma 2. L'Image-temps* (Paris: Les Éditions de Minuit, 1985).
Deleuze, Gilles, *Cinema 2: The Time-Image*, trans. Hugh Tomlinson and Robert Galeta (Minneapolis: The Athlone Press, 1989).
Deleuze, Gilles, *Gilles Deleuze: Cinéma* (Paris: Éditions Gallimard, 2006).
Deleuze, Gilles, *Negotiations: 1972–1990*, trans. Martin Joughin (New York: Columbia University Press, 1995).
Deleuze, Gilles and Félix Guattari, *A Thousand Plateaus: Capitalism and Schizophrenia*, trans. Brian Massumi (Minneapolis: University of Minnesota Press, 1978).
Déotte, Jean-Louis (ed.), *Le Milieu des appareils* (Paris: L'Harmattan, 2009).
Derrida, Jacques, 'Force of Law: The "Mystical Foundation of Authority"', *Cardozo Law Review*, 1:5–6, 1990, pp. 920–1045.
Derrida, Jacques, *Of Grammatology*, trans. Gayatri Chakravorty Spivak (Baltimore: Johns Hopkins University Press, 1997).
Derrida, Jacques, *Positions*, trans. Alan Bass (New York: Continuum, 2002).
Derrida, Jacques, *Resistances of Psychoanalysis*, trans. Peggy Kamuf, Pascale-Anne Brault and Michael Naas (Stanford: Stanford University Press, 1998).
Derrida, Jacques, *Spectres of Marx: The State of the Debt, the Work of Mourning, and the New International*, trans. Peggy Kamuf (New York: Routledge, 1994).
Derrida, Jacques, '"We Other Greeks"', trans. Pascale-Anne Brault and Michael Naas, in Miriam Leonard (ed.), *Derrida and Antiquity* (Oxford: Oxford University Press, 2010), pp. 17–39.
Derrida, Jacques, *Writing and Difference*, trans. Alan Bass (Chicago: University of Chicago Press, 1978).
Derrida, Jacques and Elisabeth Roudinesco, *For What Tomorrow ... A Dialogue*, trans. Jeff Fort (Stanford: Stanford University Press, 2004).
Descartes, René, *The Philosophical Writings of Descartes*, vol. 2, trans. John Cottingham, Robert Stoothoff and Dugald Murdoch (Cambridge: Cambridge University Press, 1984).
Dosse, François, *History of Structuralism: The Rising Sign, 1945–1966*, vol. 1, trans. Deborah Glassman (Minneapolis: University of Minnesota Press, 1997).
Droit, Roger-Pol, *Michel Foucault, entretiens* (Paris: Éditions Odile Jacob, 2004).
Eastwood, Clint (dir.), *Mystic River* [film], 2003.
Eiseley, Loren, *Darwin's Century: Evolution and the Men Who Discovered It* (Garden City, NY: Anchor Books, 1961).
Eiseley, Loren, *The Firmament of Time* (Lincoln: University of Nebraska Press, 1999).

Elias, Norbert, *Time: An Essay*, trans. Edmund Jephcott (Oxford: Blackwell Publishing, 1993).
Elsaesser, Thomas, *Fassbinder's Germany: History, Identity, Subject* (Amsterdam: Amsterdam University Press, 1996).
Eribon, Didier, *Michel Foucault*, trans. Betsy Wing (Cambridge, MA: Harvard University Press, 1991).
Fabiani, Jean-Louis, 'Sociologie et histoire des idées', in *Les Enjeux philosophiques des années 50* (Paris: Éditions du Centre Pompidou, 1989), pp. 115–30.
Fassbinder, R. W., *The Anarchy of the Imagination*, ed. Michael Töteberg and Leo A. Lensing (Baltimore and London: Johns Hopkins University Press, 1992).
Fassbinder, R. W. (dir.), *Lili Marleen* [film], 1981.
Finley, Moses I., *Ancient Slavery and Modern Ideology* (Princeton: Markus Wiener Publishers, 1998).
Finley, Moses I., *Democracy Ancient and Modern* (New Brunswick and London: Rutgers University Press, 1988).
Finley, Moses I., *Politics in the Ancient World* (Cambridge: Cambridge University Press, 1983).
Flusser, Vilém, *Towards a Philosophy of Photography*, trans. Anthony Mathews (London: Reaktion Books, 2000).
Flynn, Bernard, 'Derrida and Foucault: Madness and Writing', in Hugh J. Silverman (ed.), *Derrida and Deconstruction* (New York: Routledge, 1989), pp. 201–18.
Focillon, Henri, *Vie des formes* (Paris: Presses Universitaires de France, 1943).
Foucault, Michel, *Aesthetics, Method, and Epistemology (Essential Works of Foucault, 1954–1984)*, ed. James D. Faubion (New York: The New Press, 1998).
Foucault, Michel, *The Archaeology of Knowledge*, trans. A. M. Sheridan Smith (London: Tavistock, 1972).
Foucault, Michel, *The Birth of the Clinic* (New York: Routledge, 1976).
Foucault, Michel, *Discipline and Punish: The Birth of the Prison*, trans. Alan Sheridan (New York: Vintage Books, 1977).
Foucault, Michel, *Dits et écrits*, vol. 1: 1954–1969 (Paris: Éditions Gallimard, 1994).
Foucault, Michel, *Dits et écrits*, vol. 1: 1954–1975 (Paris: Éditions Gallimard, 2001).
Foucault, Michel, *Dits et écrits*, vol. 4: 1980–1988 (Paris: Éditions Gallimard, 1994).
Foucault, Michel, *Foucault Live: Collected Interviews, 1961–1984*, ed. Sylvère Lotringer (New York: Semiotext(e), 1996).

Bibliography

Foucault, Michel, *The Foucault Reader*, ed. Paul Rabinow (New York: Random House, 1984).
Foucault, Michel, *The Government of Self and Others: Lectures at the Collège de France (1982–1983)*, trans. Graham Burchell (New York: Picador Reading Group, 2011).
Foucault, Michel, *Histoire de la folie à l'âge classique* (Paris: Éditions Gallimard, 1972).
Foucault, Michel, *History of Madness*, trans. Jonathan Murphy and Jean Khalfa (London and New York: Routledge, 2006).
Foucault, Michel, *Language, Counter-Memory, Practice: Selected Essays and Interviews*, ed. Donald F. Bouchard (Ithaca, NY: Cornell University Press, 1986).
Foucault, Michel, *Mental Illness and Psychology*, trans. Alan Sheridan (Berkeley: University of California Press, 1987).
Foucault, Michel, 'Of Other Spaces', *Diacritics*, 16, Spring 1986, pp. 22–7.
Foucault, Michel, *The Order of Things: An Archaeology of the Human Sciences* (New York: Vintage Books, 1994).
Foucault, Michel, *The Politics of Truth*, ed. Sylvère Lotringer (Los Angeles: Semiotext(e), 2007).
Foucault, Michel, 'Postface à Flaubert', in *Die Versuchung des Heiligen Antonius (La Tentation de saint Antoine), Dits et écrits*, vol. 1: 1954–1969 (Paris: Éditions Gallimard, 1994), pp. 293–325.
Foucault, Michel, *Power: The Essential Works of Foucault, 1954–1984*, vol. 3, ed. James D. Faubion (New York: The New Press, 2000).
Foucault, Michel, *Security, Territory, Population*, trans. Graham Burchell (New York: Picador, 2007).
Foucault, Michel, 'Space, Knowledge, and Power', in *The Foucault Reader*, ed. Paul Rabinow (New York: Pantheon Books, 1984), pp. 239–56.
Frampton, Kenneth, *Modern Architecture: A Critical History* (London: Thames and Hudson Ltd, 1992).
Fraser, Nancy, *Justice Interruptus: Critical Reflections on the 'Postsocialist' Condition* (New York and London: Routledge, 1997).
Freud, Sigmund, *Civilisation and Its Discontents*, trans. James Strachey (New York: W. W. Norton & Company Inc., 1961).
Gadamer, Hans-Georg, *Truth and Method*, trans. Joel Weinsheimer and Donald G. Marshall (New York: Continuum, 1989).
Gauchet, Marcel, Pierre Manent and Pierre Rosanvallon (eds), *Situations de la démocratie* (Paris: Seuil/Gallimard, 1993).
Ghirardo, Diane (ed.), *Out of Site: A Social Criticism of Architecture* (Seattle: Bay Press, 1991).
Giroux, Henry A., *Disturbing Pleasures: Learning Popular Culture* (New York and London: Routledge, 1994).

Gordon, Lewis R. and Jane Anna Gordon (eds), *Not Only the Master's Tools: African-American Studies in Theory and Practice* (Boulder: Paradigm Publishers, 2006).

Graeber, David, *Possibilities: Essays on Hierarchy, Rebellion, and Desire* (Oakland: AK Press, 2007).

Graubard, Stephen R., 'Democracy', in Philip P. Wiener (ed.), *Dictionary of the History of Ideas*, vol. 1 (New York: Charles Scribner's Sons, 1973), pp. 652–67.

Greenburg, Jan Crawford, Howard L. Rosenberg and Arianne de Vogue, 'Bush Aware of Advisers' Interrogation Talks', ABC News, 11 April 2008, <http://abcnews.go.com/TheLaw/LawPolitics/story?id=4635175> (last accessed 11 January 2016).

Gros, Frédéric, *Foucault et la folie* (Paris: Presses Universitaires de France, 1997).

Gusdorf, Georges, *Introduction aux sciences humaines: Essai critique sur leurs origines et leur développement* (Paris: Éditions Ophrys, 1974).

Habermas, Jürgen, *The Structural Transformation of the Public Sphere: An Inquiry into a Category of Bourgeois Society*, trans. Thomas Burger (Cambridge, MA: The MIT Press, 1991).

Hall, Jacquelyn Dowd, 'The Long Civil Rights Movement and the Political Uses of the Past', *The Journal of American History*, 91:4, March 2005, pp. 1233–63.

Hall, Stuart, 'Brave New World', *Socialist Review*, 21:1, 1991, pp. 57–64.

Hallward, Peter (ed.), *Think Again: Alain Badiou and the Future of Philosophy* (London: Continuum Books, 2004).

Hartog, François, 'Régimes d'historicité: Entretien avec François Hartog', conducted by Annick Louis, *Vox-Poetica*, <http://www.vox-poetica.org/entretiens/intHartog.html> (last accessed 11 January 2016).

Hartog, François, *Régimes d'historicité: Présentisme et expériences du temps* (Paris: Éditions du Seuil, 2003).

Harvey, David, *The Condition of Postmodernity* (Oxford: Basil Blackwell, 1989).

Hays, K. Michael (ed.), *Architecture Theory since 1968* (Cambridge, MA: The MIT Press, 2000).

Hegel, G. W. F., *Introduction to the Lectures on the History of Philosophy*, trans. T. M. Knox and A. V. Miller (Oxford: Clarendon Press, 1985).

Heidegger, Martin, *Nietzsche Volume IV: Nihilism*, trans. Frank A. Capuzzi (New York: Harper & Row, 1982).

Heinich, Nathalie, *L'Élite artiste: Excellence et singularité en régime démocratique* (Paris: Éditions Gallimard, 2005).

Heinich, Nathalie, *Être artiste: Les Transformations du statut des peintres et des sculpteurs* (Paris: Éditions Klincksieck, 1996).

Herder, Johann Gottfried, *Another Philosophy of History and Selected Political Writings*, trans. I. D. Evrigenis and D. Pellerin (Indianapolis: Hackett Publishing, 2004).

Hitchcock, Alfred (dir.), *The Wrong Man* [film], 1956.

Hobbes, Thomas, *Leviathan*, ed. Edwin Curley (Indianapolis: Hackett Publishing Company, 1994).

Hughes, Robert, *The Shock of the New: The Hundred-Year History of Modern Art – Its Rise, Its Dazzling Achievement, Its Fall* (New York: Alfred A. Knopf, 1996).

Hugo, Victor, *Les Misérables*, trans. Lee Fahnestock and Norman MacAfee (New York: Signet Classics, 2013).

Imrie, Rob and Emma Street, 'Regulating Design: The Practices of Architecture, Governance and Control', *Urban Studies*, 46:12, 2009, pp. 2507–18.

Irigaray, Luce, *An Ethics of Sexual Difference*, trans. Carolyn Burke and Gillian C. Gill (Ithaca, NY: Cornell University Press, 1993).

James, William, *Pragmatism* (New York: Dover, 1995).

Jones, Paul, 'Putting Architecture in Its Social Place: A Cultural Political Economy of Architecture', *Urban Studies*, 46:12, 2009, pp. 2519–36.

Judovitz, Dalia, 'Derrida and Descartes: Economising Thought', in Hugh J. Silverman (ed.), *Derrida and Deconstruction* (New York: Routledge, 1989), pp. 40–58.

Kaika, Maria and Korinna Thielen, 'Form Follows Power: A Genealogy of Urban Shrines', *City*, 10:1, 2006, pp. 59–69.

Kant, Immanuel, *On History*, ed. Lewis White Beck (New York: Macmillan Publishing Company, 1963).

Kant, Immanuel, *Practical Philosophy*, trans. Mary J. Gregor (Cambridge: Cambridge University Press, 1996).

Karsenti, Bruno, *D'une philosophie à l'autre: Les Sciences sociales et la politique des modernes* (Paris: Éditions Gallimard, 2013).

Karsenti, Bruno, 'Rencontre à l'Atelier de Théorie Critique', 11 July 2014, <http://criticaltheoryworkshop.com/video-gallery> (last accessed 11 January 2016).

Keaton, Diane and Gus Van Sant, 'Elephant: Interview with Gus Van Sant and Diane Keaton', <http://www.aboutfilm.com/features/elephant/feature.htm> (last accessed 11 January 2016).

Kerbrat-Orecchioni, Catherine, *La Connotation* (Lyon: Presses Universitaires de Lyon, 1977).

Klein, Joe, 'The Benetton-Ad Presidency', *Time*, 164:26, 27 December 2004–3 January 2005.

Klein, Naomi, *No Logo* (New York: Picador, 2002).

Knox, Paul L., 'Symbolism, Styles and Settings: The Built Environment and the Imperatives of Urbanised Capitalism', *Architecture & Comportment*, 2:2, 1984, pp. 107–22.

Koselleck, Reinhart, *Futures Past: On the Semantics of Historical Time*, trans. Keith Tribe (New York: Columbia University Press, 2004).

Kracauer, Siegfried, *History: The Last Thing Before the Last* (New York: Oxford University Press, 1969).

Kubrick, Stanley (dir.), *The Shining* [film], 1980.

Lamont, Michèle, 'How to Become a Dominant French Philosopher: The Case of Jacques Derrida', *The American Journal of Sociology*, 93:3, November 1987, pp. 584–622.

Lang, Fritz (dir.), *You Only Live Once* [film], 1937.

Laniel, Bertlinde, *Le Mot 'democracy' et son histoire aux États-Unis de 1780 à 1856* (Saint-Étienne: Publications de l'Université de Saint-Étienne, 1995).

Laruelle, François, *Philosophies of Difference: A Critical Introduction to Non-Philosophy*, trans. Rocco Gangle (London: Continuum International Publishing, 2010).

Laruelle, François, *Philosophy and Non-Philosophy*, trans. Taylor Adkins (Minneapolis: Univocal, 2013).

Leach, Neil (ed.), *Rethinking Architecture: A Reader in Cultural Theory* (London and New York: Routledge, 1997).

Le Corbusier, *Vers une architecture* (Paris: Flammarion, 1995).

Lefort, Claude, *Essais sur le politique: XIXe–XXe siècles* (Paris: Éditions du Seuil, 1986).

Lévêque, Pierre and Pierre Vidal-Naquet, *Clisthène l'athénien: Sur la reproduction de l'espace et du temps en Grèce de la fin du VIe siècle à la mort de Platon* (Paris: Éditions Macula, 1964).

Levi, Albert William, *Philosophy as Social Expression* (Chicago: University of Chicago Press, 1974).

Lévinas, Emmanuel, *Otherwise than Being or Beyond Being*, trans. Alphonso Lingis (Dordrecht: Kluwer Academic Publishers, 1991).

Lévinas, Emmanuel, *Totality and Infinity: An Essay on Exteriority*, trans. Alphonso Lingis (Pittsburgh: Duquesne University Press, 1969).

Lévi-Strauss, Claude, *Myth and Meaning: Cracking the Code of Culture* (New York: Schocken Books, 1979).

Lévy, Edmond, *La Grèce au Ve siècle: De Clisthène à Socrate* (Paris: Éditions du Seuil, 1997).

Locke, John, *The Second Treatise on Government* (New York: Macmillan Publishing Company, 1952).

Lyotard, Jean-François, *The Differend: Phrases in Dispute*, trans. Georges Van Den Abbeele (Minneapolis: University of Minnesota Press, 1988).

Lyotard, Jean-François, *Heidegger and 'the Jews'*, trans. Andreas Michel and Mark S. Roberts (Minneapolis: University of Minnesota Press, 1990).

Lyotard, Jean-François, *Political Writings*, trans. Bill Readings and Kevin Paul (Minneapolis: University of Minnesota Press, 1993).

McClelland, Charles E., *State, Society, and University in Germany 1700–1914* (Cambridge: Cambridge University Press, 1980).

McCumber, John, *Time in the Ditch: American Philosophy and the McCarthy Era* (Evanston: Northwestern University Press, 2001).
McGrane, Bernard, *Beyond Anthropology: Society and the Other* (New York: Columbia University Press, 1989).
Maldonado-Torres, Nelson, 'Post-Continental Philosophy: Its Definition, Contours, and Fundamental Sources', *Worlds and Knowledges Otherwise*, 1:3, Fall 2006, pp. 1–29.
Malraux, André, *Le Musée imaginaire* (Paris: Éditions Gallimard, 1965).
Manicas, Peter T., *A History and Philosophy of the Social Sciences* (Oxford: Basil Blackwell, 1987).
Marcuse, Herbert, *One-Dimensional Man* (Boston: Beacon Press, 1964).
Margot, Jean-Paul, 'La Lecture foucaldienne de Descartes: Ses présupposés et ses implications', *Philosophiques*, 11:1, April 1984, pp. 3–39.
Maschino, Maurice T., 'Les Nouveaux Réactionnaires', *Le Monde diplomatique*, October 2002.
Mignolo, Walter D. and Arturo Escobar (eds), *Globalisation and the Decolonial Option* (New York: Routledge, 2010).
Montesquieu, Charles de, *Persian Letters*, trans. Margaret Mauldon (Oxford: Oxford University Press, 2008).
Montesquieu, Charles de, *The Spirit of the Laws*, trans. A. M. Cohler, B. C. Miller and H. S. Stone (Cambridge: Cambridge University Press, 1989).
Moore, Michael (dir.), *Bowling for Columbine* [documentary], 2002.
Mouffe, Chantal, *The Democratic Paradox* (London and New York: Verso, 2000).
The National Security Strategy of the United States of America, September 2002, <http://www.state.gov/documents/organization/63562.pdf> (last accessed 11 January 2016).
Nesbitt, Kate (ed.), *Theorising a New Agenda for Architecture: An Anthology of Architectural Theory 1965–1995* (New York: Princeton Architectural Press, 1996).
Nietzsche, Friedrich, *Twilight of the Idols*, trans. R. J. Hollingdale (Harmondsworth: Penguin Books, 1983).
Nkrumah, Kwame, *Consciencism: Philosophy and Ideology for De-Colonisation* (New York: Monthly Review Press, 1970).
Paine, Thomas, *Common Sense, Rights of Man, and Other Essential Writings of Thomas Paine* (New York: The Penguin Group Inc., 2003).
Palmer, R. R., 'Notes on the Use of the Word "Democracy" 1789–1799', *Political Science Quarterly*, 68:2, June 1953, pp. 203–26.
Park, Peter K. J., *Africa, Asia, and the History of Philosophy: Racism in the Formation of the Philosophical Canon, 1780–1830* (Albany: State University of New York Press, 2013).
Parry, Gerry, *Political Elites* (London: George Allen and Unwin Ltd, 1969).

Pinto, Louis, *Les Philosophes entre le lycée et l'avant-garde: Les Métamorphoses de la philosophie dans la France d'aujourd'hui* (Paris: L'Harmattan, 1987).
Pinto, Louis, *La Vocation et le métier de philosophe: Pour une sociologie de la philosophie dans la France contemporaine* (Paris: Éditions du Seuil, 2007).
Pinto, Louis, 'Volontés de savoir: Bourdieu, Derrida, Foucault', in Louis Pinto, Gisèle Sapiro et al. (eds), *Pierre Bourdieu sociologue* (Paris: Librairie Arthème Fayard, 2004), pp. 19–48.
Poulot, Dominique, *Musée, nation, patrimoine 1789–1815* (Paris: Éditions Gallimard, 1997).
Ramond, Charles (ed.), *Alain Badiou: Penser le multiple* (Paris: L'Harmattan, 2002).
Rancière, Jacques, 'The Aesthetic Revolution and its Outcomes', *New Left Review*, 14, March–April 2002, pp. 133–51.
Rancière, Jacques, *The Aesthetic Unconscious*, trans. Debra Keates and James Swenson (Cambridge: Polity, 2009).
Rancière, Jacques, *Aesthetics and Its Discontents*, trans. Steven Corcoran (Cambridge: Polity, 2009).
Rancière, Jacques, *Aisthesis: Scenes from the Aesthetic Regime of Art*, trans. Zakir Paul (London: Verso Books, 2013).
Rancière, Jacques, *Aux bords du politique* (Paris: La Fabrique Éditions, 1998).
Rancière, Jacques, *Chronicles of Consensual Time*, trans. Steve Corcoran (London: Continuum, 2010).
Rancière, Jacques, *Chroniques des temps consensuels* (Paris: Éditions du Seuil, 2005).
Rancière, Jacques, 'Le Coup double de l'art politisé: Entretien avec Gabriel Rockhill', *Lignes*, 19, February 2006, pp. 141–64.
Rancière, Jacques, *Le Destin des images* (Paris: La Fabrique Éditions, 2003).
Rancière, Jacques, *Disagreement: Politics and Philosophy*, trans. Julie Rose (Minneapolis: University of Minnesota Press, 1999).
Rancière, Jacques, 'Les Écarts du cinéma', *Trafic*, 50, Summer 2004, pp. 159–66.
Rancière, Jacques, 'Entretien avec Jacques Rancière' (by Nicolas Poirier), *Le Philosophoire*, 13, Spring 2008, pp. 29–42.
Rancière, Jacques, *Film Fables*, trans. Emiliano Battista (New York: Berg, 2006).
Rancière, Jacques, *The Flesh of Words: The Politics of Writing*, trans. Charlotte Mandell (Stanford: Stanford University Press, 2004).
Rancière, Jacques, *The Future of the Image*, trans. Gregory Elliott (London: Verso, 2009).
Rancière, Jacques, *La Haine de la démocratie* (Paris: La Fabrique Éditions, 2005).
Rancière, Jacques, *Hatred of Democracy*, trans. Steve Corcoran (London: Verso, 2014).
Rancière, Jacques, *The Ignorant Schoolmaster: Five Lessons in Intellectual Emancipation*, trans. Kristin Ross (Stanford: Stanford University Press, 1991).

Rancière, Jacques, *L'Inconscient esthétique* (Paris: Éditions Galilée, 2001).
Rancière, Jacques, 'An Interview with Jacques Rancière: Cinematographic Image, Democracy, and the "Splendor of the ..."', *Sites*, 4:2, Fall 2000, pp. 249–58.
Rancière, Jacques, 'Literature, Politics, Aesthetics', *SubStance*, 29:2, 2000, pp. 3–24.
Rancière, Jacques, *Malaise dans l'esthétique* (Paris: Éditions Galilée, 2004).
Rancière, Jacques, *Mallarmé: La politique de la sirène* (Paris: Hachette Livre, 1996).
Rancière, Jacques, *La Mésentente* (Paris: Éditions Galilée, 1995).
Rancière, Jacques, *Les Mots de l'histoire: Essai de poétique du savoir* (Paris: Éditions du Seuil, 1992).
Rancière, Jacques, *Mute Speech*, trans. James Swenson, with an introduction by Gabriel Rockhill (New York: Columbia University Press, 2011).
Rancière, Jacques, *The Names of History*, trans. Hassan Melehy (Minneapolis: Minnesota University Press, 1994).
Rancière, Jacques, 'Les Nouvelles Fictions du mal', *Cahiers du cinéma*, 590, May 2004, pp. 94–6.
Rancière, Jacques, *On the Shores of Politics*, trans. Liz Heron (London: Verso, 1995).
Rancière, Jacques, *La Parole muette* (Paris: Hachette Littératures, 1998).
Rancière, Jacques, 'Penser entre les disciplines: Une Esthétique de la connaissance', in Tobias Huber and Marcus Steinweg (eds), *Inaesthetik – Nr. 0: Theses on Contemporary Art* (Zurich and Berlin: Diaphanes, 2008), pp. 81–102.
Rancière, Jacques, *The Politics of Aesthetics*, ed. and trans. Gabriel Rockhill (London and New York: Continuum, 2004).
Rancière, Jacques, 'The Politics of Literature', *SubStance*, 33:1, 2004, pp. 10–24.
Rancière, Jacques, *Politique de la littérature* (Paris: Éditions Galilée, 2007).
Rancière, Jacques (ed.), *La Politique des poètes: Pourquoi des poètes en temps de détresse?* (Paris: Albin Michel, 1992).
Rancière, Jacques, 'Le Scandale démocratique', *Libération*, 15 December 2005.
Rancière, Jacques, 'Ten Theses on Politics', *Theory & Event*, 5:3, 2001, pp. 1–33.
Robespierre, Maximilien, *Textes choisis* (Paris: Éditions Sociales, 1994).
Robinet, André, *Le Langage à l'âge classique* (Paris: Éditions Klincksieck, 1978).
Rockhill, Gabriel, 'L'Écriture de l'histoire philosophique: L'Éternel retour du même et de l'autre chez Lévinas', *Philosophie*, 87, Fall 2005, pp. 59–77.
Rockhill, Gabriel, *Logique de l'histoire: Pour une analytique des pratiques philosophiques* (Paris: Éditions Hermann, 2010).
Rockhill, Gabriel, *Radical History and the Politics of Art* (New York: Columbia University Press, 2014).

Rockhill, Gabriel, 'Vers une critique historique de l'imaginaire politique contemporaine en France', *L'Homme et la société: Revue internationale de recherche et de synthèse en sciences sociales*, 159, January–March 2007, pp. 191–8.

Rockhill, Gabriel and Alfredo Gomez-Muller (eds), *Politics of Culture and the Spirit of Critique: Dialogues* (New York: Columbia University Press, 2011).

Rockhill, Gabriel and Philip Watts (eds), *Jacques Rancière: History, Politics, Aesthetics* (Durham, NC: Duke University Press, 2009).

Rorty, Richard, Jerome B. Schneewind and Quentin Skinner (eds), *Philosophy in History* (Cambridge: Cambridge University Press, 1984).

Rossiter, Clinton (ed.), *The Federalist Papers* (New York: The Penguin Group Inc., 1993).

Rotzer, Florian, *Conversations with French Philosophers*, trans. Gary E. Aylesworth (Atlantic Highlands, NJ: Humanities Press International Inc., 1995).

Rousseau, Jean-Jacques, *The Basic Political Writings*, trans. Donald A. Cress (Indianapolis: Hackett Publishing Company, 1987).

Rousseau, Jean-Jacques, *The Discourses and Other Early Political Writings* (Cambridge: Cambridge University Press, 1997).

Rousseau, Jean-Jacques, *The Social Contract and Other Later Political Writings*, ed. Victor Gourevitch (Cambridge: Cambridge University Press, 1997).

Rush, Julian, 'Downing St Dossier Plagiarised', Channel 4 News, 6 February 2003, <http://www.channel4.com/news/articles/politics/domestic_politics/downing%2Bst%2Bdossier%2Bplagiarised%2B%2B%2B/253293.html> (last accessed 11 January 2016).

Said, Edward, *Orientalism* (New York: Vintage Books, 1994).

Sartre, Jean-Paul, *Situations, III* (Paris: Éditions Gallimard, 1949).

Scott, David, 'Criticism and Culture: Theory and Post-Colonial Claims on Anthropological Disciplinarity', *Critique of Anthropology*, 12:4, 1992, pp. 371–94.

Scott, David, 'Culture in Political Theory', *Political Theory*, 31:1, February 2003, pp. 92–115.

Scott, David, 'Toleration and Historical Traditions of Difference', in Partha Chatterjee and Pradeep Jeganathan (eds), *Community, Gender and Violence* (New York: Columbia University Press, 2000), pp. 283–304.

Serres, Michel and Bruno Latour, *Conversations on Science, Culture, and Time*, trans. Roxanne Lapidus (Ann Arbor: University of Michigan Press, 1995).

Shakespeare, William, *Hamlet* (New York: W. W. Norton & Company Inc., 1992).

Shakespeare, William, *The Norton Shakespeare: Based on the Oxford Edition*, ed. Stephen Greenblatt (New York and London: W. W. Norton & Company Inc., 1997).

Sheridan, Alan, *Michel Foucault: The Will to Truth* (London and New York: Tavistock, 1982).

Shiner, Larry, *The Invention of Art: A Cultural History* (Chicago: University of Chicago Press, 2003).
Shivani, Anis, 'A Left Critique of Multiculturalism', *CounterPunch*, 19 October 2002, <http://www.counterpunch.org/2002/10/19/a-left-critique-of-multiculturalism> (last accessed 11 January 2016).
Soulié, Charles, 'Le Destin d'une institution d'avant-garde: Histoire du département de philosophie de Paris VIII', *Histoire de l'éducation*, 77, January 1998, pp. 47–69.
Spivak, Gayatri Chakravorty, 'Can the Subaltern Speak?', in Cary Nelson and Lawrence Grossberg (eds), *Marxism and the Interpretation of Culture* (Urbana and Chicago: University of Illinois Press, 1988), pp. 271–313.
Stein, Jonathan, 'The Best Part of Obama's Multicultural Cabinet: The Effortlessness of It', *Mother Jones*, 11 December 2008, <http://www.motherjones.com/mojo/2008/12/best-part-obamas-multicultural-cabinet-effortlessness-it> (last accessed 11 January 2016).
Stein, Jonathan, 'Bush's Biggest Achievements', *Mother Jones*, 25 August 2008, <http://www.motherjones.com/politics/2008/08/bushs-biggest-achievements> (last accessed 11 January 2016).
Sullivan, Louis H., *The Autobiography of an Idea* (New York: Press of the American Institute of Architects Inc., 1924).
Taguieff, Pierre-André, *Force of Prejudice: On Racism and Its Doubles*, trans. Hassan Melehy (Minneapolis: University of Minnesota Press, 2001).
Taguieff, Pierre-André, 'Le Néo-racisme différentialiste: Sur l'ambiguïté d'une évidence commune et ses effets pervers: L'Éloge de la différence', *Langage et société*, 34:1, December 1985, pp. 69–98.
Takács, Ádám, 'Between Theory and History: On the Interdisciplinary Practice in Michel Foucault's Work', *MLN*, 119:4, September 2004, pp. 869–84.
Thiem, Annika, 'Queering Philosophy: How Can Queer Theory Inform and Transform the Practice of Philosophy?', <http://thephilosopherseye.com/2015/06/11/queering-philosophy-how-can-queer-theory-inform-and-transform-the-practice-of-philosophy> (last accessed 11 January 2016).
Tocqueville, Alexis de, *De la démocratie en Amérique I* (Paris: GF Flammarion, 1981).
Tocqueville, Alexis de, *Democracy in America*, trans. Gerald E. Bevan (New York: Penguin, 2003).
Tonka, Hubert, '*Vérité ou radicalité de l'architecture?* de Jean Baudrillard', *Le journal de la philosophie*, 18 July 2013, <http://www.franceculture.fr/emission-le-journal-de-la-philosophie-verite-ou-radicalite-de-l-architecture-de-jean-baudrillard-201> (last accessed 11 January 2016).
Trier, Lars von (dir.), *Breaking the Waves* [film], 1996.
Trier, Lars von (dir.), *Dancer in the Dark* [film], 2000.

Trier, Lars von (dir.), *Dogville* [film], 2003.
Trier, Lars von (dir.), *Manderlay* [film], 2005.
Van Sant, Gus (dir.), *Elephant* [film], 2003.
Van Sant, Gus, 'Rencontre avec Gus Van Sant', *Elephant*, Edition Collector, 2 DVD set (Paris: MK2 S.A., 2004).
Vattimo, Gianni, *The Adventure of Difference: Philosophy After Nietzsche and Heidegger*, trans. Cyprian Blamires (Baltimore: Johns Hopkins University Press, 1993).
Vico, Giambattista, *The New Science of Giambattista Vico*, trans. T. G. Bergin and M. H. Fisch (Ithaca, NY: Cornell University Press, 1948).
Vico, Giambattista, *On the Study Methods of Our Time*, trans. Elio Gianturco (Ithaca, NY: Cornell University Press, 1990).
Vidal-Naquet, Pierre, *Le Chasseur noir: Formes de pensée et formes de société dans le monde grec* (Paris: La Découverte, 2005).
Virilio, Paul, 'Critical Space', *Log*, 13–14, 2008, pp. 29–31.
Wagner, Peter, *A History and Theory of the Social Sciences: Not All that Is Solid Melts into Air* (London: SAGE Publications, 2001).
Wallerstein, Immanuel, *Unthinking Social Science: The Limits of Nineteenth-Century Paradigms* (Philadelphia: Temple University Press, 2001).
Wallerstein, Immanuel, *World-Systems Analysis: An Introduction* (Durham, NC: Duke University Press, 2004).
Wallerstein, Immanuel et al., 'The Historical Construction of the Social Sciences, from the Eighteenth Century to 1945', in *Open the Social Sciences: Report of the Gulbenkian Commission on the Restructuring of the Social Sciences* (Stanford: Stanford University Press, 1996), pp. 1–32.
Weber, Samuel, 'Afterword: Literature – Just Making It', trans. Brian Massumi, in Jean-François Lyotard and Jean-Loup Thébaud, *Just Gaming*, trans. Wlad Godzich (Minneapolis: University of Minnesota Press, 1985), pp. 101–20.
West, Cornel, *Democracy Matters: Winning the Fight against Imperialism* (New York: Penguin Books, 2004).
West, Cornel, *Race Matters* (New York: Vintage Books, 1994).
Williams, Raymond, *Keywords* (Oxford: Oxford University Press, 1985).
Wittmann, Reinhard, 'Was There a Reading Revolution at the End of the Eighteenth Century?', in Guglielmo Cavallo and Roger Chartier (eds), *A History of Reading in the West* (Amherst, MA: University of Massachusetts Press, 2003), pp. 284–312.
Ziolkowski, Theodore, *Clio the Romantic Muse: Historicising the Faculties in Germany* (Ithaca, NY: Cornell University Press, 2004).
Ziolkowski, Theodore, *German Romanticism and Its Institutions* (Princeton: Princeton University Press, 1990).
Žižek, Slavoj, 'Multiculturalism, or, the Cultural Logic of Multinational Capitalism', *New Left Review*, 1:225, September–October 1997, pp. 28–51.

INDEX

1968 Paris uprisings, 141, 252
7000 Eichen, 204

abyss, the, 147, 160n, 163n
Adorno, Theodor, 23, 217, 243
advertising, 128
aesthetic revolution, 100–10, 112n
The Aesthetic Unconscious (Rancière), 85n
aesthetics, 21, 171, 175, 194–204, 207, 214–34, 238–9n
Aesthetics and Its Discontents (Rancière), 114n, 220–1
Agamben, Giorgio, 19, 40
Ahmadinejad, Mahmoud, 241n
Alcoff, Linda Martín, 9, 29n
Al-Qaeda, 127
Altes Museum, 105–6
Althusser, Louis, 166
amens, 71
American Philosophical Association, 10
anthropology, 7
anti-aestheticism, 205
anti-Semitism, 131
Aragon, Louis, 251
Arcades Project (Benjamin), 249
The Archaeology of Knowledge (Foucault), 51–2, 78, 84n
architecture, 243–55; *see also* art
Arendt, Hannah, 114n, 254
Aristotle, 196, 202
arithmetic, 153
art, 105–6, 155, 163n, 176, 196–9
　high and low, 23, 202–3, 256
　history of, 100, 111n
　installations, 245–6
　and politics, 100, 110n, 223–34

　public, 104–7, 246–7, 249, 252
　see also architecture; film
Arts and Crafts movement, 253
Aufklärung see Enlightenment
autonomy, 143–5, 153, 155, 157
avant-garde, 198–9, 257

babies, and psychic identity, 149–50
Bacon, Francis, 48
Bacon, Kevin, 227
Badiou, Alain, 18, 22, 137n, 166, 171
　(lack of) debate with Rancière, 193–208
　Being and Event, 194, 208n
　The Century, 198, 212n
　Ethics, 208n
　Handbook of Inaesthetics, 197–8, 208n, 210–11n
　Logic of Worlds, 199
　Manifesto for Philosophy, 194, 208n
Balibar, Étienne, 193
Ballanche, Pierre-Simon, 174
banlieues, autumn 2005 unrest, 173, 186n
Barney, Matthew, 246
Barthes, Roland, 23, 87n, 200, 214
　Camera Lucida, 217
　The Degree Zero of Writing, 200, 214–15
　Mythologies, 215, 217
Baudelaire, Charles, 246
Baudrillard, Jean, 244
Bauhaus, 253, 255
Being and Event (Badiou), 194, 208n
Bell, Daniel, 166
Benetton, 128
Benjamin, Walter, 23, 203, 216, 244, 246, 249

Berlin, 105–6
Beuys, Joseph, 204
Beyond Anthropology (McGrane), 132
binaries, 120, 155
biology, 152–3
Birch, Anthony H., 176, 187n, 236n
The Birth of the Clinic (Foucault), 78
Bloy, Léon, 216
Borges, Jorge Luis, 55, 211n
Bourdieu, Pierre, 20, 24n, 32–3n, 90n, 205, 216
Bowling for Columbine (film), 231–2, 240–1n
breast, 149–50
Buddhism, 30n, 155
bureaucracy, 139
Bürger, Paul, 257
Bush, George W., 126–7, 136n

Camera Lucida (Barthes), 217
Canguilhem, Georges, 44
capitalism, 6, 7, 128
Cartesianism *see* Descartes, René
Castoriadis, Cornelius, 21, 24n, 29n, 133–4n, 139–64
    Eurocentrism, 156–8
    Figures of the Thinkable, 142
The Century (Badiou), 198, 212n
Cervantes, Miguel de, 102
chaos, 147–8, 160n, 163n
Chardel, Pierre-Antoine, 17
Chauvet-Pont-d'Arc, 199
China, 7
Christianity, 101
chronology, 42–3
CIA, 127
citizenship, 177
The City of God (Augustine), 201
Civil Rights Movement, 138n
class, 254
clitoridectomy, 129
cogito, 65, 68, 92n
'Cogito and the History of Madness' (Derrida), 78, 86n, 89n, 92–4n
Cold War, 27n
colonialism, 6–7, 25–6n
commitment, 200, 234n
commonwealths, 178
conjuncture, 3, 11–12, 16, 19, 44, 47, 51, 156, 177, 202, 222

contemporariness, 38–41
Le Corbusier, 247, 255
crafts, 253
creation, 142–5, 155–6, 161n
Critical theory, 10, 18, 244, 246, 253, 254

Dadaism, 198
Dahl, Robert, 180, 188n
dance, 196–7, 260n
Danto, Arthur, 203–4
Davidson, Martin, 128
deconstruction, 85n, 92n, 142
The Deer Hunter (film), 224
The Degree Zero of Writing (Barthes), 200, 214–15
Déjeuner sur l'herbe (painting), 107
Deleuze, Gilles, 31n, 118, 121, 125, 135n, 166, 193, 209–10n, 219
demens, 71
democracy, 100, 131, 133, 144–6, 149, 165, 175, 221–3, 236n
    in ancient Greece, 176–7
    hatred or distrust of, 175, 178–82
    history of, 176–80
    pseudo-, 145–6
    Rancière on, 165–82
    as subjectivisation, 170
    substantialist conception, 167
Democracy Now! 136n
Derrida, Jacques, 18, 20, 22, 60, 118, 121, 134n, 136n, 193, 260n
    debate with Foucault, 57–69, 78–82, 88–9n
    on Descartes, 57–77, 80–3, 95n
Descartes, René, 6, 9, 11, 20, 30n, 55, 57–66, 80–3, 95n
design, 243, 246–7; *see also* architecture; art
desire, 149
determinism, 122
Dickson, Scott, 247
différance, 73, 77, 92n, 94n, 121, 124
difference, 21, 38, 45, 93n, 118–32, 133–4n, 138n, 141, 219–20, 235n
Disagreement (Rancière), 168, 170, 172, 183n, 218–19
Discipline and Punish (Foucault), 250–1
disciplines, 5–11, 17, 22, 25–6n
Distinction (Bourdieu), 205
diversity, 126–7

Index

Dogville, 227, 229–30, 240n
Dovey, Kim, 247
dreams, 81
Durkheim, Émile, 243

École des Hautes Études en Sciences Sociales, 140
economics, 7–8
l'écriture, 200
Elephant (film), 227, 230–3, 238n, 240–2n
Enlightenment, 38, 40, 43–9, 178, 254
'ensidic', 153, 155
epistemes, 200–1, 211n
epochal thought, 40–1, 47–9
Erlich, Leandro, 246
Ernst, Sophie, 246
Ethics (Badiou), 208n
Eurocentrism, 14–15, 31–2n, 131–2, 156–8, 162n
events, 195
evil, 124, 133
exegetical thought, 154
existentialism, 21, 141

fashion, 249
Ferry, Luc, 141
fiction *see* literature; novels
Figures of the Thinkable (Castoriadis), 142
film, 197, 210n, 212n, 237–9n
　Rancière on, 224–33
　see also art
Finkielkraut, Alain, 166
Finley, Moses, 164n, 180, 188n, 236n
Flaubert, Gustave, 107, 212n, 216
　Madame Bovary, 203–4
Flusser, Vilém, 13
Foucault, Michel, 19, 20, 23, 37–40, 78, 106, 121, 244
　The Archaeology of Knowledge, 51–2, 84n
　debate with Derrida, 57–62, 88–9n
　Discipline and Punish, 249–50
　The Government of Self, 53n
　History of Madness, 55–9
　influence on Rancière, 193, 200, 204
　on Kant, 38–9, 43–4, 47, 51–2
　Language, Counter-Memory, Practice, 24n
　'My Body, This Paper, This Fire', 79–80, 92n, 98n

　ontology of contemporary reality, 38–41, 45
　on 'police', 168–9
　'Reply to Derrida', 78
　on science, 151
　'What is Critique?', 52n
　'What is Enlightenment?', 52n
Frampton, Kenneth, 244, 246, 260n
France, 21, 25n, 44, 78, 82, 139, 166, 180, 182n, 193, 200, 214, 252
Frankfurt School, 243
Fraser, Nancy, 31n, 131, 138n, 235n
French Revolution, 101, 189n, 195, 249
Freud, Sigmund, 24n, 89n, 149, 216, 239n
functionalism, 141

Gaudi, Antoni, 257
gender, 254
genealogy, 103
Geneva Convention, 127
geography, 31n, 43
German Romanticism, 203
Gesamtkunstwerke, 245
Ghirardo, Diane, 255, 260n
Gilbert, Félix, 254
Giroux, Henry, 128
globalisation, 128, 136–7n
God, 65, 92n, 144, 201
Godin, Jean-Baptiste, 251
Gonzales, Alberto, 127
government, forms of, 178–9
Greece (ancient), 144–6, 155–7, 162–3n, 222
　historical specificity of democracy in, 163n, 176, 188n
Gropius, Walter, 245
groundless, the, 147, 160n, 163n
Gulbenkian Commission, 6, 25n

Habermas, Jürgen, 104–5, 109, 259n
Hamilton, Alexander, 180
Hamlet (Shakespeare), 48
Handbook of Inaesthetics (Badiou), 197–8, 208n, 210–11n
happenings, 246
Hartog, François, 103, 109, 111n, 113n
Harvey, David, 244
Hatred of Democracy (Rancière), 22, 165–6, 222, 236n

Haussmann, Georges-Eugène, 249
hedonism, 146
Hegel, G. W. F., 11–12, 28n, 45, 92n
Heidegger, Martin, 93n, 125, 135n, 175, 209n, 260n
Herder, Johann Gottfried, 19, 47
hermeneutics, 4, 9, 11–17, 27n, 83, 157, 198, 202, 206, 221–34, 238n
   illustrative, 22, 206, 212n
heterogeneity, 120–2
Hirschhorn, Thomas, 246
historical causality, 104
historical logic *see* logic, of history
historical order *see* logic, of history
historicism, 16, 103, 109, 168, 175
historiography, 45
history, 7–8, 11, 22, 19, 43–5, 48, 61, 80, 101, 108, 155–6, 175, 222
History of Madness (Foucault), 55–9, 73, 94n
History: The Last Things Before the Last (Kracauer), 42–3
homophobia, 131
Horace, 49
Horkheimer, Max, 243
Hughes, Robert, 257
Hugo, Victor, 44–5, 246
Hussein, Saddam, 127, 241n
hybris, 70

'identitary', 153
identity, 118, 123, 131, 149, 219–20, 235n
The Ignorant Schoolmaster (Rancière), 172
imaginary, the, 80, 142–7, 154–5
imagination, 155–6
Imrie, Rob, 247
inaesthetics, 198
incommensurability, 118–19
India, 7
Industrial Revolution, 6
insanus, 71
interdisciplinarity, 4–5
interpretation, 1–3, 216
intervention, 1–5, 15, 18, 20–1, 24, 156, 166, 181, 183, 185n, 195, 208–9n, 234
Iran, 241n
Iraq, 127, 241n
isonomy, 177, 188n

Jackson, Andrew, 180
James, William, 103–4
Jameson, Frederic, 31n, 244

Kaika, Maria, 248
Kant, Immanuel, 11, 19, 203
   on the *Aufklärung*, 46
   Conflict of the Faculties, 26n
   critique of democracy, 179
   Foucault on, 38–9, 43–4, 51–2
   on Herder, 47
knowledge, 194
Knox, Paul, 251
Koselleck, Reinhart, 108, 254
Kracauer, Siegfried, 19, 259n
   History: The Last Things Before the Last, 42–3
Kubrick, Stanley, 232
Kuhn, Thomas, 151

Lacan, Jacques, 206
Lacoue-Labarthe, Philippe, 125, 193
language, 95n, 200–1, 215
   and art, 196–7
   and madness, 71–6
   and meaning, 65, 121
Laniel, Bertlinde, 178, 180
Leach, Neil, 243
Lefebvre, Henri, 23, 244
Lefort, Claude, 139, 184n
Lévi-Strauss, Claude, 20, 90n, 97n
Lévinas, Emmanuel, 118, 121–2, 125, 138n
liberalism, 8, 146, 177
liberty, 251
libraries, 106–7, 113n
Lili Marleen (film), 225–7, 237–8n
literature, 108, 176, 202, 214–15, 253
Locke, John, 178, 188n
logic, 21, 153
   of history, 19, 50, 123, 155
Logic of Worlds (Badiou), 199, 213n
Logique de l'histoire (Rockhill), 6, 28n, 33n, 52n, 86n, 131, 176
love, 194–5
Lukács, Georg, 23, 243
Lyotard, Jean-François, 23, 118, 120–1, 125, 135n, 166–7, 186n, 193, 217, 219, 243

Index

Macbeth (Shakespeare), 147–8, 231–2, 241n
McGrane, Bernard, 132, 138n
Madame Bovary (Flaubert), 203
Madison, James, 180
madness
  and Cartesian doubt, 62–9
  Derrida's debate with Foucault, 62–77, 80–1
  Foucault on, 55–69, 62–77, 87n
  and language, 71–6, 84n
Malraux, André, 106, 109
Manet, Édouard, 107
Manifesto for Philosophy (Badiou), 194, 208n
Marcuse, Herbert, 26n, 243
Marx, Karl, 24n, 216
Marxism, 100, 139, 167, 183n, 198
mathematics, 152–3
meaning, 65, 95n, 124
  intentional, 86–7n
Meditations (Descartes), 6, 57–9
  Derrida's reading of, 61–82
  Foucault's 'double reading', 80
Mendelssohn, Moses, 46
Meno (Plato), 70
metaphilosophical critique, 15, 17, 21, 33n
metaphilosophy, 17, 20–3, 27, 32n, 83, 118–20, 124–6, 130, 132
metaphysics, 12, 28n, 95n, 142
metastatic transformation, 16, 50, 176
Milner, Jean-Claude, 166–8
Les Misérables (Hugo), 44–5
misogyny, 131
Miyakawa, J., 78
Modern Architecture: A Critical History (Frampton), 244
Modern Movement, 245
modernism, 100, 205, 257
modernity, 7, 19, 25n, 39, 45, 47, 106–7
Montesquieu, Baron de, 7, 19, 49, 53n, 179, 188–9n
Moore, Michael, 231
multiculturalism, 126–8, 136–7n
museums, 101, 105–9, 112–13n, 253
music, 196–7, 211n
Mute Speech (Rancière), 112n, 169, 201, 210n
Mystic River (film), 227–9
Mythologies (Barthes), 215, 217

Nakano, Mikitaka, 78
Nancy, Jean-Luc, 118, 125, 193
narcissism, 146
nature, 144
neoliberalism, 146
New Tradition, 245
New Wave, 214
Newton, Isaac, 152
Nietzsche, Friedrich, 29n, 45, 195
nouveau roman, 214
novels, 101, 108, 202, 211n
Nuremberg, 246

Of Grammatology (Derrida), 78, 85n, 93n, 98n
oligarchy, 145–6, 174
Olympia (painting), 107
On the Shores of Politics (Rancière), 172, 218–20
On the Study Methods of Our Time (Vico), 49
ontological illusion, 23, 225
ontology, 19, 38–48, 51, 141, 152, 155, 207–8, 209n, 224–7
  historical, 19, 21, 142–4
The Order of Things (Foucault), 78
Organisation for Economic Co-operation and Development (OECD), 139–40, 159n
Orientalism, 7, 25n

Paideia, 78
Paine, Thomas, 180
painting, 107, 197, 199
Palmer, R. R., 180
Paris, 139, 193, 208n, 246, 249, 252
paternalism, 129
Le Paysan de Paris (Aragon), 251
Pearl Roundabout, Manama, 252
Peloponnesian War, 177
Penn, Sean, 227
performance art, 246
Persia, 7
Persian Letters (Montesquieu), 49
Phaedrus (Plato), 70
phallogocentrism, 14
phase, 50–2, 176, 222

Philippe, Louis, 249
philology, 49
philosophy, 6–12, 27–8n, 76, 82, 87n, 144
  conditions and constraints of, 59, 117–18, 194
  focus on history and hermeneutics, 11, 62
  as a profession, 6–10, 13–14, 17, 24n, 48, 117, 154
  and social sciences, 83
  and science, 6, 151–2
  teaching and practice in France, 78
physics, 152
Picasso, Pablo, 199
planning *see* urban planning
Plato, 70, 167–8, 177, 195–6, 202, 204–5, 209n
pleasure, 150
Poetics (Aristotle), 196
poetry, 112–13n, 194–7, 205, 209n, 212n
police, 168–9, 175, 183–5n, 218–19
politicity, 224, 237n, 247, 251–2, 258–9
politics, 7–8, 145, 177, 194
  and art, 199–200, 212n, 215
  and the built environment, 247
  definition, 184n, 234n
  revolutionary, 253
  and subjectivity, 173
The Politics of Aesthetics (Rancière), 111–12n
positivism, 195
postmodern break, 204
post-structuralism, 20, 60, 83, 97n, 100, 141, 193, 214
Powell, Colin, 127
power, 131, 138n
The Power of Nightmares, 136n
pragmatism, 103–4
printing, 108
Protagoras (Plato), 70
psychic monad, 149–50
psychoanalysis, 21, 85n, 89n, 140, 149, 198
  as emancipatory, 149–51
  treatment and 'cure', 150–1
Puerta del Sol, Madrid, 252

quantum mechanics, 152

Rabinow, Paul, 251
race, 14, 131, 138n, 185n
radical historicism, 16, 175
Rancière, Jacques, 18, 20, 23, 85n, 100–10, 112–14n, 133n, 165–90, 243
  (lack of) debate with Badiou, 193–208
  on aesthetics, 175, 199–204, 238–9n, 259n
  Aesthetics and Its Discontents, 220–1
  Disagreement, 168, 170, 172, 183n, 218–19
  Hatred of Democracy, 22, 165–82, 222, 236n
  on the hermeneutics of art and political history, 214–34
  The Ignorant Schoolmaster, 172
  Mute Speech, 169, 201, 210n
  On the Shores of Politics, 172, 218–20
  'Ten Theses on Politics,' 183n
Raymond Roussel (Foucault), 78
reason, 201
recognition, limitations of, 130–1
religion, and art, 105
Rémusat, Charles de, 216
Renaut, Alain, 141
'Reply to Derrida' (Foucault), 78–82, 85n, 87–8n
republicanism, 173, 180
Rethinking Architecture (Leach), 243
revolutions, 109, 178
Rice, Condoleezza, 127
Riefenstahl, Leni, 246
rights, 131
Robbins, Tim, 227
Robespierre, Maximilien de, 180
Robinet, André, 201, 211n
Rockhill, Gabriel, 84n, 89n, 211n
  Logique de l'histoire, 28n, 33n, 52n, 131, 176
  Radical History and the Politics of Art, 33n
Rondinone, Ugo, 246
Rosanvallon, Pierre, 180
Rousseau, Jean-Jacques, 7, 49, 179, 189n

St Augustine, 201
Sarkozy, Nicolas, 174, 186n
Sartre, Jean-Paul, 21, 23, 140–1, 214, 216, 225, 234n, 243
  What is Literature? 196, 200, 214

Index

Saunders, Frances Stonor, 27n
Schiller, Friedrich, 203–4
Schinkel, Karl Friedrich, 105–6
Schlegel, Friedrich, 113n
science, 6, 11, 22, 147, 151–2, 194
sculpture, 244
self-creation, 143
Serres, Michel, 133–4n
sexuality, 150
Shakespeare, William, 19
  Hamlet, 48
  Macbeth, 147–8, 231–2, 241n
The Shining (film), 232
silence, 73–4, 76–7, 96n
Situationism, 198, 259–60n
social epoché, 23, 256
social politicity *see* politicity
social sciences, 6–8, 11, 101
socialisation, 150
socialism, 139
Socialisme ou barbarie, 139
sociology, 7
sociophilosophie, 17
Socrates, 69–70, 177
sophism, 195
space, 31n, 47, 50, 53n
Speech and Phenomena (Derrida), 78
Speer, Albert, 246
Spiel, 203
Street, Emma, 247
The Structural Transformation of the Public Sphere (Habermas), 104–5, 109
structuralism, 20, 60, 83, 85n, 90n, 141, 201, 214
subject-centred philosophy, 11
subjectivisation, 170, 237n
suicide bombings, 129
Sullivan, Louis, 248
Symposium (Plato), 195

Tahrir Square, Cairo, 252
Taksim Square, Istanbul, 252
Taliban, 127, 129
Talisman complex, 256
Tel Quel, 60, 200, 214
terrorism, 129, 131, 133
textolatry, 13

theatre, 197
theism, 11
Thielen, Korinna, 248
time, 42–3, 47, 50
Time magazine, 127
Tocqueville, Alexis de, 109, 113n, 236n
Tonka, Hubert, 244
Total Theatre, 245
totalising, 123
transcendentalism, conceptual, 171–2
trees, 204
Triumph des Willens (film), 246
truth, Badiou on, 194–5, 197–8, 209n

unconscious, 149
United States, 126–7, 131, 178, 180
University of Paris VIII, 171, 193, 208n
urban planning, 244, 246

Van Sant, Gus, 231–2, 240–2n
Vico, Giambattista, 7, 19, 43, 48–9, 102
Vietnam War, 224
Villar, Alex, 246
Villepin, Dominique de, 174, 186n
Virilio, Paul, 244, 252
voting, 146
voyeurism, 129

Wahl, Jean, 60
Wallerstein, Immanuel, 7, 25n
War on Terror, 131, 133
Warhol, Andy, 203–4
Washington, George, 180
Weber, Samuel, 120–1
West, Cornel, 24n, 31n, 131, 138n
What is Literature? (Sartre), 196, 200, 214
Williams, Raymond, 178, 180, 236n, 254
Wollstonecraft, Mary, 7
World War II, 245
writing, 202, 214–15
Writing and Difference (Derrida), 60, 78

xenophobia, 131

Ziolkowski, Theodore, 26n, 105–6, 112n
Žižek, Slavoj, 137n, 206, 260n
Zucotti Park, New York, 252

EU representative:
Easy Access System Europe
Mustamäe tee 50, 10621 Tallinn, Estonia
Gpsr.requests@easproject.com

www.ingramcontent.com/pod-product-compliance
Lightning Source LLC
Chambersburg PA
CBHW061707300426
44115CB00014B/2593